DATE DUE

~~NO 20 '99~~		
~~May 91~~		

Demco, Inc. 38-293

E...ve

Su...ion

W. Fred Wegener, D.P.A.
Indiana University of Pennsylvania

anderson publishing co.
p.o. box 1576
cincinnati, oh 45201-1576
(513) 421-4142

since 1887

Effective Police Supervision, Second Edition

ISBN 0-87084-593-4
Library of Congress Catalog Number 95-80143

 The text of this book is printed on recycled paper.

Cover design by Edward Smith Design, Inc.   *Managing Editor* Kelly Grondin

Foreword

At my first job interview, well over a quarter of a century ago, a very wise yet practical school superintendent related something to me that I have never forgotten. He said that when he was my age, he thought he was going to change the world. After 35 years, he realized that he hadn't changed very much at all. When I entered law enforcement and later migrated to academia, I really thought I was going to change the world. Now, as I look back over my career, I can say the same thing.

But, in retrospect, I now realize that even a little change, a little improvement makes a difference. This particular text can make a difference. The world as we know it is changing rapidly. Advances in technology are occurring at a phenomenal rate while urban dynamics are being drastically altered forever. American law enforcement must be able to adapt to these changes. Today, the police supervisor must be a skilled and knowledgeable manager with the ability to implement policies while dealing with the myriad of organizational and personnel problems that occur on a daily basis.

Government, frustrated by crime, continues to look toward the criminal justice system for solutions. Yet, the public's view is often skewed by the creative misconceptions in the media and the wishful thinking of politicians. The system, far from perfect, was never designed to solve the nation's social ills and yet it has been thrust into the front line of this struggle. As crime continues to expand and the system becomes even more overwhelmed, the frustrations of citizens, lawmakers and police officers will continue to grow. Police managers, including first-line supervisors, are not immune. They are caught between noble ideals and the cold, harsh realities of contemporary life.

The quality of police service is directly related to the first-line manager's ability to function successfully. It takes ability, human skills and a considerable amount of job-related knowledge on the part of supervisors to make a constructive and positive difference in the day-to-day operations of the police department. Making the police organization more reflective, more responsive and more effective in meeting the needs of the community is no small task. But it is absolutely essential.

The success or failure of a police organization often hinges on the sergeant's managerial abilities in dealing with people and problems. Understanding the elements of effective supervision is the key to sound management. By utilizing the information contained in *Effective Police Supervision*, sergeants will be better prepared to fulfill their role as a critical component in modern, professional law enforcement.

Joseph Bogan
Chair/Professor
Department of Criminology
Indiana University of Pennsylvania

Preface

The success or failure of a police organization is determined by the quality of management within the organization. Management experts acknowledge that the basic foundation of managerial effectiveness is at the supervisory level, and the best law enforcement agencies view the supervisor as an integral part of the managerial process.

The early assumption that the sergeant was really an extension of line personnel has been soundly rejected. Slowly but surely, the position of sergeant has been merged into management. The outstanding law enforcement agency is one in which sergeants, as first-line supervisors, perform managerial functions.

When supervisors are allowed to engage in activities best described as knowledge-, human-, conceptual- and affective-based, they are applying skills that can only be described as integral parts of the processes of management. While it must be acknowledged that supervisors or sergeants apply the skills differently than police managers of higher rank, the fact remains that the effective police organization integrates supervisors into the management team.

Today's police supervisor has to develop behavioral and social skills in order to deal effectively with a rapidly changing society. When police executives integrate the position of supervisor into the managerial process, the organization is in a position to improve both its internal and external adaptive capabilities.

The primary aim of this book is to help current or potential supervisors to understand the differing beliefs and assumptions which they hold about themselves, other officers, the organization and society at large. The end result is a focus on effectiveness and participation by supervisors in the creation of an effective organization.

Each chapter has been updated to reflect current research and knowledge. Two chapters have been eliminated. In their place, the reader will find "Community Policing" and "Supervising the Difficult Employee," which are two pivotal areas that supervisors must understand if they are to make a significant contribution to management of the law enforcement agency.

In Community Policing, officers and citizens work together to identify problems and prepare solutions by marshalling community resources. Effective community policing demands significant change in an organization, and in particu-

lar, the operating style of each supervisor must change radically. Risk-taking, originality, creativity and problem solving become part of the optimal operating style.

On the other hand, a supervisor cannot overlook the necessity, on occasion, of dealing with recalcitrant and difficult employees. These employees can test the skills of the best supervisor. Many contemporary police agencies are plagued by such problems as low morale, high job stress, exceedingly high turnover, absenteeism and internal conflict. These problems are best resolved when managers of police departments become fully conversant with the elements of organizational behavior. The new chapter titled "Supervising The Difficult Employee" identifies problems and discusses means that supervisors can utilize to resolve these enigmatic problems.

This book combines state-of-the-art behavioral theory with numerous cases that allow the reader to identify and resolve personal and organizational problems. Each chapter contains three case studies, for a total of 42, that translate theory into practice. The cases serve as a base for classroom discussion and provide the reader with a means of interpreting the behavioral theory discussed in each chapter.

Tables and figures augment and strengthen important elements presented in each chapter. As a means of facilitating the learning process, each chapter contains a Summary, Key Concepts, Discussion Topics and Questions, and in the For Further Reading section, the reader will find an annotated list of material for those who want to extend their knowledge in selected areas.

The design of the text is user-friendly, pragmatic, and realistic. It also transcends the difficult problem that many texts in this area have by describing current behavioral theory and demonstrating how it relates to an operating agency. The primary goal of the text is to address vital topics of interest to every manager by questioning the traditional means of supervision.

Effective Police Supervision has become a vital tool in preparation of officers for promotion and is on the recommended reading lists of numerous police departments. Users of the first edition have provided important feedback, and numerous suggestions have been incorporated into the second edition. Special recognition and thanks must again be extended to our wives, Ginger and Cheryl, for their assistance, patience and support during the preparation of the manuscript.

Harry W. More
Santa Cruz, California

W. Fred Wegener
Indiana, Pennsylvania

Contents

6   Discipline—
An Essential Element of Police Supervision   **133**

7   Performance Appraisal—
The Key to Police Personnel Development   **165**

11   Internal Discipline—
*   A System of Accountability*   **285**

12   Labor Relations—
*   Problem Solving through Constructive Conflict*   **321**

Supervision—

The Management Task

1

Introductory Case Study

Sergeant Robert Toms

Robert Toms graduated with honors from the local university in Administration of Justice and then attended a special foreign language program. He passed all aspects of the recruitment process with flying colors and became an officer in the Midtown Police Department.

After completing the police academy, Toms was selected by his peers and the academy staff as the outstanding graduate. He completed the field training program without difficulty and was assigned to the south side barrio because of his fluency in Spanish. Other officers constantly called upon him as a translator, and he always responded with enthusiasm. Within three years he developed into a most competent officer.

Toms is very outgoing and liked by everyone. Highly agreeable and amiable, he finds he is readily accepted by other officers. He is an excellent team player and shares credit with others. Toms is a proficient report writer, and his incident reports clearly identify all officers who participated in joint investigations. He is a good listener and respects the judgment of others.

Toms and his girlfriend of three years anticipate marriage as soon as she graduates from college next year. Their lives revolve around fellow officers and their families, but their involvement in the community-at-large is quite limited.

Toms initially approached his new position with a great deal of enthusiasm. However, within a short period of time he found he was having difficulties with what his subordinates expected of him and what his superiors viewed as his responsibility to management. Toms enjoys action and found it difficult to remove himself from situations that could be handled by the officers he supervises. Yet, he knows that he must become proficient at managing people, not just things or situations.

Prior to his promotion, Toms had socialized exclusively with fellow officers, but he realized a few of them were having a great deal of difficulty accepting him as a supervisor. They wanted special favors that Toms could not

---

extend. Because of his desire to be liked, Toms has difficulty in providing job performance feedback to subordinates, especially when their work is below an acceptable level.

If you were Sergeant Toms, how would you deal with the conflict between what your subordinates and management expect from you? What steps might you take to ensure that you perform well as a supervisor? What should you do to extend your contacts beyond members of the police department?

Effective police departments throughout the nation seem to have one thing in common—good supervision. In recent years, the first-line supervisor has become an integral part of management, and directly responsible for improving the quality of working life. When supervisors perform effectively, departmental and personal goals are achieved, the community is better served and officers find themselves functioning in a positive working environment (Mendofix, 1994).

Police work has become increasingly complex, so today's police supervisor deals with problems and challenges totally unheard of several years ago. For example, officers are more demanding and express a desire to become more involved in the decision-making process; affirmative action plays an increasingly important part in both the selection of officers and promotions. Additionally, police departments have become increasingly cosmopolitan, and more reflective of the ethnic composition of the community. Also, a rapidly growing drug culture has not only altered the selection process, as more applicants have either used or experimented with drugs, but also has forced the police supervisor to respond to on-the-job officer drug use.

The composition of communities has changed radically. Minorities now make up the majority in 1,930 cities and 186 counties across the nation (Lewis, 1993). Many police tasks must be performed in an exceedingly violent environment where increasing numbers of officers have been injured on the job. Hostages are being taken more frequently, altering the way officers respond to this type of conflict. Barricaded suspects are becoming increasingly common, and many departments utilize SWAT teams to effectuate arrests and serve search warrants. Drugs have completely altered many neighborhoods, and in recent years, gangs have become a major problem in cities and are starting to emerge in rural communities. Drive-by shootings are increasing rapidly and car jackings occur throughout the nation. Life has become cheap in the eyes of some, and violent crimes occur with increasing frequency. A violent crime rate of 758 per 100,000 inhabitants was registered nationwide in 1992. This was a 41 percent increase above the 1983 figure (Federal Bureau of Investigation, 1993).

In municipal law enforcement agencies with 100 or more sworn officers, 96 percent have a special drug enforcement unit, and 97 percent participate in a

drug asset forfeiture program (Reaves, 1992). The amount of money generated through the sale of illegal drugs has created a situation whereby officers who are involved in narcotic investigations are faced with such temptation that an increasing number have become illegally involved (McAlary, 1988). The profits are so great that in one large city an officer was arrested for leading a ring of drug dealing officers (Arizona Daily Star, 1993). In another case, seven sheriff's deputies were charged with skimming more than $1.4 millon during narcotics raids. These officers were viewed as having turned the war on drugs into their own personal piggy banks (Merina, 1990). The federal law enforcement level is not exempt from the inimical influence of drug monies. In a U.S. Customs sting operation, one FBI agent and three customs agents were arrested for stealing and laundering $200,000 (Arizona Daily Star, 1993).

Bomb emergencies have also presented new tactical considerations. The field supervisor is generally involved in such incidents at the initial stage and in many instances coordinates rescue and the investigation of the crime scene. In 1992 there were 1,911 bombings and 582 incendiary bombings in the United States. Forty-five individuals were killed and 469 injured (Bureau of Alcohol, Tobacco, and Firearms, 1992). The same can be said for hazardous material spills. After responding, the first-line supervisor must evaluate the situation and give consideration to evacuation if the circumstances dictate. This is a far cry from a few years ago when many material spills were treated as a nuisance and the items were kicked to the side of the road.

All these situations present new challenges to the first-line supervisor, and it seems reasonable to assume that the problems will not only increase in number but will become more complex. This means, then, that the supervisor must respond to these critical issues as they arise, and address them with a great deal of imagination and innovation. The supervisor is at the organizational focal point between officers and other police managers. If the police organization is to become more effective, the first-line supervisor must play a major role in responding to change that impacts the organization.

If supervisors are successful in the performance of their duties, it follows that the organization will become more effective and the potentiality of attaining goals will be enhanced. Good supervision does not just happen: it has to be cultivated. Until recently, newly appointed supervisors were left to fend for themselves, but supervisory training courses are becoming more common and an essential component of career development. In some states, improved performance has resulted because each newly appointed supervisor must complete a training program within a specified period of time after being promoted.

Transition

The transition from a line position to first-line supervisor brings numerous rewards, but it also exacts a price. These factors are set forth in Figure 1.1. However, in addition to an increase in pay, the supervisory position is marked by prestige both within and outside the department. Administratively, the super-

visor usually heads a given operation, is more involved in the decision-making process and at the same time becomes a part of management.

If there is any issue that causes a new supervisor a great deal of difficulty, it usually is learning how to be an effective disciplinarian, especially when having to discipline a former fellow line officer.

Figure 1.1
Transition from Line Officer to First-Line Supervisor

ADVANTAGES:
1. An increase in salary.
2. A feeling of accomplishment.
3. Gained prestige within and outside the department.
4. A step up in the organization.
5. A greater opportunity to provide input to the decision-making process.
6. An opportunity to have more control over the type of police service provided to the community.
7. An opportunity to be in charge of an operation.
8. Receiving a broader perspective of department's overall operation.
9. Recipient of additional training.
10. Different assignments.

DISADVANTAGES:
1. A greater degree of commitment to management.
2. One step removed from line operations.
3. Must function as a disciplinarian.
4. Positioned in the middle, between the line and top management.
5. Goals must be achieved through others.
6. Accountable for work (or lack thereof) performed by subordinates.
7. Must implement policy not personally supported.
8. Difficult or impossible to return to former position if being a supervisor is undesirable.
9. At the bottom of the seniority level in shift and work assignments.

This list was compiled by first-line supervisors attending a training program.

Further adjustment may be required as the new supervisor finds it necessary to attain goals through the efforts of subordinates, being held responsible for their success or failure. The transition from being responsible primarily for oneself to slowly becoming a more integral part of management requires a greater degree of commitment to the managerial process.

The transition to the position of first-line supervisor may be fraught with difficulty depending on the individual, but most agree it presents a real challenge and demands the ability to accept and adapt to change. A new supervisor

immediately knows the ecology of the organization is extremely important and is a dynamic social system.

Officers have personal needs and objectives that the supervisor helps to fulfill while simultaneously ensuring they do not conflict with the attainment of organizational objectives. Human behavior is what most first-line supervisors deal with in the work place. The greater the supervisor's knowledge in this area, the greater the prospect that both individual and organizational goals will be attained.

A supervisor soon becomes aware of the need to develop a range of skills if officers are to be highly productive and achieve the goals and objectives of the department. Good supervision is the result of the serious application of one's knowledge about human behavior to the work situation (Wadia and Kolender, 1988).

Supervisory Skill Areas

Once an individual assumes the position of supervisor, the role changes to such an extent that there is limited comparison to the tasks performed as a patrol officer. The supervisor is a manager and must perform managerial type activities. Certainly one technique of motivating employees is for a supervisor to show officers how something can be done by actually performing the activity, such as making a number of DUI (driving while under the influence) arrests or conducting a number of FIs (field interviews). While such activity might accomplish an immediate goal, it represents only a small part of the things a supervisor does to be effective.

The selection of the best worker for the position of supervisor is a common agency practice that can prove to be disastrous. The temptation to improve one's salary, to enhance one's position and to achieve a rank attained by few is seldom rejected by a highly competent patrol officer. In many instances, however, this practice results in a feeling of having divided loyalties.

In some instances the newly appointed supervisor performs so poorly, it becomes necessary to seek employment elsewhere or be demoted. Some play the supervisory game well enough to get by, but they become marginal supervisors and, in the long run, are of limited value to the organization.

A supervisory position is not for everyone. It is a demanding job and can create stress. The increase in pay and status can never compensate for the psychological conflict possibly occurring if one is inadequately prepared or lacks supervisory skills.

Supervisors should emphasize the development of the skills of their subordinates, rather than trying to do everything themselves. Needless to say, the supervisor could probably accomplish the task in half the time in many instances. The time-worn theory, "I would rather do it myself," must be changed when one becomes a supervisor.

As a means of maximizing effectiveness, a supervisor must work to attain objectives through the efforts of others, preferably by becoming operationally effective in one or more of the following skill areas:

1. Knowledge
2. Human
3. Conceptual
4. Affective

Figure 1.2
Supervisory Skill Areas

| KNOWLEDGE |
| HUMAN |
| CONCEPTUAL |
| AFFECTIVE |

The skill areas are closely interrelated and overlap in their application. There is common agreement that knowledge-based skills are more important at the supervisory level than they would be to the chief of police, whereas human skills are vitally important at every managerial level (see Figure 1.2). At the same time, managers at all levels must be concerned with applying some degree of conceptual and affective skills.

There is a continuing need for the integration of knowledge, human and conceptual skills as modified by the emotionally based or affective characteristics that are constantly conditioning the managerial process (Imundo, 1991).

Much of the literature written about management makes a basic distinction between humanitarian and analytical supervision approaches. The **human skills approach** deals with emotions, values and attitudes. The organization is viewed as a social system, not simply a law enforcement enterprise staffed by

individuals. It is necessary to consider both the social needs of the officers and the tasks to be performed. Figure 1.3 lists the supervisory functions.

Figure 1.3
Supervisory Functions

Knowledge	Human	Conceptual	Affective
Scheduling	Motivating	Analysis	Attitude
Evaluating	Communicating	Interpreting	Values
Organizing Work	Leading	Solving Problems	Fairness
Training	Resolving Conflict	Identification of Objectives	Equality
Directing	Integrating	Assessment	Inter-relationships

Modified from: Dan L. Costley and Ralph Todd, *Human Relations in Organizations*, St. Paul, MN: West Publishing Company, 1978.

The **analytical approach** views supervision problems as being conceptually based. Beyond achievement of agency goals, the key is the identification, analysis, interpretation and resolution of issues. In every instance, it involves the utilization of past and current police knowledge with a consideration of the future.

Knowledge-Based Skills

At the time of appointment, the supervisor is usually endowed with all kinds of knowledge-based skills because of extended duty as a patrol officer (see Figure 1.4). In most instances, promotion to the initial managerial level has been predicated on success as a patrol officer or investigator. Unfortunately, the skillful application of operational techniques can seldom ensure successful performance as a first-line supervisor. The skills are entirely different and the situation can become somewhat tenuous if, during the transition period to this newly acquired position, the new sergeant fails to adopt a managerial perspective. A manager can only succeed if results are obtained through the efforts of others. The supervisor must realize the employee is a most precious resource (Imundo, 1991).

Figure 1.4
Supervisor's Knowledge-Based Skills

1. Provides officers with appropriate administrative and technical support.
2. Knows each officer's workload.
3. Reviews officers' reports for accuracy, thoroughness and quality.
4. Demonstrates a real interest in seeing that officers do a good job and carry out their assignments.
5. Fairly implements departmental policies, rules and regulations.
6. Capable of doing all tasks an officer must perform.
7. Scheduling of officers according to organizational priorities.
8. Training and development of officers.
9. Organizing work in such a way as to effectively and efficiently achieve objectives and goals.

Human Skills

At the core of successful police supervision is a consideration of **human skills**. Employees have to be motivated, appraised and counseled. Standards must be established, tasks analyzed and expectations communicated. Officers must be trained, developed and (even though distasteful) occasionally disciplined. All those tasks are an effort to meet organizational objectives (see Figure 1.5). These activities demand the application of human skills predicated on the absolute belief that employees will work hard and diligently if incentives are such that they become highly motivated (Hawkins, 1992).

A first-line supervisor must become personally acquainted with each employee and treat each one as an individual. It is imperative for work to be accomplished through people; this can only be done when the supervisor is thoroughly acquainted with the capabilities and limitations of each employee. The supervisor should set high standards for the officers supervised and those standards should be applied to each employee.

In one supervisor/subordinate attitudinal survey it was found that in responding to the statement "My supervisor really understands and appreciates my problems," 100 percent of the supervisors thought line officers would agree with the statement whereas in fact only 39 percent did. Such a disparity clearly reflects the importance of human skills and the need to understand the dynamics of human relationships if employees are to be successfully integrated into the organization.

Conceptual Skills

Conceptual skills consume the least amount of the first-line supervisor's time. However, these skills are essential ingredients of the managerial process. The newly appointed supervisor, whether assigned to patrol or investigations,

must integrate personal activities into the total organizational plan so agency goals can be attained.

The relationship of patrol to other specialized units (such as service or investigation) can be tenuous; therefore, it is absolutely necessary for the first-line supervisor to be capable of understanding the complexities of the interrelationship of specialized units to the total organization (see Figure 1.6).

To conceptualize is to form new ideas or concepts. The first-line supervisor is in the best position to identify and resolve conflict between specialized police units by using conceptualization techniques.

The supervisor also must continuously evaluate new tasks and reevaluate old assignments in an effort to meet explicit organizational goals (Imundo, 1991). It is readily apparent that knowledge-based skills are more important to the first-line supervisor than to the chief executive or the staff, but conversely, conceptual skills dominate those skills needed to be an effective top cop.

Figure 1.5
Supervisor's Human Skills

1. Listens and discusses problems with subordinates.
2. Deals with each officer as an individual.
3. Develops a rapport with officers.
4. Lets officers know where they stand.
5. Performs as a professional and sets the standards for employees.
6. Works with officers to increase positive attitudes and counsels them in a positive manner.
7. Gives praise when appropriate.
8. Motivates employees.
9. Resolves conflict.
10. Tells employees when they have not met performance standards.

Figure 1.6
Supervisor's Conceptual Skills

1. Demonstrates the ability to analyze data and make decisions.
2. Works to eliminate errors and improve proficiency.
3. Develops and shares information.
4. Identifies emerging problems and works for their resolution.
5. Utilizes all sources in an effort to deal with the positive interpretation of information.
6. Identifies objectives.
7. Assesses performance.
8. Conceptualizes the technical and human aspects of the work environment.

Affective Skills

The fourth set of managerial characteristics are **emotion-based**. They interact with and modify all the other characteristics (see Figure 1.7). The supervisor (by actions) modifies the attitudes, emotions and values of employees. At the same time, the interaction modifies the supervisor's personal view of the managerial process and their own self-concept (Handy, 1993).

Figure 1.7
Supervisor's Affective Skills

1.	Integration of organizational and community value systems.
2.	Creation of an environment based in a belief in equality and the opportunity for all to succeed.
3.	Fairness in relationships with subordinates.
4.	Values employees and their potential contribution to the organization.
5.	Awareness of personal strengths as well as limitations.
6.	Acceptance of responsibility.
7.	Developing interrelationships based on equal treatment.

The emotion-based skills of the supervisor have to be utilized to the maximum. The first-line supervisor has to accept responsibility for errors and should never allow subordinates to be criticized for a mistake outside their control.

It does not take an alert supervisor long to realize they are not knowledgeable in every area, and that they have weaknesses as well as strengths. Weaknesses can be numerous including a lack of sensitivity, emotional immaturity, a lack of drive or the clashing of personalities. Effective supervisors apply numerous skills and perform several functions. An important function is to perform with fairness and equity. If an organizational value based on fairness and equity are to be communicated, it has to be on a continuous basis, demonstrated to each and every employee by ensuring that everyone is treated as an equal with absolute fairness. In a supervisor/subordinate attitudinal survey it was found that in responding to the statement, "My supervisor is only concerned about the few mistakes I make. Supervisors never see the things I do right," it was found that supervisors thought 33 percent of line officers would agree with that statement while, in fact, 61 percent agreed.

Obviously this demonstrates the difference in line officers' and supervisors' perception of fair treatment. Further indication of this difference is found in the response to the following statement "I usually feel comfortable in front of my boss." The supervisors thought that 92 percent would agree with the statement, but it actually was favored by only 51 percent. Thus, there is apparently a barrier possibly precluding the successful communication of organizational values and their integration into the community value structure.

Case Study

Sergeant Roger Knapp

Roger Knapp was an excellent patrolman. Considered by his peers to be a real "street cop," he knows criminal law and traffic law forward and backward. In his application of the law, Knapp is very legalistic and a stickler for applying the letter of the law. For the last three years he worked the swing shift on the toughest beat in the city. He had more felony arrests than anyone else in patrol during the last year.

Roger is clearly a highly competent and capable officer. He passed both the written and oral parts of the promotional examination with flying colors and was number one on the promotions list. After being promoted to sergeant, the honeymoon period lasted for several months, but gradually the officers under his command have begun to complain about his style of leadership. Roger's reaction is defensive and he resents the patrol officers questioning his ability as a supervisor.

Subordinates are constantly criticized by Roger for their limited knowledge of the law. No matter what they do, they feel they cannot achieve the level of excellence demanded of them.

Sergeant Knapp expects every employee to perform at a superior level and nothing less is acceptable. The characteristics Roger exhibited as a patrolman allowing him to be an exceptional performer (such as being a stickler for details and a perfectionist) cause him to falter as a supervisor. In other words, his efforts to mold everyone in his own image prohibited him from performing well as a supervisor.

The transition from employee to supervisor is generally a difficult one and Sergeant Knapp has based his supervisory style on knowledge-based skills and seemingly ignores human, conceptual and affective skills. He demonstrates an unwillingness to accept performance not based on solving problems through the precise application of rules and regulations.

How can Sergeant Knapp deal directly with his poor performance as a first-line supervisor? What skills should he develop if he is to obtain results through the efforts of others?

If employees perceive that managers refuse to acknowledge weaknesses and are always looking for a scapegoat, then the supervisors' affective skills will be muted and achievement of organizational goals can be jeopardized.

One can apply knowledge-based human relations and cognitive skills. but the affective variable serves as a modifier and allows a manager to become aware of personal limitations as well as strengths. This activity allows the supervisor to recognize and accept responsibility to make necessary decisions and be able to acknowledge the needs of peers and employees (Stone, 1989).

The supervision of line employees is readily acknowledged as highly complex and (in the view of many) the most difficult function performed by managers (Imundo, 1991).

Self-Appraisal

The initial and highly significant dilemma in becoming a truly competent supervisor is sorting through all the different supervisory techniques to select the approach(es) compatible with one's own temperament and personality. It is necessary to ask such questions as: What is an acceptable level of conflict between employees? Can personal needs be made compatible with organizational needs? What managerial style will officers find most acceptable? How does one become an effective disciplinarian? Should one go by the book when enforcing rules and regulations? Can officer discretion be accepted as an integral part of the job?

It is vital, for several reasons, for supervisors to have a clear idea of what they are doing and what is expected of them. First, it allows them to operate as professionals, and above potential conflict. Second, they are less apt, in the hectic day-to-day operation, to delude themselves into believing there is only one potential solution to every problem, and that all officers can be treated the same.

Each officer is a distinct human being with varying skills, abilities and personality, and is entitled to be treated as an individual. By accepting everyone as an individual and dealing with them on that basis, supervisors can reduce the potential for making errors and arrive at decisions suitable for both the individual and the organization (Raterman, 1992).

The pivotal factor is to understand the real attitudes toward line officers and their capacity to work. Are they viewed as having the potential to become producers, or are they regarded as "drones"? The real issue, then, becomes crystal clear: the way employees are treated by their supervisor is strongly influenced by the way the supervisor views the officers.

Most assuredly, the best supervisors adopt a managerial style acknowledging individual differences and they work diligently to tailor the style to the situation and the individual.

If the supervisor is better at conceptualizing than motivating, it becomes readily apparent that his or her approach to a supervisory problem will be entirely different than when the individual excels at motivating.

Possibly the two skill areas can be combined by emphasizing conceptual skills, carefully setting forth a plan to resolve a problem and then utilizing moti-

vational skills to implement the program. For example, a plan can be devised, focusing on improving the working relationship between the line officers and detectives assigned to investigate residential burglaries. In the plan, emphasis can be placed on expanding the role of field officers as a means of improving preliminary investigations and demonstrating to the detectives its potential impact on the clearance rate (Tracey, 1990).

If the supervisor's anxiety threshold is high, it may be more comfortable to resolve a problem with a knowledge skills base rather than a human skills approach. In other words, one can view an issue as a simple rule or regulation violation or it can be approached as a conflict-resolution problem with a goal of maximizing human relations skills. In application, it can become an integration of the two approaches, but it actually is a matter of fitting the style to the situation.

No supervisory philosophy works all the time. It is essential to be acutely conscious of an approach giving flexibility. Accomplished supervisors combine different approaches. It is what John Naisbitt identified as network management in his landmark publication *Megatrends* (Naisbitt, 1982).

Managerial networking at the supervisory level is concerned with the integration of each officer into the organization. Efforts are directed toward true communication, the sharing of ideas, information, and resources. It is the focus on decisionmaking that improves work-life and productivity.

Networks exist to foster self-help, exchange information and share resources. The problem is focused upon, and networking enhances the ability of each individual to respond to the problem. In fact, the individual is the most important element of the network. The value of networking is rooted in informality, equality and true acceptance.

Management Expectations of the Supervisor

Management expects results (not excuses), so it is the responsibility of the first-line supervisor to perform. The supervisor must develop the ability to identify those duties directly related to the management of people and place an emphasis on them (Moody, 1994). Vocational duties must be subordinate to getting work done through employees. One expert suggests asking the question, "What kind of employee would I like to have working for me?" The response to that question provides the subordinate a standard by which to work and live (Broadwell, 1984).

Positive Attitude

Everyone likes to be around people who are positive. It can be contagious. It will have a strong influence on working relationships. Think of how much

better it is to be involved with people who obviously enjoy work and the challenges it presents.

When a new general order or policy is promulgated, the best way to react to it is positively. Response should be based on a critical evaluation of ways that will ensure the policy is workable. Everyone must refrain from finding reasons why it will not work (Dobbs and Field, 1993).

The supervisors should train themselves to think about the good side of an idea or suggestion rather than the bad aspects. It is fundamental to human nature that the boss will respond to recommendations suggesting "Here is what it will take to make this work" rather than "Here is why that cannot be done" (Broadwell, 1984).

The boss's ideas may still be questioned, but at the proper time and place. This simply means the idea should be carefully evaluated and constructively criticized, but not rejected simply because it has never been done that way before.

Individuals who think positively are *results-oriented*—a characteristic management is actively seeking. The supervisor must view each obstacle as an opportunity and a challenge. It is like looking at a half-filled glass of water and trying to determine whether it is half-full or half-empty. It is obvious that the positive thinker views the glass as half-full.

Positive thinking is a way of dealing with obstacles in a constructive manner. It actually is a way of viewing life. The nature of circumstances, places, things and attitudes toward people can always be affirmative if one wants to view them as such. Since desirable attitudes can be cultivated, the new supervisor should strive to identify means of finding workable solutions to conflict, starting with developing a positive attitude toward employees (Moody, 1994).

Loyalty

Middle and top management want to feel that rules, regulations, policies and decisions coming down through channels are supported by first-line supervisors.

The supervisor should realize that policies set at one or two levels above them will in many instances lose some of their significance. In fact, their actual need for existence might be questioned. A policy may be viewed as unreasonable when it is not fully explained. The first-line supervisor is seldom in a position to know all the facts and rationale for a new policy. The view from the top or middle of the organization is very seldom duplicated at the supervisory level. Only so much information can be sent down through channels. Most managers do not have the time to explain in depth the rationale for each policy. Normally, managers are making decisions based upon more factual material, possibly unavailable at the operational level.

If some information is needed before a new policy can be explained to subordinates, then the supervisor must ask for clarifying information. When one

accepts the position of supervisor, they accept the obligation of being part of the team, not apart from it. This is not an easy task to accomplish but it must be done if the supervisor is to be successful in performing required duties.

Supervisors translate and implement policy and procedures within the organization. The supportive supervisors should ask themselves, "How can this policy be implemented in the shortest period of time with assurance of complete compliance?" The important factor in this situation is to find the solution that is best for the department. In addition, middle and top managers dislike being referred to as the "they" who take all those unreasonable stands and demand nonachievable performance. Managers at higher levels have a need for personal loyalty from supervisors, and this should be reciprocated. Loyalty works both ways. First-line supervisors want to feel they have the support and backing of their immediate supervisor.

Performance

Managers expect (and indeed have a right to demand) the thorough completion of tasks on time. Supervisors should do everything asked of them. If an assignment cannot be completed on time, the immediate supervisor needs to be consulted with an explanation of the reason(s). Maybe more time is needed or help is required in understanding the problem or completing the task.

There are very few managers who will not accept a request for help if assistance is necessary in completing an assigned project. Asking for help is not an admission of incompetence; it is an acknowledgment that the manager has an expertise as yet unacquired by subordinates.

Every manager expects personnel to be on time and to take appropriate coffee or meal breaks. Supervisors should set the standard not only for their officers, but also for everyone else in the department.

First-line supervisors have to accept their being at the fulcrum point between management and line operations. If problems occur, first-line supervisors are usually the first to know. Supervisors also have a responsibility to identify problems and respond to subordinate complaints.

It is a supervisory responsibility to function as the go-between. No one else can effectively accomplish the tasks of interpreting rules, regulations, policies and translating organizational demands for the cooperative attainment of agency goals (Stone, 1989).

Responding to Management

Since management is continually in need of information, supervisors must submit a wide range of requested reports in order to adequately reflect the tasks being accomplished by subordinates. Reports must be completed on time and

must be comprehensive. There is nothing worse, in the view of most managers, than a poorly prepared or late report. The nature of police work is such that most supervisors are assessed largely on the basis of reports submitted. While supervisors might have continuing contact with their immediate manager, other management superiors might only use the written work submitted by a supervisor as a means of evaluation. In fact, in many medium- or large-sized agencies, supervisors have little or no contact with the "brass." Therefore, it behooves them to do everything possible to ensure completeness and accuracy of any report. Special care should be taken whenever a report is to be submitted to other city departments or to the prosecuting attorney's office so these reports reflect favorably on the department (see Figure 1.8).

Figure 1.8
**What Management Wants
from First-Line Supervisors**

1. Meet with management, as needed, in order to resolve specific problems or concerns.
2. Communicate subordinates' concerns, desires and suggestions to management.
3. Render testimony at disciplinary hearings.
4. Respond in writing to various requests from management.
5. Prepare and submit budget requests.
6. Complete assigned investigations.
7. Prepare written employee evaluations.
8. Comply with procedures and policy.
9. Transmit the organizational value system to the members.
10. Take action contributing to organizational improvement.

If there is any doubt as to when a report is due, supervisors should ask their immediate superior for clarification. If the manager wants reports done in a certain way, compliance with the requirement is essential.

In order to work well with an immediate supervisor, an effort should be made to determine what is expected. Supervisors must refrain from stereotyping the manager, and learn to look upon the person as a unique individual. This is especially imperative when it comes to determining the type of report the immediate supervisor wants in particular situations. Some managers are listeners and prefer, whenever possible, to have certain reports given orally. Others react best to written reports, allowing them time to assess and evaluate the information presented. The preference of one method over the other depends upon the nature of the problem or the type of information being reported. With this in mind, supervisors should determine their managers' strengths and weaknesses, work habits and needs, before responding accordingly.

When establishing and maintaining a good working relationship with the boss, never modify a report so it appears more favorable than it should. If something is wrong, state this. Be frank, open and honest with reporting. To do less is to court disaster. Law enforcement is a process of responding to and resolving conflict. Naturally, mistakes will be made and in some instances supervisory judgment, or that of subordinate(s), may not be what it should be. A boss is human also. Most bosses are dedicated and have a definite sense of responsibility toward their work and challenge not only themselves but all personnel (Dobbs and Field, 1993). A supervisor should work with, not against, a boss. If it is obviously a situation that will be controversial, be sure to provide information leaving the individual in a position to resolve the situation. Prior field experience will (in all probability) tell supervisors when management will be forced to respond to higher authorities or the press.

Most departments have a policy requiring a written report to be submitted when any unusual occurrence happens. It is at this time that the supervisor can extend a helping hand to management by submitting a detailed report taking into consideration every possible question that might arise from the incident. The application of this technique methodically, and in a nonmanipulative fashion, produces a supervisor who accepts what may be a management problem, as a personal one. When this has been accomplished, management will start to see its supervisors not only as valuable resources, but as helpful colleagues and trustworthy professionals who are part of the management team (Couper, 1993).

Subordinate Expectations of the Supervisor

If every subordinate worked to maximum capacity, if errors were never made, if all goals were achieved on time, and if organizations were perfect there would not be a need for first-line supervisors. Obviously, such is not the case. Law enforcement agencies are composed of human beings who deal with human problems in an imperfect environment. It logically follows that supervisors will continue to be an integral part of the managerial process in the years ahead.

Supervisors have to deal with numerous demands from varying sources both from within and outside the department. One that can be the most demanding is the subordinate. In fact, if there were no line personnel to be supervised, the position of supervisor would, in all probability, never have come into existence. Hence, the question has to be asked "What should subordinates expect from a supervisor?"

The answer is not simple because of the human equation involved. Supervisors and subordinates are all different. While they are all members of the human race, they are still distinct and unique as individuals with varying needs. The primary reason for the existence of the supervisory position is the

need for work to be effectively accomplished. If goals are not achieved, then there seems to be little reason for the continued existence of the organization.

The important consideration then is to maximize the talents of each and every subordinate. What could be worse than a supervisor ignoring the skills possessed by subordinates? A supervisor certainly must utilize every skill and every bit of knowledge a subordinate possesses. This is not a simple task. It is one demanding a continual appraisal and reappraisal of each employee's capabilities. Those abilities must then be directed toward the accomplishment of tasks essential to the attainment of organizational goals.

Subordinates have needs that, organizationally, must be met and satisfied (Broadwell, 1984). From an optimistic point of view, all those needs can be handled within the working environment, but usually this is not possible. If needs are met by the job then the job is readily identified as an excellent source of motivation. If needs are not being met on the job then the question arises as to why the job is inadequately responding to employee needs.

Under no circumstance does this mean the supervisor has to accept a person's actions or inactions as an excuse for poor performance. A failure to perform at acceptable levels must always be addressed and resolved in favor of the organization. Generally speaking, it can be assumed that 85 percent of employees will respond to positive efforts by the supervisor. This is the group with which the supervisor should expend extra time and energy. Unfortunately, the remaining 15 percent of the subordinates (who for whatever reason are "poor" employees) will generally consume most of the supervisor's time. Eventually, that time will be nonproductive (except that employees who should never have been employed will be eliminated, or employees will receive assistance to such an extent they will become productive employees).

It is important for a supervisor to realize that people, time and places have changed. Things are not the way they used to be. The authoritarian management approach should have been dispensed with long ago, but is still in limited use and is definitely not as viable of a managerial approach as it once was. The old assumptions about employees' lack of desire and inability to work no longer apply. As a group, officers cannot be classified as lazy, indifferent or indolent. In fact, the constituency to be supervised is generally willing and capable of working (see Figure 1.9), but for different reasons and with different expectations than their predecessors.

A large problem facing police organizations today is that many officers do not feel they are a part of the organization. Officers want job satisfaction and this can only be provided by allowing officers to achieve individual needs while organizational needs are satisfied.

When the working environment limits the opportunity for satisfying personal goals, officers can become alienated from the organization. When an officer rejects the work situation, it can result in a lowering of work standards, general apathy and a lessening of interest in the job.

Discontent with the job has traditionally resulted in absenteeism, tardiness and low-quality work. Now, however, officers have expressed this discontent by becoming more active in unions, engaging in work slowdowns, using alcohol and drugs to a greater extent, and lastly, leaving the police field in increasing numbers.

Figure 1.9
Officer Behavior

1970s-1980s	1990s-2000s
passive	involved
dependent	independent
subordinate	equal
lack of trust	mutual trust
ordered	self-directed
autocracy	democratic work place
closed communication	open communication
acceptance	commitment
conventionality	spontaneity
conforming	nonconforming
rules dominate	goal attainment dominates
quantity	quality
personal goals ignored	personal goals attained
value neutral	value oriented

Many younger officers have rising expectations and are not willing to accept the demands of a traditionally managed police organization. The bureaucratic model of management is the antithesis of everything they want from an organization. In the past, officers sought job and financial security and the job took precedence over outside interests. Today, however, career-minded individuals have listed the following factors as important when selecting a career (Laird, Laird and Fruehling, 1983):

1. A challenging job
2. An opportunity to make a contribution
3. Self-expression
4. Free time for outside activities

Those changing attitudes toward work suggest that younger officers want a more well-rounded lifestyle. They will work and give their best efforts for a certain number of hours if they have a positive working environment. The successful police organization of the future will integrate the individual into the organization, and individual as well as organizational goals will be attained.

It is quite apparent that the composition of most law enforcement agencies will change dramatically (if it has not occurred already). Affirmative action mandates have changed hiring practices. In the years ahead, more minorities and women will enter the law enforcement ranks. This is true because the current intent of Affirmative Action is to correct any imbalance between the proportion of racial minorities and women in a community as compared to the proportion of sworn officers (Commission on Accreditation for Law Enforcement Agencies, 1993). These new employees and their white, male counterparts will become a new breed of individuals with a different attitude toward work and a changing need structure.

Participation

A new set of values has entered the organizational setting, and it strikes right at the heart of the supervisor-subordinate relationship. In the past, employees have been acted upon rather than reacted to. Except for a few instances, police employees have been passive rather than reactive. Today things are different. Most police officers want a part of the action. Progressive police organizations open the decision-making process to employees. That is not to say every employee is involved in every policy decision, but participation is allowed at all levels where employees are in a position to have first-hand information and are given an opportunity to study problems coming to the attention of the organization.

The idea of worker participation requires a redefinition of work and working relationships. It might even require a fundamental change in one's view of employees and what they can contribute to the department. One expert espouses that true participation will reduce the number of traditional managers needed by most agencies but increase the need for leaders (Pascarella, 1984).

Supervisors must learn that real participation means power must be shared, not hoarded. As the old authoritarian leadership style is discarded, it must be replaced by an insight into and a deeper understanding of human needs and expectations. Participative management will not become operational overnight. In fact, it will undoubtedly be resisted by some in the years ahead and in a few instances, never adopted. However, as individuals change, then organizations must change. As everyone knows, change can be pleasant or it can be painful. Without a doubt, supervisors from the old school will be the recipients of high levels of stress as their work experience, training and education are diametrically opposed to the demands of modern leadership.

The transformation of relationships between working employees and supervisors does not require an overhaul of human nature. Quite the contrary. It requires the elimination of distorted and outdated opinions of how one views human nature (Dessler, 1993). When supervising the new breed, the task is that of facilitator, not power broker. The real by-product of participative supervision

is the creation of a working environment in which the officers want to work. It is absolutely necessary for the supervisor to create a psychological ambiance projecting an air of caring for people, and striving to do everything possible to make the department a pleasant place to work. This is accomplished by being constantly available for help or guidance, accepting and solving problems as they occur, making decisions based on knowledge and exhibiting a genuine desire to empower employees to accomplish assigned tasks (Dessler, 1993).

Conflict Resolution

When first-line supervisors were asked to identify the most important functions they performed it was found that the vast majority had to do with the resolution of conflict (see Figure 1.10). Subordinates constantly turn to supervisors as conflict resolvers.

Figure 1.10
**Functions Performed by Supervisors
When Relating to Subordinates**

1. Provide feedback to subordinates regarding job performance.
2. Conduct investigations of incidents in which subordinates are involved (in shootings or accidents).
3. Conduct investigations of observed or reported subordinate conduct that may have vicarious liability involved.
4. Train and develop subordinates.
5. Personally conduct investigations of alleged subordinate misconduct.
6. Resolve citizen/officer conflicts.
7. Respond to subordinates' inquiries (policy, law, alternative courses of action, etc.).
8. Conduct internal investigations in accordance with rules prescribed in the Officer's Bill of Rights.
9. Assist subordinates with personal and job-related problems.
10. Serve as an archetype of professionalism in all relationships with subordinates.

Conflict cannot be ignored but has to be accepted as a certain consequence of human interaction. Subordinates expect and, in fact, demand that supervisors deal with and resolve conflict.

The nature of police work is such that conflict is inevitable. Line personnel are confronted with conflict daily and the first-line supervisor is not exempt from the realities of conflict.

Conflict must be resolved both internally and externally to the department. Citizens file complaints which must be investigated. It even occurs between officers and likewise has to be met and resolved.

Conflicts in this area range from a failure to respond rapidly when providing back-up, to taking too much time for a meal break. In some situations, gripes about another employee can fester to such a point that it impedes the accomplishment of tasks. The supervisor must listen to such complaints and work toward their reduction or elimination.

The first-line supervisor must learn to distinguish between real employee complaints and petty bickering. A certain amount of griping can actually prove to be beneficial, but if it becomes excessive it can be inimical to personal relationships, and to organizational well-being. Additionally, when officers engage in activities creating a vicarious liability they must be investigated.

Subordinates can become involved in shootings or accidents and the supervisor becomes a key factor in the investigation of such incidents. This is especially true when a firearm is discharged and someone is injured or killed. In agencies not having an internal affairs unit, the first-line supervisor is generally held responsible for conducting such an investigation.

Supervisors are the lead investigators in efforts to resolve conflicts as described above. One study reflected that 73 percent of a supervisor's time was spent in resolving conflict. Without a doubt the supervisor's position is primarily one of conflict identification and resolution.

Peer Expectations of the Supervisor

Successful accomplishment of tasks and goal attainment requires cooperation and coordination between supervisors. Supervision is a joint effort by numerous individuals and not the sole priority of any one first-line supervisor. Functions performed by one have a direct impact on every other supervisor in the department.

Getting along with and supporting fellow supervisors creates a more pleasant place to work. Occasionally someone will allow the desire to get ahead (or a strong drive to compete) get in the way of positive working relationships. Other supervisors may view their duties and responsibilities differently. If the differences are to be resolved, supervisors must make an effort to understand and get along with each other.

Supervisors have to recognize that peers have objectives to be met and commitments to be honored. They have problems that have to be dealt with and they may know best how to solve those problems. The first-line supervisor should always consider how their actions affect the duties of others.

If it is possible to make a helping decision rather than one that hinders, then it should be done. If it appears a decision will result in conflict for another supervisor, an attempt should be made to resolve the problem by direct communication. Talk over the differences and make a sincere effort to find a solution beneficial to both (Weiss, 1988).

Reciprocal, positive relationships between peers are those where experiences are shared. At the end of a shift, situations that occurred can jointly be

discussed along with views on how they were resolved. Ideas and opinions should be "thrown out on the table" for discussion (and even debate) when needed.

When the occasion demands, supervisors must meet with other supervisors to resolve problems, share information and coordinate work activities. This might be especially pertinent when there is an ongoing investigation that cannot be completed on one shift.

A good supervisor does not wait for someone else to take action when a problem occurs requiring consultation with peers. The offer to help should be extended and, if necessary, a meeting should be set up to discuss and resolve the problem. There are many instances when an end-of-shift briefing does not allow adequate time for dealing with the problem at hand.

This is best illustrated by the conflict arising when a new policy is implemented. Policies are open to interpretation and when one supervisor stringently enforces a new grooming policy and another ignores it, there will be an immediate reaction from line personnel. Such a situation is best handled by reviewing the policy in a conference setting and allowing adequate time for discussion in order to resolve differences in interpretation.

Positive relationships with peers can take many avenues, but those that have proven to be successful focus on the work to be accomplished rather than the personalities of those involved. It is not necessary to like someone in order to work with them. Personal feelings should be set aside and the need to get the job done should dominate peer relationships.

The ability to get along with people is the hallmark of the professional. It is a sign of maturity. Going out of your way to share credit and praise people when the situation dictates is vital. Everything possible should be done to develop positive working relationships, and this usually involves communication. Peers need to explain actions, share information, let others know what is going on, send a memo and make it a personal policy to maximize communication. In other words, take the extra step.

It should be expected that peer criticism will occur on occasion. Despite ultimate personal efforts, someone will find fault or be critical of the manner in which something is being done. Employees must try not only to accept criticism but to learn from it.

Summary

Attainment of the rank of sergeant in a police department is one that is not achieved by everyone who enters law enforcement. In fact, it is a position that few attain. Such an achievement has its blessings and at the same time exacts its toll. It is nice to have an increase in pay and the added prestige that goes with the stripes, but not everyone enjoys enforcing policies or disciplining officers.

A first-line supervisor is part of management. Consequently work has to be accomplished through the efforts of others. At the same time, a first-line super-

visor must engage in the specific application of skills making up the management process: knowledge-based, conceptual, human and affective.

The supervisor's success depends upon the qualities and qualifications brought to the managerial process, and the methods utilized in resolving conflict. There is no one best way to supervise. Management is an art, not a science.

Management's expectations of the supervisor will vary from agency to agency, but usually include such variables as a positive attitude, accomplishment of tasks, loyalty to the department and responding to requests from management.

Subordinate expectations of management range from simply the need for feedback to assistance in interpreting policy or analyzing court decisions. The new breed of officers wants to be involved. These officers want a say in the decision-making process, especially when the decision affects line performance. This idea of worker participation requires a redefinition of work and working relationships. First-line supervisors must learn that real participation means power must be shared.

Expectations of the supervisor's peers include joint resolution of problems, sharing of information and the coordination of work activities. The successful accomplishment of tasks and goal attainment requires cooperation and coordination between first-line supervisors. If there is a key to supervisory achievement it is being a part of the management team and attaining goals through the efforts of others.

Case Study

Sergeant Ronald Lee

Sergeant Ronald Lee has been a sergeant for 18 years and has only three years remaining until retirement. Lee is from the "old school" of law enforcement. At the very least he could easily be described as legalistic and feels there is little room for social work: what is needed is "real police work."

While he projects a front of being a real hard-nose, he is in fact a very compassionate individual and frequently provides less fortunate people with whom he comes in contact, with funds to "tide them over." He buys meals for transients and is especially protective of children who are in trouble.

Sergeant Lee has worked in every major division of the department including investigative, administrative and field operations. He is currently assigned to patrol and works the midnight shift in the most crime-ridden district of the city.

He is well-liked by his men and is continually asked by other first-line supervisors for advice and assistance. When a new policy is implemented, the other sergeants turn to him for help in interpreting the policy in an effort to insure uniformity and fairness. When a new grooming policy was implemented, all the sergeants working the midnight shift sat down in a conference setting and resolved differences in the interpretation of the policy. It was soon

apparent the other two shifts were not conforming with the new departmental grooming standards stating:

1. Male officers shall keep their hair neat, clean, well-groomed and properly trimmed at all times while on duty. The hair shall be moderately tapered, shall not extend below the top of the shirt collar, nor cover any portion of the ears, and shall not interfere with the proper wearing of the uniform cap.

2. The hair of female officers shall be neatly shaped and arranged in an attractive feminine style. Hair styles that do not allow for the proper wearing of the cap are prohibited. Hair may touch the collar but may not fall below the collar's lower edge.

The other sergeants on the midnight shift asked Sergeant Lee to intercede on their behalf with supervisors on the other two shifts to see if the new policy could be applied uniformly.

If you were Sergeant Lee, how would you go about dealing with this problem? What approach would you use when meeting with the other first-line supervisors? How would you maximize communications?

Key Concepts

affective skills
conceptual skills
conflict resolution
human skills
knowledge-based skills

loyalty
management's expectations of the supervisor
participation
peer's expectations of the supervisor
subordinate's expectations of the supervisor

Discussion Topics and Questions

1. Why do some line officers find it difficult to become effective first-line supervisors?

2. What is the difference between human and affective skills as utilized by first-line supervisors?

3. Discuss the process of self-appraisal a supervisor can utilize.

4. Describe a common interpretation of knowledge-based skills and how a supervisor could apply them.

5. Discuss management's expectations of the supervisor.

6.   How can one create a truly participative organizational setting?

7.   An officer has charged favoritism in scheduling. How might this problem be resolved?

8.   What can supervisors do to maximize communications between themselves?

For Further Reading

Cordner, Gary W. (1992). "Human Resource Issues." In Larry T. Hoover (ed.) *Police Management, Perspectives and Issues*. Washington, DC: Police Executive Research Forum.

> This article emphasizes the need for police agencies to effectively manage human resources. Discusses such current issues as women in policing, minorities in policing, employment of the disabled, higher education, intelligence, psychological testing, physical fitness testing, assessment centers, performance evaluation, and patrol scheduling.

Imundo, Louis V. (1991). *The Effective Supervisor's Handbook*, 2nd ed. New York: American Management Association.

> Presents an excellent discussion of management and the supervisor's role. This text identifies the cornerstones of effective supervision such as trust, competence, fairness, respect, and confidence. The author takes the position that a supervisor is a manager. Of special interest is the chapter describing the process by which an employee becomes a supervisor.

Moody, Bobby D. (1994). "Is This Any Way to Run a Police Department?" *The Police Chief*, Vol. LXI, No. 1, 46-48.

> Positions the line officers at the top of the organizational structure rather than at the bottom and charges the officers with the responsibility of performing effectively in a professional manner. Holds the first-line supervisor responsible for effective and open communications. Supervisors are responsible for devoting their time to subordinate development.

Raterman, Max (1992). "Contingency Management for Line Level Supervisors." *Law and Order*, Vol. 40, No.5, 39-42.

> Supports contingency management as a viable technique to be used by first-line supervisors. Recommends considering each unit and each group of people as a unique management situation. Lists factors to consider when selecting a management style.

References

Arizona Daily Star (1993). "Four Federal Agents Charged in Drug Money Case." Jan. 28, A13.

Arizona Daily Star (1993). "N.Y.C. Panel Faces Tough Task of Curtailing Police Corruption." Oct. 10, A11.

Broadwell, Martin M. (1984). *The Practice of Supervising: Making Experience Pay*. Reading, MA: Addison-Wesley Publishing Co.

Bureau of Alcohol, Tobacco and Firearms (1992). *Explosives Incident Report*. Washington, DC: Bureau of Alcohol, Tobacco and Firearms, Treasury Department.

Commission on Accreditation for Law Enforcement Agencies (1993). *Commission Update,* No. 52, April.

Costley, Dan L. and Ralph Todd (1978). *Human Relations in Organizations.* St. Paul, MN: West.

Couper, David (1993). "Leadership for Change: A National Agenda." *The Police Chief,* Vol. LX, No. 12.

Dessler, Gary (1993). *Winning Commitment: How to Build and Keep a Competitive Workforce.* New York: R. R. Donnelley & Sons Co.

Dobbs, Carl and Mark W. Field (1993). "Rational Risk: Leadership Success or Failure?" *The Police Chief*, Vol. LX, No. 12.

Federal Bureau of Investigation (1993). *Crime in the United States 1992*. Washington, DC: U.S. Government Printing Office.

Handy, Charles B. (1993). *Understanding Organizations.* New York: Oxford University Press, Inc.

Hawkins, Jeff (1992). "Officer Motivation." *Law and Order*, Vol. 40, No. 10.

Imundo, Louis V. (1991). *The Effective Supervisor's Handbook,* 2nd ed. New York: AMACOM.

Laird, Donald A., Eleanor C. Laird and Rosemary T. Fruehling (1983). *Psychology: Human Relations and Work*. New York: McGraw-Hill Book Company.

Lewis, Marilyn (1993). "Minorities Now Make up Majority in 1,930 Cities." *San Jose Mercury News*, June 9: 1A and 12A.

McAlary, Mike (1988). *Buddy Boys*. New York: G.P. Putnam's Sons.

Mendofix, Paul J. (1994). "Reflections on Leadership." *FBI Law Enforcement Bulletin*, Vol. 63, No. 8.

Merina, Victor (1990). "Deputies Described as Corrupt." *Los Angeles Times*, Nov. 28: B3.

Moody, Bobby D. (1994). "Is This Any Way to Run a Police Department?" *The Police Chief*, Vol. LXI, No. 1.

Naisbitt, John (1982). *Mega Trends: Ten New Directions Transforming Our Lives.* New York: Warner Books.

Pascarella, Perry (1984). *The Achievers*. New York: The Free Press.

Raterman, Max (1992). "Contingency Management For Line Level Supervisors." *Law and Order*, Vol. 40, No. 5.

Reaves, Brian A. (1992). *Law Enforcement Management and Administration, 1990: Data for Individual State and Local Agencies with 100 or More Officers*. Washington, DC: U. S. Department of Justice.

Stone, Florence M. (1989). *The AMA Handbook of Supervisory Management*. New York: AMACOM.

Tracey, William R. (1990). *Leadership Skills: Standout Performance for Human Resources*. New York: AMACOM.

Wadia, M.S. and William Kolender (1988). "Holistic Management: A Behavioral Theory of Successful Leadership." *The Police Chief,* Vol. LV, No. 4.

Weiss, W. H. (1988). *Supervisor's Standard Reference Handbook*. Englewood Cliffs, NJ: Prentice-Hall, Inc.

Community
Policing—

Serving the Neighborhoods

2

Introductory Case Study

Sergeant Chris Eck

Chris Eck was elated to become a sergeant after five years as a patrol officer. He is a graduate of a local university with a degree in humanities and foreign languages. He speaks four languages fluently and frequently serves as an interpreter. Departmental policy allows him to earn an extra five percent monthly pay as a translator. He has averaged six hours each week serving as an interpreter for interviewing witnesses and victims, or interrogating suspects.

Sergeant Eck has a pleasing personality and a very good sense of humor. He has a positive working relationship with upper management, as well as with peers and those he supervises. In his new assignment to field operations he supervises nine officers on the swing shift in a high crime area.

After his promotion, Eck meticulously reviewed the personnel jackets of the officers under his supervision, and determined three of the officers had records requiring disciplinary action. The infractions included reporting to work late, spending too much time on breaks, and not responding rapidly when backing up other units.

The personnel jackets of the other six officers reflected semiannual performance ratings ranging from average to superior. After consulting with each officer, Eck determined that each of the three previously disciplined officers opposed community policing. Eck's team had been selected as the pilot team for the implementation of community policing. Eck decided to change the days off for the disciplined officers to reduce the time they would be working together. Hopefully this would lessen the impact of opposition to the new program.

Eck feels the decision is necessary because of his desire to see that the new program is successful. It reduces the potential for supervisory problems, and allows the team to perform more effectively.

The immediate reaction from the three disciplined officers was that, while consultation occurred, they really had no part in the decision-making process. They admitted they did not think community policing was a viable policing

technique, but they stated they would not oppose or impede its implementation. Additionally, they objected to having their days off changed because of their previous conduct rather than present conduct.

If you were Sergeant Eck, what would you do? Was Eck in error when he limited his contact with the three officers to consultation, but did not allow them to participate in the final decision? How should Sergeant Eck involve the three officers in the community program?

Law enforcement is changing its mode of operations, and community policing is the byword of the day. It grabs headlines throughout the nation, and articles extol its virtues (Skolnick and Bayley, 1988). Police conferences discuss it in depth, and special training prepares attenders to implement problem-solving programs. It has reached the point where it is almost a game of one-upmanship as police leaders describe their community policing programs. Unfortunately, there is a lack of consensus in defining community policing. Some view it as a traffic program (Sweeney, 1992), gun tip program (Shaw, 1993), gang control (Bloom, 1992) or citizens on patrol (Windham, 1994). Others create a special police unit similar to those occurring when community relations was in vogue. In the past the community relations unit was a status symbol. It was an indicator that the agency was responding to the needs of the community, and was part of the vanguard of professional law enforcement. One can only wonder if community policing in some cities is a hollow effort to keep up with what is a momentous shift in policing. Others view it as the ideology underpinning the agency, suggesting that it provides the reason for the existence of the department. Philosophically it can be a significant change in the provision of police services (Vaughn, 1991). At the least it is semantical gamesmanship and at the most it requires radical change, wherein personnel work with the community in determining the delivery system for police services (Trojanowicz and Bucqueroux, 1994; Bobinsky, 1994). Community policing provides officers with an opportunity to move closer to the community. It is a process wherein the police become organizers, advocates, and protectors (Couper, 1994; Stern, 1991).

At this point it is appropriate to suggest a working definition of community policing in Figure 2.1. Key elements of this definition include: (1) officers work jointly with community residents, (2) consideration is given to the needs of the community, (3) the causes of crime are agreed upon, and (4) community resources are marshalled to solve community problems.

Community policing, if it is to be successful, demands radical change over time, if there is to be a significant alteration in the way the organization attains goals. If change is to occur it has to be leader centered and engendered (Seagrave, 1994). The historical nature of police work, with its quasi-military orientation, mandates the need for change to emanate from top management (Rush, 1992). The values of community policing must be communicated to every

level and everyone in the organization (Overman, 1994). It is a transitional process wherein the chief executive officer removes barriers that impede change, fostering the development of a culture in which actions contrary to traditional working methods are stimulated (Cunningham, 1994). In community policing, top management must articulate the values of community policing and communicate them to every level and everyone in the organization (Overman, 1994; Rush, 1992). The police become an integral part of the community culture and members of the community help in defining future priorities and distributing resources (Bureau of Justice Assistance, 1994). It differs substantially from traditional models of policing and places considerable power and authority at the lowest level of the organization. Line officers and supervisors are the recipient of this significant shift of power and authority.

Figure 2.1
Definition of Community Policing

Community policing is a philosophy of policing in which officers work closely with community residents, developing a sense of the character of the neighborhood through regular, informal contacts with residents and institutions serving the area. Law enforcement officials address not just crimes but their causes; they identify problems and work with community residents to marshal community resources to solve those problems.

Adopted from National Crime Prevention Council, *National Service and Public Safety: Partnerships for Safer Communities,* Washington, D.C.: Presstar, Inc. 1994.

Empowerment

Risk-taking, originality, creativity, individuality and problem solving are essential characteristics of officers and supervisors operating in a community policing organization. Every aspect of the organization must foster the development of these skills in its officers. This is the only way the organization can respond to the need to promote public safety and enhance the quality of life in neighborhoods. Communities are changing rapidly and so are the characteristics of crime and violence, which are affecting neighborhoods (Bureau of Justice Assistance, 1994).

Empowerment of line personnel and first line supervisors is an essential ingredient of community policing. If it is missing, it is not really community policing even though it might involve some degree of citizen participation. Empowerment allows personnel to arrive at decisions based upon delegated power and authority. Empowerment is the conscious decision of the chief executive officer to allow others to assume decisionmaking (Johnson, 1994). It is the placing of authority and responsibility at the lowest levels of the organization. The exercise of judgment by the first line supervisor calls for superior decisionmaking when developing a problem-solving program. Instead of making

decisions, the supervisor coaches, supports, and helps officers in planning, analyzing and solving community problems. With such a process supervisors foster a working environment that increases officer discretion (Cunningham, 1944).

Community policing envisions the empowerment of officers so they can take independent action to solve problems, work with community leaders and improve the social environment of the neighborhoods they serve (Meese, 1993). Empowerment is the opposite of a supervisor encouraging officers to "stay out of trouble" or "not bother " their sergeant. Challenged with enigmatic problems not responsive to routine solutions, officers can be empowered by sergeants to search for imaginative solutions to problems rather than responding in rote fashion (Kelling, Wasserman and Williams, 1988). Additionally, the supervisor functions as a mentor, motivator and facilitator. Obviously all of this calls for a significant change in attitudes and methods of supervision. Constant and close supervision and the restriction of discretion are no longer the parameters of effective police supervision. The community police officer does not just take reports and pass on information so others in the chain of command can make decisions. Instead, the officer becomes a decisionmaker, solves the problem if possible, or at the least participates in decisions leading to problem resolution (Meese, 1993).

When empowerment occurs, community policing flourishes. Significant decisionmaking becomes the responsibility of line personnel and first-line supervisors rather than the sole property of police bureaucrats. With the eradication of red tape and the elimination of delays, those who are really familiar with community problems have the power of real input based on their knowledge of the local environment (Cunningham, 1994).

Quality Supervision

The first-line supervisor is at the focal point of change with the introduction of community policing into a department. Expectations are varied and include those set forth in Chapter 1 identifying the anticipations of subordinates, management and peers. To these we must add the expectations of the public as they join forces with the police in an effort to identify and solve community problems. It is necessary to understand the needs and perceptions of the public. This demands a constant interaction with members of the public to determine the services needing improvement, and whether there is a need for new services (Wycoff and Skogan, 1993).

Figure 2.2 lists several activities a supervisor must engage in when working within the parameters of community policing. Some of these are discussed below. **Quality supervision** envisions shared decisionmaking, teamwork, creativity and innovation. It involves commitment to the philosophy of community policing. The supervisor must personify the attributes of a facilitator, coach, role model, communicator and coordinator if community policing is to succeed.

Case Study

Sergeant Lara Buchanan

Sergeant Lara Buchanan is the supervisor of eight police officers. She has been a supervisor for three years. She is a graduate of the local college (with a major in psychology) and worked as a patrol officer for four years before her promotion. Her peers, as well as the officers under her supervision, find her to be a person that is easy to work with and for. She works in a somewhat marginal area of the city that has many policing problems. The sector contains two adjacent public housing projects, many small businesses, residential properties, apartment houses and some light industry. The sector has the third highest crime rate in the city, and most of the neighborhoods are deteriorating. Residents of the single dwellings have lived in the neighborhoods for many years and find themselves faced with changes that are causing them considerable discomfort and concern for their safety.

Officer James Wong has asked for help in dealing with the problem at one of the major intersections. There is a liquor store at the corner of Roma and Vista streets (an area causing police problems for many years). Vagrants and inebriates gather on the corner, especially in front of the liquor store. The police receive disturbance calls, on a daily basis, for this location. Customers buy cheap wine from the store, consume it on the adjacent sidewalks, and harass anyone using the sidewalk. They also wave down cars to talk with friends or complete strangers. All this results in traffic-flow problems at the intersection. In the evenings, the crowd at the intersection grows larger, and the drinkers often become rowdy and noisy. Fights are a common occurrence, and drug dealings are becoming increasingly frequent.

Three abandoned buildings near the intersection are a source of additional problems. These buildings have deteriorated considerably and are full of garbage. They are a health hazard, are structurally unsafe and present a real eyesore. Drug dealers often hide stash amid the rubble and debris, drug users get high in the buildings and women addicts often trade sex for drugs inside the buildings.

In the past, calls for service have resulted in the corner not receiving adequate police attention. In most instances the single officer assigned to the beat was responding to calls away from the intersection. When the beat officer visited the intersection he dispersed loiterers, and when appropriate made arrests. Charges ranged from disorderly conduct to possession of a controlled substance.

If you were Sergeant Buchanan, how would you go about helping Officer Wong? Would you analyze the problem and design a response or would you have Officer Wong do this? Why? Based on the information provided, what is the problem? What data would you collect? What resources would you use? What style of leadership would you use with Officer Wong?

Figure 2.2
Responsibilities of a First-Line Supervisor in Community Policing

1. Ensure the retention of beat integrity when problem solving.
2. Monitor the creation of beat profiles to insure they have identified critical problems.
3. Work with officers and community residents to create a system for the allocation and use of resources.
4. Work with officers and community members to develop, implement and manage problem-solving systems.
5. Collaborating with other agencies that can work together in solving community problems.
6. Depersonalize failure and judge events–not people.
7. Motivate personnel to serve as catalysts when dealing with and solving community problems.
8. Function as a process facilitator by providing officers with support and guidance, acting as a liaison, and running interference when needed.
9. Encourage officers to take risks when solving problems.
10. Foster inventiveness when problem solving.
11. Represent the unit within the department.

Process Facilitation

The supervisor must convey the importance of community policing especially in convincing police officers that community engagement and problem solving are **real** police work (Bureau of Justice Assistance, 1994). If community policing is to succeed, the supervisor must genuinely support organizational changes. In some instances the change might include organizational structure and at the very least it will include new service policies and procedures. It is essential to articulate and reinforce the philosophy of community policing. Supervisors must become knowledgeable about the duties expected of them. Initially, a supervisor might be unfamiliar with the working implications of the new service style. They must therefore make an effort to perform the role as expected (Wycoff and Oettmeier, 1994). In this respect the goal is for the supervisor to become comfortable in the new role. Finally, as a **process facilitator**, a supervisor must communicate openly, become a team member and encourage officers to participate actively in problem solving.

Building Partnerships within the Police Department

The vital responsibility of building **partnerships** has several dimensions, including serving as a conduit by relaying information up the chain of command, explaining problems and finding the means for resolving them. Additionally, efforts to build partnerships within the department, as a task, provides the supervisor with an opportunity to explain how community policing works cooperatively with other units as well as requesting assets needed to resolve problems. This includes resources such as traffic officers, detectives, patrol officers, juvenile investigators or a narcotics unit. It also involves relaying information to other unit supervisors about criminal activities that would be of interest to them, mediating conflict between units and integrating unit activities with others. This activity involves not only sharing information but a form of salesmanship wherein the supervisor tries to secure the commitment of resources to implement effective problem-solving strategies (McElroy, Cosgrove and Sadd, 1993). These efforts are needed to encourage a spirit of cooperation throughout the ranks and foster the commitment of every officer to the community policing process (Stipak, Immer and Clavadetscher, 1994).

Of special importance is the working relationship between patrol officers and detectives. Under community policing it is necessary to reduce the isolation between the two units. Officers can use neighborhood-based information for follow-up investigation including the arrest of offenders (Meese, 1993). Information will become available (that was not available before) because of the continuing and constant contact between community police officers and members of the community. The supervisor should ensure that feedback is given to the officers by detectives when information results in the successful conclusion of an investigation. This reinforces the relationship between the two groups and motivates officers to continue to provide information. It is possible to describe the relationship between specialized units of a police agency and the officers responsible for community policing by means of a medical model (Meese, 1993):

> [T]he patrol officer in a specific neighborhood or beat area is like a general practitioner physician who has the principal interface with the individual citizen. Surrounding and supporting the police general practitioner is a series of specialists–detectives, juvenile investigators, narcotics officers, headquarters staff officers, and others–who are available for consultation or referral of the case.

It is this medical model that the first-line supervisor should foster and cultivate. The line officer remains as the key to community policing and all other units should support problem-solving efforts.

Collaboration

A basic tenet of community policing is to work with a wide variety of resources needed to resolve identifiable problems. Employing external resources may range from making a referral to another agency to actually asking an agency to engage in a cooperative effort. Figure 2.3 lists several potential public and private resources. The identification of available and pertinent resources is a major phase in the development of a positive problem-solving program. If a department is fortunate enough, it will have a resource manual listing agencies, contact persons and brief synopses of the services offered by the agencies (Bureau of Justice Assistance, 1993). First-line supervisors should begin by contacting government and private agencies to collect information and develop responses to identifiable problems. Or, if required, ask a commanding officer to make official contact. This allows supervisors to screen and identify viable agencies and it reduces the number of individuals who are contacting other agencies. In fact, in some communities agencies encourage contact by appointed individuals.

Liaison and follow-up activities are essential if **collaboration** is to be effective. This is true both for units within the police organization, and other city departments. Figure 2.4 is a Community Enhancement Request Form that an officer can use to request specific services from city agencies to handle conditions that may result in crime or community decay. Monitoring of follow-up requests is mandatory and if the problems are not addressed within a reasonable time, the first-line supervisor should stimulate the needed response and provide feedback to line officers. This function is critical to community policing because it proves that something can happen when citizens complain. It also directly affects the credibility of the line officer as well as that of the police department (Meese, 1993). Other city agencies have been especially effective at removing abandoned vehicles, enforcing parking regulations, and demolishing vacant buildings. They can also control vendors and eliminate hazardous conditions on private property. One police department obtained the permission of owners of abandoned buildings (by working with the department of building and safety) to enter each building and evict trespassers prior to the demolition of the buildings. In another instance, a city housing department actively helped apartment owners obtain loans to rehabilitate property, thus improving the quality of housing and setting a new standard for the community (Margolis, 1994). The Code Enforcement Team of Fort Lauderdale is another example of cooperative efforts in this area. The team is composed of one member each from the police, fire, and building and zone departments. During 1992 this team inspected approximately 2,500 dwellings, issued 21,600 citations, and boarded up or demolished 60 structures (Donisi, 1992).

Supervisors can reinforce the collaboration process of problem solving by checking the efforts of officers. Members of other agencies can be contacted to determine how well subordinates have performed in a collaborative effort. If the supervisor finds the officer has functioned poorly, effort should be expended to provide the officer with assistance and guidance to resolve the problem (Bureau of Justice Assistance, 1994).

Figure 2.3
A List of Potential Collaborative Agencies

Police Departments	Sheriff's Departments
State Police	Federal Agencies
Community Centers	Neighborhood Associations
Judicial System	Prosecutor's Office
Public Defender's Office	Mediation Centers
Probation Office	Parole Agency
Correctional Facilities	Social Services
Counseling Services	Health Services
Transit Companies	Teachers
Boards of Education	School Principals
Agencies Serving the Elderly	Housing Authorities
Businesses	Local United Way
YMCA/YWCA	Civic Clubs
Fraternal Clubs	Social Clubs
Boys & Girls Clubs	Big Brothers/Big Sisters
Youth Membership Groups	Womens/Mens Clubs
Victim Service Agencies	Public Libraries
Mayor or County Executives	City or County Councils
Chamber of Commerce	Local Utility Companies

Adopted from National Crime Prevention Council, *National Service and Public Safety: Partnerships for Safer Communities,* Washington, D.C., National Crime Prevention Council, 1994.

Supervising Community Police Officers

Community policing involves giving officers greater control over their working conditions. This requires a **new style of supervision**. The authoritarian supervision style is unacceptable. No longer is it permissible to give an order and expect an officer to respond with absolute obedience. There are many intrinsic rewards to officers who work in a problem-solving police department. An officer has greater control over the work performed coupled with increased responsibility and a higher degree of autonomy. The most significant feature is the involvement of line officers in the decision-making process as a result of increased participation in the problem-solving process. All of these lead to improved job satisfaction (Bureau of Justice Assistance, 1993). A community supervisor's typical day is set forth in Figure 2.5 listing tasks performed. Supervisors can provide expertise needed to identify and solve neighborhood problems or provide assistance to residents (McElroy, Cosgrove and Sadd, 1993). A supervisor can also help officers to manage their available time so they might adequately handle problems. Some agencies authorize first line supervisors to schedule "flex time" permitting officers to amend their work hours as necessary and balance demands between calls

Figure 2.4
Community Enhancement Request Form

City Police Department
COMMUNITY ENHANCEMENT REQUEST

❑ Citizen Request   Date & Time Rec'd/Obs'd
❑ Business Request
❑ Officer Initiated

PERSON REPORTING SECTION
(Leave Blank When Officer-Initiated)

Last Name, First, Middle

Residence Address   Zip

Business Address   Zip

Residence Phone No.   Business Phone No.
( )   ( )

Location of Activity/Problem   RD   Area

Completing Officer   Serial No.

TYPE OF REQUEST FOR SERVICE

Department of Building and Safety:
❑ Abandoned/junked vehicle on private property
❑ Unkept conditions on private property
❑ Hazardous conditions on private property
❑ Vacant buildings/houses
❑ Vendors on private property/parking lots
❑ Other (Explain in information section below)
Department of Transportation:
❑ Abandoned vehicles on street
❑ Parking enforcement
❑ Other (Explain in information section below)
Department of Public Works (Street Maintenance):
❑ Street repair
❑ Sidewalk repair
❑ Tree trimming
❑ Vacant lot cleanup
❑ Street lighting
❑ Graffiti
❑ Other (Explain in information section below)
Department of Public Works (Sanitation):
❑ Trash collection (street/sidewalk/parkway)
❑ Other (Explain in information section below)
Police Department (Confidential):
❑ Gang activity
❑ Drinking in public
❑ Other (Explain in information section below)
Other City Department

_____

Additional Information _____
_____
_____
_____

SUPERVISOR/OFFICER MAKING REQUEST

Name   Serial   Date

CITY DEPARTMENT NOTIFIED

Department   Time

Employee   Ph. Ext.

FOLLOW-UP INFORMATION

Date   City Employee   Ph. Ext.

Findings: _____
_____
_____
_____
_____
_____

If the complaint was initiated by a citizen, was
the original PR contacted?
        ❑   Yes   ❑   No

Was the PR satisfied with the response to the
complaint?
        ❑   Yes   ❑   No

Comments of PR (optional): _____
_____
_____
_____
_____
_____

for service and problem solving. Some departments allow officers to consult with other officers and a supervisor to work cooperatively by changing days off or changing schedules to help in addressing a problem (Wycoff and Skogan, 1993).

Computer software is available that materially helps a supervisor by forecasting officer and vehicle needs by beat and neighborhood, generating alternative officer schedules that optimize services, and redesigning beats to optimally balance workloads and communities. Additionally, this software can automatically detect and rank problems by geographical areas and tie them to demographics, crime reports, patterns and known offenders (Analysis Central Systems, 1994).

Supervisors will normally meet with officers at daily briefings to discuss scheduling, personnel problems, problem-solving techniques, resources, and other matters of mutual interest. Sergeants should spend most of their time working with officers in the neighborhoods. This allows them to become familiar with not only the neighborhoods but the problems facing the officers, so help can be provided as needed.

Successful community policing requires the supervisor to relay information up the change of command about problem-solving efforts as well as requests for needed resources. It is also an excellent time to reinforce the importance of community policing by indicating its contributions to the attainment of departmental goals.

Figure 2.5
A Community Supervisor's Day

In addition to responding to calls for service where backup is needed, a typical day might include:

1. A meeting with a neighborhood group, along with the beat officer about drug activity.
2. Preparing the weekly work schedule.
3. A meeting with the Health Department about a communicable disease problem in one of the neighborhoods.
4. Briefing command personnel on needed resources to deal with community problems.
5. Preparation of a performance evaluation for one of the officers.
6. Upon request, working with an officer in the analysis of school dropout, truancy information, and census data regarding a neighborhood juvenile vandalism problem.

Managing Failure

The first-line supervisor must manage in an informal manner. Community policing is new ground and problem solving is a new technique. It is not uncommon for mistakes to precede innovative results. In the struggle to resolve problems officers will make mistakes and proposed solutions will fail. When risks occur and innovative solutions are sought the margin for error increases dramatically as officers proceed through the learning curve. **Managing and controlling failure** can result in positive results. Supervisors have to develop an attitude of tolerance and accept honest failure (Wycoff and Skogan, 1993). Management of the total department begins with the attitude that positive failures can become the power that propels the organization toward the attainment of goals.

When failure occurs, the supervisor should work with the officer and document the reasons for failure. Circulation of this information to all interested parties is an essential part of the learning process. This critique process will undoubtedly identify training needs or other errors subject to correction. The supervisor should arrange for additional training, or provide feedback in order to reduce future errors. A teamwork philosophy should replace power-oriented supervision emphasizing an atmosphere of risk taking, creativity and the acceptance of errors in decisionmaking.

When managing failure you must engage in a process of depersonalizing the failure and judging the actual event rather than the involved individual. Failure should lead to growth, not recriminations or punishment (Bennett, 1993).

Summary

Community policing is fast becoming the mode of operation for many police departments. It is a philosophy of policing wherein officers work closely with citizens to identify and deal with neighborhood problems. The police actually become a part of the community culture to promote public safety and enhance the quality of life in neighborhoods.

Empowerment of line personnel and first-line supervisors is an essential ingredient of community policing. It permeates the entire organization and is the conscious decision of the chief executive officer to allow others to assume decision-making power. Under empowerment the first-line supervisor functions as a mentor, motivator and facilitator.

The supervisor should articulate the philosophy of community policing through every action. This involves communicating openly, becoming a team member, and encouraging officers to solve community problems. The supervisor must genuinely support this new philosophy.

All supervisors must become familiar with a wide variety of resources that can help in the process of problem solving. First-line supervisors should initiate direct contact with governmental and private agencies to ask for a cooperative effort. The process of collaboration clearly enhances the potential for success.

In community policing, officers have greater control over decisionmaking, a higher degree of autonomy, and additional responsibility. Supervisors can help officers by managing their available time to allow them to handle problems, and meeting with officers frequently to discuss scheduling, personnel problems, available resources, and problem-solving techniques.

Lastly, supervisors must learn to manage failure and turn it into a positive learning experience. When risks occur and creativity is instituted failures should be expected. Failure management is a process of depersonalizing failure and judging the event rather than the individual.

Case Study

Sergeant Ralph Armstrong

Sergeant Ralph Armstrong has been in the Rose Heights Police Department for four years. He previously worked in another department for five years and transferred laterally with the rank of sergeant. He has a BA degree in criminology, is currently enrolled in a master's degree program, and has completed twelve units of graduate work. He is a very outgoing person and well-liked by peers and the officers he supervises. The department is just in the process of beginning a community policing program and every member of the team has completed the required training course.

He has eleven officers on his team that services a racially mixed sector in a bedroom part of the city. Part of the sector contains several theaters and nightclubs frequented by the younger set, especially on Friday and Saturday nights. Residents in the area have complained about the noise, drinking and fighting. Young adults cruise the nearby neighborhoods, disturbing the peace, and committing acts of vandalism. In the area of the night clubs, drugs are readily available. The city has a population of 54,000 and is part of the metropolitan area. Residential burglary has increased dramatically along with thefts from automobiles. A citizens committee, supported by local churches, has demanded action. Sergeant Armstrong has verified the increase in crime from departmental records. Additionally, he visited the troubled beats and discussed the problem with the assigned officers. He plans to meet with the committee and discuss the problem.

If you were Sergeant Armstrong, how would you conduct the meeting? What police personnel would you have at the meeting? What departmental, city, and community resources would you expect would be involved in the analysis phase? Why?

Key Concepts

collaboration

community enhancement

empowerment

managing failure

partnerships

process facilitation

quality supervision

supervisory techniques

Discussion Topics and Questions

1. What is the principal difference between community policing and the professional model of policing?

2. What are the key characteristics of empowerment?

3. What distinguishes quality supervision from command and control supervision?

4. Discuss how process facilitation works.

5. What are the responsibilities of a first-line supervisor in community policing?

6. How does a supervisor build partnerships within the police department?

7. What is collaboration?

8. Discuss how a supervisor manages failure.

For Further Reading

Bureau of Justice Assistance (1994). *Understanding Community Policing: A Framework for Action.* August. Washington, DC, U.S. Department of Justice.

> This monogram provides a conceptual framework useful to practitioners interested in implementing or expanding community policing. The roots of community policing are traced, and community partnership and problem solving are discussed in depth. Basic organizational and operational elements are reviewed in terms of implementing community policing. Finally, the monogram reviews the criteria for assessing the progress of a community policing program.

Overman, Richard (1994). "The Case for Community Policing." *The Police Chief,* Vol. LXI, No. 3.

> Reviews the value of community policing and the importance of mobilizing the community to protect and help themselves. Recommends communicating the need for implementing community policing and involving people in the planning. Suggests creating a citizens' police academy and holding regular community meetings. Recommends decentralization, and finding ways to get officers out of cars and close to the community. Finally, the author supports the need to be results-oriented.

Trojanowicz, Robert and Bonnie Bucqueroux (1994). *Community Policing: How to Get Started.* Cincinnati, OH: Anderson Publishing Co.

> This book contains sections ranging from theory and definition of community policing to the actual duties of the officer, and how to evaluate officers. Of special interest is the section on supervision that includes a wide range of topics such as: internal functions, sources of resistance, external relationships, and measurable activities performed by a first-line supervisor.

Wycoff, Mary Ann and Wesley K. Skogan (1993). *Community Policing in Madison: An Evaluation of Implementation and Impact.* Washington, DC: National Institute of Justice, U.S. Department of Justice.

> This study concludes that it is possible to change a traditional department to one where employees become members of a team, and participate in decisionmaking. Discusses the change process and supports the need for quality leadership. Reviews the consequences of change for officers and citizens.

References

Analysis Central Systems (1994). "Community Policing Software." *The Police Chief,* Vol. LXI, No. 10.

Bennett, Charles W., Jr. (1993). "The Last Taboo of Community Policing." *The Police Chief,* Vol. LX, No. 8.

Bloom, Lynda (1992). "Community Policing Nips Gang Problem in the Bud." *Law and Order,* Vol. 40, No. 9.

Bobinsky, Robert (1994). "Reflections on Community-Oriented Policing." *FBI Law Enforcement Bulletin,* Vol. 63, No. 3.

Bureau of Justice Assistance (1993). *Problem-Oriented Drug Enforcement: A Community-based Approach for Effective Policing.* Washington, DC: U.S. Department of Justice.

Bureau of Justice Assistance (1994). *Neighborhood-Oriented Policing in Rural Communities: A Program Planning Guide.* Washington, DC: U.S. Department of Justice.

Bureau of Justice Assistance (1994). *Understanding Community Policing: A Framework for Action.* Washington, DC: U.S. Department of Justice.

Couper, David C. (1994). "Seven Seeds for Policing." *FBI Law Enforcement Bulletin,* Vol. 63, No. 3.

Cunningham, Scott A. (1994). "The Empowering Leader and Organizational Change." *The Police Chief,* Vol. LXI, No.8.

Donisi, Joseph M. (1992). "Fort Lauderdale's Code Enforcement Team." *FBI Law Enforcement Bulletin,* Vol. 61, No. 3.

Johnson, Robert A. (1994). "Police Organizational Design and Structure." *FBI Law Enforcement Bulletin,* Vol. 63, No. 6.

Kelling, George L., Robert Wasserman and Hubert Williams (1988). *Police Accountability and Community Policing.* Washington, DC: U.S. Department of Justice.

McElroy, Jerome E., Colleen A. Cosgrove and Susan Sadd (1993). *Community Policing: The CPOP in New York.* Newbury Park: Sage Publications.

Margolis, Stephen (1994). "Blythe Street Team Makes an Impact." *The Police Chief,* Vol. LXI, No. 10.

Meese, Edwin III, (1993) *Community Policing and the Police Officer.* January. Washington, DC: U.S. Department of Justice.

National Crime Prevention Council (1994). *National Service and Public Safety: Partnerships for Safer Communities.* March. Washington, DC: U.S. Department of Justice.

Overman, Richard (1994). "The Case for Community Policing." *The Police Chief,* Vol. LXI, No. 3.

Rush, George E. (1992). "Community Policing: Overcoming the Obstacles." *The Police Chief,* Vol. LIX, No. 10.

Seagrave, Jayne (1994). "Accounting for Police Resistance to Change: The Benefits of Integrating (Theoretical) Police Subculture Literature with (Pragmatic) Organizational Culture Literature." *Western Criminologist.* Spring.

Shaw, J. Wilford (1993). "Community Policing to Take Guns off the Street." *Behavioral Science and the Law,* Vol. 11, No.4.

Skolnick, Jerome H. and David H. Bayley (1988). *Community Policing: Issues and Practices Around the World.* May. Washington, DC: U.S. Department of Justice.

Stern, Gary (1991). "Community Policing Six Years Later: What Have We Learned?" *Law and Order,* Vol. 39, No. 5.

Stipak, Brian, Susan Immer and Maria Clavadetscher (1994). "Are You Really Doing Community Policing?" *The Police Chief,* Vol. LXI, No. 10.

Sweeney, Earl M. (1992). "Community-Oriented Traffic Policing." *The Police Chief,* Vol. LIX, No. 7.

Trojanowicz, Robert and Bonnie Bucqueroux (1994). *Community Policing: How to Get Started.* Cincinnati, OH: Anderson Publishing Co.

Vaughn, Jerald R. (1991). "Community Oriented Policing...You Can Make it Happen." *Law and Order,* Vol. 39, No.6.

Windham, Thomas R. (1994). "Code Blue: Citizens on Patrol." *The Police Chief,* Vol. LXI, No. 5.

Wycoff, Mary Ann and Timothy N. Oettmeier (1994). *Evaluating Patrol Officer Performance Under Community Policing: The Houston Experience.* February. Washington, DC: U.S. Department of Justice.

Wycoff, Mary Ann and Wesley K. Skogan (1993). *Community Policing in Madison: Quality from the Inside Out.* December. Washington, DC: U.S. Department of Justice.

Interpersonal Communications—

Striving for Effectiveness

3

Introductory Case Study

Sergeant Lou Duton

Sergeant Duton, a supervisor on the midnight shift, is under pressure to resolve a conflict. He has received an increasing number of complaints from Officer Jim James that his partner Sarah Hawks is a chain smoker and she refuses to quit smoking in the patrol car. James finds cigarette smoke exceptionally irritating and it makes his eyes water. In fact, he stated on occasion he feels nauseous because of cigarette smoke and even opening the automobile windows does very little to reduce the feelings of discomfort. Officer James has become increasingly insistent that Sarah Hawks refrain from smoking, but her position is she has a right to smoke and Officer James should not infringe on her rights.

Up to this point, Sergeant Duton has left the resolution of the problem up to the two officers, hoping their differences were minor enough to be worked out. Since the two officers are working partners, Duton felt it was up to them to resolve their dispute. Unfortunately, the two officers have been unable to solve the problem amicably.

The conflict between the officers has not affected their work, yet; however, it seems this could occur at any time because the participants are making their positions known to other members of the shift in an effort to gain support. An immediate solution to the conflict would be to assign each of the officers another partner, but the current scheduling cannot be changed because it would cause an undue hardship on others.

There is no departmental policy regarding smoking so neither the officers nor the sergeant can refer back to a precedent as a means of resolving the problem. The sergeant must resolve the problem before the situation deteriorates to the extent their work performance is affected. If at all possible, a solution has to be found, resulting in a situation in which each of the employees' needs are met, as well as those of the department.

Normally it would seem such a problem could be resolved with ease, but in this case each of the employees has become overwhelmed by their emotions.

> *Since the two officers cannot resolve their problem, how would you, as Sergeant Duton, proceed? What would you do to ensure communications are reopened between the two officers? Is it a problem of inadequate information or decoding? Explain. What could be done to improve two-way communications?*

If police executives could identify one characteristic that "excellent" supervisors have in common, it is the ability to communicate. In law enforcement agencies, the first-line supervisor engages in a number of activities, the first of which includes the translation of the organization's managerial values, mission, goals, objectives and operational policies into day-to-day decisions and operational activities (Southerland, 1992). Secondly, a supervisor utilizes communication to train, discipline and motivate each officer in an effort to improve performance and provide for a more secure community. Lastly, the supervisor plans and organizes work, gives directions and orders, and controls employee performance, all in an effort to improve the effectiveness of the organization.

There is an unquestionable need for supervisors who understand the intricate nature of the communication process and vigorously foster a working environment encouraging open communication (Gaines, Southerland and Angell, 1991).

The Importance of Communication Skills

Within police agencies the need for good communication skills has become increasingly important as the tasks performed have become more complex and demanding. It is difficult to imagine a professional law enforcement agency without advanced communications, computer-aided dispatching and microcomputers for the analysis of data and the preparation of a budget. In fact, law enforcement has readily adopted hardware, but there is a clear-cut need for improved interpersonal and organizational communication.

Interpersonal communication exists at every level of any organization, but is most prevalent at the operational level where there is a continual interaction between supervisors and line personnel. When there is good communication, it is a result of effective supervision. Communication is an integral part of our everyday life and it is difficult to imagine an organization not fostering and encouraging strong communication skills. At the very least, communication is the lifeblood of an organization. It is the process tieing the whole organization together. When a mishap occurs, the immediate reaction is to blame it on an inability to communicate effectively.

A breakdown in communication is an inevitable consequence of our inability to properly interpret what is said. It is easier to blame failures on poor or inadequate communication than deal with the problem directly. When one becomes a first-line supervisor it does not confer upon them the ability to be an effective communicator. It takes time to develop communication skills and assume the posture of a good communicator. It can be learned.

If communication is to be effective it must be nurtured by all levels of management, from the top down. As previously stated, first-line supervisors are managers, and an integral part of the management team. They are the only ones who are in constant contact with operational personnel. It is the most strategic and important position in any law enforcement agency.

Supervisors spend a large part of their working hours engaged in tasks clearly identified as communicating. A recent study of first-line supervisors in municipal law enforcement agencies reflected that 55 percent of their communication time involved tasks related to subordinates, 26 percent concerned superiors, 15 percent related to the public and 4 percent involved other supervisors. These percentages are set forth in Figure 3.1.

Figure 3.1
Supervisor's Communication Tasks by Level

Level	Percentage
Subordinates	55
Superiors	26
Citizens	15
Other Supervisors	4
	100

Additional support which delineates the importance of communication for supervisors was reflected in a task analysis study of the first-line supervisor's position. In considering 53 specific tasks, 51 percent involved communication. These tasks, rated in terms of their importance, included such activities as:

1. Providing feedback to subordinates regarding job performance.

2. Responding to subordinates' inquiries.

3. Meeting with and providing direction to subordinates regarding particular incidents or investigations.

4. Meeting with managers to resolve specific problems or concerns.

5. Resolving citizen/officer conflicts.

6. Meeting with and resolving disputes among subordinates.

It is amazing, when one stops to think of it, that so much of a human's waking time is spent communicating. This is noticed especially in the work environment, and law enforcement is no exception. The first-line supervisor must understand the importance of verbal/nonverbal communication, the art of listening and

the processing of information. The interaction between sergeants and subordinates succeeds or fails as a direct result of their ability or inability to communicate.

Effective communication means getting the meaning across. In many instances this can prove to be a difficult barrier to surmount. When analyzing the reasons one supervisor is a better communicator than another, one characteristic stands out: an awareness of the need to communicate well. A successful communicator is one who is not concerned about personal self-esteem. When communication falters, they don't look for someone to blame; they work to resolve the problem. If they know they have done a poor job in explaining something, good communicators will admit they have erred and start over. It boils down to wanting to communicate well.

A good communicator avoids meaningless or imprecise words. Today, much of our communication is impaired by wordiness. Often the erroneous assumption is made that a lot of words will clarify a situation and the problem will be resolved. The poor communicator fails to realize that, more often than not, words can confuse, confound or mislead. Supervisors who have the reputation of being good communicators are known as individuals who have something to say. When it is necessary to communicate, they respond accordingly, whether it is on a one-to-one basis or in a group. A good communicator is a respectable and valuable member of the law enforcement community.

The Communication Process

Defining communication might seem to be an easy and straightforward task; however, it has confounded experts for years. In fact, one study reviewed managerial literature and found 94 different definitions of the word communication. If nothing else, this clearly demonstrates the complexity of the actual communication process. The dictionary defines communication as a process by which information is exchanged between individuals through a common system of symbols, signs or behavior. If communication is to be effective, however, there is definitely a need to have something more than just the exchange of information.

The sender of a message must make a sincere effort to affect the behavior of the recipient. Effective person-to-person communication involves:

1. Transmission of a message.

2. Decoding the message.

3. The recipient correctly interpreting and understanding the message.

On the surface the process seems quite simple, but a careful analysis of the components indicates a number of places where the message can become misconstrued, garbled or even ignored. It is somewhat similar to talking with someone from another culture who has a limited knowledge of English.

The recipient of the message may continually nod his or her head, look you straight in the eye and seemingly absorb every word and respond to every nuance. However, if one asks the listener even the most simple question, it is readily apparent that while the message was transmitted, it was definitely not decoded. Keep in mind the same thing can also occur between two individuals who are fluent in the same language (see Figure 3.2).

The communication process is exceedingly complex, especially when one takes into consideration the fact that both the sender and the recipient of a message are affected by attitudes, skills, knowledge, opinions and other forces existing before, during and after the message is transmitted.

Figure 3.2
Simplistic Communication Process

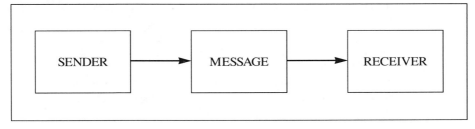

Interpersonal communication requires two or more people. Participants in a conversation send messages by verbal as well as nonverbal channels. The characteristics of senders and receivers can substantially influence the communication process—a continually changing one. For example, the sender may want to change the opinion, perception or behavior of the receiver and will send a message in an effort to accomplish a specific goal. A problem can occur when the goals of the two individuals involved are in conflict. When this happens there is a strong possibility of distortion and misunderstandings occurring. When goals are compatible, there is a greater possibility that a message will be interpreted accurately.

The sender of a message determines the relevancy of each and every message. This is generally known as gatekeeping inasmuch as the sender determines the importance and relevancy of information. The sender, therefore, exercises complete control over the flow of information. This is especially noted when supervisors, by virtue of their position in a police organization, operate as the primary communication point between upper management and the line. Operational autonomy, with the primary guidance coming from departmental policy, places the first-line supervisor in the position of controlling the amount and the nature of information entering the information system. Decisions are constantly made as to the need for passing information into the system. At the same time, the supervisor is in a position to control the amount of information subordinates will receive.

This is really pertinent when the supervisor presides at the roll-call session preceding each shift. It can be a real learning process for the officers or it can be conducted in a perfunctory manner with a limited exchange of information. Many first-line supervisors believe that proper communication has occurred when they have simply told a shift of officers what to do. It is difficult to believe that anyone who has been in an organization for a year or more has not heard either, "I told you what the new policy was," or "Why didn't you tell me?" It seems the message transmission could be accomplished without difficulty, but it is soon obvious that encoding the message can and will, in all probability, become complex.

Communication is an exchange of information involving two or more parties and all must participate. It is a process modified or constrained by such features as those listed here:

1. Inadequate information will seldom produce a desired result.

2. The receiver of the message determines the accuracy of the message through decoding.

3. The receiver of the message, as a result of attitudes, experiences and motivations, determines whether the message is decoded in the way intended by the sender.

Each person involved in a communication situation both encodes and decodes messages simultaneously. It is a continuous process and as information is received it is decoded. From the standpoint of the first-line supervisor, answers should be sought to the following type of questions:

1. What is the real message to be encoded?

2. Is there data supporting the message's theme?

3. Does the message imply anything?

4. Can the message be misinterpreted?

5. What type of reaction will result from the message?

6. Will the message produce results?

Each supervisor should make a conscious effort to deal with the practical problems readily identifiable from the above questions. With practice, a supervisor can soon develop messages that are clear, have content, and will obtain results (see Figure 3.3).

Another element of the communication process is the channel through which the message travels from the sender to the receiver. The term channel usually refers to one or more of the human senses. This obviously involves both verbal

and nonverbal aspects of communication, although the first-line supervisor usually deals with oral communication.

Failure to acknowledge the importance of nonverbal communication and its impact on the receiver(s) will often cause problems. This was especially apparent in one agency when top management instituted a new policy prohibiting officers from carrying "second weapons." At the roll call where the new policy was discussed, one of the senior sergeants made light of the new policy, leading everyone in attendance to believe the policy would never be enforced and officers could continue the past practice of carrying "second weapons."

Figure 3.3
Realistic Communication Process

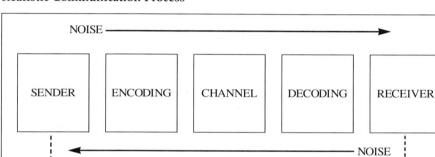

After an unfortunate shooting incident in which an officer used a "second weapon," an internal investigation concluded the shooting was justified and conformed with the departmental use of deadly force policy, but suspended the officer for two weeks for carrying a "second weapon." The investigation also recommended that the sergeant who had failed to explain and support departmental policy be suspended for two weeks. The chief of police, after an appropriate hearing, demoted the sergeant.

The distorted message sent by the sergeant in this situation proved disastrous for the officer as well as the supervisor. The *content* of the sergeant's presentation to the officers was clear and concise, but the *context* in which it was delivered proved to be the most persuasive part of the message. The context of any message cannot be ignored for it can prove to be more meaningful than content.

Once the message has been sent, it is up to the receiver to decode the message and attach significant meaning. There are six aspects to consider at this point (Naval Education and Training Program, 1984):

1. What the sender INTENDED to say.

2. What was ACTUALLY said.

3. What the receiver HEARD.

4. What the receiver THINKS was heard.

5. What the receiver SAID.

6. What the sender THINKS the receiver said.

These six modifiers of the communication process are involved in every message and the receiver reacts, based upon personal experiences, viewpoints, knowledge and frame of reference. It is apparent that a failure in communication can occur at numerous points. With feedback, the cycle becomes a viable two-way process. *Feedback* (because of its type) can vary greatly. It can be as simple as a nod of the head or as complex as a multiple-paged report. For example, the receiver could respond with a request for clarification: "As I understand it you want me to notify every liquor store on my beat about the two armed robbers. Is that correct?" Such a technique can leave no doubt as to what was meant by the sender and whether the message was understood.

Noise is the last feature of the communication process. It is anything reducing the accuracy of a communication. An awareness of how noise affects communication will allow one to take steps to reduce it, thereby improving the accuracy of each communication. Noise can be present at any point in the communication process, but the greatest problem area is with the use of language.

Some people seem to have the ability to explain things clearly and with a great deal of simplicity. At the same time, another individual never seems to be able to find the correct expressive words and even a simple thought becomes tangled up in complicated details. In a police department, written and verbal skills play an important part in one's success. Those who develop those skills are easily identified. Articulate individuals are generally at ease when discussing issues, seem to influence others easily and get their way more often than not.

Individuals should assess their own verbal capacity and evaluate their ability to organize information and present it clearly to others. Some things one might want to consider include (Albrecht, 1979):

1. Start all discussions at a level where there is absolute certainty of mutual understanding.

2. If the topic is new, lay a foundation by providing information to bring the receivers up to the same level of understanding.

3. Carefully screen all information and provide only essential information.

4. When making a presentation, move from generalities to specifics.

5. Never assume the receivers are as knowledgeable about a subject as the presenter.

6. The greater the complexity of the data being presented, the greater the need to present the information step by step in a logical manner.

7. Summarize the salient features of the presentation before accepting questions.

8. Videotape lectures and review them with a sincere intent to improve the method of presentation.

The above factors delineate how to improve communication and how a supervisor can (by following these general guidelines) more effectively convey thoughts, ideas and decisions when engaged in the managerial activities of controlling and directing.

First-line supervisors in law enforcement agencies are task-oriented: results are what count. Line officers work within operating procedures (with limited supervision), so they have considerable decision-making discretion. In fact, the application of discretion consumes a large part of the average officer's time, and when difficulties occur, officers consult their first-line supervisor. As pointed out earlier, supervisors spend 55 percent of their communication time communicating with the officers they supervise.

The realistic supervisor works with subordinates in an effort to develop them to the point where they can become committed and motivated to such an extent that they are "self-supervised." Within this context, one study showed that when ranking communication tasks, first-line supervisors listed the following items in terms of importance:

1. Provide feedback to subordinates regarding their job performance. This should include such things as identifying strengths, weaknesses, and exceptional or poor performance.

2. Prepare written employee performance evaluations.

3. Respond to subordinates' inquiries regarding departmental policy, legal questions and the application of discretionary decision-making.

4. Meet with and provide direction to subordinates regarding particular violations, investigative techniques and case processing.

5. Brief subordinates on new or revised policies and procedures.

6. Communicate subordinates' concerns, desires and suggestions to management.

Each of these items emphasizes the importance of the superior/subordinate relationship and alludes to the complexity of the communication process. A supervisor must be continually aware of the need to develop and maintain communication skills because it is the most significant managerial tool.

Communication Patterns

Communication is defined as the exchange of information between individuals, implying it can be either one-way or two-way. Traditionally, **one-way communication** has dominated supervisory relationships with subordinates. The sender, in this situation, communicates without expecting or receiving feedback from the recipient. Typical of this type of communication activity is when the sergeant tells the officers what will be done and how to do it, without any degree of feedback.

Two-way communication occurs when the receiver provides feedback to the sender. An example would be when, during roll call, the sergeant discusses a new policy, then asks for feedback. Another example would be the creation of a task force consisting of line officers who are assigned to develop a new grooming policy for officers and prepare a report for management.

Each of these methods has its advantages. One-way communication is preferable when:

1. Speed is imperative.

2. Orderliness is significant.

3. Compliance is imperative.

When one-way communication is selected as the appropriate means to be utilized, the sender must spend a great deal of time preparing what will be said because there is no feedback to clarify issues or correct errors. It does protect the sender's authority and power because mistakes are never acknowledged. Line officers might criticize the sergeant, but with one-way communication the potential criticism by subordinates is not allowed.

When a sergeant utilizes one-way communication the assumption is that one's responsibility ends there and it is the responsibility of the listener to receive and decode the message. It is a simple one-way street and blame can be placed on the receiver for failure to understand the message. The sergeant can say, "I explained it to you and there is no reason why you did not understand the message."

The problem is obvious. A message can be transmitted but there is no real communication unless the message is understood by the receiver. The sender is responsible for seeing that a message is understood and this can only be done if the message is received and there is an opportunity for feedback.

This is where two-way communication becomes useful. It is readily apparent that when one engages in two-way communication there is not only a message sent, but there is feedback allowing for the modification and correction of the initial message. This is exactly the opposite of the classical one-way communication process.

The drawback to two-way communication is that one must accept some risk and share power and authority. The sender's position may be subject to scrutiny by subordinates, and an awareness that the sender is not completely knowledgeable in the subject area may develop. Two-way communication requires less planning because of the built-in opportunity for feedback and the subsequent correction of errors or the clarification of issues. For this to work, it is imperative for the sender to listen and understand the feedback provided by the receiver; otherwise there is just the facade of two-way communication.

The success of two-way communication depends upon mutual understanding as an integral part of the communication process. The desire is to communicate, not to find fault or place blame. If there is a lack of understanding, everyone works to correct errors and clarify issues.

It is apparent from the above discussion that the advantages of two-way communication include (Naval Education and Training Program, 1984):

1. Improved accuracy.

2. Sharing of authority and responsibility.

3. Greater understanding.

4. Acknowledgment of the importance of communicating.

5. Recognition of subordinates' need to know what is expected of them.

Barriers to Communication

An officer never reacts to a message in isolation. There is always a reaction to the relationship between the actual situation, the content of the message and the receiver. An officer must feel free to discuss issues with superiors. Unfortunately, this is not always the case. If an officer is concerned about a negative reaction from a superior, then the officer is less likely to bring up the issue for discussion.

The **barriers to communication** are numerous, but generally include a concern about one's knowledge of a subject, the probability of being looked upon with displeasure, jeopardizing one's status, environmental influences, personal expectations and semantics.

Some officers will assume that asking for clarification on any issue will be immediately interpreted by the supervisor as not being as knowledgeable as they should be. There is a concern that one might be viewed as less than a "real" offi-

cer who is aware and streetwise. Survival in the organization suggests that under no circumstances should officers leave themselves in a position where their ability is called into question, especially if it might jeopardize favorable consideration when choice assignments are handed out.

Subordinates are reticent to discuss personal goals and aspirations if there is any question in their mind that the supervisor might not be receptive. They often feel expressing concerns about the job or the need to learn something new can be taken as a sign of weakness and used against them. With inadequate two-way communication, actions taken by a supervisor are viewed as detrimental and the subordinates will, in all probability, grudgingly accept and implement them with a complete lack of enthusiasm. These actions may even be sabotaged (Bradford and Cohen, 1984).

Physical barriers in any given situation may block or lead to garbled transmission of messages. These barriers might be the result of a poor radio transmission, a poorly written note or even the incorrect use of the "Ten Code." Whatever the barrier, it should be identified. Steps should then be taken to ensure the blocks or distortions to effective communication are eliminated.

Psychological barriers include an individual's beliefs, judgments, values, bias, needs, life-experiences, emotions, education, training and goals. All these combine to form a frame of reference for both the sender and the receiver of any message. Inasmuch as everyone has distinctive combinations of the above characteristics, it should be readily apparent that everyone has the potential of seeing and hearing the same situation from different perspectives (Overton and Black, 1994).

Another barrier to effective communication is *semantics*. There are many words having multiple meanings that can vary with each situation. For example, to "take one into custody" can have a number of meanings ranging from an actual arrest to protective custody. Effective communication can only take place when the actual symbolic meaning of words is shared. Telling a subordinate to "hit the bricks and get with it" communicates little or perhaps nothing. Is it a meaningless instruction or does it mean there is a need to be more productive in terms of issuing more citations or conducting more field interviews? How will it affect the behavior of each officer? (Carter, 1994). Figure 3.4 lists the major barriers to communication.

Figure 3.4
Communication Barriers

1. One's fear of being viewed as having a limited knowledge about a subject.

2. One's fear of being looked down upon.

3. Concern about jeopardizing one's status.

4. Physical influences.

5. Psychological factors.

6. Semantics.

Case Study

Sergeant Paul Iley

Sergeant Paul Iley has been with the police department for 10 years, the last three of which were as a records supervisor. He has just been transferred to the detective division as the supervising sergeant. In the records division, Sergeant Iley spent a great deal of time reviewing investigative reports, and going to the trouble of listing the most common errors found in the reports. These errors ranged from basic grammar errors to the failure to follow up what appeared to be investigative leads.

Sergeant Iley is the replacement for a sergeant who just retired and had the reputation of being a lax supervisor who allowed officers to do just about whatever they wanted to do. Iley's predecessor allowed case due dates to slip by and his management style could best be described as indifferent. Everyone knew he was just waiting out his time until the magic date of retirement arrived.

Iley soon realized the extent of the work ahead of him as he assumed the new position. His first step was to send each investigator a memorandum identifying both specific errors he had found in their investigative reports and investigative leads they had failed to follow up. The memorandum requested each officer to make an appointment to see Iley within two weeks and discuss the previously submitted reports. After three weeks, not one of the eight investigators has requested an appointment and it appears they are going to ignore the request.

When talking with one of the senior investigators regarding the situation, it became readily apparent the other investigators were threatened by the memorandums. Some of them are even fearful the new sergeant might request their transfer from the detective division back to the patrol unit. In fact, there is a rumor that all the officers are to be transferred.

Assignment as an investigator is a coveted position in the department and all the investigators feel they have done their stint in patrol and are entitled to remain in their present position. There is an obvious communication barrier to be overcome if Sergeant Iley is to function successfully as a supervisor. At this point, communication has been limited to one-way, but there is an obvious need for two-way communication.

What would you do to improve communications between Sergeant Iley and the investigators? How might Sergeant Iley develop an atmosphere of trust? What is the real crux of this communications problem? Is it the lack of a supportive relationship or a lack of awareness of subordinate expectations? Explain.

A word is not a complete representation of reality. It is a symbol that can be manipulated without regard to what is factual. Language can be used to distort facts or be used according to the whim of the sender.

Another semantical problem occurs when a supervisor makes use of jargon or esoteric language known as *argot*. A supervisor (when dealing with subordinates) will sometimes assume everyone is familiar with legal terms. Consequently the process of communication may become clouded, if not completely distorted. At other times, jargon of the trade can be used to impress someone or to exclude them from a discussion.

Words will often have strong symbolic significance, so using them as labels should be done with a great deal of caution. For example, using such terms as "punks," "pukes" or "dirt bags" should be avoided, since such labeling can give officers the impression that these uniquely identified individuals can be treated differently and not accorded their complete constitutional rights.

Overcoming Communication Barriers

Many officers have had supervisors who have said, "Come into the office and let's talk it over." Or they have had a memo placed in their mailbox, "See me." Messages like these can evoke all types of reactions ranging from an open and honest discussion to the subordinate simply not expressing thoughts and feelings at all (see Figure 3.5).

Figure 3.5
Overcoming Communication Barriers

1. Creation of a supportive relationship.
2. Awareness of subordinate needs and expectations.
3. Maximum use of feedback.
4. Continual use of face-to-face communication.
5. Acute awareness of semantics.
6. Constant use of direct and simple language.
7. Repetition of communication when needed.
8. Development of an atmosphere of mutual trust.

Some officers will withdraw and turn the discussion into a one-way communication process where the sergeant does all the talking. Or the officers will say things they believe the sergeant wants to hear. In either case feedback does not occur, so the sergeant is limited in accurately appraising or evaluating the situation (Naval Education and Training Program, 1984).

A supervisor can only obtain sound feedback when there is reason for officers to dispel fears and concerns impeding or impairing valid two-way communication. A superior must, due to the position of power, deal with the fears or misgivings of subordinates and work diligently to dispel them. This must be accomplished not only by words but also by actions.

A supportive relationship, if it is also to be a viable and a positive working relationship, is one where the subordinate is allowed to influence the supervisor. The foundation for real two-way communication occurs when the subordinates accept a supervisor as someone who assists and supports rather than one who forces, demands or orders. It cannot be a relationship where communication is limited to such one-way positioning as "Do it now" or "I said do it and that is the way it is going to be."

Subordinate involvement in a real working relationship where there is true commitment requires some degree of power sharing. If subordinates have little or no power, or if they cannot either disagree or vigorously support an opposing position, there clearly is not a viable supportive relationship. An effective relationship can occur only when there is a genuine acceptance of each other, a concern for the needs of others and a feeling of absolute trust and mutual respect (Bradford and Cohen, 1984).

Supervisors' lives would be very simple if they did not have to work diligently to listen to subordinates' ideas and thoughts, strive to share power, create a base for compromise and conciliation, and give feedback that leads to solving interpersonal problems. Supervision is hard work. Positive supervision maximizes the use of human resources— it does not waste them. A supervisory style must be adopted that not only allows for individual differences but views them as valuable assets contributing to the success of the organization.

A supervisor can do many things to insure that individual differences do not impact negatively on superior/subordinate relationships. Many times success is a combination of what the supervisor does and the way it is done. When a supervisor views each officer as a potential member of the team, then there is the beginning of a positive working relationship. A supervisor must focus on bringing each officer into a working relationship, avoid making negative personality judgments and stress strengths rather than weaknesses.

It is best to focus on things to do to resolve problems rather than employing criticism for the sake of criticism. Emphasis should be placed on reaching out to each employee to understand his or her situation better. The goal is to build a working relationship, allowing for a continual exchange of opinions and information. This process can be enhanced by stressing tasks performed by subordinates rather than their personalities. Effective leadership involves viewing personnel in a positive light.

Employees have a right to know where supervisors are coming from. A supervisor will be judged by the nature and quality of communications. If one treats every officer as fairly as possible and does not show favoritism, these actions will support the creation of a positive working relationship. A supervisor will probably feel more comfortable with some officers than with others, but it

will be incumbent upon a supervisor to perform in such a way that individuals are not singled out for preferential treatment. Fairness is the leadership attribute to be followed.

A supervisor should also vary the assignments of the officers so their performance can be improved and boredom reduced. In a police department, the third watch is normally less active, so one should feel obligated to distribute assignments to enhance working conditions and demonstrate equitable treatment.

Whenever possible, the supervisor should recommend additional training. Most employees like to be placed in a learning environment to give them additional skills. Also, it will serve to make the officer more valuable to the organization. It is equally imperative for supervisors to keep abreast of changes in order to improve subordinate training.

If one of the officers does an excellent job, a direct compliment should be given and it should be done as soon as possible. In addition, the supervisor should send a note to higher management levels pointing out the significance of the contribution to the organization. It carries a lot more impact when the recognition of a job well done is made a part of the subordinate's personnel file. A sincere word of appreciation for excellent work can go a long way in building a supportive working relationship with subordinates.

Successful supervisors give serious consideration to creating a working environment where there is mutual respect and trust between themselves and subordinates. It is not a matter of blindly trusting every officer and having faith that the task to be accomplished will be completed, for there will always be a time and place where an officer will fail to follow instructions or complete a task as required by departmental policy. A supervisor has to be willing to accept a certain factor of risk because the positive results will generally exceed the errors or mistakes inevitably occurring.

Trust and respect are prerequisites to any working relationship. These qualities must come before there is anything possibly resembling candid and open communication (DeVito, 1992).

Every officer must have the right to openly approach and resolve all interpersonal and task problems as they occur. One should be allowed to express true feelings and expect they will be heard by the supervisor. Officers should always be able to anticipate an impartial and fair consideration of the issues (Naval Education and Training Program, 1984).

A good supervisor's actions lets every officer know they are being treated fairly and equitably. Every action taken must convey that supervisors always keep their word, are concerned about employee welfare and are willing to work with their officers to resolve problems. In a working relationship where trust and mutual respect are part and parcel of everyday activities, officers will have no need to be guarded or suspicious of each other or their supervisor, and energies can be directed to task achievement (Bradford and Cohen, 1984).

If there is but one supervisory principle a sergeant should follow, it is to communicate. This is an essential aspect of any leadership style and must be instituted at every opportunity, even to the point of over communicating.

Officers are more secure when they know what is going on and have the feeling of being in control of their lives.

In many situations it is necessary to communicate by memorandum, but whenever possible, face-to-face communication is strongly recommended. Feedback can be immediate and more accurate, resulting in the reduction of conflict. Most people are more accustomed to expressing themselves with a greater degree of freedom when talking rather than when writing. The spoken word, in contrast to the written, reinforces supportive relationships and helps in the creation of an atmosphere of mutual trust and confidence.

Feedback

In any working relationship it is essential for a sergeant to develop skills and techniques to provide officers with **feedback** regarding their performance. This can range from praising someone's work to telling an officer what they have done wrong.

The utility of feedback is limited unless it is viewed as a process intended to help the receiver understand the communication. When time allows, it is up to the supervisor to take the time to analyze the message. This can be done by asking the question, "Will what I am going to say really help the officer or will it confuse the issue?" Self-examination is clearly needed so emotions, feelings and values will not interfere with the transmission of the message. Careful consideration should be given as to how to approach an officer with feedback, keeping in mind that part of the role of a supervisor is to be a trainer.

Feedback acknowledging subordinates' importance can serve to build a foundation of trust between the supervisor and officers. However, if one resorts to an extremely critical assessment of every subordinate activity, engaging in strictly one-way communication, or constantly pulling rank, then feedback will soon be nonexistent because the foundation of trust will be eradicated (see Figure 3.6).

Another feature of feedback is that it should be specific. A specific and detailed discussion of the issue under consideration is needed. For example, if a supervisor feels one of the officers should respond more quickly when providing backup for another officer when traffic stops are being made, it is best to recall definite instances when the officer was late in responding to the scene. It is entirely possible that a valid reason for the delay (of which others were not aware) will be given. At the same time, by recalling the date, time and place of the officer's tardiness, it helps to focus upon the problematic issue and not on personalities. Feedback should be provided as soon as possible after the occurrence, while it is still fresh in everyone's mind.

In the above situation the aspect of validity was pointed out. It should be emphasized that it is important to be sure of one's facts before providing feedback. It can be most embarrassing, if not harmful to a working relationship with a subordinate, if the facts of a situation have not been verified before bringing up the issue.

Figure 3.6
Features of Feedback

1. Personal relationship based on trust.

2. Treated equitably and fairly.

3. Specific not general.

4. Appropriate time and place.

5. Issue-oriented.

6. Based on fact not personality.

7. Selective in nature.

When feedback is provided, it should be descriptive and nonjudgmental. Most people find it difficult to accept negative feedback concerning their performance; therefore, when an incident is described (putting it into a context of time and place), there is a greater possibility of dialogue occurring rather than a one-way communication.

A good part of a supervisor's time is spent evaluating the conduct and actions of subordinates. Therefore, a good part of feedback is either instructive or corrective. This places an extra burden on the supervisor to ensure that when feedback is given, the officer is in a position to accept it. If the officer is mentally or emotionally unable to receive the transmission, then there is little gained in giving negative feedback at that time. This does not mean negative feedback is inappropriate, but there is a time and place for everything. Many things occur in police work that may temporarily leave an officer angry, confused, distraught or defensive. These feelings can be the result of a situation involving an abused child, an injury at an accident or an abusive drunk. Any of these or similar situations could call for a delay in providing negative feedback (Naval Education and Training Program, 1984).

Feedback should be selective and limited to the issue at hand. It should never be a situation where every past omission or commission is brought to light and the supervisor "dumps" on the officer. At the very best, constructive criticism is difficult to accept, so it is essential to give it at an appropriate time and place. The ultimate goal is an improvement in performance.

The Art of Listening

Good supervisors generally practice one of the hardest skills there is to learn: the **art of listening.** Books are written on the subject, but apparently few have read them. We should never underestimate the value of developing the ability to listen. If there is but one pet peeve in interpersonal relationships, it is that one party does not listen. This is why some of the most successful supervisors are also the best listeners.

To become a good listener requires work; there is no one sure path to success. Just hearing what someone has said does not mean the real message has been properly received. Listening is an active process that requires one's intellectual capacity of comprehension and evaluation.

A good listener makes a sincere effort to get the message. It might involve taking notes to insure accuracy, asking the individuals to repeat themselves, asking for clarification or restating what the person said. Whatever the method or technique, the focus is on the message, insuring the correct information has been received.

The first tenet of the art of listening is to pay attention to the speaker. As simple as this seems, the precept is violated a great deal. When an officer wants to talk with the supervisor, the officer should be made to feel that no one else will be allowed to interfere with the discussion. Giving someone undivided attention can only be accomplished by shutting out all the extraneous things. An easy way to do this is to look directly at the person with whom you are conversing. In other words, be alert to what is being said and how it is being delivered. How often has a supervisor tried to tell someone something and it was blatantly obvious that the other person was actually not listening? Or, in other instances, it is clear that the supervisor refuses to listen to a subordinate.

Listening is as much a persuasive art as speaking, but it must be developed. A successful listener should strive to keep an open mind and be fully cognizant of his or her own biases and preconceptions (Nierenberg, 1986). An emotional block cannot be allowed to impede communication. If the officer being dealt with is someone personally disliked or has certain annoying mannerisms, the effect of these things can be minimized by analyzing the reasons for the negative emotional block. A good supervisor does not allow these personal feelings to prevent communication, but addresses the situation intellectually so the officer's ideas might be heard and understood (Naval Education and Training Program, 1984).

One way to respond intellectually rather than emotionally is to concentrate on the conversation and to look for value and meaning in what is being said. Listen and wait. Take time to understand what is being said and then evaluate the content of the message. Use the time to listen for what the officer might really be trying to say. Another useful technique is to try to listen for what is not being said. Look for implications or inferences telling what the person really wants to say. A good listener waits until the sender completes a message before responding. This suspends judgment, reduces errors in interpretation and allows one to concentrate on the entire message rather than jumping to a conclusion.

A supervisor can work to improve listening effectiveness by following the recommendations listed in Figure 3.7 (U.S. Department of Health and Human Services, 1981).

Figure 3.7
Techniques that can be Utilized to Improve Listening Effectiveness

1. Give undivided attention to the speaker

   a. Maintain eye contact
   b. Show attentiveness through body language
   c. Nod approval when it is appropriate
   d. Be expressive when appropriate

2. Attempt to listen unemotionally

   a. Do not respond to emotionally laden words
   b. Withhold judgment
   c. Be patient
   d. Do not interrupt

3. Adjust to the sender's message

   a. Reflect upon the content
   b. Search for the meaning the sender does not express
   c. Review and weigh what has been heard
   d. Minimize distractions
   e. Minimize or eliminate criticism
   f. Ask questions
   g. Repeat major points of the message

Greater accuracy in communication can be gained if one works diligently at developing good listening habits. Probably the first and most important action to be taken is to stop talking. You cannot listen if you are talking (Verderber, 1992).

The art of listening requires one to expend considerable energy in order to understand and utilize the information transmitted by others. The opportunities to listen when functioning as a supervisor are considerable and it is one of the best ways to receive information from subordinates. Good listeners can easily expand their knowledge about a subject with which they have limited awareness. It is the responsibility of an effective supervisor to develop the skill of being a good listener to the highest point possible (Verderber, 1992).

Nonverbal Communication

Communication involves more than sending, receiving and assessing a message. It is a complex process extending beyond the actual message to a consideration of nonverbal aspects of communication. Feelings and emotions are important aspects of any message. Some experts have observed that it is more important to be competent in **nonverbal communication** than in actual verbal skills. There are three components of a message contributing to the communi-

cation process. In terms of impact, only 7 percent can be accredited to the actual words, 38 percent to the way it was said and 55 percent to nonverbal facets of communications (Mehrabian, 1981).

This means the stance, the gestures used, the facial expression and other nonverbal aspects of communication all have a serious impact on the communication process. Body language (kinesics) is the scientific study of nonverbal communication and concerns itself with understanding nonverbal signals. Body language needs to be accepted as an important element of the communication process if one is to be an effective supervisor. It must be remembered that many important things transpire as part of the communication process that are nonverbal (Leathers, 1992).

One expert pointed out that one's state of being can be acted out with nonverbal body language: an eyebrow can be lifted to convey disbelief; a nose rubbed to indicate puzzlement; folded arms indicate refusal or in some instances self-protection; a shrug of a shoulder might indicate indifference; a wink may convey intimacy; or a tap of the finger or a foot may reflect impatience (Fast, 1991).

Body language extends beyond these items by including a wide range of indicators such as posture, facial expressions, body movements, positioning, eye contact and body tension. All these contribute to the communication process. Be aware of the image you are projecting and realize that body language cues can be picked up. Keep in mind that any single nonverbal cue might not be especially significant, but when taken in conjunction with others it might have a great deal of significance. For example, stroking the chin accompanied by a relaxed smile will in all probability indicate that the listener's mind has been made up about the issue under discussion.

Nonverbal communication is used primarily to convey emotions, desires and preferences. Generally, nonverbal cues reinforce or contradict the feelings verbally communicated. Feelings can be expressed through various types of nonverbal behavior including facial expressions, particularly eye contact, posture and gestures (Jackson, 1988).

Eye contact can be used effectively in controlling communication. It can be used to solicit or to actually suppress the transmission of a message. It can be used to support communication, or to reinforce feedback. A supervisor can convey to a subordinate, through appropriate eye contact, a specific interest in him or her and the problem. Eye contact reinforces talking with a subordinate because they are given undivided attention. The failure to maintain sufficient eye contact can display aloofness, indirectness, a lack of confidence or anxiety. The face is the primary communicator of emotions. One expert believes there are 250,000 different facial expressions. Nonverbal messages can be conveyed by the following easily recognizable facial expressions:

1. Interest in the individual or topic.

2. Acceptance.

3. Concern.

4. An expression of anger.

5. Disapproval of one's conduct or the action taken.

6. Boredom with the problem or the topic.

The supervisor, once aware of the importance of facial expressions, can utilize cues supporting and reinforcing the communication, thereby reducing the probability the receiver will misinterpret the sender's message.

Even one's posture serves as a cue to the communication process. When conversing with a subordinate, the supervisor can convey the importance of the topic and a definite interest in the matter simply by leaning forward. One should avoid slouching, and always assume an erect but relaxed position (Verderber, 1992), The supervisor's posture can be used to reinforce other nonverbal cues and reduce the potential for any contradiction between an individual's verbal and nonverbal communication.

Gestures are the voluntary movement of a part of the body to explain, emphasize or reinforce the verbal component of a message. For the most part, gestures are made with the hands and arms to clarify a point or to indicate a transition point in the conversation. Because there is less awareness of the gestures used, in contrast to eye contact or facial expressions, it is essential to become familiar with these gestures. A supervisor must use good timing in the use of gestures, realizing they must be coordinated with the verbal message. Care also must be taken to control gestures possibly distracting from the message being transmitted. For instance, stroking the chin, folding the arms or rubbing the nose can either reinforce or distract from the message. A simple technique for determining the extent and nature of gestures is to videotape a five-minute presentation and then review it, identifying specific gestures and determining their relationship to specific verbal points.

One should immediately be able to determine whether a conflicting message is being sent. When this is done it can confuse officers. The nonverbal message communicates emotions so it is essential to accurately reflect the intent of your message. Supervisors can ask such questions as: Does the body language support and reinforce the verbal message? Are conflicting messages being sent? Do actions convey a genuine and sincere interest in my subordinates? It is important to respond to these questions and do everything possible to ensure that effective communication occurs.

The Dilemma of Communicating with Non-English Speaking Individuals

The communication process becomes increasingly complex and difficult when an officer deals with witnesses, victims or individuals seeking assistance or help who do not speak English. Traditionally, this problem was dealt with by

obtaining the assistance of a neighbor, a friend or a relative of the individual being interviewed who could act as translator. Many officers have utilized the talents of younger individuals as interpreters since, in many instances, they have been found to be bilingual in contrast to their older family members who have not learned English.

In some departments, officers who are bilingual serve as translators when the occasion arises. In fact, it is becoming increasingly common for police departments to hire bilingual officers and in a few instances they are paid a bonus for the additional skill. In one police department, with approximately 1,000 sworn officers, the federal court ordered the department to give preference during hiring to candidates who were fluent in Spanish. Thus, the availability of Spanish-speaking officers increased dramatically.

In many areas, community colleges have responded positively to police department needs and have developed special foreign language courses for officers. Typical of this is a three-unit class entitled Spanish for Law Enforcement Officers.

Another innovative approach, which illustrates what can be done to obtain expert assistance when language is a barrier, is the arrangement made by one department whereby foreign language instructors at a governmental agency are available as interpreters. Their expertise ranges from Arabic to Swahili.

In the event a first-line supervisor encounters a foreign language barrier and an interpreter is not available within the department, consideration should be given to identifying interpreters who are employees of other city or county agencies. For example, in one library system, individuals were identified who spoke 20 different languages and a memorandum of understanding was agreed to, so officers could utilize their expertise. The opportunities for such arrangements are extensive and departments should not overlook the language expertise to be found in high schools, colleges or some business establishments.

The Hearing-Impaired

In the United States it is estimated that 21 million people have some degree of **hearing impairment**, and a large number of these individuals are completely deaf. This can be a serious problem for law enforcement officers when they are faced with someone whose communication is limited because of such an affliction. Supervisors who take the time to learn sign language can become a valuable departmental resource and assist other officers.

The hearing-impaired can usually be identified by careful and sensitive observation of an individual. Some actions facilitating this identification are set forth in Figure 3.8.

Figure 3.8
Techniques for Recognizing the Hearing-Impaired Person

1. The person appears alert but fails to respond to any sounds, such as surrounding noises or spoken language.

2. The person points to the ears, or to the ears and mouth with an index finger.

3. The person moves his or her lips without making any sound.

4. The person speaks in a flat, harsh or unintelligible monotone.

5. The person gestures in a manner suggesting a desire to write something.

6. A person moving fingers and hands in repetitive patterns could be using sign language, hoping to be understood.

7. Repeating a sequence of body movements, or gestures, may be an attempt to communicate an unspoken thought or idea.

8. The individual appears unusually alert and follows every move with his or her eyes.

Some deaf persons express themselves orally or they may combine the use of speech with signing. The latter technique is described as a form of manual communication, in which the individual uses movements of the body, hands and face to convey messages (Traub, 1989). It is estimated there are at least 500,000 deaf people who communicate by utilizing American Sign Language as their primary method of communication.

Lipreading (speech-reading) is another technique used by the hearing-impaired. This is the process of recognizing spoken words by watching the speaker's facial expressions, lip movements and/or body language. A deaf person must have a number of skills, including good visual acuity, knowledge of the language and the ability to distinguish between words looking similar when they are spoken. Unfortunately, the task of effectively reading someone's lips can be complicated by the speaker who has a beard or moustache or speaks with an accent. When communicating with a deaf person, the supervisor should (Commission on Peace Officer Standards and Training, 1987):

1. Face the individual and look directly at him or her. Refrain from smoking, placing hands in front of the face or doing anything to distract from the communication process.

2. Speak slowly and as clearly as possible, but always keep in mind that overemphasizing words or distorted lip movements will undoubtedly make lipreading more difficult.

3. Get the deaf person's attention before speaking.

4. Whenever possible use pantomime, body language and facial expressions to enhance communication. All these techniques reinforce the communication process.

5. Maintain as much eye contact with the deaf person as possible.

6. If it is apparent the deaf person does not understand, rephrase the sentence or question.

7. When things are not working, communicate in writing. The significant factor is getting the message across by any method that works.

8. Remember every deaf person is a unique individual and his or her communication skills will vary extensively.

9. Realize techniques utilized by a deaf person to communicate will vary extensively. For example, some will use speech only, others will use sign language, or there may be a combination of techniques including body language, facial expressions and written communication.

Interpreters

Interpreters facilitate communication between hearing and deaf persons. Operationally, there are two types of interpreters. The first is a sign language interpreter, who listens to the speaking person and informs the deaf person of the content of the message by using sign language. The second is an oral interpreter, who repeats an officer's word without using voice. The words are mouthed and the deaf person speech-reads the interpreter.

A U.S. Department of Justice regulation directs law enforcement agencies to ensure hearing-impaired individuals can be communicated with effectively. They are also encouraged to utilize qualified interpreters who are registered with a local or state chapter of the Registry of Interpreters of the Deaf (RID). This agency has the responsibility of certifying individuals as qualified interpreters.

Interpreters should be present when a hearing-impaired individual is informed of rights, when being questioned and when a statement is taken (Traub, 1989). When a hearing-impaired individual is arrested, they should be provided with a printed form of the Miranda warning (a statement setting forth the obligation of the law enforcement agency to obtain an interpreter), and they should be told that interrogation will be delayed until an interpreter is present.

Summary

A supervisor interacting with a subordinate elicits some kind of response or triggers a feeling. If supervisors are successful, the desired impression is creat-

ed and conveyed. At other times, the officer responds to behavior in a way the supervisor did not anticipate. One's interpersonal effectiveness depends upon the ability to communicate a point clearly and influence another person in a manner desired.

Police supervisors spend a majority of their working hours communicating. In fact, one task analysis study showed they were involved in communication activities more than half the time they were at work. While some communicating is represented by written reports, the majority is interpersonal.

The communication process is highly complex and modified by the following variables: what the sender intended to say, what was actually said, what the receiver heard, what the receiver thinks he or she heard, what the receiver said and what the sender thinks the receiver said.

While one-way communication has its uses, it is readily apparent that two-way communication should dominate the supervisory/subordinate relationship. Its advantages far outweigh the disadvantages. It improves accuracy, provides for shared authority, produces greater understanding and acknowledges the importance of the communication process.

The barriers to communication are numerous, but those found to be of greatest concern include an anxiety about one's knowledge of a subject, the probability of being looked upon with displeasure, jeopardizing one's status, environmental influences, personal expectations and semantics.

Barriers to communication can be overcome if the first-line supervisor follows the leadership mandate of always communicating, even to the point of over-communicating. The problems resolved by this method clearly outnumber the problems that can be created. Today's officers want to know what is going on. They want to feel they are in control of their lives and are part of the system.

Feedback is one of the sergeant's most important communication tools and should be offered in a specified way, conveyed fairly, selective in nature and based on fact (not personality). Its ultimate goal is to improve performance.

Some of the most successful supervisors are also the best listeners. The opportunities to listen when functioning as a supervisor are considerable and it is one of the best ways to receive information from subordinates. It is the responsibility of the supervisor to develop, to the highest point possible, the skill of being a good listener.

Nonverbal aspects of communication constitute a major proportion of the communication process. This means the way one stands, the gestures used, facial expressions and other nonverbal expressions have a serious impact on the communication process.

Clearly, the ability to communicate is a requisite for success as a first-line supervisor, for virtually everything a supervisor does depends on effective communications. Task accomplishment depends upon clear and precise communication.

Case Study

Officer Richard Mazoni

Officer Richard Mazoni has been in the department for two years. He successfully completed his probationary period six months ago and his performance ratings were excellent. Since completing the probationary period, Officer Mazoni has become increasingly vocal about his own prowess as a "street cop" and is constantly criticizing the performance of his fellow officers.

No matter what the topic, Mazoni has an opinion on the subject. He is an excellent pistol shot and perceives himself as an expert on all weapons. He is good at self-defense tactics and feels compelled to instruct others in this art. He continuously cites case law when legal matters are discussed, especially when it involves search and seizure.

Officer Mazoni constantly interrupts others in order to present his position and is always so eager to express his point of view or argument that he never listens to other officers. Fellow officers can hardly complete a sentence before they are interrupted and it is usually done in a way suggesting the other person has no idea what they are talking about.

Mazoni shows a complete lack of respect for anyone who disagrees with him and openly argues with those whose opinions differ. Officer Mazoni does everything asked of him and, other than the situation described above, is considered to be a good employee. The other officers do not quarrel with his expertise in special areas, but they find his abrasive nature and refusal to listen to the opinions of others to be totally unacceptable.

As Officer Mazoni's supervisor, you are fully aware of the importance of having good listening skills. It is your desire to work with Mazoni so he might learn to listen to others more effectively while also improving his mannerisms and general attitude. How would you work with Mazoni to alert him to his communications problem? How would you then teach him to deal with the problem?

Key Concepts

art of listening	feedback
barriers to communication	hearing impairment
communicating with non-English	interpreters
speaking individuals	nonverbal communication
communication patterns	one-way communication
the communication process	two-way communication

Discussion Topics and Questions

1. Why is interpersonal communication so important?

2. What are the differences between the simplistic and realistic communication processes?

3. What are the advantages of one-way communication?

4. Why does two-way communication work?

5. What impact does nonverbal communication have on the communication process?

6. How can one interview someone who is hearing-impaired?

For Further Reading

Carter, Carla C. (1994). *Human Resource Management and the Total Quality Imperative.* New York: AMACOM.

> This text discusses ways individuals, experienced and inexperienced, can improve communications and points out that different communications methods may be needed for each individual. The importance of measuring the effectiveness of the numerous ways messages are sent is stressed.

DeVito, Joseph A. (1992). *The Interpersonal Communications Book.* 6th ed. New York: HarperCollins Publishers, Inc.

> The author of this excellent text on interpersonal communications presents a humanistic model of interpersonal effectiveness. Five general qualities are considered: openness, empathy, supportiveness, positiveness and equality.

Genua, Robert L. (1992). *Managing Your Mouth.* New York: AMACOM.

> This book was designed to help employees improve their understanding of and skill in the forms of communication most crucial to their growth and success on the job. Of special interest is the chapter discussing the use of reverse body language.

Verderber, Rudolph F. (1992). *Inter-act: Using Interpersonal Communication Skills.* 6th ed. Belmont, CA: Wadsworth Publishing Co.

> A landmark publication on interpersonal communication. This text reviews theory and describes in detail the pragmatic application of communications at the personal level. It will serve as an excellent resource on the topic.

References

Albrecht, Karl (1979). *Stress and the Manager.* Englewood Cliffs, NJ: Prentice-Hall, Inc.

Bradford, David L. and Allan R. Cohen (1984). *Managing for Excellence: The Guide to Developing High Performance in Contemporary Organizations.* New York: John Wiley and Sons, Inc.

Carter, Carla C. (1994). *Human Resource Management and the Total Quality Imperative*. New York: AMACOM.

Commission on Peace Officers Standards and Training (1987). *Communicating with the Deaf*. Sacramento, CA: Commission on Peace Officers Standards and Training.

Department of the Army (1983). *Military Leadership*. Washington, DC: Headquarters, Department of the Army.

DeVito, Joseph A. (1992). *The Interpersonal Communications Book*. HarperCollins Publishers, Inc.

Fast, Julius (1991). *Making Body Language Work in the Workplace*. New York: Viking.

Gaines, L.K., M.D. Southerland and J.E. Angell (1991). *Police Administration*. New York: McGraw-Hill Book Company.

Jackson, Dale E. (1988). *Interpersonal Communications for Technically Trained Managers: A Guide to Skills and Techniques*. Westport, CT: Greenwood Press, Inc.

Leathers, Dale G. (1992). *Successful Nonverbal Communication: Principles and Applications*. New York: Macmillan Publishing Co.

Mehrabian, Albert (1981). *Silent Messages*. Belmont, CA: Wadsworth Publishing.

Naval Education and Training Program (1984). *Human Behavior*. Washington, DC: U.S. Government Printing Office.

Nierenberg, Gerald I. (1986). *Fundamentals of Negotiation*. New York: Nierenberg and Zeif Publishers.

Overton, W.C. and J.J. Black (1994). "Language as a Weapon." *The Police Chief*. Vol. LXI, No. 8.

Sutherland, Mittie D. (1992). "Organizational Communication." In Larry T. Hoover (ed). *Police Management: Issues and Perspectives*. Washington, DC, Police Executive Research Forum.

Traub, Jeri F. (1989). "The Hearing Impaired Individual: Suspect or Victim." In John A. Brown, Peter C. Unsinger and Harry W. More (eds). *Law Enforcement and Social Welfare: The Emergency Response*. Springfield, IL: Charles C Thomas, Publisher.

U.S. Department of Health and Human Services (1981). *EMS and the Hearing Impaired*. Rockville, MD: U.S. Department of Health and Human Services.

Verderber, Rudolph F. (1992). *Inter-act: Using Interpersonal Communications Skills*. 6th ed. Belmont, CA: Wadsworth Publishing Co.

Motivation—
A Prerequisite for Success

4

Introductory Case Study

Officers Charles Daniels and James Donald

Charles Daniels has just completed the police academy where he graduated fifth in his class. He is now on the midnight shift under the supervision of John Spock, a Field Training Officer. Daniels is 31 years old, married, has three children and resides in the suburbs. He commutes 25 miles to work. He had previously worked as a grocery clerk and a truck driver. Before that, he spent two years in the Navy.

Corporal Spock is concerned about Daniels' adjustment to certain aspects of police work. In any situation presenting a potential for physical conflict Daniels has been overly cautious. Daniels is perceived as being too self-protective. He also seems to want to avoid conflict or disputes. He is quiet and restrained and functions well in highly structured situations, especially during cases involving family disputes. He readily responds to every suggestion from the FTO and executes orders without hesitation. Officer Daniels makes every effort to function as a follower rather than a leader. Even at this early stage, Daniels demonstrates a strong tendency to go strictly by the book. The departmental operations manual is followed religiously. Routine is important and the status quo imperative.

Daniels is reluctant to take command when a confrontation occurs with a citizen. Typical of this was one incident where a customer of a restaurant refused to pay for what was found to be an inferior meal. An argument erupted between the manager and the customer and Officer Daniels did not immediately intervene as a mediator or a controller of the situation. In fact, the situation was just short of a physical confrontation before Daniels intervened.

James Donald was a graduate of the same police academy class as Daniels and graduated third in the class. He has also been placed on the midnight shift under the supervision of the same FTO as Daniels. Donald is a graduate of a local college where he majored in sociology and has always had an interest in law enforcement. He spent four years in an Explorer Scout program. He is single and resides in a garden apartment, noted for its party atmosphere.

Donald is very gregarious and strives to be accepted by everyone. He looks upon everyone as a friend and is sensitive to the needs of others. He is extremely loyal to the department and believes it is the best place in the world to work. Donald never takes an unpopular stand and is a dedicated team player. Details bore him and he is impatient with structure. As a report writer, he has a tendency to gloss over important facts and prefers to handle almost all situations informally.

When dealing with victims, Donald expresses extreme compassion and sensitivity to their needs. He readily contacts the Victim and Witness program so individuals can receive support and help. He always makes it a point to advise victims of their rights. At the same time, Donald feels many of the suspects are just misguided individuals who are the victims of society. Obviously, he is more prone to warn them and strive to find any alternative other than arrest and incarceration. He is always the first to suggest the inebriated individual be driven home or sent home in a taxi. Without question Donald has a strong desire to be accepted by everyone with whom he comes in contact.

The Field Training Officer is very concerned about the adjustment of both Daniels and Donald to police work and has discussed the problem with the sergeant in order to find ways to deal with the situation.

What should the sergeant recommend? What are the basic needs of each of these employees? What motivates them? This case study demonstrates the complexity of human behavior and how one satisfies psychological needs. Supervisors must motivate individuals so departmental objectives can be attained. This chapter discusses the theories of motivation and their application to the police field.

The majority of problems facing society are clearly those identified as phenomena involving human behavior. The advances in physical and biological technology have not even identified what constitutes human behavior, much less presented a solution to understanding this complex area. There is a need for a technology of behavior, but this has not evolved and we seem to know little more about human behavior today than we did a century ago.

The behavioral sciences trace behavior by utilizing such terms as attitudes, feelings and state of mind. These concepts can be interpreted differently; consequently, problems have been created as the field has developed. There is a continuous struggle as efforts are made to identify and measure behavior and, while a comprehensive theory of behavior has yet to be set forth, the quest goes on. In the meantime supervisors must deal with the behavior of subordinates and utilize every bit of knowledge at their disposal to motivate each employee so organizational goals can be achieved (Burg, 1991).

Successful supervisors know that in order to motivate employees, a great deal of effort must be expended. It is not just something to be turned off and on at one's leisure. Motivation is a full-time demanding process and in fact, it can be all-consuming. Employees will soon learn that a motivational speech at roll

call asking them to "go out and make those streets safe" means nothing other than the probability that it will make the supervisor feel better. Rhetoric means little if it is not accompanied by other positive reinforcements.

Why Officers Work

Behavioral scientists generally accept the proposition that behavior does not happen spontaneously—it is caused. Human behavior can be explained to a great extent by determining basic human needs (Naval Education and Training, Program, 1984). Needs are fundamental to our basic existence and they cause things to happen. Needs cause one to act in a certain manner and goal attainment can result in need satisfaction. For example, before acquiring the rank of sergeant, an officer's behavior was directed toward successfully passing examinations allowing for goal attainment.

It seems the more mankind is studied the more we realize the complexity of human behavior. In the past, it was believed reason was capable of solving all problems. Aristotle believed reason held sway over all human capacities (Nirenberg, 1986). Our current knowledge goes well beyond this. Our complexity demands a systematic procedure be followed in attempting to understand the internal and external factors motivating individuals to act the way they do. In general, behavior will follow a pattern showing that:

1. A need will mobilize the energy to reach an acceptable goal.

2. As the need increases in intensity, goal attainment is emphasized by the individual.

3. As the need increases, behavior will follow, hopefully allowing for the attainment of goals.

From the above, the characteristics of human behavior become more apparent. A need arises and one's perception mobilizes the energy needed for reaching a goal. If the goal is not attained, the person tries again, mobilizing additional energy. Additional attention is paid to excluding factors that do not foster goal attainment.

The **motivation cycle** is a vehicle aiding in the understanding of human behavior. This cycle will allow you to gain an appreciation of the interacting forces and the resultant motivated behavior. Figure 4.1 depicts motivation as a continuous process consisting of three specific steps. Step one occurs when an individual experiences a need caused by external or internal forces and those forces are mobilized. In step two, a responding behavior transpires, energy increases in intensity and satisfaction occurs. The final step (three) results in goal attainment. The completion of one cycle is not necessarily the end of the process. It can repeat itself or another need can arise.

Figure 4.1
Motivation Cycle

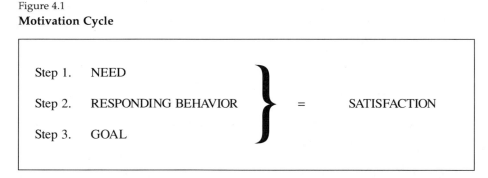

Adopted from: Associates, *A Study of Organizational Leadership.* Harrisburg, PA: Stackpole Books, 1975.

An individual's motivation to act depends upon two factors: the strength of the need and believing a certain action will lead to need satisfaction. For example, a person thought of becoming a sergeant and developed the desire to strive for the rank. The intensity of the person's motivation and the satisfaction of the need depends upon the perception of the real value of the goal. If the person's desire to become a sergeant is more than a transient one and he or she wants the extra pay, the status, involvement in the decision-making process, and the power that goes with position, the individual's motivation will undoubtedly be high (Brown, 1992).

This simple example fulfills the requirement of motivation inasmuch as the strength of the need was strong and the individual pursued a course to satisfy that need. A manager has a definitive responsibility to motivate employees. In fact, most agencies have a written directive stating supervisory personnel are accountable for the performance of employees under their immediate supervision (Commission on Accreditation for Law Enforcement Agencies, 1991). Supervisors must create conditions maximizing the productivity of the officers. Their efforts must be coordinated to achieve departmental goals. A first-line supervisor will soon acknowledge every officer as a unique individual and each individual is generally stimulated by different needs.

Officers can be motivated by one need today and tomorrow the need may reappear, or a new need may become evident. In other words, as the situation changes, the individual's wants and desires can change. It is clear that subjective and objective features affect job satisfaction (Fincham and Rhodes, 1988). Officers can be motivated by fear, values, beliefs, interests, habits, the culture, peer influence, love, moral standards or other factors. It is evident some of these factors are internal to the officer while others are external. The resultant combination of the external and internal factors determine what motivates an officer to act in a certain way in a particular situation.

Motivational experts point out that the total person is hired, not just a part. This means motivating the totality of one's drives. Motivation is as complex as human behavior. So a supervisor should keep an open mind as to the things motivating individuals and not fall victim to the desire to find the panacea to the motivational problem.

At one time in the police service the primary motivational force was based on power. If the order was to jump, the required response was, "How high?" A supervisor might have the power, but the work environment is different and the employees, for the most part, will respond better to different motivational factors. It is a supervisor's responsibility to develop officers' needs and, when appropriate, make organizational needs overcome personal needs.

Effort must be directed toward attaining organizational goals through the work of individuals and groups. In order to accomplish this immense task, a supervisor should strive to create an atmosphere in the organizational working life where most officers become self-motivated (Leonard and More, 1993).

The police supervisor who ignores the ecology of the organization will seldom be successful. A motivated employee is the product of interaction with the organization and the attitudes generated. Thus the key to motivation is not just the individual, but the department. There should be an organization norm of supervisory activities that stimulate the development and growth of every officer. Above all, this calls for a supervisor to demonstrate a consistency in performance of supervisory duties. Extremes of supervisory style such as "tough" or "lax" supervision should be avoided (Dees, 1992).

The complete individual must be motivated. If an officer can be placed in a well-structured organization with identifiable goals, where the culture is such that one can readily identify with it, where tasks are challenging and accomplished individuals are rewarded, then the organization really is motivating its employees.

Historically a number of police agencies have exhibited characteristics definitely incompatible with the above description. These agencies personify the "authoritarian mandate" of leadership style reminiscent of the time when a manager gave an order and the only response was when, where and how much. Fortunately this type of supervision is a thing of the past in most agencies.

In our society, work is fundamental, and is a natural aspect of one's daily life. In fact, work performs an exceedingly strong role in the economic, social and psychological aspect of one's life. Work is defined as effort directed to accomplish something. This definition is compatible with the concept of goals being attained through the efforts of individuals and groups.

Often an individual's sense of identity is obtained from work, as evidenced by most people describing themselves as a member of a department or agency. While this means most people identify work as having a great importance in their lives, it has to be acknowledged that there are a few individuals who view work as a necessary evil.

Work provides officers with a sense of accomplishment as well as something with which to identify. Police work especially challenges one's skill and ingenuity. For many employees the attainment of work-related goals has proven to be as important as material rewards. Most officers find police work is usually challenging and demanding. In fact, everything else can become subordinate to work. Police work provides a sense of belongingness, a sharing of duties and a unique social bond.

A legitimate supervisory role is to create a work environment resulting in officer satisfaction. Two types of feelings come into play when one considers work. The first is **global** and describes an officer's expressed feelings about the total job. The second is **facet** and reveals an officer's feelings about one specific job element (Fincham and Rhodes, 1988). An example would be where an officer feels all promotions are based on "juice" and the support of a "rabbi." Even with this as a dissatisfer, the officer expresses a positive global view of the job and feels other job factors such as importance of the work, feeling of accomplishing something, compensation, supervision and equipment are factors supporting a "good" working environment. In fact, a healthy place to work has five characteristics (see Figure 4.2).

Figure 4.2
Phrases that Describe a Good Workplace

1.   A friendly place to work.
2.   There isn't much politicking around here.
3.   You get a fair shake.
4.   More than a job.
5.   It's just like family.

Within a good working place the relationship between each employee and the organization is one of trust. When trust is present, officers get real satisfaction from the job. When managers and supervisors view the employees as an important organizational component, it results in real participation and increased productivity. Pride is another component of relationships describing a good workplace. The organization instills pride in each employee. In return, each employee feels pride in what they do. Officers enjoy working in an organization described as one where trust is present and pride dominates the style of work. Thus, the workplace becomes a place where relationships are friendly, politicking is not present and each employee is challenged to grow personally and professionally (Levering, 1988).

Motivation

If there is one word that seems to be overworked in the managerial lexicon, it is motivation. We apparently have an insatiable appetite for keeping up with the latest motivational techniques. It has reached the point where some businesses use motivational seminars extensively as a means of boosting morale and

some have even used the fire-walk as a technique. In the latter situation the participants walk across 12 feet of glowing embers, and the response of one participant was, "It was a great feeling to do something that I did not think could be done, and after doing it I felt that I could accomplish anything" (Roman, 1986). Whether this type of training produces a more productive employee or not cannot be answered at this time, but it does illustrate the extent to which some agencies will go in an effort to motivate employees.

Why is motivation so elusive? Why have we heard so much about it? Why is it accepted as a means of achieving goals or increasing productivity? Is it something magical? A basic assumption of this chapter is that managerial skills stimulating and motivating employees can be learned. They are skills that are not tenuous but real and demonstrate (without a doubt) that motivation can be managed.

Motivation can be defined as the action that causes someone's behavior to change. It is a mental process producing an attitude resulting in an action leading to a result. Why do officers respond to a motivational factor? The primary reason is they derive a benefit from the result. Interestingly enough, each person interprets and defines the reward differently. For one person it might be one thing and for another, something entirely different.

The key to motivation is not only the individual, but the organization. In practice, nearly every organization has its own approach to motivation, which is usually a difference of style, taste or emphasis rather than one of substance (Gellerman, 1992). When an individual is placed in a department where the goals and values are easily identifiable, where there is room for growth, where one is allowed to be creative and accept a challenge, and where the officer feels secure and appreciated, as well as properly rewarded, then one finds an agency where the conditions are maximized for positive motivation. Departments, however, have their own motivational norms and there are clearly those where motivation plays a very important part and those where it does not.

Where the dull are leading the dull, all the management experts in the world could not possibly improve the performance of employees. When a healthy culture evolves, it includes values, beliefs, and behaviors built upon a sound organizational base developing and fostering the creation of truly committed and highly motivated employees. When the major motivational influence in the work force is one's internal drive to achieve, supported by and developed by the organization, then morale is high and this in turn enhances performance (Aragon, 1993). When the above occurs, the organization can be described as performing successfully. In its simplest explanation, employees need to be empowered, involved, and true participants in the decision-making process. Every supervisor must work with employees in developing their abilities, skills and knowledge, and every employee needs the technical knowledge and skill to perform assigned tasks. The supervisor must also provide conceptual skill training. This is an ongoing process of developing employees who can relate their own performance to the mission and value structure of the organization. Each employee has an understanding of the organization's relationship to the community, and how change in one part can affect the rest of the organization (Grant, 1990).

In order to become an excellent supervisor, a person must develop a plan identifying obligations to both the officers being supervised and immediate superiors. Some of the more specific responsibilities include:

1. Determining exactly what is to be done.

2. Placing objectives in a time frame.

3. Making better (more sensitive) use of human resources.

4. Introducing greater democracy into the workplace.

5. Demanding high performance from yourself and employees.

6. Turning the work place into a learning place.

7. Monitoring your performance and that of supervised officers.

8. Correcting the situation immediately when something goes wrong.

9. Creating a work environment where individuals can grow and work toward self-fulfillment.

In reviewing these, notice they are all part of what can be identified as an **achievement-motivation program.** The bottom line is that everybody works with greater intensity when there is something in it for them.

Needs-Based Motivation

Probably the most widespread motivational theory in use is the one developed by Abraham H. Maslow. He postulated that people's needs were exceedingly complex and were arranged in a hierarchy. His studies were based upon a positive concept of mental health and his research cohorts were the very best individuals he could identify (Globe, 1970). These individuals were described as being **self-actualized** (S-A) and constituting a small percentage of the population (less than 1 percent). The self-actualized individual's personality was found to be more harmonious and perceptions were less distorted by fears, desires, hopes, false optimism or pessimism (Maslow, 1970).

Interestingly enough, Maslow's superior individual was found to be 60 years of age or older, and the most universal characteristic was the ability to see life clearly. The self-actualized person was creative, risk prone and possessed a low threshold for self-conflict. Additionally, the S-A individual possessed a healthy attitude toward work, finding it enjoyable to the point of actually being play. The ultimate key for a supervisor is to help employees actualize—in other words let them become all they can be (Dessler, 1993).

Based on the S-A personality, Maslow created a theory of motivation showing that human beings are motivated by a number of basic needs that are clearly identifiable as species-wide, unchanged and instinctual. This theory identified five need-categories: physiological, security, social, esteem and self-actualization (see Figure 4.3).

Figure 4.3
Hierarchy of Needs

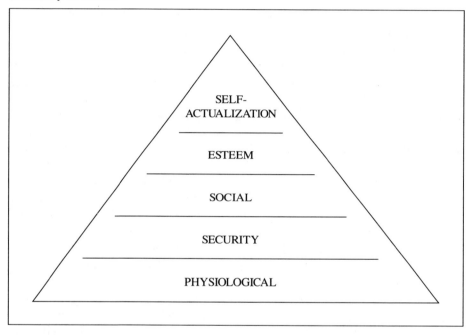

Physiological

The strongest and most fundamental needs are **physiological needs** and sustain life. These include food, shelter, sex, air, water and sleep. Maslow showed that throughout life the human being constantly desires something. Man is a wanting animal and complete satisfaction is achieved only for a short time. As soon as one desire is satisfied, another takes its place. Imagine what it would be like to really be hungry, to the point of almost feeling starved. This could cause not only physical discomfort, but could lead to impairment or illness. It can readily be seen that such a state of need will be dominant. In most areas of the United States, police officers' salaries place them beyond the point of minimum subsistence so their basic physiological needs are generally fulfilled.

From a supervisory perspective, it becomes necessary to understand the degree to which officers are motivated by physiological needs. If these needs aren't fulfilled, it becomes readily apparent that the work they are involved in has no meaning to them.

When management concentrates on physiological needs as a means of motivating officers, they have made the assumption that people work foremost for financial rewards. Emphasis is placed on wage increases, better working conditions, longer breaks and improved fringe benefits as a means of motivating officers.

Security

The **security needs** emerge once the basic needs are fulfilled. The dominant security needs are primarily the need for reasonable order and stability, and freedom from being anxious and insecure. Some officers have entered the police service because governmental agencies provide a secure and stable job. With security as a dominant need, officers will want stability and predictability above all else.

The managerial response should be one stressing rules and regulations. Emphasis should be placed on traditional union demands such as pay and fringe benefits (Ranchlin, 1993). In addition, management meeting security needs would limit efforts encouraging individual initiative, complex problem-solving situations or any type of risk-taking.

Security-minded officers want everything in black and white. The known is stressed over the unknown. Some officers never get beyond the level of satisfying security needs. Change is rejected and every aspect of their working life has to be geared to absolute safety. This creates difficulties for some officers who want things to be stable and predictable, as when courts change the time-honored practices revolving around procedures such as advising suspects of their rights on search-and-seizure techniques.

When a supervisor seeks security above all, it is obvious everything is played "close to the vest." Rules and procedures dominate and absolute adherence to time schedules is demanded. Such a supervisor is well organized to the point of rigidity. One's boss is not only omnipotent but omniscient. Everything possible is done to please and placate individuals who are higher in the chain of command. The supervisor fixated with security needs ignores the needs of subordinate officers, utilizes manipulation when necessary and the need to develop feelings of growth are rejected. Officers are viewed as having no need to control their own lives and the key to success is close supervision.

It would seem realistic to examine one's own security needs. How far should you go to cover up personal mistakes? Would you cover up mistakes made by your superiors? Would you do anything just to get promoted? Do you always agree with the boss just because that person is the boss? Whatever answers, one should know more about one's self after answering these questions.

Social

This level is a clear departure from the two basic needs discussed above. With the fulfillment of the physiological and security needs, the **social needs**

emerge. Maslow pointed out that human beings will hunger for affiliation with others, for a place in a group, and they will attempt to achieve this goal with a great deal of intensity (Globe, 1970).

When this need is not fulfilled by the organization, the officer can respond by an excessive use of sick leave and inadequate productivity. It can lead to loneliness, boredom and a low self-image affecting mental health. Most individuals want to be accepted by peers and supervisors. In fact, everyone has a strong tendency to identify with groups and some people will modify their behavior to meet the group's criterion for membership.

When a supervisor becomes aware that social needs are what are motivating officers, then every effort should be made to promote social interaction. This can be difficult to do in a patrol unit that utilizes one-person units, but the supervisor can provide backup units whenever possible. In addition, the supervisor can act in a very supportive manner whenever possible. A physical conditioning room, parties or organized sports events can all provide a means for meeting social needs.

The socially motivated supervisor emphasizes officers' needs and usually will ignore organizational needs. If options are available, the decision is always made on the side of the employee. Everything is done to insure the supervisor is part of the group. The approval of everyone is sought: subordinates, peers and bosses. Supervisors must accomplish tasks through the efforts of others, thus a good supervisor must help by supporting the efforts of those who are working to achieve departmental objectives.

What about your own social need? When you become a supervisor can you change roles and lead? How strong is your need to be socially accepted? When you are promoted, can you accept being a part of management? These are not easy questions to answer, and they demand real soul-searching to determine where you stand in relation to your needs.

Esteem

Maslow described two categories of **esteem needs**. The first was *self-esteem*, including such factors as the need for independence, freedom, confidence and achievement. The second area was identified as *respect* from others and includes the concepts of recognition, prestige, acceptance, status and reputation (Globe, 1970).

Officers who do not feel their esteem needs are being fulfilled through the job can become discouraged (if not disgruntled) employees. Officers want to be recognized for their accomplishments. This has been done in part by such things as commendations, medals and longevity stripes. Also (in some agencies) the rank of corporal is awarded for achievement, or an unusual act of bravery is rewarded by promoting the individual.

The above-mentioned external indicators of status can fulfill an officer's esteem needs, leading to feelings of worthiness, adequacy and self-confidence.

Supervisors who recognize the importance of esteem needs do everything possible to ensure that officers demonstrate self-confidence, have few self-doubts and have a positive self-image.

The supervisor whose primary drive is esteem will, in all probability, be a successful manager. Such an individual will expend a bundle of energy in order to achieve recognition. No stone will be left unturned if the results are favorable. In the final analysis, the supervisor should take the time and expend the effort to convey to every officer that he or she is an important person, doing important work in an important place (Hawkins, 1992).

Self-Actualization

Maslow points out that when most of the esteem needs are fulfilled, then "what man can be, he must be." This is the stage of **self-actualization** characterized by the need to develop feelings of growth and maturity, become increasingly competent, and gain a mastery over situations. At this level the individual reaches the point where all talents and potential are put to use. Motivation is totally internalized and external stimulation is unnecessary. Efforts of an S-A individual focus on applying creative and constructive skills to work situations, and they are never bothered by feelings of futility, alienation or bitterness.

Supervisors who manage S-A officers should do everything possible to make work meaningful. Participation should be maximized so officers can utilize their unique skills. Special assignments should be made when possible in order to capitalize on an officer's talents. When task forces are organized to deal with unique police problems, the S-A officer should be assigned. The self-actualized individual has a need to demonstrate the ability to assume responsibility and involvement at the highest possible level.

Maslow did not view the hierarchy of needs as a series of levels, totally independent. In fact, the categories overlap and are not entirely precise. He suggests it is the unsatisfied needs that influence behavior. Once a need is satisfied, it has limited effect on motivation. Maslow estimated the average person is 85 percent satisfied in physiological needs, 70 percent satisfied in safety needs, 50 percent in social needs, 40 percent in esteem needs, and 10 percent in self-actualization needs. Since the initial research, Maslow developed a new list of needs identified as growth needs (social, self-esteem and self-actualization) as compared to basic needs (physiological and safety). He believed the higher needs utilized the basic needs as a foundation. The higher or growth needs are:

1. Wholeness
2. Perfection
3. Completion
4. Justice
5. Aliveness
6. Richness
7. Simplicity
8. Beauty
9. Goodness
10. Uniqueness
11. Effortlessness
12. Playfulness
13. Truth
14. Self-sufficiency

Maslow pointed out that the growth needs are interrelated and when defining one value it is necessary to use the others. These values cannot be separated, and all values reflect the highest need category (see Figure 4.4). Maslow cautioned that we should not make the mistake of thinking good working conditions will automatically transform all employees into growing, self-actualized individuals.

Figure 4.4
Behavior when Needs are not Fulfilled

Need	Behavior
Physiological	Pain, suffering, possible impairment, discomfort or illness.
Security	Stress, anxiety, fearfulness, trepidation or fright.
Social	Feelings of being alone, remote, forlorn, sad or unloved.
Self-Esteem	Insecure, lack of a firm belief in one's own power or a lack of conviction.
Self-Actualization	Alienated, bitter, frustrated, exploited or a feeling of uselessness.

Motivational-Hygiene Theory

The hierarchy of needs motivational theory has numerous supporters, but the **motivational-hygiene theory,** while somewhat more controversial, has received increasing attention. This theory was developed by Frederick Herzberg and his colleagues. It was based upon semi-structured interviews with 200 accountants and engineers. Job satisfaction and its relationship were examined and the central question of the investigation was, "What do people want from their job?"

In this landmark study, the researchers found 155 studies addressing this vital question. They found different results were achieved when the research design was concerned with the elements making employees happy with their job, as opposed to studies stressing factors leading to job dissatisfaction. In the Herzberg study, workers who were found to be most happy with their jobs identified factors relating to the performance of tasks, to work events reflecting successful performance and to factors identified as growth.

The other aspect of the two-factor study related to feelings of unhappiness, and they were found to be totally unrelated to the actual accomplishment of work. These factors, identified as hygiene because they acted in a manner similar to medical hygiene, include supervision, interpersonal relations, physical working conditions, salary, company policies, administrative practices, benefits and job security (see Figure 4.5).

Figure 4.5
Motivation-Hygiene Theory

MOTIVATORS	HYGIENE
Achievement	Interpersonal Relations
Advancement	Policies and Administration
Recognition	Salary and Benefits
Responsibility	Security
Work Itself	Working Conditions

Case Study

Officer Charles Edwards

Officer Charles Edwards has been in the department for three years, during which time he has had mixed performance reviews. He is married and has two children. A graduate of a local college, he has continued his education and is currently enrolled in a graduate program, taking two classes each semester. He entered the department after serving in the Army for two years. He received a commission upon graduation from college and is currently assigned as a First Lieutenant in a Military Police unit.

Edwards socializes very little with his peers and does not engage in extracurricular activities such as softball or bowling. He is boastful and flaunts his education and the rank he has attained in the Army Reserve. He is not only boastful but also is dogmatic and highly opinionated. He holds strong opinions on everything from politics to economics.

He values status above everything else and prefers to deal only with those who have power or influence. He has no difficulty in overstating his qualifications or monopolizing conversations, and is most skillful at building up his own image. Edwards is adept at putting others down, and never blames himself for failures. He only praises others when it is to his advantage.

As Edwards' supervisor what would you do to make him a more productive employee and a member of the team? What basic needs motivate this officer? These are key questions and typical of those that confront a supervisor on a daily basis.

Motivational factors are readily identifiable because they either relate to work itself or they revolve around such things as advancement, responsibility or recognition. The hygiene factors are either determined by the organization or occur as a result of a "memorandum of understanding" negotiated by a police union. They are generally restricted to working conditions and policies, in contrast to the motivational factors that stimulate the individual. It is easy to see an immediate parallel between Maslow's concepts of self-actualization and esteem needs. What the employee wants is either growth or recognition (Bergland, 1993).

The factors that address the needs of employees resulting in **job satisfaction** tend to satisfy an officer's needs over an extended period of time, in contrast to

Figure 4.6
Comparison of Job Satisfiers and Dissatisfiers

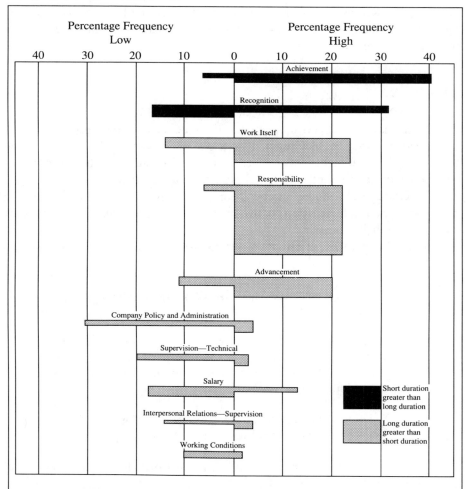

Adopted from Frederick Herzberg, et al., *The Motivation to Work.* New York, John Wiley and Sons, Inc., 1969. Reprinted by permission of John Wiley and Sons, Inc.

hygiene factors that are usually more short-lived. A unique characteristic of Herzberg's theory is that motivators can result in a positive feeling toward work, but at the same time, some individuals respond negatively.

Both the motivators and the hygiene factors meet employee needs, but it is primarily the **motivators** that result in job satisfaction. The workers studied by Herzberg and his collaborators found, for example, that achievement was present in more than 40 percent of what were identified as satisfying situations, and in less than 10 percent of dissatisfying situations. In terms of recognition, more than 30 percent of the situations were satisfying and less than 20 percent were dissatisfying (see Figure 4.6).

Herzberg viewed **satisfiers** and **dissatisfiers** as separate and distinct entities. Simultaneously, one can be satisfied and dissatisfied. This means hygiene factors cannot increase job satisfaction, but only affect the amount of job dissatisfaction.

There are definite differences between the theories of Maslow and Herzberg, as well as similarities as noted by the fact that both theories identify motivational factors (see Figure 4.7). Herzberg creates a different category identified as hygiene factors (non-motivators).

Theory X—Theory Y

Others have developed motivational theories. One of the best known was developed by Douglas McGregor. It is a straightforward theory and is based upon the belief that managers conduct themselves according to the assumptions, generalizations and hypotheses they have about human behavior.

The employees' attitudes and behavior are viewed by McGregor as being in response to management's perspective of their own job and their basic mind-set about human behavior.

The traditional view of direction and control identified as **Theory X** stresses that:

1. The average employee really dislikes work and will do whatever is necessary to avoid it.

2. If employees dislike work, then in order to direct activities toward the accomplishment of organizational objectives, most employees will have to be coerced, controlled, directed or threatened with punishment.

3. Security is important to the average employee. This type of individual has little ambition, and would rather be told what to do.

This view of human behavior is still somewhat prevalent in the police field and is reminiscent of autocratic leadership. What are the consequences of such assumptions about human behavior? What roles are supervisors and officers forced to take? While human behavior is most complex, it would seem appro-

Figure 4.7
Comparison of Maslow and Herzberg

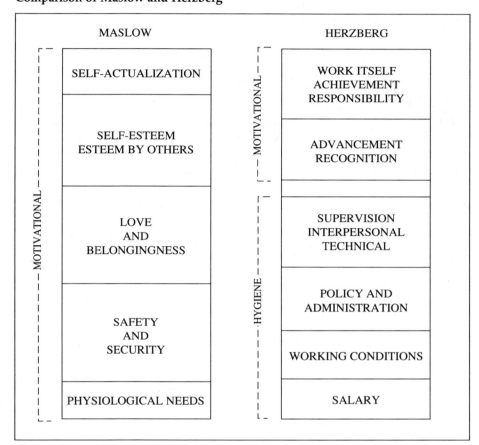

Adopted and modified from J.G. Hunt and J.W. Hill, "The New Look in Motivational Theory for Organizational Research," *Human Organization*, Vol. 28, No. 2 1969, cited in Associates, 1976, *A Study of Organizational Leadership*, Harrisburg, PA., Stakepole Books.

priate to suggest unequivocally that Theory X can explain the behavior of a few employees, but certainly not the majority.

Closely paralleling Theory X is another motivational theory called the *carrot and stick*. Both theories seem viable when meeting an employee's basic needs at the physiological and safety levels. The job itself, working conditions and fringe benefits can be very strong control features when officers are struggling to just get by, but when basic need levels are reasonably satisfied and officers become motivated by higher needs, the theories leave a lot to be desired.

If managers view employees as a necessary evil, they actually view themselves as the chosen ones possessing special abilities. They view the majority of individuals as having limited abilities. Thus, employees are viewed as fundamentally lazy, preferring to have decisions made for them and readily accepting (and actually wanting) forceful leadership. Employees will continually take

advantage of the work situation and have no concept of the factors constituting a fair day's work. If supervisors hold to Theory X it will be reflected in every contact with those supervised.

Theory X places a strong emphasis on control and direction (Von der Embse, 1987). Procedures are devised for providing officers with close supervision (determining whether the task has been accomplished) and the creation of a means for providing rewards and punishments.

With the increasing emphasis on the professionalization of law enforcement and an improved standard of living, the fundamental needs (physiological and safety) have become less of a managerial issue. Thus control becomes fundamentally inadequate as a means of motivating employees when they have developed a social esteem or self-actualization need (Handy, 1993).

This means a supervisor should consider a new generalization about the management of human resources, namely the assumptions outlined by **Theory Y**:

1.   The majority of employees will respond as positively to work as they do to play or rest.

2.   Control and direction are not the only techniques used to achieve departmental goals. Employees will, when truly committed to an objective, exercise self-control and self-direction.

3.   Commitment to departmental objectives is a function of the rewards associated with the attainment of objectives.

4.   Avoidance of responsibility, an accentuation on security and limited drive are, for the most part, consequences of experience, not fundamental characteristics of human nature.

5.   The ability to exercise a high degree of imagination, ingenuity and creativity, when striving to solve an organizational problem, is a widely distributed talent among the population.

6.   With industrial life conditions as they are, the intellectual potential of the average employee is only partially utilized.

A careful analysis of the above factors clearly suggests management should respond to the employees with an enlightened strategy. The managerial perspective will have to be creative, discover new organizational principles, and develop new means of directing employees. It should be acknowledged, while the perfect organization might not be attainable, there is certainly room for improvement.

McGregor pointed out that the complete integration of individual and organizational goals was not realistic. The ultimate goal for which we strive should be a degree of integration whereby workers can attain their own goals by directing their efforts toward the success of the organization. Workers must be encouraged to develop to their highest capacity by acquiring knowledge and skills to make the organization successful.

Interestingly enough, when a supervisor accepts Theory Y it does not imply the abdication of one's responsibilities or what has become known as "soft" management. This idea stems from traditional control procedures emphasizing authority above all (Vail, 1993). Theory Y assumes employees will exercise self-direction and self-control if they are committed to departmental objectives. If commitment is slight or nonexistent then self-direction and self-control will be slight or nonexistent. External influences will have to be exerted in order to achieve goals. If the commitment is great, then external influences should be minimal or better yet, nonexistent.

An appropriate application of Theory Y reduces the need for external control and relies upon other managerial techniques for successfully reaching organizational goals. Generally, authority will prove to be an inappropriate technique for obtaining departmental goals, but it has to be pointed out that authority is definitely something that has to be utilized when an organization cannot get a genuine commitment to departmental objectives. Theory Y assumes that authority is not appropriate for all situations.

It can readily be seen that when a supervisor applies the concepts predicated by Theory Y, each employee is viewed as a real asset. Officers have a definite capacity for growth and development. The sky is the limit. Employees can be highly creative and will willingly accept responsibility. It is the supervisor's job to create such a working environment that the real potential of every officer can be tapped. Unquestionably, employees are not indolent, stupid, irresponsible or hostile. The supervisor accepts that there will always be a few such officers, but they are the exception, not the rule.

Such an orientation requires the supervisor to be primarily concerned with the quality of interpersonal relationships. One's effort is directed toward developing an organizational atmosphere fostering a commitment to departmental goals. Each employee is given an opportunity to become self-directing, innovative and growth-oriented.

There are definitely contrasting sets of attitudes when one compares Theory X and Theory Y. What then is the answer? What theory should a supervisor follow? Not surprisingly, neither theory can be applied in every managerial situation. A supervisor probably functions at some point in between the two extremes. When an officer is on probation and new to the job, a Theory X approach may be more appropriate until the officer is capable of functioning alone. During a narcotics raid is not the proper time for each individual to question what is being done or take it upon themselves to deviate from the prescribed procedures. Safety is imperative and officers must follow orders.

On the other hand, as an officer grows and develops, control can be reduced and the officer can be given a greater opportunity for self-direction and self-control. The assumptions a supervisor makes about what theory to use depends upon a detailed evaluation of each officer's abilities and qualifications. The more knowledgeable and competent officers can be extended a great deal of freedom in their work environment. When these conditions are not met, the supervisor must emphasize control and dependent subordinate behavior.

Expectancy Theory

Predicting behavior in organizations has always challenged behaviorists. A model predictor holding promise is one developed by Victor H. Vroom. This model is predicated on the concept that it is the internal state as well as external forces impinging upon individuals that will enable them to act in a specific manner. In the final analysis, a worker will be motivated to put forth the necessary effort when it will result in the attainment of desired goals.

There are four basic assumptions about human behavior serving as the foundation of the **expectancy theory**. They demonstrate the complexity of not only human behavior but of motivation.

The first assumption is that behavior is not determined exclusively by the individual. It is a product of the vitality of an individual and the environment, and within this context, each individual will develop a preference for available objectives. When the preference is high, the acceptance will be greater. On the other hand, the employee will definitely avoid undesirable consequences. If an individual values promotion over everything else, behavior will be adjusted accordingly in order to meet that need.

Secondly, employees have expectancies about outcomes. Or to put it another way, each person anticipates what will occur. If the results are not compatible with efforts then the activity is ignored or avoided. Expectations vary from individual to individual. What one police officer feels is important might be unimportant to another officer. Some individuals feel job security is important above all else, while others want to perform demanding and challenging tasks.

One aspect of expectancy is termed *effort-performance* (E-P), which refers to an individual's motivation to choose a specific performance objective and the relationship of effort to that objective. The factors affecting an individual's expectancy perception include such things as self-esteem, previous experience in similar situations, one's capability and the style of supervision. This list is not meant to be comprehensive, but it does illustrate the range of such factors. It is believed each individual seeks to increase self-esteem by searching for **psychological success**. One experiences psychological success when (Handy, 1993):

1.   A personal challenging goal is set.

2.   Methods of achieving that goal are set.

3.   The goal is relevant to one's self-concept.

When an officer experiences psychological success, the officer feels more competent. The more competent one feels, the more apt that person is to take risks in perceived areas of importance. On the other hand, when one is not psychologically successful it can lead to the lowering of personal goals as the person strives to protect his or her self-concept (Handy, 1993). While the importance of self-esteem is evident, the whole process should be approached with

some degree of caution, especially if there are other influencing factors such as limited manpower or inadequate equipment. All the desire in the world cannot achieve the impossible.

Another aspect of expectancy is *performance-outcome* (P-O), which deals with an officer's anticipation of performing at a specified level and the outcome of those efforts. This can best be illustrated by a situation where an officer may feel a superior effort will result in different outcomes. Such efforts can undoubtedly result in unintended consequences. While a merit increase might be forthcoming, it might also foster resentment from peers and cause difficulties at home because of excessive absence from the family. It is clear then that any single outcome might be positive in some ways and negative in others.

Needless to say, one conceptual way of analyzing motivation is to view the consequences resulting from expectancies and valences. Then motivation can be viewed as:

$$\text{Motivation} = \text{E (Expectancy x Valence)}$$

Valence is defined as the strength of an individual's desire for a particular outcome. Other words possibly substituting for valence include drive, incentive or desire. Valences range from -1.0 to 1.0 and when the valence is in the negative range, the officer does not want to reach or attain the objective. When the valence is positive, the outcome is highly desirable. When the valence is zero, the officer is indifferent to the outcome (Luthans and Kreitner, 1985). It is important to realize the factor really counting is the employee's perception of what will occur.

Supervisors seem to continually underrate the factors necessary for motivating employees. They forget it is the officer's perception that counts, not the supervisor's perception. The **expectancy motivational model** combines the previously discussed needs theory with the concept of perceived outcomes. Officers are motivated, for example, by satisfying their esteem needs such as receiving a promotion or obtaining a preferred assignment to a special unit (such as a SWAT team). They can be motivated by the successful completion of the probationary period because of the security it will provide. The interplay occurring between officers who are involved in team policing can fulfill one's need for socialization.

Another study revealed that when studying three levels of employees (low, middle and upper) there was hardly any difference between the levels when they rated the importance of needs (security, social, esteem, autonomy and self-actualization). The real difference came when the three levels rated the degree to which needs were satisfied. Lower-level employees were much less satisfied with the amount of higher order needs being met on the job (Hawkins, 1981). The most successful supervisors will concentrate on helping officers to clarify their needs and become aware of how officers perceive those needs. Once this is accomplished, the expectancies of outcomes can be dealt with through such techniques as training, delegation, acknowledgment of a job well-done or the granting of greater autonomy.

How to Motivate

The above-mentioned theories have their place, and supervisors have been successful in varying degrees in the application of these theories to the work environment. If there is a drawback in this application, it is that they are somewhat subjective. This is readily apparent when one closely examines the theories and such related terms as needs, satisfaction, psychological success, self-concept and expectancies.

In analyzing the behavior of officers, it is necessary to study what will happen if a certain action is taken. It is important to determine what the officer believes the consequence of the act will be, not what the supervisor thinks. A supervisor, utilizing the concept of **behavior modification** shapes behavior based on the belief that when an activity results in a positive consequence, the activity is apt to be repeated. Or, if the activity results in a negative consequence, the activity tends not to be repeated (Williams, DuBrin and Sisk, 1985).

Within the framework of behavior modification, the supervisor works to influence officer behavior in such a way that organizational objectives and goals are attained (Laird, Laird and Fruehling, 1983). The advantage of this approach is that the supervisor does not need to become aware of such things as officer needs or motives, but can limit efforts to altering the behavior by manipulating some aspect of the reward system.

If, in the judgment of the officers, the consequences are important, then behavior can be viewed as being based upon the following two principles:

1.   Officers will continue any behavior when it results in a positive consequence.

2.   Officers will cease or curtail a specific behavior when the result is negative.

On the surface, behavior modification seems to be quite simple, but in application, it becomes somewhat complex. A behavioral psychologist, Karen Brethower, has expanded the theory and applied it to the job situation:

1.   If a specific behavior is asked for, but another behavior results in a positive consequence, then the second behavior will become dominant.

2.   When officer behavior results in a positive consequence in a specific instance, but negative consequences under another set of conditions, the positive behavior will dominate.

3.   When the job does not require a specific type of behavior, or has no consequence, such behavior will eventually cease.

4.   When the consequence of a certain behavior is far removed (in time) from the behavior, there will be a lessening in the effect consequences will have on the behavior.

By utilizing the two principles and the four corollaries discussed above, a supervisor can respond to the tasks performed by officers, and engage in reinforcing activities including such things as praise, recommending a commendation, special assignment or additional training. Officers usually have a good understanding of what management expects from them (in terms of job performance) and so they act accordingly.

If behavior is to be modified, consequences must occur when a behavior occurs, not days or months afterward. To delay responding either leads to officer indifference, or their refusal to engage in such activities. Positive behavior must always be rewarded, not ignored. Ignored negative behavior will, in all probability, either harm the supervisor or the department.

In other words, when reinforcement is utilized to modify behavior, it must be done continuously and consistently. Any given task performed by a police officer can be performed as management desires, or in an unacceptable way. Supervisors actually want officers to perform their duties with reasonable dispatch and effectiveness. If reinforcement is to work, it must be *response-contingent.* Any response to officer activity should be clearly and definitely related to performance. Otherwise the effort to reinforce will be blunted or possibly even meaningless.

Positive reinforcement works because there is a greater probability that desirable behavior will occur. It is direct, simple, clear and highly practical. Above all, it is not encumbered by negative side effects. If there is a problem with managing with a reinforcement focus, it is that our society in general deals with most negative performance by punishment or criticism. If a supervisor has been reared in a family where punishment dominated, and schools as well as the job reinforce this negative approach, it becomes readily apparent that when this individual becomes a manager, his or her first instinct is to deal with all undesirable behavior by punishing.

Punishment is viewed by some as the quickest and most effective way of obtaining compliance, but in reality it is seldom long-lasting and when used exclusively is generally ineffective. Another problem is, unpredictable punishment can easily lead to more negative consequences such as reinforcing the schism between the department and a police union.

Initially, punishment will eliminate or reduce undesirable behavior, but managing fear, coercion or threats as a means of getting work done serves only to alienate officers from managers and the department itself. Punishment is usually based on power and the individual's task is to conform or punishment will occur (Handy, 1993). In many instances, officers actually feel they are not extended the common courtesy of being treated as a human being let alone an individual. As one expert pointed out, some supervisors, wanting to improve the performance of officers they are supervising, are so effective at punishing that they actually reinforce alienation. Viewed realistically, the officer who is treated with contempt and disdain by an immediate supervisor can be expected to react negatively (Nirenberg, 1986).

At some point, some employees will have to be punished, but it should be as a last resort, not a supervisory style. Certainly punishment will provide a less-

ening of undesirable behavior, but once the punishment is eliminated from the supervisory process, the employee can resume unacceptable behavior. A punishing style of leadership requires the supervisor to operate continuously from a negative managerial style and always be alert to correct unacceptable officer behavior. It actually means the supervisor must watch employees so closely that, in many instances, the officers are forced to react defensively and production is reduced, not increased.

Punishment as a managerial style can, and most often will, lead to a negative emotional reaction in which an officer can react with anger, become hostile, act out aggression or withdraw. Any or all these reactions can create a working environment in which it becomes uncomfortable to work, personal satisfaction of doing a good job becomes unimportant, and the total atmosphere is void of positive motivational factors.

In police work, an additional consequence of a punishing atmosphere can be one where the officers respond by becoming totally inflexible in their enforcement of the law and officer discretion becomes nonexistent. In this instance, the public loses, and in the long run the department loses. As one officer pointed out, "If they want conformity that's what they are going to get: absolute conformity. Go by the book, and toe the line as that is the only way to keep out of trouble."

A supervisor, using reinforcement techniques, is attempting to actually shape behavior. If the process is to be successful, it is necessary to utilize reinforcement thoughtfully and systematically. Initially, a supervisor must recognize that changing behavior at the outset is more difficult than sustaining and supporting the change once it has been put in place. This means the supervisor should apply the greatest amount of reinforcement during the early stages, and the frequency of reinforcement should be greater during this time period. If the initial employee efforts go unnoticed or are ignored by the supervisor, those efforts, in all probability, will not be sustained.

It is also important for a supervisor to respond to behavior after the fact, not before. If reinforcement is utilized before the desired behavior it will not shape behavior. Reinforcement must be tied to a specific act by the employee, and should occur immediately after the specific activity. This is one reason the annual or semi-annual performance reviews generally prove to be ineffective in changing job behavior. Short-term behavior changes may occur as a result of a performance review, but the change in behavior seldom lasts more than two or three months. Lasting changes in behavior can only be accomplished by immediately responding to an act, not waiting until the next review which might be one year away. A supervisor should reinforce every performance improvement, no matter how slight. When the desired behavior becomes an established pattern, reinforcement then can be used periodically or randomly.

When instituting a behavior modification program, a supervisor should consider the following (Williams, DuBrin and Sisk, 1985):

1. Positive reinforcement will result in improved performance.

2. While punishment is required in some instances, it has numerous harmful side effects.

3. Response to behavior changes should be immediate.

4. Officers need to know what is expected of them.

5. Positive reinforcement should be consistent and continuous.

6. Reinforcement should be response-contingent.

7. Feedback is essential. Officers need to know what they are doing (right or wrong).

8. Training should not be confused with a need to reinforce positive behavior. If officers are performing poorly because of lack of knowledge, they should be trained.

Reinforcement will modify behavior. It is a technique whereby officers can be motivated to work harder and with a great degree of effectiveness. This can result in an improvement in organizational pride and loyalty, and a working environment stimulating officers to achieve their potential.

Summary

If there is any clear-cut task with which first-line supervisors must deal, it is motivating officers or civilians under their immediate supervision. Employees must be motivated so departmental objectives can be met. The motivation of employees is a demanding and time-consuming task and one in which a supervisor must engage at all times.

Of primary importance to a supervisor is striving to create a quality of working life where most officers become self-motivated. This is done by viewing motivation as not only eclectic but synergistic. The supervisor should have an in-depth knowledge of motivational theories such as needs-based, motivation-hygiene, Theory X—Theory Y and expectancy. This knowledge must be applied judiciously.

The key to motivation is the integration of the individual into the organization. Each organization approaches motivation differently, in terms of style and emphasis rather than actual substance. As the one who deals constantly with operational personnel, the sergeant becomes a key figure in the motivational process.

The sergeant who strives for excellence must develop a motivational plan identifying responsibilities to both officers supervised and to superiors. The goal is to create a department where goals are easily identifiable, where there is room for growth, and officers feel secure and appreciated as well as properly rewarded.

Case Study

Officer Stanley Rogers

Officer Stanley Rogers has been in the department eight years. During this time he has received annual performance ratings of satisfactory or higher. Rogers is married and has no children. His wife works as a loan officer for a local savings and loan company and her annual income exceeds Rogers.

Officer Rogers is an avid golfer and his off-duty time is spent (as much as possible) playing in tournaments throughout the surrounding area. He is a scratch golfer who wins most of the tournaments he enters, or at least comes out in one of the top ten positions. The fact is, he also wins considerable money on side bets.

Rogers has taken the promotional test for sergeant twice. The first time was four years ago and he failed to receive a passing score of 70. He finished the second promotional test nine months ago and although he passed the examination this time it is apparent he is so low on the list he will not receive a promotion prior to the expiration date for the promotional list.

Since the last examination, Rogers' work performance has been barely adequate. He shuns special assignments and performs most tasks in a perfunctory manner. He has become argumentative and rejects others' ideas out-and-out. He takes a fixed position on almost any topic and is not in the least bit open to new or different ideas. He points out it has always been done this way, so why change?

You are Rogers' sergeant and you are due to prepare his efficiency report in three months. You can sympathize with his failure to score well enough on the promotional test, but his work performance (if it continues at the same level) will, in all probability, result in an unsatisfactory rating.

What would you do to improve his performance? What might you do to motivate Rogers to improve his performance? What basic need behavior is Rogers exhibiting?

Key Concepts

achievement-motivation program
behavior modification
dissatisfiers
esteem needs
expectancy motivational model
expectancy theory
facet feelings
global feelings
human behavior
hygiene
job satisfaction

motivation cycle
motivators
physiological needs
positive reinforcement
psychological success
satisfiers
security needs
self-actualized needs
social needs
Theory X–Theory Y
valence

Discussion Topics and Questions

1. Why is it difficult to define motivation?

2. What are the limitations in utilizing any single motivational theory?

3. Discuss Maslow's and Herzberg's motivational theories.

4. Identify two major aspects of expectancy theory. Which one precedes the other?

5. What are the key characteristics of Theory Y?

6. Why do some line personnel find it difficult to find an opportunity to achieve self-actualization on the job?

7. How can officers be motivated to work with greater effectiveness?

For Further Reading

Bergland, Shelia (1993). "Employment Empowerment." *FBI Law Enforcement Bulletin,* Vol 62, No. 12.

>   This article discusses the process whereby the goals of the agency can be attained by balancing the needs of employees with organizational demands. When empowered employees actively participate in setting and achieving departmental objectives, they feel a sense of ownership and pride in the tasks they perform. The position is taken that organizational improvement will occur when consideration of people is given priority.

Dessler, Gary (1993). *Winning Commitment: How to Build and Keep a Competitive Workforce.* New York: R. R. Donnelley & Sons Co.

>   Addresses actualization as a key to commitment. Describes a developmental program allowing employees to use all their skills and become all they can be. Suggests work be designed so it enriches and empowers employees.

Grant, Philip C. (1990). *The Effort-Net Return Model of Employee Motivation: Principles, Propositions, and Prescriptions.* Westport, CT: Greenwood Press, Inc.

>   This text has an excellent chapter on motivation utilizing the effort-net return model. Of particular interest is the proposition that employees must perceive they have, or can easily acquire the ability to perform well. Includes recommendations to help employees build their self-confidence.

Handy, Charles (1993). *Understanding Organization.* New York: Oxford University Press, Inc.

>   Briefly reviews early motivational theories including: satisfaction, incentive and intrinsic. Presents a motivational model emphasizing that each individual has a set of needs and desired results can be identified. Discusses three categories of psychological contracts: coercive, calculative and cooperative.

References

Aragon, Randall (1993). "Positive Organizational Culture." *FBI Law Enforcement Bulletin,* Vol. 62, No. 12.

Associates (1976). *A Study of Organizational Leadership.* Harrisburg, PA: Stackpole Books.

Bergland, Shelia (1993). "Employment Empowerment." *FBI Law Enforcement Bulletin,* Vol. 62. No. 12.

Brown, Michael F. (1992). "The Sergeant's Role in a Modern Law Enforcement Agency." *The Police Chief,* Vol. LIX, No. 5.

Burg, Mike (1991). "Goal Setting for First Line Supervisors." *Law and Order,* Vol. 43, No. 5.

Commission on Accreditation for Law Enforcement Agencies (1991). *Standards for Law Enforcement Agencies.* Fairfax, VA: Commission on Accreditation for Law Enforcement Agencies, Inc.

Dees, Timothy (1992). "Identifying and Solving Morale Problems." *Law and Order,* Vol. 40. No. 9.

Dessler, Gary (1993). *Winning Commitment: How to Build and Keep a Competitive Workforce.* New York: R. R. Donnelley & Sons Co.

Fincham, Robin and Peter S. Rhodes (1988). *The Individual, Work and Organization.* London: Weidenfield and Nicolson.

Gellerman, Saul W. (1992). *Motivation in the Real World: The Art of Getting Extra Effort From Everyone–Including Yourself.* New York: Dutton.

Globe, Frank G. (1970). *The Third Force.* New York: Pocket Books.

Grant, Philip C. (1990). *The Effort-Net Return Model of Employee Motivation: Principles, Propositions, and Prescriptions.* Westport, CT: Greenwood Press, Inc.

Handy, Charles (1993). *Understanding Organizations.* New York: Oxford University Press, Inc.

Hawkins, Brian L. (1981). *Managerial Communication.* Santa Monica, CA: Goodyear Publishing Company.

Hawkins, Jeff (1992). "Officer Motivation." *Law And Order.* Vol. 40, No. 10.

Herzberg, Frederick (1969). *The Motivation to Work.* New York: John Wiley and Sons, Inc

Hunt, J.G. and J.W. Hill (1969) "The New Look in Motivational Theory for Organizational Research." *Human Organization.* Vol. 28, No. 2. In Associates (1976). *A Study of Organizational Leadership.* Harrisburg, PA: Stackpole Books.

Laird, Donald A., Eleanor C. Laird and Rosemary T. Fruehling (1983). *Psychology: Human Relations and Work Adjustment,* 6th ed. New York: McGraw-Hill Book Company.

Leonard, V.A. and Harry W. More (1993). *Police Organization and Administration,* 8th ed. Westbury, NY: The Foundation Press, Inc.

Levering, Robert A. (1988). *A Great Place to Work.* New York: Random House.

Luthans, Fred and Robert Kreitner (1985). *Organizational Behavior Modification and Beyond: An Operant and Social Learning Approach.* New York: McGraw-Hill Book Company.

Maslow, Abraham H. (1970). *Motivation and Personality,* 2nd ed. New York: Harper and Row.

Naval Education and Training Program (1984). *Human Behavior.* Washington, DC: U.S. Government Printing Office.

Nirenberg, John (1986). "Motivation as if People Matter." *Supervisory Management,* Vol. 26.

Ranchlin, Harvey (1993). "A National Review of Wages and Benefits." *Law and Order,* Vol. 41, No. 11.

Roman, Mark B. (1986). "Beyond the Carrot and the Stick." *Success,* Vol. 33, Number 8.

Vail, Chris (1993). "Supervision Requires 'More' in Policing." *Law and Order,* Vol. 41, No. 5.

Von der Embse, Thomas J. (1987). *Supervision: Managerial Skills for a New Era.* New York: Macmillan Publishing Co.

Williams, J. Clifton, Andrew J. DuBrin and Henry L. Sisk (1985). *Management and Organization,* 5th ed. Cincinnati, OH: South-Western Publishing Company.

Leadership—

The Integrative Variable

5

Introductory Case Study

Sergeant Rob Robbins

Sergeant Rob Robbins is a patrol supervisor on the swing shift in a medium-sized police department and is one of 11 fulfilling that operational position. There are nine officers under his immediate supervision, but only two have more than two years of field experience.

Officer salaries are 20 percent lower than those in the major department in the metropolitan area. Therefore it has become almost customary for officers to get some primary experience, then enter the larger department via lateral transfer.

Sergeant Robbins feels the constant personnel turnover places an excessive burden on supervisors and serves to diminish operational effectiveness. During the last three months, Robbins has been forced to operate with a shortage of from one to three officers and the calls for service continue to backlog to such an extent they cannot be handled effectively. Service is seriously impaired. Felony arrests are down 12 percent as compared to the same period the previous year, and several major cases have been lost in court because of poor preliminary investigations conducted by officers under his supervision.

The city council is adamantly opposed to raises and the departmental administrators have taken the position that they have done everything they could possibly do to improve salaries. Supervisors are told to do the best they can and wait for a change in the composition of the city council in the hope they will be more enlightened when it comes to providing the department with adequate funds.

Sergeant Robbins has become increasingly punitive in his supervision by resorting to assigning the poorest officers to the most difficult tasks and then criticizing their actions and rejecting their investigative reports. It has become quite common for reports to be rejected three or four times. Officers are subjected to very close supervision and everything (including making a felony arrest) must be approved by Sergeant Robbins.

> *Describe the supervisory power sources Sergeant Robbins is utilizing when dealing with his subordinates. How might Sergeant Robbins work to resolve the leadership problems confronting him? Could reward of referent power sources be utilized in this situation? How?*

If there is but one important characteristic of a well-managed police department, it is leadership. Effective leadership can transform a marginal organization into a successful one. It gives life and reinforces an organization in its efforts to achieve agency goals and objectives. While it is an intangible quality, it must be present if officers are to be controlled and directed.

Inspired leadership can be extremely contagious and cause officers to achieve high levels of quality production. Undoubtedly, leadership makes the difference (Garner, 1993). If a person has ever worked for a "good" leader it has undoubtedly proven to be an exhilarating experience. If one has hopes of becoming a supervisor or is currently at that level, it would behoove them to accept the challenge to work diligently at becoming a truly positive leader (Cox and Hoover, 1992).

One thing a person does not want to be is an incompetent boss. Horror stories abound in the police field about supervisors who are ignorant, dictatorial, egomaniacal, domineering, manipulative, power-happy or just unfit. Such supervisors, whatever the label attached, can destroy or severely impede the effectiveness of line officers. In fact, officers can (and do) become the victims of exploitative leadership styles, and such a working environment has led to the resignation of many competent officers or the creation of a situation whereby officers conform to meet their supervisors' low expectations and become minimally effective. Few officers work effectively when constantly under abusive stress. An incompetent supervisor can soon dampen enthusiasm and constrict even those who are highly motivated.

The key question then is, "What makes one supervisor competent and another incompetent?" Needless to say, if we had the answer to that question there would be no more incompetent supervisors.

Taking on a position of leadership rather than being a follower involves a definite shift in the way people view themselves and the way they operate. A newly promoted supervisor generally has the experience of moving from being a highly proficient employee to one who is less sure of him or herself. Operational skills are still important but other skills must now be applied in order to be an effective supervisor.

Reliance on knowledge, methods and techniques that dominated work in a line position and allowed performance of specific operational tasks must now be shifted to a greater consideration of human and conceptual skills (see Figure 5.1).

Figure 5.1
Supervisory Skills

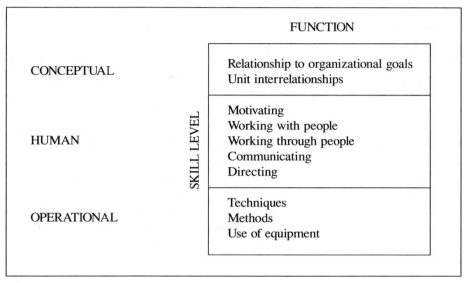

Varying demands on one in a supervisory position call for a different mix of supervisory skills. In one situation, instructing others on how to conduct a lineup or a field sobriety test will call for some reliance upon **operational skills**. In another instance, **human skills** may dominate as in a situation where a supervisor combines directing with motivation in an effort to control the behavior of one or more officers.

Lastly, while it does not occur as often as operational or human situations calling for the application of differing skills, the supervisor will be required to handle instances entailing the application of **conceptual skills**. The most common situation probably occurs where there is conflict between the goals of individual officers and the primary objective of the department. One's knowledge of the overall organization, and awareness of how the unit fits into this organization, will allow the supervisor to work toward the enhancement of organizational life and increased efficiencies (Dobbs, and Field, 1993).

When one analyzes the first-line supervisory position in law enforcement, it is readily apparent that human skills dominate. An effective supervisor must develop the ability to understand why people behave as they do and work toward the development of effective means of changing, directing and controlling behavior.

First-line supervisors in police agencies exceed the number of managers in all other administrative positions. In a nationwide survey, 111 police departments indicated the median percentage of personnel in the rank of sergeant was 9.67 while there were only 6.23 percent of sworn personnel in the combined ranks of lieutenant, captain and major (Police Foundation, 1981). This means the organizational pyramid becomes increasingly constricted, and if (as a first-line

supervisor) one envisions rising higher in the organization, the characteristics that will set this person apart from contemporaries will be leadership skills.

It is a stimulating experience when one meets or works for someone who exhibits genuine leadership skills. There is an increasing awareness of the importance of leadership. When leadership is missing or ineffectual then the organization is generally ineffective. Problems develop that are seldom resolved, and chaos is most likely to occur. When there is positive leadership present, operational tasks are completed and objectives attained. Above all else, the effective leader is responsible for the attainment of clearly specified tasks (Cox and Hoover, 1992).

The discharge of leadership responsibilities is a demanding role and forces a supervisor to make decisions, apply discipline or control behavior—which arouses feelings as well as responses. Whether or not leadership is effective involves a complex interrelationship of leaders, followers and situations.

The studies on leadership are numerous, extending over a considerable period of time, and cover every probable phase of leadership. In fact, there are so many studies it is difficult to assimilate them in any reasonable period of time. It can easily be suggested that the more one studies leadership, the more it can be seen as an inexact science (Fetherolf, 1994).

In recent years emphasis has been placed on the critical roles leaders should assume in order to deal with the organizational environment and the continuing and constantly changing demands of the community. This has resulted in the identification of four roles critical to effective leadership. These are directional setter, change agent, spokesperson, and coach (Nanus, 1992).

A good definition of leadership proves to be elusive. For purposes of this chapter, the most comprehensive definition is utilized. Leadership is defined as the process of influencing group activities toward the achievement of goals. There are a number of implications to this definition and it must be recognized as a process of influencing which can include such activities as telling, selling, ordering, coaching, joining or consulting. At the same time, influencing others must be directed toward the achievement of some objective or goal, otherwise it can be an exercise in futility. Whatever the objective, whether it is an arrest or assisting a lost child, the first-line supervisor is responsible for ensuring the attainment of the objective.

Another aspect of the definition is that the first-line supervisor is no longer primarily a doer, but a coordinator of other people's activities. Group members respond to and willingly accept directions from someone who has a leadership style emphasizing the coordination of subordinates. This means a supervisor should comply with the 50-percent rule. Supervisors should spend one half of their time managing others rather than being just another employee (Von der Embse, 1987).

Finally, the definition demonstrates that the leader operates from a position of power based on the authority delegated to the supervisor. The position has numerous power sources including reward, coercive, legitimate, referent and expert (French and Raven, 1959). These sources are listed in Figure 5.2.

Figure 5.2
Supervisory Power Sources

POSITIONAL	Legitimate Coercive Reward
PERSONAL	Expert Referent

Power

Within a police agency, power plays a very important role. In fact, the national accreditation program specifically calls for written directives addressing the position of supervisor. First, it is recommended there be one written directive setting forth the need for supervisory personnel to be held accountable for the performance of employees under their immediate supervision. Another directive should point out that, in order to permit effective supervision, direction and control, employees should promptly obey any lawful order of a superior (Commission on Accreditation for Law Enforcement Agencies, Inc., 1994). Figure 5.3 is an example of a policy statement suggesting partial authority for a first-line supervisor.

Beyond formally derived power, the first-line supervisor can **extend power** by utilizing a number of techniques when dealing with others. Figure 5.4 lists things a supervisor can do to expand power (Covey, 1991). Persuasion is such a technique. It is imperative that the supervisor share reason and justification when exerting influence over others. At the same time the supervisor should genuinely demonstrate an interest in each officer's ideas and position. Officers should be told why as well as what needs to be done.

Patience is another technique to be emphasized when relating to subordinates. Consideration must be given to the shortcomings and weaknesses of each employee and these must be balanced against an immediate desire to attain objectives. Short-term impediments and in some instances actual opposition must be dealt with, placed in proper perspective and balanced against a realistic commitment to the achievement of objectives and goals.

Another technique is to be enlightened. Supervisors seldom have the "best" answer to every problem or situation. One should accept and value the insights, discernment and seasoning of those being supervised.

The technique of openness serves as a vehicle for communicating with subordinates. Officers should be accepted not only for who they are now but what they can become as growth occurs. A supervisor's perspective should be based

on accurately acquired information about each officer to include an awareness of goals, values, desires and intentions. In some instances, actual behavior can become secondary as the supervisor strives to increase power.

Consistency is another technique a supervisor should follow in order to increase power. This means doing what is expected of you so subordinates will always know where you are coming from and never have to feel like they are being manipulated. A leadership style reflecting consistency will then become a manifestation of one's true character reflecting values and personal code.

Lastly, integrity is a technique resulting in the extension of power. Officers know when they are working for someone who is honest and demonstrates a real concern for others. A supervisor should constantly strive for control that can only be interpreted as fair, impartial and nonmanipulative (Covey, 1991).

Figure 5.3
Policy Statement

Compliance with Lawful Orders

The department is an organization with a clearly defined hierarchy of authority. This is necessary because unquestioned obedience of a superior's lawful command is essential for the safe and prompt performance of law enforcement operations. The most desirable means of obtaining compliance are recognition and reward of proper performance and the positive encouragement of a willingness to serve. However, negative discipline may be necessary where there is a willful disregard of lawful orders, commands or directives.

Adapted from: Harry W. More and O.R. Shipley, 1987, *The Police Policy Manual—Personnel*. Springfield, IL, Charles C Thomas, Publisher.

Figure 5.4
Techniques for Extending Power

Persuasion

Patience

Enlightenment

Openness

Consistency

Integrity

Legitimate

The above reference to written directives provides a clear-cut example of what is known as **legitimate power.** The directives spell out not only the responsibility of the supervisor for subordinate performance but the requirement that

subordinates comply with lawful orders. Officers are well aware of the first-line supervisor's status in the organization and the support of other managerial positions. At the same time, the officers are fully aware that the incumbent of a supervisory position has the formal right to exercise influence.

Expert

If the sergeant has had previous experience in either patrol or investigation and is currently supervising in that area, then there is a vast reservoir of special knowledge and expertise (**expert power**) to be called upon when supervising officers. Subordinates will respond to supervisors who possess this greater amount of knowledge, knowing it insures the successful completion of tasks. Expertise in law enforcement is coveted and officers continually strive to improve their operational skills. A knowledgeable supervisor who demonstrates the ability to implement, analyze, evaluate and control situations and resolve problems is readily accepted.

Expert power is extremely narrow in scope. If it is to be a continuing source of influence it is imperative for the possessor to stay abreast of new developments because one's expertise can become diluted rapidly in many areas. An example of this is in criminal law where court decisions can alter criminal procedures in one sitting of the U.S. Supreme Court.

Referent

An additional source of influence a supervisor can call upon is **referent power.** It is the only aspect of a potential power base that is not directly attributable to the position the supervisor holds. It is a type of power that is associated with the leader's personality. Some would identify it as charisma. Whatever the description of this quality, it is something that makes the supervisor likable, and subordinates respond by imitating the style of the leader or struggling to accomplish tasks in order to receive the leader's approbation.

An additional source of referent power for a supervisor is a good reputation, especially when it is based on effective police work. This power is evident when subordinates refer to a supervisor as a real police officer and respond accordingly. Acts of heroism and bravery or outstanding performance accompanied by departmental citations go a long way in establishing a base of referent power.

Coercive

Coercive power is that which is based on fear and the ability of the supervisor to administer some type of punishment. A first-line supervisor in law enforcement has coercive power, but usually much less than other managerial

positions. This type of power is subject to review depending upon the nature and type of disciplinary action taken. As noted in Chapter 6, it can be construed as being totally negative and it may not result in the desired behavior. Supervisors have power that should be used with care, ensuring adequate employee performance (Hudson, 1994).

In some instances coercive power can be applied without taking formal disciplinary action, such as assigning an officer to an undesirable work assignment or enacting a closer supervisory pattern. Reports written by officers can be reviewed with an emphasis on minutiae and returned to the officer for correction. These actions, as well as numerous others, are extensions of the formal coercive power circumscribing the relationship between a superior and a subordinate. It is also an example of how a supervisor can extend personal power beyond that which is assigned to the position.

Reward

Reward power is somewhat limited in law enforcement because promotions are usually based on service regulations, hence the supervisor's role in the process is limited. It might also refer to annual raises (until an officer is at the top step) or for cost-of-living raises which usually are automatic.

Officers are more likely to respond to reward power when the authority of the supervisor impacts upon operational working conditions. Officers will comply when the supervisor has the authority to give out preferential work assignments, influence the assignment of officers to special training programs or support such things as transfer requests. Compliance results in a reward and the officers respond accordingly.

Power (to be useful to a supervisor) should be viewed positively. It is something to cultivate, not ignore. Power is the base that legitimizes the supervisor's position. When the five power sources are analyzed, it is obvious each of them has limitations, but they must be developed and utilized if a supervisor is to maintain an effective relationship with subordinates.

Theories of Leadership

The theories of leadership are as numerous as the number of individuals who have investigated the topic in an effort to determine why one individual is effective and another is ineffective. The approaches to this important topic can be grouped into three categories: (1) trait theories, (2) behavioral theories, and (3) contingency theories.

Trait Theory

The trait theory of leadership identifies distinguishing qualities or characteristics a person possesses when functioning as an effective leader. It has been widely accepted because it is appealing, simple and straightforward (Daresh, 1989). Clearly, the abilities, skills and personality traits found in successful leaders are not present in poorly functioning leaders.

The number of traits manifested by successful leaders varies considerably from a few to as many as 56. It is quite improbable that every trait identified could be possessed by any one individual. Typically a list of traits may include:

1. Courage	6.	Initiative
2. Decisiveness	7.	Intelligence
3. Determination	8.	Optimism
4. Energy	9.	Self-assurance
5. Enthusiasm	10.	Sociability

The possession of specific traits creates an impossible ideal. There are numerous examples of supervisors who do not exhibit these qualities but who have proven to be highly successful (Handy, 1993). Notwithstanding the criticisms of the trait approach, it still is accepted by many managers. One large police department has identified the following traits as qualities required of a good supervisor:

1. Cooperative	6.	Prompt
2. Courteous	7.	Reliable
3. Energetic	8.	Resourceful
4. Fair	9.	Tolerant
5. Open minded		

Numerous problems become readily apparent if one is to use traits as a means of identifying potential leaders. In many instances, it is difficult to determine whether the leadership position results in the development of the traits or if the individual had the traits before becoming a leader (Johns, 1983). Also, trait theory studies do not weigh the relative importance of each characteristic. In other words, if being tolerant is believed to be an essential trait of a good police supervisor, one must determine how much tolerance is needed before an individual becomes a good supervisor.

Finally, the trait approach does not acknowledge the complex interaction between the actions of the leader and the situation. It is clear the situation modifies the interaction between the supervisor and the follower. In many instances the environment modifies the leadership process. This is especially evident during police emergencies.

From the discussion of the supervisor's role in Chapter 1, it is apparent that supervisors deal with three types of skills: knowledge, human and conceptual. All are conditioned and reconditioned by the uniqueness of each situation. Acknowledging the limitation of studies of the trait approach to leadership qualities, one researcher has identified five groups of traits found to be associated with leadership effectiveness. After the analysis of thousands of articles and books, Ralph Stogdill found a relationship between leadership capacity, achievement, responsibility, participation and status (Stogdill, 1974). See Figure 5.5 for an explanation of each of these variables.

Figure 5.5
Leadership Traits

	Leadership Traits
CAPACITY	Intelligence Mental alertness Verbal ability Originality Judgment
ACHIEVEMENT	Knowing how to work in a group Ability to present ideas Attainment of good school grades Successful in athletics
RESPONSIBILITY	Dependability Willingness to assume responsibility Initiative Persistence Self-confidence Desire to excel
PARTICIPATION	High activity level Sociability Cooperation Adaptability
STATUS	Social position Economic position Popularity

These leadership traits clearly illustrate the importance of groups and the need for the leader to become involved in the group. It is also definitely supportive of our definition of leadership, which is the process of influencing group activities toward the achievement of goals (Couper, 1994).

Behavioral Model

A great deal of research has focused on the actual behavior of leaders rather than upon the trait model. Under the direction of Carroll Shartle, the studies at Ohio State rejected the concept of leadership behavior occurring on a single continuum and, after having subordinates describe the behavior of superiors, concluded there were two basic types of leadership behavior (Johns, 1983).

The two factors are identified as **initiating structure** and **consideration**. The concept of initiating structure is defined as "the leader's behavior in delineating the relationship between himself and members of the work group and in endeavoring to establish well-defined patterns of organization, channels of communication and methods or procedures." Consideration is defined as "behavior indicative of friendship, mutual trust, respect and warmth in the relationship between the leader and all members."

The Ohio State leadership studies resulted in a model of four quadrants plotted on two separated axes identifying the two principal aspects of leadership behavior defined in the preceding paragraph as initiating structure and consideration, and are discussed in Figure 5.6.

Figure 5.6
Leadership Behavior

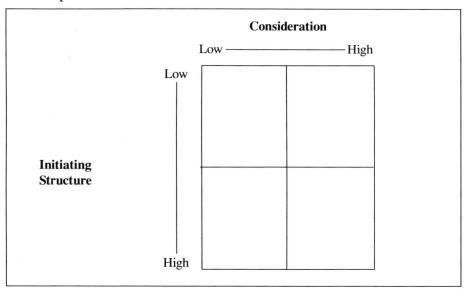

The studies at Ohio State noted that leadership styles vary considerably from individual to individual. Some leaders are characterized as being task-oriented and rigidly structure subordinate activities. On the other hand, there are leaders who demonstrate (through their behavior) the capacity to build and maintain good personal relationships. Finally, other individuals exhibit a leadership behavior that is a mixture of consideration and initiating structure.

A supervisor who feels comfortable emphasizing consideration as a leadership approach is more likely to utilize two-way communication (See Chapter 3), show respect for officers' ideas and work best when there is a feeling of mutual trust. This style is especially applicable when officers are well trained and the goals and methods of performing tasks are clear-cut and not the least bit ambiguous (Johns, 1983). Such a leader continually demonstrates a concern for the needs of each officer when there is a high degree of consideration. When there is a low degree of consideration, the supervisor is more impersonal and shows less concern for the needs of those supervised.

When a supervisor emphasizes initiating structure, objectives are attained by carefully structuring a subordinate's role. Activities are carefully planned and communicated. Deadlines are established and giving instructions dominates the interpersonal relationship between the sergeant and the officers. Tasks are scheduled and rules and regulations are adhered to in an effort to ensure a high standard of performance. In fact, the task proves to be more important than the needs of the officers.

If there is a limitation to the Ohio State studies, it is their ignoring the influence of the situation and concentrating on the relationship between the leader and the follower.

Contingency Model

Proponents of the contingency model of leadership hold that the leader's style (if it is to be effective) must match the demands of the specific situation. The situation causes the leader to utilize the qualities ensuring success. The situationist makes the assumption that the leader will emerge from the situation. This approach broadens the scope of leadership beyond the trait or the behavioral approaches.

Fred Fiedler and his associates, in landmark research, developed the first contingency model of leadership. This theory postulated three factors of major importance and identified them as (1) the leader's position power, (2) the structure of the task, and (3) the interpersonal relationship between the leader and members.

Position Power. This term is defined as the degree to which the position itself confers upon the leader the capacity to get officers to accept and comply with directions.

Position power can be measured. Fiedler and his associates have developed an 18-item checklist incorporating various indices of power such as:

1. Leader has official rank and status.

2. Leader is knowledgeable in terms of the position and work of subordinates.

3. Leader can recommend punishments and rewards.

4. Leader's knowledge allows for a decision concerning how a task is to be done.

The value of position power for a supervisor is readily apparent. The rank and status provide the leader with the tools to get the officers to perform their tasks. While the sergeant does not possess the position power that can be attributed to lieutenants or those of higher rank, the power is enhanced because the first-line supervisor has more frequent and intense contact with line personnel.

Task Structure. Task structure is the extent to which a task is routine and structured as compared to an ambiguous and poorly defined task. When tasks are carefully defined it is much easier for a supervisor to control operational duties and officers can be held responsible for their actions or inactions. In many law enforcement agencies, standard operating procedures abound and policy manuals can take up a substantial part of a bookcase shelf.

Routine police tasks are mostly highly structured and circumscribed by numerous legal requirements. Consequently, there is little or no reason for an officer to question the right of a supervisor to give instructions supported by departmental policy. Fiedler states that the structured task is enforceable while the unstructured, ambiguous task is difficult or impossible to enforce.

Personal relationships. When the relationship between subordinates and a leader can be described as a good working relationship, the leader is in a favorable position to influence behavior (Johns, 1983). This is due to the trust developing between them because of positive personal relations.

In most instances the newly appointed supervisor, because of position power, is acceptable to a certain degree, and the conduct of the supervisor is seldom questioned unless the supervisor's conduct is clearly inept. The interpersonal relationship developing between a leader and followers is in part dependent upon the personality of the leader. Of the three factors, personality has been found to be the most important in terms of the leader's capacity to influence a group of officers.

When a sergeant is totally acceptable from the officer's viewpoint, loyalty is inspired, compliance is generated from the interpersonal relationship, giving rank and position power a limited meaning. When a supervisor and the officers get along reluctantly, to the point where friction is readily apparent, compliance may be obtained, but in many instances it is done with reservation. When there is such a strained relationship, it can result in a lessening of the leader's influence.

When the first-line supervisor is rejected by the followers and strife prevails, it comes down to basic survival from the leader's point of view. Considerable effort must be expended if even a margin of productivity is to be achieved. Control becomes the means essential to ensure attainment of goals and ordering officers to do something usually gets immediate results.

Fiedler points out, quite candidly, it is much easier to work with followers who are loyal and devoted than those who are tolerant or antagonistic. Also the life of a leader supervising the latter group will prove to be most difficult.

If effective leadership is to prevail, it is necessary for the leader's guidance style to be congruent with the demands of the specific situation. Fiedler identified two basic styles of leadership. One style is **task-oriented** and the leader's satisfaction is generated by effective task accomplishment. The second leadership style is predicated on the desire to achieve personal acceptance and is identified as **relationship-oriented**. By themselves neither of these styles can be described as effective; they depend upon the favorableness of the situation as modified by the three dimensions discussed above. When there is mutual trust and respect and the task is highly structured, the supervisor has high position power and the situation can then be considered favorable. However, if the leader is not respected and has limited support, the position power is weak, the task will be unstructured and vague, creating an unfavorable situation.

The effectiveness of a leadership style is highly variable. In all probability you will find that, in one situation, it might be most effective to be task-oriented while in another, it might be effective if a relationship-oriented style is utilized. In other words, there is no one style consistently successful all of the time with supervising different officers.

For the newly appointed supervisor whose influence is (in all probability) limited, the task-oriented leadership style will be most effective. When situations are moderately favorable in terms of influence, the best leadership style has been found to be relationship-oriented. If a supervisor is a failure, it is probably due to an inability to adapt to the situation. A supervisor's position demands considerable flexibility when it is compared to a line officer's position. As pointed out in Chapter 1, a line officer's position is dominated by the need to achieve tasks while the first-line supervisor's position requires a response to situations where human relations becomes more important. The situation clearly changes when it becomes necessary to accomplish objectives through the efforts of others.

There are times in a police organization when both relationship-oriented and task-oriented supervisors have been found to function effectively under certain conditions, but are less than effective under other circumstances. If a supervisor fails to function effectively it is usually not a question of intelligence or innate ability, but the development of a different situation where the leadership style proves to be inappropriate.

In some situations the supervisor can change the leadership style by utilizing positive features of the hierarchical organization and structuring the tasks more carefully. This will result in a greater compliance with departmental policy. In addition, the supervisor can make more decisions, initiate a closer review process of certain calls for service or let the officers know where they stand when faced with certain situations. For example, the supervisor can provide backup in certain types of situations, review all felony arrests or carefully scrutinize reports submitted by the line officers.

A first-line supervisor may find, in some situations, the working environment is tense, and the interpersonal relationships are less than adequate. It would seem the task-oriented leadership has contributed to the situation. The supervisor should then implement a relationship-oriented leadership style. Emphasis

can be placed on such things as lessening close supervision activities (allowing line officers more discretion in specific situations), involving subordinates in the decision-making process, or in general, doing whatever is necessary to create a relaxed working environment.

The question then might be, "How does one measure one's leadership style?" Fiedler's contingency model utilizes an instrument called "The Least Preferred Coworker (LPC) Scale," which is presented in Figure 5.7. When completing the scale, an individual is required to think of all the people with whom they have worked and then think of the person with whom they can work least well. When completing the instrument this person is identified on the scale by placing an "X" in the appropriate place. The scale consists of 18 pairs of words, diametrically opposed, and the score obtained by adding the responses becomes a measure of one's leadership style.

When the total score is 64 or above, it indicates the leader is relationship-motivated and has the tendency to be most concerned with maintaining good interpersonal relations, sometimes even to the point where the job to be done received limited attention.

If the score is 57 or below, it is an indication that the leader will place primary emphasis on the performance of the task. This leader tends to be a no-nonsense individual who works best by going by the book. If the situation is at all ambiguous, this type of leader will generate rules and regulations to control the situation.

Figure 5.7
Least Preferred Coworker (LPC) Scale

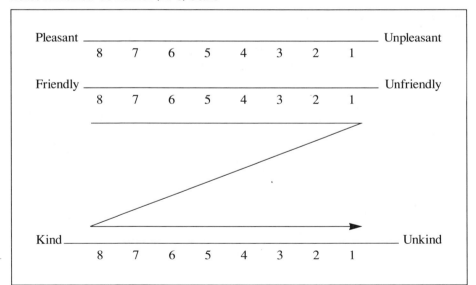

Adopted from Fred E. Fiedler, Martin M. Chemers and Linda Maher, *Improving Leadership Effectiveness: The Leader Match Concept.* New York, John Wiley and Sons, Inc., 1976, p. 8. (Note: The actual scale has 18 variables.)

When the score is between 58 and 63, the individuals completing the scale will have to determine for themselves which classification they favor (Fiedler, Chemers and Maher, 1976).

Whether a first-line supervisor is task-motivated or relationship-motivated, it is necessary to consider three different kinds of leadership situations:

1. The high-control situation provides the leader with a working environment where there is all of the control and influence needed to direct the activities of others.

2. In the moderate-control situation the leader is presented with mixed signals wherein interpersonal relations are less than adequate, but the task is structured and position power is high. On the other hand, the situation might be such that the relationships are good, position power is low and the task is unstructured.

3. In a low-control situation the leader is not supported by the group causing control and influence to be low. At the same time, influence is not provided by either the task or position power.

The interaction of the leadership style, extent of control and the situational dimension result in a position whereby the relationship-motivated leader is most effective in a moderate-control situation, and the task-motivated leader is most effective in high- or low-control conditions.

Leadership Continuum

The success of a first-line supervisor depends upon numerous factors. The relationship between a supervisor and subordinates is best described as existing along a **leadership continuum**. Some researchers have identified two basic types of leadership and identified them as autocratic and democratic. Another researcher's list expands on this and lists five styles: authoritarian, democratic, laissez-faire, bureaucratic and charismatic.

Other experts have stressed sharing power in the decision-making process and described seven types of leadership behavior in which the style is increasingly subordinate-centered. Whatever the number of leadership styles, it seems readily apparent a supervisor does not consistently utilize any single leadership style. Seldom is any style found in its pure form because the supervisor's behavior varies depending on the situation.

Most supervisors, in fact most individuals, are not capable of being infinitely flexible in applying leadership styles, but they can employ styles that are consistent with their personality. Leadership is highly personal and projects one's innermost beliefs and feelings. For the purposes of this discussion it is best to describe three types of leadership behavior that can be used when a supervisor wants to influence the behavior of line officers: directive, consultative and participative.

Directive

Many supervisors feel most comfortable when exerting a **directive** leadership behavior. In many instances, the supervisor who practices this style of leadership was previously supervised by someone who relied upon a directive style of leadership. Other terms used to describe a directive type of leadership behavior include autocratic and dictatorial, indicating the variability of behavior and that leadership styles are best represented on a continuum.

While some suggest directive leadership is on the decline, this is certainly not the case in many law enforcement agencies. In fact, the working environments of some police departments are such that it is very difficult for a supervisor to operate with any leadership style other than directive.

The directive supervisor exhibits little concern for officers and allows little or no involvement in the decision-making process. The supervisor makes the decision and insures it is implemented. This type of leader will, if the situation dictates, listen to questions, but never for the purpose of altering the decision. Control dominates the situation and "Do as I say" is the prevailing philosophy.

A first-line supervisor, by virtue of position power, is firmly entrenched in a position of unquestioned authority and will wield the power necessary to accomplish assigned tasks. To show weakness to subordinates is to give them an opportunity to undermine one's authority, so this is never done.

Knowledge of the task to be performed is used to support position power and status. Whenever possible, assignments to special details and tasks can bolster a positive response to authority. The description of Theory X, as set forth in Chapter 4, holds that a directive supervisor perceives line officers as being lazy and untrustworthy. Consequently, officers should be told what to do and their conduct and activities should be monitored closely.

A directive leadership style places emphasis on a combination of things, such as structuring the tasks in such a way as to easily control officers. A supervisor who uses this style uses the authority inherent in the position as the basis for subordinate obedience. If deviation occurs from the desired behavior, then the supervisor controls the subordinates by assigning blame. Control is maintained by relying upon rules and regulations as a means of ensuring compliance.

Close attention is paid to adhering to schedules. Progress reports are required to be on time; late or inadequate reports constitute reasons for immediate discipline. Failure to comply with standard operating procedures results in closer supervision and will, in all probability, result in disciplinary action.

Directive leadership, because it is authoritarian in type, relies on position power to reduce or suppress conflict. Authority should never be questioned and absolute obedience is required. Decisions are made by the supervisor and input is never allowed. The primary concern is to get the job done and such things as social interaction are ignored unless it enhances goal attainment. What this means is that personal needs are subordinate to departmental needs.

This type of task-oriented behavior for the supervisor certainly lets the officers know what is expected of them. It also ensures the use of uniform proce-

dures and eliminates or substantially reduces officer discretion. The advantages and disadvantages set forth in Figure 5.8 make it readily apparent that the directive style of leadership is not without drawbacks. The style of leadership used by a supervisor must vary with the individual and the situation.

Figure 5.8
Directive Leadership

Advantages	<ul><li>Focuses on goal attainment.</li><li>Subordinates know what has to be done.</li><li>Decisions are made quickly.</li><li>Decisions are not challenged.</li><li>It is a logical extension of position power.</li><li>Maximizes control of subordinates.</li><li>Enhances compliance with departmental rules and regulations.</li></ul>
Disadvantages	<ul><li>It isolates the supervisor.</li><li>Negative feelings can be generated.</li><li>Minimal compliance.</li><li>Stressful for the supervisor.</li><li>It can be punitive and seldom rewarding.</li><li>It may result in a lowering of morale.</li><li>Stifles creativity.</li><li>Limits two-way communication.</li></ul>

Consultative

If everyone in a police organization worked at his or her maximum capacity, there would probably be limited need for a supervisor. However, such is not the case. Problems have to be resolved and conflict reduced, hence the need for supervisors. **Consultative** is the second style of leadership and represents an additional description of leadership behavior. In recent years it has become an increasingly popular approach used by police supervisors.

It is, in reality, a leadership position adopted by a supervisor as a compromise position when it has become apparent that line officers have values and attitudes different from those held by older police officers. A conscious decision is hereby made by the supervisor indicating officers can no longer live in the past. It is then necessary to acknowledge existing changes in working conditions and proceed to make needed adjustments.

The supervisor cannot completely abandon the directive style of leadership because it is the type higher managers expect to see in operation. However, the supervisor may believe another style of leadership will prove to be more productive while improving officer working conditions.

Case Study

Sergeant George Coats

Sergeant George Coats has worked the midnight shift for the last 10 years in a department with 49 sworn police positions. He is the only supervisor working this shift. Therefore, he is in charge of the department and makes all decisions.

It might be said he is from the "old school" and his Marine Corps training is evident in terms of his leadership style. When his decision is made it is well-known this is the way it is going to be. There is no appeal and the officers soon learn they had better do what they are told to do. There is no doubt who is in charge: Sergeant Coats. There is only one way to do things—Sergeant Coats' way.

The shift supervised by Sergeant Coats is staffed with three officers, always the newest officers in the department because of a departmental policy to put new officers on the midnight shift. Each of these officers has less than two years of service and all are graduates of the community college program in criminal justice. None are pursuing any additional education but are committed to improving their operational skills. Each has completed the 14-week basic officer training program.

Each of the three line officers find it difficult to adjust to Sergeant Coats' directive leadership style, as they find it to be foreign to them considering the way they were raised and the education they have received. Needless to say, they have spent their lifetime in a permissive atmosphere and even the academy training was nonstressful in style. It is almost a shock to them to always be told what to do and to never be involved in the decision-making process or even to be allowed to question a decision.

Sergeant Coats demands results and the working relationships are totally one-way. His leadership style emphasizes control.

There is an obvious conflict between the line officers and Sergeant Coats, and the morale of the officers is at a lower level than it should be. What is the real problem? Is it the supervisor's problem because of his leadership style, or are the officers expecting too much? What can be done to resolve the problem?

The consultative supervisor shows a concern for officers and their needs as well as organizational needs. Subordinates are allowed to participate in the decision-making process and they are accepted as part of a potential team. It is, thus, an acknowledgement that officers have something to offer and they are knowledgeable and capable.

The consultative style of leadership works best when decisions that have to be made deal with relatively simple tasks or issues. When issues are complex or there is not enough time to permit discussion and analysis, the supervisor should make the decision. This is especially true if the decision involves an emergency situation and where directive leadership would be the most appropriate response.

If the decision involves the personal or work life of an officer, then input should be sought so a mutually acceptable decision can be made. Input from subordinates should also be sought when a decision involves the behavior of one officer that affects other officers.

A supervisor should provide for officer input to the decision-making process when it is felt the process will result in a better decision. In addition, officers should be involved in the decision-making process when it is clear that group commitment and effort will be needed to implement a program or introduce a process. Providing for input will generally reduce resistance.

When situations occur where there are two or more appropriate solutions for the same problem, the decision can generally be left to subordinates. This way an arbitrary decision is avoided, and compliance is ensured. In addition, ideas and suggestions are sought on a regular basis and on occasion are accepted and implemented (see Figure 5.9). A consultative leadership style is a significant departure from the directive style, but is not fully participative.

Figure 5.9
Consultative

Advantages	<ul><li>Involves subordinates in the decision-making process.</li><li>Shows a concern for the welfare of subordinates.</li><li>Reduction in stressful situations.</li><li>Utilizes subordinate ideas.</li><li>Improves the quality of decisions.</li></ul>
Disadvantages	<ul><li>It leaves personnel in the middle and they never know what to expect.</li><li>Limited effectiveness in solving problems.</li><li>One never knows what impact a suggestion will have.</li></ul>

Participative

A **participative** leadership style can only be utilized when the supervisor has a genuine belief in and respect for subordinates. It is in sharp contrast to the Theory X view of worker and leadership behavior described as directive. The supervisor consults with subordinates and involves them in the decision-making process. Attitudes, values and officers' feelings are viewed as important and are taken into consideration.

Group involvement is sought and power is shared. Every effort is made to create a working environment where two-way communication is stressed, ideas are accepted and creativity is fostered. Officers are encouraged to develop to their highest potential, and every effort is made to get officers to accept respon-

sibility as well as handle delegated authority. The informal organization is accepted as an integral element of the formal organization, and each officer is encouraged to think critically.

A change from directive to participative leadership style can prove to be most difficult. It is usually because of the initial misunderstanding as to what participative supervision is or is not. It does not mean officers have a veto power over the decision-making process. Employees do have meaningful input to this process, but, in every instance, the supervisor or someone higher in the hierarchy makes the final decision. At the same time, the supervisor is always held responsible for the accomplishment of objectives.

Participative leadership is not permissiveness whereby leadership skills are not exercised, but exists when the recommendations of subordinates influence the decision-making process (see Figure 5.10). A truly participative leader strives to create a working environment where controls are minimized and officers develop to their highest potential. The goal is to have employees actively managing themselves (Carr, 1994).

Figure 5.10
Participative

Advantages	<ul><li>Totally acknowledges subordinate skills and abilities.</li><li>Improves working relationships.</li><li>Employees are motivated.</li><li>Better decisions.</li><li>Committed employees.</li><li>Improved communication.</li></ul>
Disadvantages	<ul><li>Slows down the decision-making process.</li><li>A true participative style takes a long time to evolve.</li><li>Raises officer expectations.</li><li>Time consuming.</li></ul>

Participative leadership integrates each officer into the work unit. A working environment is created whereby officers can achieve and master the tasks they have to perform. Traditions are continuously challenged and if circumstances warrant, modifications are introduced. When planning has to be accomplished, and circumstances permit, knowledgeable officers are consulted.

A participative manager never performs the task alone when it can be accomplished through the efforts of others. Subordinate creativity in problem solving is encouraged, and traditional control techniques rejected. Motivation of officers consumes a great deal of the supervisory working week, and emphasis is placed on recognition of good work. When appropriate, officers are given additional authority and responsibility. When officers do good work it is praised and, when praise alone will not suffice, commendations are forwarded through channels.

A participative management style works best when the department has a positive orientation toward its human resources and subordinates have some discretion when they are performing assigned tasks. When tasks to be achieved are less structured and officers are given a considerable degree of freedom to perform, they are more apt to successfully accomplish the task and will do it with a greater degree of satisfaction.

A truly people-oriented supervisor functions best for the following reasons:

1. All subordinates are treated with respect.

2. When changes are made, everyone is notified in advance.

3. Work units are consulted.

4. Officers are involved in the decision-making process.

5. When actions are taken, the reason(s) for the actions are explained.

6. A pleasant working environment is created.

7. A consensus decision process is provided for.

8. Authority and responsibility are placed at the operational level.

9. Supervision is supportive and friendly.

10. High performance standards are an integral component of a participative style.

11. Creative problem solving is encouraged and supported.

Leadership Mistakes

Functioning as a supervisor can prove to be very difficult. Often a supervisor will feel suspended somewhere between line officers and upper management. It is a difficult position to be in but one that occurs more often than one would like it to. It is imperative for a supervisor to accept being part of management, and the only way things are going to be accomplished with any degree of effectiveness is to see that proper tasks are performed by line personnel. It is the officers who are doing the work, and it is a supervisor's job to work for and with them.

This means making certain operational personnel are properly trained and equipped to perform their job. Supervisors work for both management and subordinates. Their task is not only to tell employees what to do, but to coach them when the situation dictates, consult when necessary and join with the employees

to attain objectives. Do not make the mistake of trying to change human nature. Accept each employee as a unique individual. Certainly supervisors can use power to ensure compliance, but in the long run that may prove to be detrimental. Accept individual differences and work to develop employees by improving the contributions they make to the organization. One should assist officers by really trying to understand them. Determine their needs and work to improve their self-image.

Supervisors who criticize employees in public make a serious mistake. A true mark of a competent supervisor is a strong sensitivity toward the feelings of others. When it is necessary to criticize someone, do it privately and in a sensitive manner.

Many problems facing a supervisor will stem from letting the acquisition of power become more important than the actual attainment of objectives and goals. Officers will make mistakes or errors and, by virtue of position power, you can criticize, discipline or even become involved in the dismissal of an employee (Mendofik, 1994). Excessive or improper use of power is totally unacceptable conduct. It might prove useful initially, but, over a period of time, could lead to the downfall of a first-line supervisor.

Newer supervisors sometimes have trouble with subordinates, and will do a task themselves rather than spend the time necessary to coach employees in the proper technique. This is a clear-cut failure to manage. As repeatedly stated throughout this text, as a supervisor you must accomplish goals through the efforts of others. The supervisor should ask him or herself such questions as: "Is too much expected?" or "Are requirements stated clearly?" or "Are the officers properly trained to accomplish the task?"

A supervisor should never show favoritism to one or more subordinates. One will soon find out employees have a built-in sense of what is right and wrong and strongly object when preferential treatment is extended to a few and denied to others. When rewards can be extended (such as assignments), they should be based upon merit, not likes and dislikes. It is essential for a supervisor to be perceived by subordinates as fair. A good supervisor is one who accepts the challenge of leadership with all of its problems and rewards (Cox and Hoover, 1992).

Summary

When a police department is well managed it is always found to have outstanding leadership. Effective leadership can transform a marginal organization into a successful one. Inspired leadership is extremely contagious and will cause officers to achieve high levels of productivity.

A first-line supervisor, like other managerial personnel, is concerned with the application of skills described as operational, human and conceptual. In the application of these three skill areas it is readily apparent that human skills dominate the activities performed by a supervisor.

In this text, leadership is defined as the process of influencing group activities toward the achievement of organizational goals. Of particular interest concerning this definition is that the first-line supervisor is no longer a doer but a coordinator of the activities of other employees.

Supervisory power sources vary and include those of positional and personal. Under the positional variable one will find sources including legitimate, coercive and reward. Personal sources of power include expert and referent. If a supervisor is to function effectively, it is essential these five sources of power be cultivated and utilized.

Fundamental theories of leadership abound, which fall into one of the following categories: trait theories, behavioral theories and contingency theories.

Leadership is best viewed as existing along a continuum. While the experts do not agree as to the number of leadership styles to be included on such a continuum, it would seem a minimum of at least the following three must be included: directive, consultative and participative. Leadership styles, when being implemented, are modified by the situation and a first-line supervisor will, over a period of time, utilize all the styles.

Supervisors are obligated to accept their status as part of management and are no longer strictly operational. At the same time, if a supervisor is to be effective, it is necessary to work for (and through) subordinates. When dealing with subordinates accept them as unique individuals and work to improve their self-image.

Case Study

Officer Paul Enboe

Officer Paul Enboe has been in the department for three years and recently transferred to the swing shift. He spent four years in the Marine Corps and was discharged with the rank of sergeant. He is still a member of the Marine Corps Reserve.

Enboe is most comfortable in a highly structured situation. While working on the midnight shift under a directive supervisor, he received outstanding ratings for the three years he had been in the department.

On his present shift, the supervisor's primary working style is participative. Subordinates are always consulted, except in emergency situations, before decisions are made. Group involvement is expected and power is shared. Two-way communication is encouraged. Attitudes, values and feelings are important and are taken into consideration.

Enboe feels a great deal of time is wasted when the sergeant makes a sincere effort to involve everyone in the decision-making process. It seems to Enboe that everyone is always spinning wheels and task accomplishment is delayed again and again.

Enboe is genuinely concerned that the sergeant never seems to make a decision and the shift is actually run by the officers. In fact, he thinks the line officers continually exert a veto power whenever they desire, and officers are not working to their top capacity.

Enboe's supervisor believes himself to be highly effective and thinks it is essential to create a working environment where controls are minimized and officers are allowed to develop to their highest potential.

There is a definite conflict between the leadership style utilized by the supervisor and that to which Enboe is accustomed. It seems clear that it is difficult for Enboe to work effectively when supervised by a participative leadership style. What should be done in this case? Should Enboe be transferred to another supervisor or should he be expected to adjust to this style of leadership?

Key Concepts

coercive power
conceptual skills
consideration
consultative
contingency
directive
expert power
extending power
human skills
initiating structure
leadership continuum

leadership traits
legitimate power
operational skills
participative
personal relationships
position power
referent power
relationship-oriented leadership
reward power
task-oriented leadership
task structure

Discussion Topics and Questions

1. Why does power play such an important part in a police department?

2. How can a supervisor extend power?

3. Why is the trait theory of leadership viewed as having limited application today?

4. What are the limitations inherent in emphasizing consideration as a leadership approach?

5. How does the situation affect leadership style?

6. Discuss the disadvantages of a consultative leadership style.

7. What are the limitations of the directive leadership style?

For Further Reading

Cox, Danny with John Hoover (1992). *Leadership When the Heat's On*. New York: McGraw-Hill Book Company.

> A key chapter describes leadership as being good when growth-producing techniques are carefully and strategically implemented, to the extent that employees are motivated to achieve new heights of quality in current tasks, in addition to encouraging new and innovative actions.

Carr, Clay (1994). "Empowered Organizations, Empowered Leaders." *Training and Development*, Vol. 48, No.3.

> Emphasizes that at every level in an organization leaders are actively engaged in managing themselves. Fundamental leadership functions are identified as: defining the mission, maintaining trust, coordinating activities, communicating information, ensuring learning and ensuring creativity. A realistic key is that leaders empower others rather than just running things themselves.

Garner, Ronnie (1993). "Leadership in the Nineties." *FBI Law Enforcement Bulletin*, Vol. 62, No. 12.

> Views leadership as the process of articulating the vision, mission, and values of the organization within the context of a long-ranged strategic plan and giving impetus to that plan by empowering subordinates. Without this base it is the author's position that police managers serve only as custodians of a bureaucracy preoccupying itself with the present at the expense of the future.

Nanus, Burt. (1992). *Visionary Leadership: Creating a Compelling Sense of Direction for Your Organization*. San Francisco, CA: Jossey-Bass Publishers.

> Describes leaders as being totally results oriented. They adopt challenging new visions of what is both possible and desirable, communicate their visions, and persuade others to become committed to the new directions. Describes the leadership roles of spokesperson, direction setter, coach, and change agent.

References

Carr, Clay (1994). "Empowered Organizations, Empowered Leaders." *Training and Development*, Vol. 48, No. 3.

Commission on Accreditation for Law Enforcement Agencies, Inc. (1994). *Standards for Law Enforcement Agencies*. Fairfield, VA: Commission on Accreditation for Law Enforcement Agencies, Inc.

Couper, David (1994). "Seven Seeds for Policing." *FBI Law Enforcement Bulletin*, Vol. 63, No. 3.

Covey, Stephen R. (1991). *Principle-centered Leadership*. New York: Summit Books.

Cox, Danny with John Hoover (1992). *Leadership When the Heat's On*. New York: McGraw-Hill, Book Company.

Daresh, John C. (1989). *Supervision as a Proactive Process*. White Plains, NY: Longman, Inc.

Dobbs, Carl and Mark W. Field (1993). "Rational Risk: Leadership Success or Failure?" *The Police Chief*, Vol. XLII, No. 12.

Fetherolf, Louis H. (1994). "Leadership: An Inside-Out Proposition." *The Police Chief*, Vol. XLIII, No. 1.

Fiedler, Fred E., Martin M. Chemers and Linda Maher (1976). *Improving Leadership Effectiveness: The Leader Match Concept*. New York, John Wiley and Sons, Inc.

French, J. and B. Raven (1959). "The Bases of Social Power." In D. Cartwright (ed.) *Studies In Social Power*. Ann Arbor, MI: Institute for Social Research.

Garner, Ronnie (1993). "Leadership in The Nineties." *FBI Law Enforcement Bulletin*, Vol. 62, No. 12.

Handy, Charles (1993). *Understanding Organizations*. Oxford: Oxford University Press.

Hudson, David (1994). "The Power Gap and Police Performance Failure." *The Police Chief*, Vol. LXI, No. 6.

Johns, Gary (1983). *Organizational Behavior*. Glenview, IL: Scott, Foresman and Company.

Mendofik, Paul J. (1994). "Reflections on Leadership." *FBI Law Enforcement Bulletin*, Vol. 63, No. 8.

More, Harry W. and O.R. Shipley (1987). *The Police Policy Manual—Personnel*. Springfield, IL: Charles C Thomas, Publisher.

Nanus, Burt (1992). *Visionary Leadership: Creating a Compelling Sense of Direction for Your Organization*. San Francisco: Jossey-Bass Publishers.

Police Foundation (1981). *Survey of Police Operational Administrative Practices—1981*. Washington, DC: Police Executive Research Forum.

Stogdill, R.M. (1974). *Handbook of Leadership*. New York: Free Press.

Von der Embse, Thomas J. (1987). *Supervision: Managerial Skills for a New Era*. New York: Macmillan Publishing Co.

Discipline—

An Essential Element of Police Supervision

6

Introductory Case Study

Sergeant Donna Hatfield

Donna Hatfield, an experienced juvenile officer and a recently promoted sergeant, has been named to head the department's new and overlapping 7 p.m. to 3 a.m. patrol shift. She will supervise five male police officers assigned to solo patrol vehicles. Three of the men are veterans; the other two are rookies with little more than one year on the job.

As the first-line supervisor, Sergeant Hatfield is expected to provide leadership and to take formal disciplinary action against her subordinates when the need arises. This has caused a real problem. The officers resent the fact that they have been assigned to work for the only female patrol sergeant in the department and have made it clear to everyone that they plan to give her a rough time. Their egos have become a stumbling block. While the members of the new shift are facetiously being called the "F Troop," the situation is out of hand and is beginning to cause a great deal of stress within the organization.

Since Sergeant Hatfield is a novice and has not been trained to deal effectively with this particular type of situation, she will need all the help she can get. As the senior patrol sergeant, what philosophical orientation to discipline would you recommend that she adopt? What specific actions should Sergeant Hatfield take in order to correct errant, disruptive or deviant behavior and to deter misconduct by her subordinates in the future?

The Nature of Discipline

Discipline should never be an end in and of itself. The **goal of discipline** is to produce desirable behavior. This function can be accomplished by encouraging appropriate behavior and punishing inappropriate or unacceptable behavior.

Discipline, as an operational concept, is very closely related to the other managerial aspects of first-line supervision in paramilitary-type police organizations. It should not be viewed as a derogatory term or dirty word. In fact, dis-

cipline is regarded as being the essential element in work that ensures overall productivity and an orderly environment. Unfortunately, it is the word discipline, in and of itself, that causes the problem. It has a number of different (at times conflicting) meanings and must be used carefully in order to avoid confusion.

The term *discipline* is most often used to describe an adversarial process resulting in the application of various kinds of negative sanctions or punishments. It may also refer to the state of affairs within a given organization that produces order, a shared sense of purpose and common goal-oriented behavior. In this particular context, discipline is considered to be positive and means teaching, instruction, training and remediation. Its purpose is to facilitate collective action, the internalization of self-control based on the norms and values of the work force, predictable behavior and organizational efficiency. From this perspective, the maintenance of discipline is a management function that involves conditioning subordinates to promote obedience to legitimate authority, internal self-control and the acceptance of objective and fairly administered punishments designed to help curb individual deviance or professional misconduct within a particular law enforcement agency.

Discipline in the Ranks

Human resources provide the linchpin for delivery of all public safety services in a given community. Police work is, in itself, a labor-intensive governmental activity in which personnel costs consume a lion's share of the budget. Attempting to maximize the efficiency, effectiveness and productivity of the police department while holding the line on spending is clearly a management function. It is the first-line supervisor, normally a sergeant, who has direct responsibility for accomplishing the organization's mission, goals and objectives through the collaborative efforts of immediate subordinates. Consequently, each first-line supervisor must develop those skills necessary to influence the behavior of others, to coordinate their activities and to lead or direct employees in such a way as to gain their respect, confidence, trust and positive cooperation. Supervision, based on this model, is viewed as an art rather than a science.

Sergeants, as first-line supervisors charged with getting police work done through others, play two distinct yet related roles when it comes to the on-the-job behavior of their subordinates. Sergeants are expected to nurture professionalism in the employee; on the other hand, they are responsible for initiating disciplinary measures when formal action is required to deal with individual deviance. The trick is to find the appropriate balance between employee self-regulation and organizational control (Covey, 1992).

Police sergeants, like all other first-line supervisors, find themselves sandwiched between upper management and operational personnel. While their authority is often ambiguous, sergeants are generally expected to utilize existing human resources in an effort to translate official departmental policy into both efficient and effective action on the street. In order to fulfill this awesome

responsibility and to play a meaningful role in police personnel administration, sergeants use positive as well as negative discipline. No matter which form they opt to use, the objective is always the same. Sergeants try to encourage safe, reasonable and predictable conduct in the workplace so as to create an environment in which competent, well-trained police officers "protect and serve" the community while satisfying their personal needs and achieving their professional goals. Needless to say, police sergeants play a pivotal leadership role in the administration of criminal justice. In the long run, it is the first-line supervisors who will (based on their ability, training and human relation skills) determine the success or failure of the police department in achieving its mission, goals and objectives. According to Dwight Eisenhower, "Leadership is the art of getting others to do something you want done because they want to do it!"

Positive Discipline

The words "disciple" and "discipline" have the same root meaning: to teach or mold. **Positive discipline** involves a systematic approach that is designed to instruct and/or guide employees in such a way that they become loyal, dedicated, responsible and productive members of the organization (Sherman and Lucia, 1992). From a practical point of view, discipline is considered to be positive or "good" when all police employees share a common sense of purpose, practice self-discipline and voluntarily follow the policies, procedures, rules and regulations established to promote order and to facilitate work within the department. Positive discipline is a by-product of the socialization and attitudinal conditioning used in progressive agencies to prevent deviation from group-shared expectations or to deal with maladjusted employees without resorting to punishments or other kinds of negative sanctions. This particular orientation to discipline (built on an esprit de corps) is not unique in police organizations and is based on the fundamental assumption that police personnel are no different than other employees. Police officers who have mastered their craft, who know what is expected of them as professionals and who understand the rationale behind those expectations are much more likely to identify with the department in terms of its mission, goals and objectives and to invest their time, energy, effort and expertise in work-related activities. According to the legendary O.W. Wilson, positive discipline manifests itself in the officer's willingness to conform and participate in self-restraint, based on professional dedication or a personal commitment to the ethos of the police department (Wilson and McLaren, 1977).

The most positive form of discipline is the self-discipline that is built on the human tendency to do what needs to be done, to do what is right in a given situation and to voluntarily comply with those reasonable standards of performance and conduct that are applicable to all members of the work force. Mature employees know that following instructions and obeying rules is part of the game. Responsible and cooperative behavior at work is a tacitly accepted condition of employment in virtually all organizations.

Every first-line supervisor should strive to create an environment in which self-discipline is rewarded, and external or imposed discipline is held to an absolute minimum. In modern police work, the sergeant plays a crucial role in the employee development process. It is the sergeant's job to promote professional growth and to foster a sense of self-worth in each subordinate. The success or failure of this effort will depend, in the long run, on the supervisor's technical knowledge and human skills. All first-line supervisors in healthy police organizations are multidimensional players who act as technical advisors, role models, teachers, counselors, leaders and, when all else fails, disciplinarians. They learn to accentuate the positive and to cultivate each employee's sense of competence, craftsmanship and pride through constructive interpersonal relationships built on a bedrock of empathy and mutual respect. Effective supervision and good supervisors help keep subordinates interested in their job and satisfied with working conditions (see Figure 6.1).

Figure 6.1
Basic Supervisory Roles

1.	Planner	7.	Role model
2.	Technical advisor	8.	Leader
3.	Problem solver	9.	Coach
4.	Teacher	10.	Facilitator
5.	Motivator	11.	Disciplinarian
6.	Counselor		

Even though money and other material rewards are very powerful incentives, recognition (based on sincere assessment of an employee's personal worth) can have an even more dramatic impact on job-related behavior. It costs little or nothing and yet, like money, almost everyone responds to it in one way or another. It is amazing how hard police officers will work when the psychological payoff is feeling appreciated and important. While she may have overstated the case somewhat, Mary Kay Ash, the woman who turned an idea into a $600 million-a-year cosmetic industry, believes that there are two things people want more than sex or money. They covet recognition and praise from those in a position to judge their on-the-job performance and exert a positive influence on their career (LeBoeuf, 1985).

Good supervisors are enthusiastic team players who have the skills necessary to influence their subordinates in a positive way. They help create an environment in which police personnel buy into and make a willing contribution to the organization. According to the legendary Dale Carnegie (1992), there are nine ways that a sergeant can change a person's attitudes without giving offense or arousing resentment:

1.   Begin with praise and honest appreciation.

2.   Call attention to the other person's mistakes indirectly.

3.   Discuss personal mistakes before criticizing others.

4.   Ask thoughtful questions instead of giving direct orders.

5.   Always try to let the other person save face.

6.   Praise, whenever possible, even the slightest improvement.

7.   Give the other person a fine reputation to live up to.

8.   Use encouragement and make faults seem easy to correct.

9.   Make the person happy about doing what has been suggested.

Effective supervisors have learned to criticize *the work* done by an employee rather than criticize the employee. They know what Michael LeBoeuf has called "The Greatest Management Principle": Those things that get rewarded get done. Recognition and praise are rewards.

Police departments use commendations, citations, certificates and plaques as physical indications to denote a job well done. These psychological rewards are among the most powerful motivators at the disposal of the first-line supervisor. They are the key ingredient in morale and serve as the cornerstone of esprit de corps.

Camaraderie, unity of purpose, technical expertise and effective supervision create natural parameters for accepted and expected behavior in a given organization. Once internalized and continuously reinforced with positive sanctions or rewards, these parameters form the basis for self-control. Self-control is an important trait of police professionalism. Once employees know their job and accept the standards by which their on-the-job performance will be judged, they gain a great deal of self-confidence and personal security. They feel more comfortable exercising discretion and accept the fact that there are limits beyond which they must not go. If a subordinate crosses over one of these boundaries, it must be understood that some type of legitimate disciplinary action will follow.

Total quality management (TQM) is a technique designed to assist in developing a positive performance-oriented culture as well as employee commitment within the work environment. TQM empowers employees, through meaningful participation, to become partners in making the organization work more efficiently and effectively by removing the barriers which inhibit commitment, creativity and high quality service. First-line supervisors must become facilitators who elicit from their people their maximum effort to contribute ideas, creativity, innovative thinking, attention to detail and analyses of process, products and services in the workplace (Whisenand and Rush, 1993).

From a practical point of view, all police officers must be treated as adults if that is the behavior expected in return. Supervisors can almost guarantee improvement in employee performance through use of the **PRICE protocol**. PRICE is the acronym for pinpoint, record, involve, coach and evaluate.

1. **Pinpoint**. Supervisors must continually scan the work environment in order to pinpoint performance problems that merit attention.

2. **Record**. Supervisors should record (and quantify) the current performance level of those who are having problems.

3. **Involve**. Supervisors must involve the employee and/or employees in determining the best way to deal with the problem, the coaching strategies to be used, how the supervisor will be monitoring progress and the rewards or punishments to be associated with success or failure of the corrective process.

4. **Coach**. Supervisors should implement the agreed upon coaching strategy by observing performance and providing timely advice, continuous encouragement, positive reinforcement and retraining (if and when it is necessary).

5. **Evaluate**. Supervisors must evaluate and provide feedback on a continuous basis in order to determine whether or not the goal(s) of the PRICE protocol have been achieved.

If employee performance does not reach the mutually agreed upon level, the supervisor needs to determine the cause. There may be a need to redefine goals. On the other hand, there may be a need for further assistance (Aragon, 1993). Additional time or training might be required. Police officers who "cannot" or "will not" perform at an acceptable level should be disciplined and—if necessary—separated from the police service.

Negative Discipline

In ideal circumstances, employees are expected to be willing and capable of assuming responsibility for the quantity and quality of their productive output. Under these conditions, the employee's ego satisfaction, pride in achievement, professional competence and job security become very powerful motivators and are key ingredients in a work-based reward system built on self-discipline. Unfortunately, this utopian view of on-the-job behavior is overly simplistic and, in many ways, a figment of the management theorist's imagination. As valuable as it is, self-discipline is not sufficient, in itself, to regulate behavior in complex criminal justice organizations. Consequently, the police sergeant must be pre-

pared, when circumstances warrant, to supplement employee self-discipline with external and, at times negative, imposed discipline.

Discipline that is based on the use of punishment, rather than rewards, is referred to as **negative discipline**. When used in this context, it is synonymous with the phrase "disciplinary action" and is imposed by those in authority when all positive approaches have failed to produce conformity with specific performance standards and/or behavioral expectations. Disciplinary action is adversarial in nature and is inherently punitive. It is designed to regulate work-related behavior and to safeguard the integrity of the organization. Negative discipline in the form of disciplinary action is considered a legitimate and necessary behavior control mechanism in virtually all paramilitary-type police departments.

First-line supervisors in bureaucratic police organizations spend a great deal of time and energy trying to cope with marginal employees. A marginal employee is not a deviant per se. Some individuals (for a variety of idiosyncratic or cultural reasons) simply do not measure up to reasonable expectations. These employees do the minimum amount of work to get by. They lack or have lost interest in their job and have adapted their behavior to and are comfortable with their present level of incompetence. Many marginal employees freely admit that they are just "putting in time."

Sergeants are expected to deal with employee problems, motivate marginal employees and increase the employee's productivity through effective supervision. Unfortunately, a sergeant may or may not have the diagnostic or human skills needed to accomplish this objective.

In large police departments, first-line supervisors may have access and be authorized to refer marginal employees to an Employee Assistance Program designed to deal with mental health problems, alcoholism, drug addiction, stress, domestic difficulties and so on. In smaller departments, the sergeant is the Employee Assistance Program. Problem-solving and counseling come with the stripes. As a result, we expect sergeants to have a wide range of knowledge and a knapsack full of human skills.

When all else fails, sergeants are forced to rely on the imposition of negative discipline to deal with both deviant and marginal police personnel. This tends to overload the system and is not cost effective. Discipline and morale begin to suffer when most of the sergeant's time is spent on a few deviant or marginal employees. From a practical point of view, formal disciplinary action should be the court of last resort in human resources management.

While it is clear that the vast majority of all American police personnel exercise a considerable degree of self-discipline, there are always a few (up to 15 percent) who will, for one reason or another, continue to violate departmental policies, procedures, rules and regulations even though they are aware of the potential consequences of their deviant behavior. They simply cannot or will not toe the line and accept responsibility for disciplining themselves. At this point, the sergeant, as a first-line supervisor, is obligated to initiate appropriate disciplinary action. Under these conditions, negative discipline becomes a necessary, albeit time-consuming, aspect of effective supervision.

Sergeants as Disciplinarians

Due to their position in the department hierarchy and the legitimate authority vested in their rank, sergeants play a much more important and direct role in the disciplinary process than almost any other police manager. For all practical purposes, they are the departmental disciplinarians with the power to discipline nearly every line officer engaged in the delivery of police services. Many of their subordinates are inexperienced, inadequately trained or in need of some corrective remediation. When all else fails, it is the sergeant's responsibility:

1. To identify the weaknesses, deficiencies, failure or overt behavior of subordinates that indicate the need for corrective action.

2. To analyze all of the relevant factors to determine the appropriate action to be taken.

3. To initiate and, in many cases, to carry out the disciplinary action.

4. To document the case (in terms of "cause," "analysis," "action," and the "appropriateness of the discipline") for subsequent review by superiors (see Figure 6.2).

Figure 6.2
The Sergeant's Role as Disciplinarian

---

1. Recognize disciplinary problems as they arise.
2. Gather pertinent data concerning the situation.
3. Analyze those factors relevant to the problem.
4. Determine appropriate disciplinary measures.
5. Initiate disciplinary action.
6. Discipline subordinates when authorized.
7. Document the case for subsequent review.

Sergeants, as responsible first-line supervisors, have a professional duty to act reasonably, decisively and promptly in resolving disciplinary problems. They are expected to act in the best interests of the employee, the department, the law enforcement profession and the community at large. Needless to say, all disciplinary actions should be "constructive" rather than "destructive," in the sense that they are administered in a firm, fair and impartial manner. **Constructive discipline** is built on a foundation of sensitivity and good judgment. Its goal is the correction or remediation of deviant behavior as it occurs as well as improvement in the overall behavior of the employee and other members of the police department in the future (Hilgert and Haimann, 1991).

Fair and Equitable Discipline

Disciplinary action in complex criminal justice organizations should not be an idiosyncratic or random exercise of power by those in authority. As noted earlier, it must be viewed as an essential part of a goal-oriented process designed to control the disruptive behavior of individual employees while ensuring the overall efficiency, effectiveness and productivity of the work force. Those employees who cannot measure up to reasonable performance standards, or who refuse to toe the line in terms of their on-the-job behavior, are legitimate targets for formal disciplinary action. They should be penalized in such a way that they learn to achieve acceptable performance standards and exhibit appropriate behavior. Employees who do not respond or are incapable of making a substantive change become a liability to the department and must be removed from their job for the good of the service.

Fair and equitable disciplinary procedures are necessary to protect the integrity of the service and provide an adequate frame of reference for all police personnel. Police officers (like all other employees) have emotional job-related security needs that must be considered by management. It is the sergeant, as the first-line supervisor, who has the primary responsibility for satisfying a subordinate's:

1. NEED to be treated as an individual with intrinsic value and the capacity to make a contribution to the organization.

2. NEED to know exactly what management expects in terms of work performance and on-the-job conduct.

3. NEED for regular feedback from management concerning job performance (including praise as well as censure).

4. NEED to be treated fairly and impartially by those in management.

5. NEED to be judged by management based on facts and standards rather than on personal opinion and/or assumptions.

The failure to recognize and deal with employee needs in these very critical areas often leads to job dissatisfaction, interpersonal conflict, poor performance, disciplinary problems and high employee turnover (Robbins, 1989). It represents a sergeant's dereliction of duty and the abdication of responsibility by management.

All seasoned first-line supervisors know that rationality is a prerequisite for effective disciplinary action in law enforcement. Good disciplinary systems do not materialize out of thin air; they are, in fact, very carefully crafted by management (Plunkett, 1992) and generally exhibit the following characteristics:

1. Proper assignment of personnel to jobs within the organization based on their interest, skill, utility and specialized training.

2. Necessary and reasonable job-related policies, procedures, rules and regulations formulated to govern behavior in the workplace, meet employee needs and accomplish the department's mission, goals and specified objectives.

3. Effective communication of information regarding expected performance and acceptable behavior to all employees along with an explanation of the probable consequences of noncompliance.

4. Continuous review, evaluation and appraisal of all personnel to assess strengths, detect weaknesses and identify disciplinary problems that may require immediate attention.

5. Consistent, fair and equitable enforcement of all policies, procedures, rules and regulations within the organization.

6. Mutually acceptable, institutionalized, disciplinary procedures based on a "due process" model that is in harmony with applicable civil service regulations and negotiated collective bargaining agreements.

7. A formal appeals procedure designed to ensure the fairness of all disciplinary actions and to serve as a check and balance on the imposition of punitive sanctions.

While no manager really likes the idea of being the disciplinarian, using disciplinary action is an unavoidable part of each first-line supervisor's job. No matter how alert or skillful the particular supervisor is, the imposition of discipline (in one form or another) is inevitable in virtually all work situations. Consequently, supervisors must face the fact that they will, in all likelihood, be called on to take disciplinary action against a subordinate. The imposition of punishment is normal and to be expected, though hopefully an infrequent aspect of the first-line supervisor's role in complex criminal justice organizations.

Inconsistency and favoritism in disciplining subordinates will have an adverse, potentially destructive effect on employee morale and productivity. The effective sergeant understands departmental policies, procedures, rules and regulations; trains and guides immediate subordinates; and is both fair and impartial when dispensing discipline. From a pragmatic point of view, a sergeant's actions must be legal, reasonable, consistent and timely. Employees react strongly, and frequently challenge management prerogatives in court when they believe they have been treated unfairly due to the arbitrary denial of some "due process" right. It is the sergeant, as the first-line supervisor, who is the central character in the drama to preserve management's authority to discipline errant, disruptive or deviant subordinates.

The Use and Abuse of Discipline

Although punishment might produce some negative effects (like resentment, interpersonal conflict and lower morale), it must be used, at times, simply because there is no practical alternative. Some of the adverse reactions to punishment will be tempered, however, if it is carried out in an intelligent, fair and predictable manner and the employee targeted for disciplinary action is made to understand that it was made necessary due to poor performance or misconduct, not because of someone else's behavior (Iannone, 1994).

Lack of trust is another factor that must be taken into consideration. Police officers learn to fear, lose respect for and distrust those supervisors who become entrenched in company politics, make decisions too quickly or irrationally and invoke disciplinary measures for the slightest infractions. Mature officers want their sergeants to be equitable and to act in good faith when disciplining. When their first-line supervisors fail to live up to these expectations, the dissonance created makes matters even worse.

Each sergeant's approach to the use of discipline is indicative of the sergeant's view of the administrative power inherent in the rank. If the sergeant has an authoritarian personality, misunderstands the nature of the job or lacks rudimentary leadership skills, the potential for abuse of the disciplinary apparatus is great. There is a solution for this problem, however. All newly promoted first-line police supervisors should be required to successfully complete a supervisory/ management training program designed to familiarize them with their new administrative duties, their role as a supervisor and their authority vis-à-vis the formal disciplinary system.

The imposition of disciplinary action within an organization has two distinct yet interactive objectives: (1) to reform the individual offender and (2) to deter others who may be influenced by what has happened. From this perspective, all imposed discipline has value in terms of correcting errant, disruptive or deviant behavior as well as for its future effect on those individuals involved as offenders and/or observers. Each sergeant must, in light of these objectives, determine which penalties are available, feasible and appropriate for use in a particular set of circumstances. While evaluating the alternatives, both the short-term and long-range effect that punishment is likely to have must be estimated. It is then up to the sergeant, in conjunction with superior officers, to select the most effective form of punishment. All other things being equal, the punishment should be adequate based on the offense. Excessive punishment is counterproductive and becomes a stressor in labor-management relations.

On the other side of the coin, first-line supervisors, as human beings, must avoid the pitfalls of subjectivity and continuously guard against making discipline-related decisions based on emotions. Based on the "people orientation" in contemporary applied management theory (Peters and Waterman, 1982), it is safe to say that there is no place for anger, revenge or retribution in the disciplinary process. It is illegal for supervisors to harass employees through the capricious exercise of power or to intentionally humiliate those that have been tar-

geted for disciplinary action. And finally, there is absolutely no justification for the behavior of supervisors who displace aggression by scapegoating their employees. The proper goal of imposed discipline is to make the future more satisfactory, not to vent emotions or to fulfill some abstract sense of justice (see Figure 6.3).

Figure 6.3
Objectives of Disciplinary Action

MOTIVE/GOAL	LIKELY EFFECT

Legitimate
    Reform
    Deterrence
	Improved performance or conduct.
	Prevent similar violations by others.

Unacceptable
    Revenge
    Capriciousness
    Displaced Aggression
    Humiliation
    Retribution
	Anger, provocation to more violations.
	Fear, loss of respect, distrust.
	Uncertainty, confusion, resentment.
	Anxiety, personal conflict, hatred.
	Frustration, accusations of legalism.

Modified from Aaron Q. Sartain and Alton Baker, *The Supervisor and the Job*. New York: McGraw-Hill Book Company, 1978.

Administering effective discipline is one of the most demanding aspects of any first-line supervisor's job. It is both complex and very time consuming. Based on our Anglo-Saxon heritage, the accused employee is presumed innocent until proven guilty, and in establishing that guilt (as a justification for using disciplinary action in the workplace), the burden of proof is almost always on those involved in direct supervisory management (Steinmetz and Todd, 1992). Many courts have now ruled that an employer violates an implied contract if a subordinate is disciplined without having sufficient and just cause.

In the public sector, *just cause* refers to a cause of action that is legally adequate to sustain a decision to inflict negative sanctions. At this point, sufficient and just cause clauses have been incorporated into virtually all civil service regulations and grievance procedures mandated by negotiated collective bargaining agreements. The imposition of disciplinary action without just cause is viewed by most Americans as an unconscionable and totally unacceptable abuse of authority. This type of unprofessional conduct undermines the individual supervisor's effectiveness and subjects management itself to ridicule, charges of unfair labor practices, political repercussions and civil suit. The misuse of power destroys the sergeant's credibility and diminishes legitimate authority over subordinates.

While most supervisory personnel do an adequate job, police work has its share of poor first-line supervisors. There are sergeants who are merely putting

in time and trying to survive. They take disciplinary action against coworkers only when they are forced into a corner and do not want to make waves or rock the boat unless their own career is on the line. Other sergeants are simply inept. They do not have the sensitivity, judgment, knowledge, training or human skills needed to deal effectively with recalcitrant employees. These men and women are shackled by their own inadequacy. Malfeasance, misfeasance and nonfeasance interact synergistically to produce a dual impact: police professionalism is diminished, and public safety is placed in jeopardy. It is American society, in the long run, that suffers the consequences of poor first-line supervision in law enforcement.

Saying that **firm, fair, equitable and lawful disciplinary action** is an essential ingredient in effective supervision is one thing; achieving it in a complex criminal justice organization is another matter altogether.

Keys to Effective Discipline

In order to make disciplinary action more effective, it should be proactive as well as reactive in that police sergeants must be prepared, based on their education, training and job-related supervisory experience, to detect and correct discipline problems before they become malignant and spread throughout the organization. Good supervisors know "the keys to effective discipline" (Preston and Zimmerer, 1983) and apply them as conscientiously as possible:

1. **Don't be a Discipline Ostrich.** First-line supervisors should not slip into a pattern of overlooking discipline problems. In fact, they have a duty to take immediate and appropriate action to correct the situation. Failure to act promptly and decisively tends to perpetuate the problem and sets the stage for more debilitating interpersonal conflict. In addition, other employees will begin to question the sergeant's ability and fairness if they see that disciplinary action is put off or avoided altogether. Under these circumstances, subordinates will assume that most, if not all, of the department's policies, procedures, rules and regulations are worthless. Violations may become the rule rather than the exception. This anomie or "normlessness" is inherently destructive.

2. **Become a "Caesar's Wife."** All of the sergeant's behavior must be above reproach. There can be absolutely no doubt in the subordinate's mind about the sergeant's loyalty to the organization or willingness to comply with departmental policies, procedures, rules and regulations. Employees cannot be expected to practice self-control if their immediate supervisors are poor role models who fail to set an example worthy of emulation. Sergeants lead others by example. Seeing supervisory personnel bend or break the rules promotes disruptive and deviant behavior by others in the work force.

3. **Practice the "Hot Stove" Rule.** According to this basic concept, discipline (like touching a hot stove) should be immediate, based on known rules, consistent and impersonal. While the abstract principle of "the hot stove" is easy to remember, it is much more difficult to translate into practice in complex criminal justice organizations. Under less than ideal conditions, effective discipline is largely a matter of chance.

4. **Never Lose Control.** First-line supervisors must remain calm and in control as they deal with various types of disciplinary problems. They are not expected to show emotion, to fly off the handle or to touch their subordinates. Unless the sergeant's authority is challenged publicly, employees should be disciplined in private. An open display of anger or power is normally counterproductive. It leads to resentment, game playing and lower morale. The supervisor's failure to exercise self-control and behave in a consistent and mature manner will result in a loss of respect (for the person and the rank) and the further erosion of authority.

5. **Be Instructive.** Good first-line supervisors are also teachers. Whenever disciplinary action becomes necessary, the errant, disruptive or deviant employee should be told why the discipline is being imposed and how it can be avoided in the future. Sergeants, as supervisory managers, function as culture carriers. They clarify and explain policies, procedures, rules and regulations to their subordinates. When it comes to disciplinary action, the sergeant is obligated to advise subordinates of the "due process" options available to them should they choose to challenge the propriety of the disciplinary process or the punishment. Sergeants should never hide anything from the employee. Deception will come back to haunt the supervisor. Sergeants should be open and honest with their subordinates and must impose the discipline in an intelligent, reasonable and mature manner.

6. **Be Firm but Fair.** The first-line supervisor must always be firm but fair in administering disciplinary action. If the police sergeant wants subordinates to feel that discipline is both firm and fair, the sergeant must be open, honest, reasonable and a direct approach must be used. Attitude is the key. Effective supervisors never joke about discipline; they take their responsibility as disciplinarians very seriously. They know that discipline administered in a firm, fair, consistent and impartial manner helps correct performance problems; deters errant, disruptive or deviant behavior by others; and generates respect for both the supervisor and the authority inherent in rank. Ambiguity and inconsistency will, on the other hand, destroy the sergeant's credibility and overall effectiveness as a disciplinarian.

7. **Stay Out of the Employee's Private Life.** All other things being equal, a subordinate's private life is just that, PRIVATE. Unless the employee's personal beliefs or off-the-job behavior have a direct bearing on job performance, they should not be factored into the disciplinary process. As first-line supervisors who are charged with delegating authority, sergeants are responsible for the work being done under their personal direction. It is imperative to avoid making assessments based on irrelevant types of data. Personal value judgments often lead to interpersonal conflict and covert as well as overt discrimination. The scope of provisions dealing with "conduct unbecoming an officer" has been narrowed considerably by the courts in a series of recent decisions. This is hazardous uncharted territory.

8. **State Rules/Regulations in a Positive Manner.** Effective sergeants avoid negativism and treat department policies, procedures, rules and regulations as being positive control mechanisms designed to promote order and to facilitate work related to the organization's mission, goals and objectives.

9. **Don't be a Disciplinary Magician.** A good supervisor avoids becoming the type of person who makes rules as they go along, in an effort to trap subordinates. The key to success as a disciplinarian is to ensure that all employees know and fully understand the department's policies, procedures, rules and regulations. The best advice is to be up front with all employees; don't spring new rules and/or variations of the old rules on them ex post facto. Effective supervisors give every employee an ample opportunity to comply with performance standards and behavioral expectations.

10. **Be Precise.** Sergeants, as first-line supervisors and departmental disciplinarians, must (based on the civil liability inherent in their position) comply with labor laws, collective bargaining agreements and civil service regulations. Since their actions are subject to both administrative and judicial review, sergeants must be precise in assessing job performance and taking formal disciplinary action. They must not deviate from prescribed procedures and should very carefully document all of their actions. Imprecision lessens the sergeant's credibility, weakens the case and increases the likelihood that there will be subsequent litigation of the issue or issues under civil law.

While there is really no way to avoid the use of negative discipline in complex criminal justice organizations, it can be made more effective and much less stressful if supervisory personnel use these keys to unlock the productive potential of their immediate subordinates. Once again, the sergeant is in the catbird seat and will, in the long run, determine the effectiveness of the discipline and the overall credibility of the disciplinary system.

The Hot Stove Revisited

Taking appropriate disciplinary action creates a real dilemma for first-line supervisors. Police sergeants walk a tightrope between two seemingly incongruent roles. As noted earlier, they are expected to be "teachers," "helpers" and "leaders" who nurture their subordinates; on the other hand, they are the "disciplinarians" who punish them for their errant, disruptive or deviant behavior. The trick is to balance these roles in such a way so as not to create interpersonal conflict or generate deep-seated resentment.

Douglas McGregor, a noted management theorist, provided us with a very useful analogy concerning disciplinary tasks and earned punishment. He called his idea **the Hot Stove concept** (Plunkett, 1992). It compares an organization's disciplinary system to a red hot stove and the burn victim to an employee who has earned punishment. When you touch a red hot stove, the discipline is immediate, predictable, consistent and totally impersonal.

McGregor's Hot Stove analogy is used to illustrate the essential elements of a functional disciplinary policy. It points out that when you burn your hand based on your own stupidity, you become angry with yourself. While you might be mad at the stove, the anger cannot last long because you should have known the consequences of your act. According to the Hot Stove rule, you learn your lesson quickly and effectively because:

1. The burn is IMMEDIATE, with no question as to cause and effect. The sooner the disciplinary action is taken, the more automatic it will be and the more closely it will be associated with the errant, disruptive or deviant behavior. While speed is an essential ingredient in effective discipline, undue haste should be avoided because it could lead to carelessness and the imposition of unwarranted punishments.

2. You had ADVANCE WARNING and knew (because the stove was red hot) exactly what would happen if you touched it. Unexpected discipline is almost always considered unfair and usually creates a great deal of resentment. Consequently, employees must be given a clear warning that a particular offense or type of behavior will result in disciplinary action, coupled with a definite warning as to the nature and extent of the discipline to be invoked.

3. The discipline is CONSISTENT because everyone who touches the red hot stove is burned. Consistency means that each and every time there is an infraction, appropriate disciplinary action will be taken. This helps to set internal as well as external limits in terms of what subordinates can or cannot do. Consistency also means that the punishment inflicted should be no more or no less than expected for a particular offense. Inconsistent disciplinary action, on the other hand, leads to uncertainty and confusion. It

destroys the integrity of the disciplinary process and erodes the sergeant's legitimate authority. Inconsistency produces anxiety, insecurity, interpersonal conflict, resentment and poor morale.

4. The discipline is IMPERSONAL in that victims are burned for touching the red hot stove regardless of their identity. They are on the receiving end of discipline not because they are "bad," but because of their errant, disruptive or deviant behavior. This helps to remove the personal, "You are always out to get me" element of disciplinary action because the discipline is directed against an act or unacceptable behavior, not the individual. When discipline is automatic and impersonal, it reduces resentment and clears the way for subordinates to assume responsibility for their own performance and/or job-related conduct.

Sergeants, in addition to their other supervisory responsibilities, add the human element to McGregor's Hot Stove concept. They tend the stove to make sure it operates efficiently and effectively. Under ideal circumstances, the hot stove not only serves as a deterrent against whom it is applied, but as a form of conditioning or training that will orient other police employees to the types of performance or on-the-job behavior the organization cannot and will not accept. Telling employees what is expected of them and explaining the negative consequences they may face is an absolute prerequisite for effective discipline in law enforcement (see Figure 6.4).

Figure 6.4
Discipline and the Hot Stove Analogy in Law Enforcement

1. Delineation of what is unacceptable.
2. Reasonable negative sanctions.
3. Advance warning of consequences.
4. Certainty of punishment.
5. Immediate disciplinary action.
6. Consistent application of negative sanctions.
7. Impersonal and goal-oriented discipline.
8. Adequate due process.
9. Appellate review of all disciplinary action.

Inflicting punishment is a painful experience for the employee and the first-line supervisor. In order to reduce the unpleasantness and stress associated with the use of discipline, sergeants should incorporate the Hot Stove concept into their management repertoire. The Hot Stove replaces subjectivity with a philosophy of firm, fair and impartial discipline that is designed to correct and deter the errant, disruptive or deviant behavior of subordinates (Plunkett, 1992).

Various states have adopted **peace officer bill of rights** laws that superimposes additional constraints on the disciplinary process. These laws often mandate warnings to be given and procedures to be followed when certain types of disciplinary action are anticipated. Supervisors need to know and comply with what is required if they are to prevail when it comes to the imposition of discipline (Redlich, 1994).

Case Study

Officer Leon D. Grafton

Leon D. Grafton has been with the police department for more than six years and is the department's only K-9 officer. Due to the nature of this assignment, Grafton works an overlapping 10-hour shift (8 p.m. to 6 a.m.) Thursday through Sunday.

Officer Grafton was recently divorced by his second wife. It is common knowledge that he has been under a great deal of stress. The stress seems to be having a negative effect on his performance as a police officer.

Officer Grafton has taken the maximum number of sick days and personal days. He is rapidly exhausting his accumulated vacation time. His on-the-job behavior has become erratic and his overall productivity (in terms of calls answered, arrests and traffic citations) is down significantly. On several occasions Officer Grafton was unavailable when he was paged on the police radio. Other units were required to cover these assignments for him.

According to the rumor mill, Officer Grafton has a severe drinking problem that is affecting his behavior and making him a liability to the police department. Witnesses claim that he has been drinking on the job. Something must be done.

As the midnight shift patrol supervisor, what action should you take in the Grafton case? What options do you have? What factors should you take into consideration when selecting an appropriate remedy?

Firm but Fair Disciplinary Action

Sergeants are the keystone around which the police discipline system is built and, as such, exert a tremendous influence on the disciplinary process. Consequently, they are expected to be "firm but fair" when inflicting negative sanctions on their subordinates. "Fairness" means being able to say that the punishment was warranted, justified and appropriate in terms of its goal. In order to be fair, the first-line supervisor must be sure that all employees in the work force are familiar with and understand the reasoning behind the department's policies, procedures, rules and regulations. If a subordinate's performance or job-related conduct is errant, disruptive or deviant, that person must be targeted for inves-

tigation. The sergeant should conduct an objective inquiry into the situation and must never, under any circumstances, exceed legitimate authority when punishing subordinates.

According to Steinmetz and Todd (1986), one way to ensure basic fairness is to ask certain questions concerning the need for imposed discipline or negative sanctions in a particular situation. These questions might include the following:

1. **Is the disciplinary action based on violation of a known policy, procedure, rule or regulation?** The bottom line is determining whether or not there has been a "statutory violation." In other words, is the policy, procedure, rule or regulation clearly spelled out in an employee handbook; has it been posted as a general order; or is it otherwise known to all employees within the police department? Have employees received a copy? Is the material easily understood? Is the policy, procedure, rule or regulation reasonable in terms of promoting efficiency and effectiveness within a safe and orderly environment? Is it legal in that it complies with labor laws, collective bargaining agreements and civil service regulations? Are you sure, as the responsible first-line supervisor, that there are no extenuating circumstances that may have contributed to a misunderstanding or belief that a policy, procedure, rule or regulation does not apply to the situation? If all of these questions can be answered in the affirmative, the sergeant is justified in taking action against the subordinate.

2. **What has happened to others who have knowingly violated this policy, procedure, rule or regulation?** This question is designed to help sergeants explore and understand the nature, significance and appropriate disciplinary response to errant, disruptive or deviant behavior in the workplace. Assuming the employee knowingly violated a departmental policy, procedure, rule or regulation, the next logical step is to determine the seriousness of the problem and chart a course of action to correct or deter it in the future. The sergeant must determine whether or not other employees have been disciplined under similar circumstances and ascertain the kind of disciplinary action that was taken. In order to make the punishment fit the offender as well as the crime, the sergeant should study the subordinate's background relative to the particular offense or unacceptable conduct. The worse the record in relation to others, the more severe the disciplinary action should be. Progressively severe discipline is often required because habitual offenders tend to develop a chronic attitudinal problem in which they do not care whether or not departmental policies, procedures, rules and regulations are followed.

3. **What is the subordinate's record concerning this specific policy, procedure, rule or regulation?** The sergeant must determine exactly how the employee has violated the specific policy, procedure, rule or regulation and whether there had been a prior

warning about this type of behavior. If the subordinate had, in fact, been formally warned or disciplined on previous occasions, the disciplinary action should be more severe than for those who have neither been warned or disciplined. In theory, this employee should know the policies, procedures, rules and regulations, and should understand the consequences of errant, disruptive or deviant on-the-job behavior.

4. **Has the employee ever received a written "final warning" from the supervisor?** If an errant, disruptive or deviant employee had previously been given a written final warning, the case must be treated more severely. It is the sergeant's job to ascertain whether or not the employee understood both the seriousness and consequences associated with the final warning before disciplinary action is taken. As a general rule, if the employee was given a final warning and still continues to violate the policy, procedure, rule or regulation, termination should be seriously considered as the appropriate response. The health of the organization will continue to suffer unless this type of action is taken.

5. **What caused the poor performance or unacceptable conduct?** Here again, it is the sergeant who must determine whether the errant, disruptive or deviant behavior was intentional. Was it triggered by ignorance or by maliciousness? Was it deliberate or was it caused by an oversight by the employee? In a rational disciplinary system, punishment is always contingent on and measured in relation to the offender's motive. Consequently, it is the sergeant's primary responsibility to assess the seriousness of the problem and to determine (as accurately as possible) why the subordinate is behaving in an errant, disruptive or deviant manner. This information must then be factored into the disciplinary process.

6. **What evidence is there that the employee intentionally and/or maliciously violated a departmental policy, procedure, rule or regulation?** As noted before, the accused employee is presumed to be innocent until proven guilty. It is the sergeant's job to identify disciplinary problems, analyze all of the relevant factors, initiate or carry out appropriate disciplinary action, ensure due process and document the case for subsequent administrative and/or judicial review. The sergeant, like the prosecutor in a criminal probe, builds a case designed to demonstrate the extent, seriousness and deliberateness of the errant, disruptive or deviant behavior. In addition to this prosecutorial role, the sergeant (as the first-line supervisor) is expected to discover any extenuating or mitigating circumstances that might justify lessening the punishment.

7. **Are the intended disciplinary measures appropriate for use in this particular situation?** The basic question comes down to whether the discipline to be inflicted is commensurate with the

seriousness of the errant, disruptive or deviant behavior. Is it consistent with the employee's prior record? Sergeants should base their actions (and measure the appropriateness of the discipline contingent) on how other subordinates have been treated in similar situations and how prior service to the department has been factored (positively or negatively) into the punishment. If the errant, disruptive or deviant officer has an extensive prior record, has been on the job a long time and has involved others in serious discipline problems, the punishment must be severe. If, on the other hand, the officer is relatively new, has had few problems, acted as an individual and has exhibited a cooperative attitude, the punishment should be much less severe. Progressively severe punishment is calculated to correct or deter disciplinary problems. Here again, the strategy is to use the right type and amount of punishment in a given situation to achieve the goals of the disciplinary system.

Firm but fair discipline is the ideal that each first-line supervisor should strive to achieve. Actually achieving this ideal in a complex criminal justice organization is another matter. Whether the discipline is firm and fair will depend, in the long run, on four critical factors: (1) the quality of the personnel being recruited by the department; (2) the effectiveness of the promotion system; (3) the training given to newly-promoted sergeants; and (4) the support that first-line supervisors receive from their superiors.

Types of Disciplinary Action

The decision to discipline a subordinate is not an easy one and should be made with a great deal of care. Sergeants are expected to know each employee; the employee's work record; and the nature, relative seriousness and cause or causes of the particular offense. First-line supervisors must be aware of and understand the powers laid down in their job description. In order to be effective, they must be familiar with the department's personnel policies (including applicable collective bargaining agreements or civil service regulations) as well as the basic policies, procedures, rules and regulations that govern on-the-job behavior.

Once the decision to discipline has been made, the sergeant (in consultation with superiors) must select the appropriate type of punishment. As a general rule, the different types of punishment available to the first-line supervisor are spelled out in departmental manuals, civil service regulations or labor contracts. This specificity is designed to eliminate ambiguity, ensure fair treatment and protect police employees from impulsive, arbitrary and unusually harsh punishments.

Most police departments have created discipline systems based on the idea of **progressive discipline**, which provides for an increase in punishment for each subsequent offense. Certain steps have become institutionalized as part of the disciplinary process. These steps have been incorporated into the process to

ensure fundamental fairness and to demonstrate to trial boards, arbitrators and the courts that the supervisor made a good faith effort to correct the errant, disruptive or deviant behavior through some type of remediation or rehabilitation. The normal sequencing of punishment with progressively severe discipline action is as follows: informal discussion, oral warning, written reprimand, final written warning, suspension, demotion and discharge.

1. **Informal Discussion.** If the offense is relatively minor and the employee has not been disciplined for similar misconduct in the past, an informal, friendly discussion will clear up the problem in many cases. During the discussion, the sergeant should determine the cause of the errant, disruptive or deviant behavior; reaffirm the employee's responsibility for self-discipline; and make constructive suggestions for improvement. Should this approach fail to produce the desired result, the sergeant must be prepared to give the subordinate a more formal oral warning.

2. **Oral Warning.** The oral warning is probably the most common form of punishment inflicted on employees. When subordinates fail to meet prescribed performance standards and continue to violate policies, procedures, rules or regulations, they must be put on "notice" that their behavior is unacceptable and that repetition will result in formal disciplinary action. They need to know, in no uncertain terms, that their misconduct will not be condoned and that future violations will produce more severe punishments. The effectiveness of an oral warning will generally be dependent on past experience, the strength of the supervisor-subordinate relationship and the employee's desire to conform to group-shared expectations. The spirit in which the warning is given is often more important than the oral warning itself. If the oral warning fails to correct the problem or deter an employee's errant, disruptive or deviant behavior, the sergeant must be prepared to use a formal written reprimand.

3. **Written Reprimand.** As the term implies, the written reprimand is a formal warning issued to an errant, disruptive or deviant employee by the immediate supervisor. For all practical purposes, it is the first official step in progressive discipline. No matter whether it is general or specific, the written reprimand is designed to spell out the problem, recommend corrective measures and specify the probable consequence of further misconduct. Written reprimands must not exaggerate the problem or make idle threats. They should be used sparingly in an effort to accentuate their importance. As a general rule, written warnings should be fairly simple and to the point. The original letter should be given to the employee with a copy placed in the personnel file. When appropriate, a copy of the reprimand should be sent to Civil Service or the union. The written reprimand

becomes part of the case file and can be used as evidence in a subsequent arbitration or civil action. If the written reprimand fails to correct the problem or deter further misconduct, the sergeant should issue a final written warning to the employee.

4. **Final Written Warning.** Since we live and work in a litigious environment where employees frequently challenge management's authority, the sergeant must be able to prove (based on objective evidence) that progressively more severe disciplinary action was required to correct the problem or to deter further misconduct. Keeping written records is extremely important in complex criminal justice organizations. Written records help to demonstrate that the employee was apprised of the seriousness of the situation and that notification had been given indicating there would be a significant escalation in punishment for continued errant, disruptive or deviant behavior. The final written warning becomes the bottom line, so to speak, and shifts all responsibility for compliance to the employee. If this strategy fails to resolve the problem, the sergeant has no alternative but to consider suspending the subordinate.

5. **Suspension.** The suspension, or "disciplinary layoff" as it is called in the private sector, is the next step in progressively severe disciplinary action and is not uncommon in police work. The errant, disruptive or deviant police officer who has not profited from informal discussions or a formal warning is targeted for suspension. Suspension may be with or without pay for a period ranging from a few days to a week or more. Under normal circumstances, the employee loses wages and the fringe benefits based on those wages. Suspension is viewed as being severe in that it "hits the employee where it hurts most, in the pocketbook." In addition, suspensions usually become common knowledge and the focus of peer interest. While an ill-conceived suspension can aggravate the situation and might even make the employee's behavior worse, it can, if used properly, be one of the most effective disciplinary tools available to the supervisor. It might shock the errant, disruptive or deviant officer back to a sense of responsibility. It shows that the department means business. If, on the other hand, there is no substantive change in the employee's work-related behavior, further disciplinary action must be taken. The suspension is merely a prelude to further disciplinary action in the form of a demotion or discharge.

6. **Demotion.** Due to the paramilitary structure of most police departments, demotion from a higher to a lower rank within the same department has persisted as an alternative form of disciplinary action. In highly political situations, it is common. Many police administrators, however, are beginning to question the validity of demotion as a disciplinary measure. They contend that

the negatives far outweigh the positives, and they prefer resocial-ization or retraining to demotion. Maintaining good morale is the issue. Demotees suffer from the loss of income, social status and self-esteem. They tend to become resentful, discouraged and dis-satisfied. Disgruntled personnel normally continue to challenge legitimate authority and sow the seeds of discontent. When all else fails, the errant, disruptive or deviant employee must be ter-minated or discharged for the good of the police service.

7. **Discharge.** Discharging, terminating or firing an errant, disrup-tive or deviant employee is, without doubt, the most drastic form of disciplinary action and, as such, must be reserved for only the most serious offenses. In today's legalistic environment, the employee must be given every opportunity to change that behav-ior and conform to departmental policies, procedures, rules and regulations. While it is possible under unusual circumstances, very few police officers are discharged without warning. Discharge is a costly, albeit necessary, type of discipline in some cases. The employee loses an income, seniority and, in some cases, even employability. The department, on the other hand, loses an experienced and potentially valuable human resource. It also forfeits all that has been invested in that particular employ-ee's professional development. In addition, there are costs associ-ated with recruiting, screening, training and orienting a replace-ment. Since discharge is viewed by many as a form of industrial capital punishment, it often leads to lengthy, costly arbitrations or civil court cases. This does not mean that supervisors should not recommend that management discharge an employee in appro-priate situations. There are times when the department must take a stand and serve notice to all personnel that there are certain behaviors that simply cannot or will not be tolerated. Used spar-ingly and in a judicious manner, discharge is the ultimate tool at management's disposal.

No matter what type of disciplinary action sergeants opt to use, they must be careful to observe all labor laws, collective bargaining agreements and civil service regulations. In addition, the sergeant (as the lead actor in this very com-plex drama) must pay close attention to procedural due process. Failure in either area will destroy the first-line supervisor's credibility and substantially under-mine authority.

Modern management theory has rejected the imposition of negative sanc-tions for the sake of inflicting punishment. It views disciplinary action as being an essential ingredient in a goal-oriented intervention strategy that is designed to correct problems and to deter future misconduct. Progressive discipline (see Figure 6.5) is based on the notion that the punishment should fit the crime and that progressively more severe punishment will trigger a "hedonistic calcula-tion." The repetitive or recalcitrant offender assesses the pleasure derived from the errant, disruptive or deviant behavior vis-à-vis the pain caused by the esca-

lating punishments. All other things being equal, when the perceived pain outweighs the pleasure, there will be a substantive change in the employee's behavior. Progressive discipline is not a cure-all; it is a tool.

Progressive discipline may not work with indifferent, irrational or socially maladjusted subordinates. When it becomes necessary to discharge an employee, progressive discipline is the scalpel used to excise the unhealthy tissue. While the decision to fire an employee is the prerogative of management, it is almost always based on direct input from the first-line supervisor. Here again, this awesome responsibility is part of the job and rests squarely on the sergeant's shoulders.

Figure 6.5
The Steps in Progressive Discipline

1. Informal discussion.
2. Oral warning.
3. Written reprimand.
4. Final written warning.
5. Suspension.
6. Demotion.
7. Discharge.

Making the Disciplinary Action Stick

In what some managers consider to be the "good old days," employers hired their employees at will and could discipline or fire them for any reason or for no reason at all. Employees had no right to their jobs. Consequently, they had no legal standing to sue their superiors for arbitrary or capricious disciplinary action. Needless to say, things have changed dramatically. Labor laws, collective bargaining agreements and civil service regulations are now in place to protect workers in the public sector. In addition, the courts have begun to recognize that employees have (at least to some extent) a property right to their jobs (Swanson, Territo and Taylor, 1993). This swing in legal philosophy has ushered in a new era of judicial activism. Dead and gone forever are the days when sergeants could talk tough, act on impulse and inflict punishments on subordinates without careful administrative and/or judicial review.

Even with these constraints, however, it is still possible to use disciplinary action as a tool to promote efficiency, effectiveness and productivity within the workplace. Here again, it is the sergeant (as the responsible first-line supervisor) who plays the pivotal role and, in large measure, determines whether or not the police department will face unfair labor practice charges, costly arbitrations, lengthy litigation and more union activism. According to many labor relations specialists, reasonable **disciplinary action can be made to stick** if it is fair and if first-line supervisors learn to avoid the following mistakes:

1. No Clear-Cut Misconduct or Violation. Under normal circumstances, disciplinary action is considered to be a legitimate option only when it can be tied to a specific offense.

2. Inadequate Warning. Trial boards, civil service hearing officers, arbitrators and the courts have held that police personnel are entitled to both direct and sufficient warning that their poor performance or misconduct will not be tolerated.

3. Absence of Positive Evidence. The absence of positive evidence to support the charge against the employee jeopardizes the case, subjects the sergeant's motive(s) to question and destroys confidence in the department's disciplinary system.

4. Acting on Prejudice. Real or imagined favoritism or discrimination has a debilitating effect on discipline, undermines legitimate authority and creates poor morale.

5. Inadequate Records. The value of written records of warnings and reprimands cannot be overestimated, since they are documentary evidence of the action taken to correct personnel problems and to deter further misconduct.

6. Excessive Punishment. Most civil service hearing officers, arbitrators and judges subscribe to the concept of progressive discipline and look unfavorably on punishment that is too severe, especially for first-time offenders.

7. Violation of Procedural Due Process. A lack of concern for just cause and procedural due process taints the disciplinary action and pits the employee against the employer in a struggle for power (Bittel and Newstrom, 1990).

Poorly prepared, carelessly investigated and inadequately documented cases not only reflect negatively on the first-line supervisor who conducted the inquiry but also upon the police department that based disciplinary action on it. Consequently, the errant, disruptive or deviant employee who should have been severely disciplined or even discharged for the good of the service often wins the case on appeal. More often than not, that employee returns to the job an embittered, marginal performer, who attempts to contaminate others at every opportunity. Not only does the employee's morale suffer, but the morale of all those who work with that employee suffers as well. From a very practical point of view, greater harm may result when the undeserving subordinate is returned to duty because the disciplinary action was not sustained than if that particular employee had never been disciplined at all. It is the sergeant's responsibility to take appropriate disciplinary action and to make sure it sticks. There is no acceptable alternative.

Proof of the Pudding

The lack of self-control and the absence of meaningful disciplinary action in police organizations are antithetical to the common good. When they are compounded by benign neglect or deliberate indifference on the part of police supervisors and managers, they lower the quality of service provided by a given department and undermine the integrity of the entire profession.

We have argued that disciplinary action must be prompt, sure, reasonable and fair if it is to deter misbehavior and help purge undesirables from police work. The absence of effective (positive as well as negative) discipline is the harbinger of systemic failure.

In a series of well-researched and very disturbing articles, *The Washington Post* (Flaherty and Harriston, 1994) chronicled such a failure in a large police department located in the middle-Atlantic region of the United States. The department hired nearly 1,500 new police officers in a two-year period (1989/1990). The department, for unfathomable reasons, was not effective in screening, selecting, appointing, training and evaluating many of these new officers. On-the-job supervision was lax and in many cases nonexistent. According to *The Washington Post*, inaction on the part of police supervisors and managers tacitly allowed incompetence, misconduct and corruption to flourish.

While it is impossible to quantify incompetence or to assess the impact of minor as well as unreported misconduct, there is one chilling statistic in *The Washington Post* series that should give every professional police officer cause for concern. Since 1991, 256 of the police officers who were suspended or fired have had the adverse disciplinary actions overturned by the courts or labor arbitrators solely because the department took too long to initiate formal disciplinary action. The lack of prompt and sure disciplinary action has permitted incompetents, malcontents and criminals to remain on the public payroll in critically important positions.

The Washington Post series underscores the importance of self-control and formal discipline. Poor supervision and the lack of effective disciplinary mechanisms allow "loose canons" who are in positions of power to abuse that power. We know that power can corrupt and unbridled power tends to corrupt completely.

Personal and Vicarious Liability

Failure to sustain a disciplinary action against an employee puts the supervisor at risk for a subsequent civil suit. The suit may involve abuse of authority, discrimination or defamation of character. Employers and supervisors also incur civil liability if they deprive a subordinate of some guaranteed due process right. As a general rule, police officers can go to either state or federal courts to seek monetary damages and/or injunctive relief against an employer or supervisor at any stage of the disciplinary process if it is determined that they may have been denied procedural due process.

Public employees have always been liable for their own negligent or wrongful acts. They are liable, in most situations, for compensatory as well as punitive damages. Until quite recently, however, public entities (units of state, county and local government) were considered immune from civil liability resulting from the negligent or wrongful acts of their employees. Once again, things have changed rather drastically. While the individual employee is still liable, the courts, based on case law and recently enacted statutes, have held that public agencies are often liable for compensatory damages when the wrongful acts or omissions occur while employees are acting within the scope of their employment. Based on the fact that government is perceived as having "deep pockets" and a virtually inexhaustible source of revenue, suits for **vicarious liability** have become commonplace. If the litigant can show by a preponderance of evidence that the police department failed to train, supervise or discipline errant, disruptive or deviant employees properly, the department may be held liable. It will pay for the misconduct of its personnel when that misconduct (violation of policies, procedures, rules or regulations) causes injury to others. Recent monetary judgments have been enormous. Some local governments have been forced into bankruptcy. It is in the police department's best interest, then, to promote only competent employees to the rank of sergeant and to strengthen the internal disciplinary system (Iannone, 1994).

Summary

As noted earlier in this chapter, discipline is the essential element in productive work that produces an orderly environment, cooperative goal-oriented behavior and esprit de corps. There are two types of discipline: internal (positive) and external (negative). Internal discipline is the self-discipline learned from significant others and acquired through the socialization process. While self-discipline is tucked away in the subconscious mind, it controls behavior and produces willing conformity to various group-shared expectations. External or negative discipline, on the other hand, is imposed on the errant, disruptive or deviant employee from the outside by someone in a position of authority. Negative discipline (in the form of disciplinary action or punishment) is a tool used by supervisors to correct existing personnel problems or to deter these problems from occurring again in the future. As a general rule, the amount of external discipline required by an employee will vary inversely with the degree of self-discipline exercised by the individual.

Effective disciplinary action is always based on just cause, is appropriate in terms of the offense and the needs of the offender, and becomes progressively more severe if the subordinate fails to change his or her errant, disruptive or deviant behavior. According to the Hot Stove concept, punishments must be immediate, with advance warning, consistent and impersonal. Punishments must also be reasonable, lawful and commensurate with the offense. In order to be effective disciplinarians, sergeants must be firm, impartial and fair to their employees. Anything less distorts the process and undermines the entire discipline system.

There is probably no area in supervisor-subordinate relationships that creates more of a challenge than the administration of discipline. In this context, discipline means strict and regular training for obedience and efficiency; a system of planning, orderly control and appropriate conduct; and the use of rewards and progressively more severe punishments. Discipline must be insisted upon and sustained before there can be any continuous and cooperative effort to accomplish the organization's mission, goals or objectives. On the other hand, the growing emphasis on employee rights and freedom in the workplace runs counter to the prerogatives of management in the area of behavior control. The challenge is clear. It is up to the first-line supervisor, the sergeant, to maintain control while encouraging self-discipline, and to take appropriate disciplinary action in such a way as not to threaten but to enhance the employee's self-esteem, sense of worth and job-related productivity. The goal is total quality management.

Capricious and excessive discipline has provided much of the impetus for the unionization of police personnel. It has also led to the enactment of peace officer bill of rights laws. The labor relations movement and its impact on the American law enforcement establishment is explored in Chapter 12 of this text.

Case Study

Sergeant Howard P. Ziegler

Sergeant Howard Zeigler, a 20-year veteran, is the permanent midnight shift patrol supervisor in a relatively small police department. Based on the collective bargaining agreement, all new police personnel are assigned to work on his shift during their probationary period. It is Sergeant Zeigler's job to mold these inexperienced men and women into efficient, effective and productive police officers. He takes this responsibility seriously and has developed a reputation as a no-nonsense police professional.

Rookie patrolman Bobby Pastorie is having problems adjusting to the demands of police work. He has inadvertently violated several departmental policies and frequently disregards standard operating procedures. During a recent crime scene search, for example, Pastorie handled a murder weapon improperly. He obliterated latent fingerprints and legally contaminated the evidence. The case was thrown out of court.

When he was asked about the incident, Officer Pastorie lied to Sergeant Zeigler. He claimed that someone else must have destroyed the evidence and steadfastly refused to accept responsibility for his error. Sergeant Zeigler now has two problems. He must develop a strategy to upgrade Bobby Pastorie's on-the-job performance and determine the appropriate disciplinary response to the officer's deception.

If you were Sergeant Zeigler, what factors would you take into consideration before taking disciplinary action? Do you think that progressively more severe disciplinary action might help to deter future misconduct? How would you ensure that the punishment fits the crime? What can be done to sustain the disciplinary action and to convert it into a positive rather than a negative experience?

Key Concepts

constructive discipline
disciplinary action
disciplinary action made to stick
firm, fair, equitable and lawful
    disciplinary action
first-line supervisors as disciplinarians
goal of discipline
the Hot Stove concept
negative discipline

objectives of the discipline system
peace officer bill of rights
positive discipline
PRICE protocol
progressive discipline
total quality management (TQM)
types of discipline
vicarious liability

Discussion Topics and Questions

1. Compare and contrast the concept of positive discipline with that of disciplinary action.

2. Explore the PRICE protocol and show its relationship to the concept of total quality management (TQM).

3. Explain the sergeant's role as a disciplinarian within the police hierarchy.

4. What are the two basic objectives of any disciplinary system?

5. What is the "Hot Stove" concept and how has it been adapted to law enforcement?

6. In order to be fair, what factors should a sergeant take into consideration before recommending or imposing disciplinary action on a subordinate?

7. Trace the "steps" involved in progressive disciplinary action.

8. Identify and discuss the various types of disciplinary actions that are commonly used as corrective mechanisms in American police departments.

9. Why has it become increasingly difficult to enforce disciplinary action in police agencies covered by civil service, collective bargaining agreements or peace officer bill of rights laws?

For Further Reading

Bennett, Wayne W. and Karen M. Hess (1992). *Management and Supervision in Law Enforcement.* St. Paul, MN: West Publishing Company.

    Comprehensive exploration of discipline and related processes as applied to the complexities of supervision and self-control in modern police work. The authors present very specific guidelines for administering negative discipline in a constructive rather than a destructive manner.

Fulmer, Robert M. (1988). *The New Management*, 4th ed. New York: Macmillan Publishing Co.

> Analysis of management's role in controlling on-the-job behavior and using disciplinary action, where appropriate, to enhance efficiency, effectiveness and productivity. This is a general management text emphasizing basic principles applicable to the use of discipline in police work.

Walsh, William F. and Edwin J. Donovan (1990). *The Supervision of Police Personnel: A Performance Based Approach*. Dubuque, IA: Kendall/Hunt Publishing Company.

> Practical guide to discipline and the use of disciplinary action to help police personnel accomplish the organization's mission, goals and objectives. It offers a no-nonsense, performance-based approach to discipline within the context of administrative due process.

References

Aragon, Randall (1993). "Positive Organizational Culture: A Practical Approach." *FBI Law Enforcement Bulletin,* Vol. 62, No. 12.

Bittel, Lester R. and John W. Newstrom. (1990). *What Every Supervisor Should Know,* 6th ed. New York: McGraw-Hill Book Company.

Carnegie, Dale (1992). *The Dale Carnegie Course* (syllabus). New York: Dale Carnegie and Associates.

Covey, Stephen R. (1992). *Principle-Centered Leadership.* New York: Simon and Schuster.

Flaherty, Mary Pat and Keith Harriston (1994). "Law and Disorder; The District's Troubled Police." *The Washington Post.* Aug. 28-31: Section A.

Hilgert, Raymond L. and Theo Haimann (1991). *Supervision: Concepts and Practices of Management,* 5th ed. Cincinnati, OH: South-Western Publishing Company.

Iannone, Nathan F. (1994). *Supervision of Police Personnel,* 5th ed. Englewood Cliffs, NJ: Prentice-Hall, Inc.

LeBoeuf, Michael (1985). *GMP: The Greatest Management Principle in the World.* New York: Barkley Books.

Peters, Thomas J. and Robert H. Waterman, Jr. (1982). *In Search of Excellence: Lessons from America's Best-Run Companies.* New York: Warner Books, Inc.

Plunkett, Richard W. (1992). *Supervision: The Direction of People at Work,* 6th ed. Boston: Allyn and Bacon, Inc.

Preston, Paul and Thomas W. Zimmerer (1983). *Management for Supervisors,* 2nd ed. Englewood Cliffs, NJ: Prentice-Hall, Inc.

Redlich, James W. (1994). "Disciplinary Interrogations: Which Warnings Apply? And When?" *The Police Chief,* Vol. LXI, No. 6.

Robbins, Stephen P. (1989). *Organizational Behavior,* 4th ed. Englewood Cliffs, NJ: Prentice-Hall, Inc.

Sartain, Aaron Q. and Alton W. Baker (1978). *The Supervisor and the Job,* 3rd ed. New York: McGraw-Hill Book Company.

Sherman, Mark and Al Lucia (1992). "Positive Discipline and Labor Arbitration." *Arbitration Journal,* Vol. 47, No. 2.

Steinmetz, Lawrence L. and H. Ralph Todd, Jr. (1986). *First-Line Management: Approaching Supervision Effectively,* 4th ed. Plano, TX: Business Publications, Inc.

Steinmetz, Lawrence L. and H. Ralph Todd, Jr. (1992). *Supervision: First-Line Management,* 5th ed. Boston: Richard D. Irwin, Inc.

Swanson, Charles R., Leonard Territo and Robert W. Taylor (1993). *Police Administration* 3rd ed. New York: Macmillan Publishing Co.

Whisenand, Paul M. and George E. Rush (1993). *Supervising Police Personnel,* 2nd ed. Englewood Cliffs, NJ: Prentice-Hall, Inc.

Wilson, O. W. and Roy C. McLaren (1977). *Police Administration,* 4th ed. New York: McGraw-Hill Book Company.

Performance Appraisal—

The Key to Police Personnel Development

7

Introductory Case Study

Sergeant Herman Pulkowski

Sergeant Herman Pulkowski, a well-respected patrol supervisor in a relatively small and economically distressed city, is a member of the management team trying to hammer out a new collective bargaining agreement with the Police Benevolent Association. The union is demanding a pay raise, improved benefits and more job security. The city, based on Pulkowski's recommendation, has countered with a proposal to increase police productivity. It calls for creation of a personnel development program keyed to regular performance evaluation. They have been unable to reach agreement on any of these issues.

At a recent bargaining session, "all hell broke loose." Stefan Altman, the union's chief negotiator, voiced vehement opposition to the city's proposal and called it a sneak attack on seniority. After several misstatements of fact, he berated Sergeant Pulkowski for supporting such a "harebrained" scheme and went so far as to question the sergeant's professional integrity. Altman charged that the city's proposal amounted to an unfair labor practice.

It is obvious that Officer Altman does not understand the concept of personnel development and that he is being overly defensive about the city's desire to implement a formal performance appraisal program. He has allowed anxiety, emotion and unwarranted fears to color his judgment.

If you were Sergeant Pulkowski, how would you handle this situation? What steps would you take to ensure that Officer Altman understands the philosophy of personnel development, the objectives of performance evaluation and the linkage between performance appraisals and increased police productivity? Given the fact that an objective, fair and equitable performance evaluation process zeroes in on job-related performance and not the subordinate's personality, how would you help Altman deal with the insecurity, anxiety and fear generated by the proposed performance enhancement program?

People Power

Police work is a unique multi-billion dollar labor-intensive industry built around order maintenance, law enforcement and the provision of other essential government services. By the early 1990s, for example, more than 17,000 police agencies at all levels of government spent over $31.8 billion "to protect and serve" their constituents. Most of these funds, 80 to 90 percent, went to cover salaries and benefits for more than 850,000 full- and part-time law enforcement personnel. Municipal governments spend more than 20 percent of their total budgetary outlay on police services. The per capita expenditure for police service in cities more than 10,000 ranges anywhere from $81.78 to $224.36 a year (U.S. Department of Justice, 1994). It is estimated that it now costs between $280,000 and $320,000 a year to field an additional fully equipped and professionally trained police officer around-the-clock in urban high crime areas (Hamblin, 1994).

In light of these phenomenal costs, local governments are now beginning to realize that they have a vested interest in recruiting, hiring and retaining only the most efficient, effective and productive personnel. Police managers are being sensitized to the fact that numerical strength alone does not guarantee the quality of service. Quality is much more likely to be determined by the intelligence, ability, skill, experience, integrity and dedication of the police department's human resources. Consequently, police managers are forced into being much more *personnel conscious*.

Many observers have come to the conclusion that personnel development may be the only truly viable solution to those problems caused by an erosion of the tax base and dwindling resources in the public sector. Personnel development focuses on the employee. It is a management strategy designed to improve both the quantity and quality of each individual's output while ensuring that employees work collaboratively (in groups) to achieve the organization's mission, goals and objectives. Based on modern management theory, personnel development is an ongoing process that begins on the day the rookie police officer joins the police department and continues throughout the career.

Systematic performance appraisal is regarded as the key to employee development and is now viewed as the centerpiece of an effective police personnel system.

Performance Appraisal

The evaluation of job performance is a managerial task that is normally delegated to first-line supervisors in healthy work-based organizations. Formal (objective) **performance appraisal** has been emphasized in government and has become the standard by which we judge the legitimacy of any public sector personnel system.

Many police supervisors do not fully understand the purpose of or need for regular performance appraisal. They approach the evaluation of subordinates in

a negative manner. Evaluation becomes an unpleasant and stressful chore requiring them to assume the awesome responsibility for honestly assessing the job-related strengths and weaknesses of their fellow police officers. Some police supervisors are simply not prepared to take on this very important role-related responsibility.

In a generic sense, there are seven common justifications used by management for requiring first-line supervisors to evaluate their personnel. They are summarized below:

1. To determine whether or not subordinates are doing the job they were hired to do.

2. To measure the quantity of work and quality of performance and provide rewards for those who are doing well.

3. To correct specific problems and improve the employee's overall performance.

4. To estimate employee potential and prepare that employee for promotion within the organization.

5. To assess employee attitudes and strengthen each supervisor's understanding of subordinates.

6. To let employees know exactly how they are doing, where they stand and what they can do to improve their own on-the-job performance.

7. To provide supervisors (and management) with sufficient objective data to make and, if necessary, to defend decisions concerning personnel within the agency.

In addition to these specific objectives, many management theorists contend that an objective and fair performance appraisal tends to fortify and enrich supervisor-subordinate relationships in the workplace (Swanson, Territo and Taylor, 1993).

A great deal of time, effort and creative thought has gone into the search for a comprehensive, multipurpose, performance-appraisal process designed to give police managers objective data that can be factored into administrative decisions concerning salary increases, promotions, transfers, discipline or personnel development. While progress is being made, no such process exists at this time and it is doubtful that one will be perfected in the near future.

Many personnel specialists, or human resources managers as they are now called, really feel that the achievement of multiple objectives is not feasible and believe that a performance appraisal system should be limited to one (and only one) objective: to inform employees about the quality of their work so they might strive to improve their own performance. This is commonly referred to as

"developmental" as opposed to "judgmental" performance appraisal (Steinmetz and Todd, 1992).

According to Raymond Hilgert and Theo Haimann (1991), the purpose of a formal merit rating, performance review or employee appraisal is to synthesize, in objective terms, the performance, experience and capabilities of individual employees and to compare them with the requirements of a particular job. This assessment is almost always based on observable criteria like cooperation, dependability, productivity, quality of output, follow-through, judgment or safety. Regularized performance appraisal provides rank-and-file police officers with some assurance that they are not being overlooked and that the supervisors, managers and various superiors within the police organization know something about them as individuals.

The key to effective performance appraisal is knowing exactly *who* is responsible for doing *what* and *how* it (the job) is to be done. The essential components or elements of the total job must be carefully identified and communicated to the subordinate personnel. The most important elements of performance appraisal have the following characteristics:

1. They are job-centered and focus on the specific task or tasks to be performed.

2. They are clear and simply stated.

3. They are observable as well as objective.

4. They target actual on-the-job performance.

5. They are measurable in terms of predetermined performance standards.

The second step in effective **performance evaluation** is applying a standard designed to specify the minimum level of acceptable performance for each particular job. This standard becomes critically important as a performance-measuring device. It clearly delineates what is expected from the police officer in terms of productivity, accuracy, completeness, timeliness, dependability or safety. It is the first-line supervisor, normally a sergeant, who is in the best position to utilize the information concerning elements of the job, performance standards and objective appraisal criteria to forge a meaningful composite which accurately reflects each subordinate's job performance (Iannone, 1994). The performance profile is an invaluable source of information for management decisionmaking.

There are literally thousands of different performance-appraisal instruments in use today. Virtually all of them incorporate elements of the job (based on a job description), some type of gradated performance measurement and objective evaluative criteria. Needless to say, none are perfect.

The four universal aspects of performance appraisal are (1) a performance goal, standard or plan; (2) measurement of job-related performance; (3) com-

parison of employee performance with the goal, standard or plan; and (4) the use of corrective action as required in a given situation (Walsh and Donovan, 1990). These represent the conceptual pillars upon which the employee evaluation process is built.

The Employee Evaluation Process

While the actual mix may differ from one jurisdiction to another, there are nine basic steps in most formal employee-evaluation systems. These steps have been summarized below.

1. Preparing a detailed job description and specifying minimum performance requirements. In other words, local management determines what is to be done and how well each employee is expected to do it.

2. Discussing the job, acceptable performance standards and the formal evaluation process with the employees, and making adjustments if necessary.

3. The employee does the work. How well it is done will be influenced by personal ability, training, adaptability, time, resources and an error factor based on chance.

4. Observing and evaluating the employee's job performance by appropriate supervisory personnel. This will be influenced by the skill of the evaluator, the frequency of the observation, the predispositions of the supervisor and random error.

5. Evaluative data derived from objective criteria are recorded on an appraisal form designed to measure the quantity as well as the quality of an employee's work vis-à-vis very specific performance standards.

6. Explaining the mechanics of the particular evaluation and discussing the contents of the evaluative report with each employee.

7. Forwarding the evaluative report to the central personnel unit and/or the appropriate manager where it is interpreted from an organization-wide perspective.

8. Alternative responses are considered and appropriate administrative action is taken.

9. An appeals process is made available to ensure administrative due process and to safeguard the rights of the employee.

These steps have become institutionalized in public sector personnel administration. In police work, for example, they have become an integral component of all civil service systems, collective bargaining agreements and municipal human resources management programs. From a management perspective, performance appraisal is necessary in order to (1) allocate resources, (2) reward competent employees, (3) provide valuable feedback to workers and (4) maintain fair relationships and communication bonds (Fulmer, 1988).

Police officers, first-line supervisors and managers play very distinct yet interrelated roles in performance appraisal. They are assigned specific responsibilities but must work cooperatively to ensure the success of the evaluative process (see Figure 7.1). Unity of purpose is a critical variable.

While performance evaluation is always a major undertaking in complex criminal justice organizations, it is an absolutely essential component of managerial control. Job performance must be observed, compared with objective standards, and evaluated so that police supervisors and managers can implement effective strategies designed to mitigate performance problems or remove those employees from the work force who cannot or will not change their unacceptable job-related behavior.

Frequency of Evaluation

The National Advisory Commission on Criminal Justice Standards and Goals emphasized the importance of regular performance appraisal in law enforcement. According to Standard 17.1, every police agency should adopt a policy of retaining and/or promoting to higher ranks

> . . . only those personnel who successfully demonstrate their ability to assume the responsibilities and perform the duties of the position to which they will be promoted or advanced. Personnel who have the potential to assume increased responsibilities should be identified and placed in a program that will lead to full development of that potential (United States Government, 1973).

The key ingredient in this type of screening process is an accurate assessment of the employee's past performance, initiative in the area of self-development and the person's potential for advancement within the organization. Standardized performance appraisal for both probationary and certified police personnel has become the norm in progressive police departments.

While conscientious supervisors continuously evaluate the performance of their subordinates, formal objective evaluations like those discussed earlier are much less frequent. From a very practical point of view, formal evaluations should be performed on a predictable schedule. Sequencing is critical. If employees are evaluated too often, the supervisor is likely to place undue emphasis on and be swayed by normal day-to-day occurrences. If, on the other hand, they are infrequent, evaluators tend to forget critical incidents and much of the data that should be factored into the appraisal.

Figure 7.1
Roles and Responsibilities in the Evaluation Process

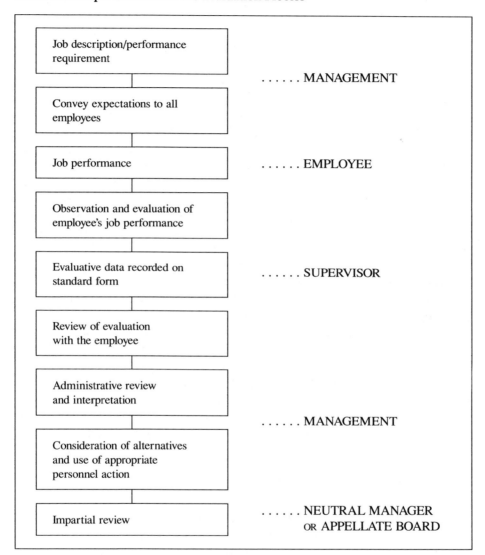

Modified from: Richard W. Holden, *Modern Police Management,* Second Edition, Englewood Cliffs, NJ, Prentice-Hall, Inc., 1994.

As a general rule, police departments evaluate their permanent personnel once a year. Due to the nature of the work and the value that we, as members of a free society, place on proper performance of the police role, it would be a better and much more reliable practice to evaluate certified police officers once every six months. More frequent evaluation would provide management with an accumulative data-base upon which to make decisions concerning the individual employee.

No matter how careful a department has been in selecting its new personnel, there is a continuing need for quality control. Probably the most valuable technique for determining a rookie's suitability for police service is actual trial on the job. Police managers and seasoned first-line supervisors firmly believe (almost as an article of faith) that a probationary period is an absolutely essential element in the personnel screening process. It gives them the necessary time to judge the new employee in terms of ability and character. It also allows them to assess the recruit's capacity to cope with the demands of police work and to detect those deficiencies that manifest themselves only under actual working conditions.

Probation, if it is to fulfill its role in quality control, must be predicated on a very careful, consistent and objective evaluation of each new employee's on-the-job performance. Those men and women who are truly unsuited for a career in law enforcement should be separated from police service (Gaines, Southerland and Angell, 1991) as quickly as possible. While it has been customary in many civil service systems to evaluate probationary employees once or twice before they are certified and given permanent status, most management theorists and many practitioners now recommend more frequent evaluation. Under ideal circumstances, police departments should require at least two years of probation with rookie police officers evaluated every six months. After four objective and very thorough evaluations by a competent first-line supervisor or group of supervisors, it is usually clear to supervisory personnel, management and the employee whether the awarding of permanent status will be in the best interests of the police department. The department should be given the benefit of the doubt in all borderline cases (Leonard and More, 1993).

Objective, thorough and frequent performance appraisals help to ensure the quality of police service. They protect the public and promote professionalism within the ranks. When used regularly and in an appropriate manner, performance reviews foster professional growth and create a genuine esprit de corps.

The Sergeant's Role

Sergeants, as first-line supervisors, play a leading role in the employee evaluation process. Based on their strategic position in the management structure, they are responsible for appraising the on-the-job performance of almost all line personnel. For all practical purposes, they provide quality assurance within the police establishment. The assessment of human resources, then, goes with the turf.

As noted before, many sergeants do not fully understand or appreciate their unique role in the evaluative process. They perceive it as a difficult and distasteful part of their job. Consequently, they attempt to insulate themselves from the stress associated with performance appraisal. If they cannot avoid it altogether, they elect to approach it as perfunctory and adopt a blasé attitude. This is very unfortunate because apathy is normally a precursor to deterioration in police service.

Many sergeants (due to insecurity, the lack of maturity, poor training or the inability to cope with criticism) fear the thought of judging their subordinates and use all sorts of excuses to avoid it. They claim that it takes too much time away from their other duties, strains personal relationships, is ignored by management and is almost always perceived by fellow employees as an unwarranted intrusion in their professional lives. These rationalizations are unacceptable. Sergeants must be prepared to accept responsibility for meaningful performance appraisal.

Accepting sergeants' stripes means more than merely an increase in pay. It represents an advancement in rank that thrusts the newly promoted noncommissioned officer into a different, very demanding role within the organization. Sergeants are expected to assume the risks inherent in the evaluative function. They must honestly assess how well each employee is doing the job and articulate, in meaningful terms, what they feel about that person's overall performance as a police officer. Once again, personnel evaluation goes with the territory.

Not everyone has the inclination and/or the talent to be a good evaluator. In fact, whether or not a particular first-line supervisor becomes a competent evaluator will, in the long run, depend on that person's:

1. Ability to be firm, fair and impartial when dealing with other human beings.

2. Orientation to and understanding of the personnel evaluation process.

3. Self-confidence in making judgments about the strengths and weaknesses of other people.

4. Human relations and communication skills.

5. Capacity to empathize with subordinates.

6. Knowledge of the assigned tasks performed by the employee.

7. Training as an evaluator.

8. Experience with performance appraisal.

9. Ego strength when it comes to dealing with disagreement or criticism expressed by significant others within the police organization.

Being a good evaluator requires natural talent, knowledge and the acquisition of special skills. Personnel evaluation is one of the most difficult aspects of an otherwise very complex job.

Human factors alone cannot guarantee the success of a particular performance appraisal program. **Institutional support** is absolutely essential. First-line supervisors exhibit enthusiasm for and derive satisfaction from their

role as evaluators when they are given adequate support from management. Genuine support does not come from professional rhetoric; it comes from action.

In order to do their job effectively, sergeants need to have clear-cut authority based on department policies, procedures, rules and regulations to do a meaningful evaluation of subordinates. They must also believe that their assessment will be accepted and respected by their superiors as a professional judgment concerning the competence of the employee. Unless police sergeants are given time, training and access to adequate institutional resources, performance appraisal becomes a sham. It is nothing more than window dressing. Ritualistic performance evaluations which lack relevance are an unwelcome burden that help to destroy the supervisor's morale and undermine the credibility of management (see Figure 7.2).

Figure 7.2
Institutional Support for Performance Appraisal

1. Role—A job description outlining the sergeant's role in performance appraisal.

2. Authority—Formal department policy granting first-line supervisors authority to evaluate immediate subordinates.

3. Procedure—Mutually acceptable procedures specified in department manuals, civil service regulations or collective bargaining agreements.

4. Relevance—A clear-cut statement concerning how the evaluative data will be factored into administrative decisions concerning personnel.

5. Resources—Supervisor training and career development opportunities.

6. Utility—Evaluative data factored into the actual decision-making process.

7. Stature—Sergeants accepted as members of the management team who make valuable contributions to the department through their quality control and personnel development function.

First-line supervisors in healthy work-based organizations take their job very seriously. Top-notch sergeants evaluate their employees, and they do it frequently. They accept performance appraisal as a challenge and are willing to take the risks associated with it because it gives them an opportunity to provide both form and substance to the department's human resources. They help weed out incompetent personnel, identify those employees who need assistance and provide positive reinforcement for good workers. Police sergeants are in a key position to influence the efficiency, effectiveness and productivity of the individual employee as well as the police department as a whole.

While performance evaluation protocols differ in design, they have three common objectives:

1. To assess each and every employee's contribution to the organization.

2. To provide employees with valuable feedback concerning their on-the-job performance.

3. To develop a mutually acceptable plan for correcting those performance-related problems that are found.

The evaluation process itself consists of: (1) the assessment, (2) an evaluation interview and (3) remediation. The sergeant is a central figure in the evaluation process.

Methods of Appraisal

There is no real consensus concerning the single best way to approach performance appraisal in complex criminal justice organizations. In fact, there are several competing schools of thought. Some of the important ones are outlined below.

Graphic Rating Scale. The graphic rating scale is probably the most frequently used performance assessment device. Each characteristic or trait that is to be evaluated is represented by a line (or scale) on which the evaluator indicates the degree to which it is believed the person possesses that particular trait or characteristic. Scales represent a graphic continuum that ranges from one extreme (negative) to another (positive). A space for rater comments is found on most graphic rating scales. This gives a supervisor the opportunity to support a rating with facts (see Figures 7.3, 7.4, 7.5). There are a number of advantages associated with a graphic rating scale:

1. It is fairly simple to design and construct.

2. It is easy for supervisors to use.

3. Interpretation is not particularly difficult.

4. Employees can be compared based on a composite score.

There are disadvantages as well. Rigidity, rater error and intentional manipulation can skew the results. They undermine the credibility of the evaluation process and strain interpersonal relations within the organization.

Figure 7.3
Performance Evaluation Report

INSTRUCTIONS
FOR USE OF THE PERFORMANCE EVALUATION REPORT FORM

GENERAL:

1. Using preliminary draft sheet and pencil, complete Section A first, then other appropriate sections. The rater should review the draft report with his own supervisor. Markings and comments should then be typed or inked in on the final form. Either the rater or reviewer (or both) should then review the rating with the employee in a private interview. All signatures shall be in ink. Changes and corrections shall be initialed by the employee.

2. If space for comments is inadequate, dated and signed attachments may be made (either typewritten or in ink).

3. Due dates shall be observed, and are particularly important for final probationary reports. Filing dates for these are flexible, and both the first and the final reports may be filed any time between the receipt and the printed due date.

4. All probationers (either entrance level or promotional) shall be evaluated at the end of each month of probationary service. Probationers may be separated at any time such action is deemed necessary by the Township Manager, through use of either a scheduled or an unscheduled performance evaluation report.

5. All permanent employees and entrance level probationers in their second year shall be evaluated annually as of the printed due date.

6. The "Guide to Performance Evaluation" should be consulted for suggestions, definitions, interpretations and further instructions.

7. The main purposes of this form are to inform the employee of his performance, to improve performance when possible, and to sustain superior performance.

SECTION A: Check one column for each factor. Column (5) may be checked when a factor is not considered applicable to a particular job. Additional spaces have been provided to write in any additional factors. Each check mark in Columns 1 and 2 requires specific explanation in Section E. In the absence of specific standards for a factor, use your own opinion as to what constitutes standard performance. Standard does not mean average; in fact, standard performance can often be higher than average performance.

Exceeds Standards: Total performance is well above standards for the position. This evaluation should be reflected by marks for critical factors in Section A, and superior or excellent performance should be noted in Section B. Only a few employees would normally qualify for this rating.

Effective—Meets Standards: Consistently competent performance meeting or exceeding standards in all critical factors for the position. If margin is narrow and standards barely met, explain in Section E. Most employees would be rated in this category.

Some Improvement Needed: Total performance occasionally or periodically falls short of normal standards. Specific deficiencies should be noted in Section E. This evaluation indicates the supervisor's belief that the employee can and will make the necessary improvements.

Not Satisfactory: Performance clearly inadequate in one or more critical factors as explained or documented in Section E. Employee has demonstrated inability or unwillingness to improve or to meet standards. Performance not acceptable for position held.

SECTION B: Must be used to describe outstanding qualities or performances when check marks are placed in Column 4. Use this section to record other progress or improvements in performance resulting from employee's efforts to reach previously set goals.

SECTION C: Record agreed-upon or prescribed performance goals for the next evaluation period.

SECTION D: Use for describing standard performance.

SECTION E: Give specific reasons for check marks in Columns 1 and 2. Record here any other specific reasons why the employee should not be recommended for permanent status, or—if the employee is already permanent—any specific reasons for required improvement.

SIGNATURES: Both the rater and the employee shall sign the report. The employee's signature indicates that the conference has been held and that he has had an opportunity to read the report. If he refuses to sign for any reason, explain that his signature does not necessarily imply or indicate agreement with the report, and that space is provided for him to state any disagreement. Further refusal to sign shall be recorded in the report, after which it shall be forwarded.

ROUTING: Keep the preliminary draft at the division level until the next rating period and then discard. Route the permanent copy through channels to the Township Manager's Office.

Figure 7.3, *continued*

PERFORMANCE EVALUATION REPORT

EMPLOYEE NAME (Last) (First) (Initial)	EVALUATION NO.	DEPARTMENT	DIVISION
POSITION TITLE	EMPLOYEE STATUS	ASSIGNMENT	**DUE DATE:**

SECTION: 1 NOT SATISFACTORY / 2 SOME IMPROVEMENT NEEDED / 3 MEETS STANDARDS / 4 EXCEEDS STANDARDS / 5 DOES NOT APPLY

FACTOR CHECK LIST
Immediate Supervisor Must Check Each Factor in the Appropriate Column

1	2	3	4	Factor	5
				1. Observance of Work Hours	
				2. Attendance	
				3. Grooming & Dress	
				4. Compliance with Rules	
				5. Safety Practices	
				6. Public Contacts	
				7. Employee Contacts	
				8. Knowledge of Work	
				9. Work Judgments	
				10. Planning and Organizing	
				11. Job Skill Level	
				12. Quality of Work	
				13. Volume of Acceptable Work	
				14. Meeting Deadlines	
				15. Accepts Responsibility	
				16. Accepts Direction	
				17. Accepts Change	
				18. Effectiveness Under Stress	
				19. Appearance of Work Station	
				20. Operation & Care of Equipment	
				21. Work Coordination	
				22. Initiative	
				23. [Additional Factors]	
				24.	
				25.	
				26.	
				27.	
				28.	
				29.	

FOR EMPLOYEES who SUPERVISE OTHERS

1	2	3	4	Factor	5
				30. Planning & Organizing	
				31. Scheduling & Coordinating	
				32. Training & Instructing	
				33. Effectiveness	
				34. Evaluating Subordinates	
				35. Judgments & Decisions	
				36. Leadership	
				37. Operational Economy	
				38. Supervisory Control	
				39. [Additional Factors]	
				40.	
				41.	

CHECKS IN CODE 1 AND 2 MUST BE EXPLAINED IN SECTION E

SECTION B Record job **STRENGTHS**, superior performance incidents, progress achieved, or checks in Col. 4.

SECTION C Record specific GOALS or IMPROVEMENT PROGRAMS to be undertaken during next evaluation period.

SECTION D Describe STANDARD performance.

SECTION E Record specific work performance of DEFICIENCIES or job behavior requiring improvement or correction. (Explain checks in Col. 1 and 2.)

OVERALL RATING

Not Satis.	Needs Imp.	Meets Std.	Exceeds Std.

RATER: I certify this report representing my best judgment. ☐ I DO ☐ I DO NOT recommend this employee be granted permanent status. (For final probationary reports only).

(RATER'S SIGNATURE) (TITLE) (DATE)

REVIEWER: (IF NONE, SO INDICATE)

(REVIEWER'S SIGNATURE) (TITLE) (DATE)

EMPLOYEE: I certify that this report has been shown to me and/or discussed with me. I understand my signature does not necessarily indicate agreement. ☐ I wish to discuss this report with the reviewer.

Comment:

(EMPLOYEE'S SIGNATURE) (DATE)

–SEE INSTRUCTIONS ON REVERSE SIDE–

Figure 7.4
Performance Evaluation Report

PERFORMANCE EVALUATION REPORT NON-SUPERVISORY

NAME		CLASS TITLE	DIVISION

PERIOD COVERED BY EVALUATION REPORT
FROM: TO:

ASSIGNMENT

RATING INSTRUCTIONS:
1. Check each item box.
   - ◆ STRONG   ✓ STANDARD
   - – WEAK   N NOT OBSERVED
2. Rate each factor by circling the appropriate number.
3. Multiply the circled number by the weight for each factor and write the results in the "score" column.
4. Add the "score" column and record the sum.

RATINGS

Column headers (vertical): 1 = UNSATISFACTORY, 2 = IMPROVEMENT NEEDED, 3 = COMPETENT, 4 = HIGH COMPETENT, 5 = OUTSTANDING, WEIGHT, SCORE (RATING X WEIGHT)

Use spaces below for comments. Ratings other than competent should be substantiated in writing. Use reverse side for additional space.

PERFORMANCE FACTORS	1	2	3	4	5	WEIGHT	SCORE
QUANTITY ☐ AMOUNT OF WORK PERFORMED ☐ COMPLETION OF WORK ON SCHEDULE	1	2	3	4	5	25	.
QUALITY ☐ ACCURACY ☐ NEATNESS ☐ THOROUGHNESS ☐ ORAL EXPRESSION ☐ WRITTEN EXPRESSION	1	2	3	4	5	25	
WORK HABITS ☐ PUNCTUALITY ☐ ATTENDANCE ☐ COMPLIANCE WITH ORDERS ☐ INTEREST ☐ INITIATIVE ☐ RESOURCEFULNESS ☐ AGGRESSIVENESS	1	2	3	4	5	15	
PERSONAL TRAITS ☐ EMOTIONAL STABILITY ☐ MATURITY ☐ ATTITUDE ☐ COMPATABILITY WITH OTHERS ☐ PERSONAL APPEARANCE ☐ COMMAND PRESENCE ☐ LOYALTY	1	2	3	4	5	15	
ADAPTABILITY ☐ PERFORMANCE IN NEW SITUATIONS ☐ PERFORMANCE UNDER STRESS ☐ PERFORMANCE WITH MINIMUM INSTRUCTIONS ☐ ABILITY TO LEARN	1	2	3	4	5	10	
JOB KNOWLEDGE ☐ TECHNIQUES ☐ PROCEDURES ☐ SKILLS	1	2	3	4	5	10	
						100 SUM	SUM

1. Examples of work well done; Superior performance:
_____

2. Performance deficiencies; Suggestions for improvement or continuing development:
_____

3. General comments (e.g., over-all performance, progress since last report, plans, goals; any other remarks):
_____

This report represents my best judgement of the employee's performance based on my observations and knowledge.

RATING
SUPERVISOR _____ DATE _____

I have read and approved this report.

DIVISION
COMMANDER _____ DATE _____

This report has been discussed with me.

EMPLOYEE'S
SIGNATURE _____ DATE _____

F 2021-54

Figure 7.5
Performance Evaluation Report

PERFORMANCE APPRAISAL REPORT FOR POLICE OFFICER

EMPLOYEE _____ DATE OF EVALUATION _____

JOB TITLE _____ FROM _____ TO _____

DEPARTMENT _____ PURPOSE OF EVALUATION: Probationary _____ Annual _____ Special _____

Performance Measures and Evaluation

	ALWAYS DOES IT	USUALLY DOES IT	SELDOM DOES IT	NOT APPLICABLE	COMMENTS
1. EMERGENCY CALLS FOR SERVICE					
a. Responds quickly but safely when dispatched within established "Code 3" procedures					
b. Exercises reasonable caution in response to emergency calls for service					
c. Gains effective and prompt control of the situation and properly utilizes necessary supporting resources					
d. Exhibits calm, tactful, deliberate, organized and poised demeanor when handling emergency situations					
2. GENERAL ASSISTANCE CALLS	ALWAYS DOES IT	USUALLY DOES IT	SELDOM DOES IT	NOT APPLICABLE	COMMENTS
a. Responds within a reasonable time and safely when dispatched in conformance with established procedures					
b. Minimizes "out of service" time and completes the assignment within an acceptable time period					
c. Exhibits concern and interest in the call even when routine and maintains a highly professional manner					
3. COMMUNITY AND HUMAN RELATIONS	ALWAYS DOES IT	USUALLY DOES IT	SELDOM DOES IT	NOT APPLICABLE	COMMENTS
a. Projects a positive image to individuals and groups as a professional, competent and helpful police officer					
b. Communicates effectively and openly with all types of individuals and groups					
c. Relates well to people even in stress situations					
d. Exhibits sincere interest in, and concern for, the problems and viewpoints of others					
e. Takes proper care of equipment and vehicles and pride in their appearance					
f. Maintains effective working relationships with co-workers and supervisors					
4. CASE INVESTIGATION	ALWAYS DOES IT	USUALLY DOES IT	SELDOM DOES IT	NOT APPLICABLE	COMMENTS
a. Uses productive techniques in case investigations Recognizes and carefully collects and preserves all evidence					
b. Prepares clear, concise, accurate and logical reports for department and court use					
c. Exhibits a professional and poised demeanor in court and functions well as an objective witness					
d. Maintains acceptable clearance and complaint issuance level					
e. Works cooperatively and constructively with other organizations and resources					
5. ARREST PROCEDURES	ALWAYS DOES IT	USUALLY DOES IT	SELDOM DOES IT	NOT APPLICABLE	COMMENTS
a. Protects the safety of himself/herself and others in the apprehension process					
b. Utilizes only reasonable and legal levels of force and restraint in accordance with department policy in arrest situations					
c. Makes "quality" arrests which are compatible with departmental or team goals					
d. Respects the civil rights of persons placed in custody					
6. TRAFFIC CONTROL	ALWAYS DOES IT	USUALLY DOES IT	SELDOM DOES IT	NOT APPLICABLE	COMMENTS
a. Maintains acceptable enforcement levels and relates activities to the location, time and causes of serious accidents					
b. Gains effective and prompt control at an accident scene and properly utilizes necessary supporting resources					
c. Minimizes citizen friction and complaints in traffic law enforcement					
d. Maintains an acceptable record of judicial support of citations issued					
7. CRIME PREVENTION	ALWAYS DOES IT	USUALLY DOES IT	SELDOM DOES IT	NOT APPLICABLE	COMMENTS
a. Keeps abreast of crime problems, hazards, and prevention priorities in assigned patrol sector					
b. Maintains acceptable and productive levels of field activity, including "on-view" stops and arrests, which can actually impact crime levels					
c. Exercises initiative in finding and developing resources in the community to help in crime prevention					
d. Makes citizens aware of their crime prevention responsibilities and assists them in reducing hazards					

The accuracy of a particular scale (in assessing an employee's performance) is almost always contingent on the selection of identifiable and measurable on-the-job traits, the design of the rating instrument and the competence of the person doing the rating. The rater's knowledge, training and inclination to take a risk are critical variables that actually may determine the success or failure of the performance evaluation process. Unless sergeants take responsibility for performance appraisal and play their role as first-line supervisors very skillfully, performance evaluation will become just another element in mutual admiration that perpetuates mediocrity. Sergeants should not forget that excellence is the by-product of selectivity and that they are in a position to mold the department's human resources into a more efficient, effective and productive work force.

Critical Incident Method. The critical incident method involves identifying, classifying and recording significant employee behaviors. A critical incident can be favorable or unfavorable, but both must be recorded accurately. The events chosen by the supervisor for analysis must be concrete indicators of effective or ineffective performance on the job. The three basic steps in the critical incident approach to performance appraisal are:

1.   Gather and record accurate information about critical incidents involving employees.

2.   Abstract the information into a manageable number of categories describing significant job behaviors.

3.   Provide the evaluator with a list of categories and a form on which to record an analysis of the employee's performance during various critical incidents.

The worksheet becomes an accurate record of actual behavior and gives management a profile of each employee in terms of that employee's performance-related strengths and weaknesses. The critical incident method has a number of distinct advantages. It deals with factual situations, zeroes in on positive and negative aspects of behavior and is well-suited for the employee-counseling aspects of performance assessment. On the downside, the critical incident method has several disadvantages. It takes a lot of time, specialized training and management oversight to do it right.

The critical incident approach to performance evaluation is much more subjective when compared to the use of graphic rating scales. It requires a great deal of interpretive skill and introspection on the part of the evaluator. The sergeant must know how the critical incident should have been handled as well as have the expertise to judge the performance of subordinates in relation to that standard. This requires professional competence and confidence in the supervisor's ability to evaluate the on-the-job performance of working police officers. Critical incidents, if evaluated objectively, help alert supervisors to problems and raise "red flags" that tell a great deal about that employee's ability to function as a police officer. These red flags often indicate the type of remediation that may

be necessary to correct a performance deficit. While the critical incident method has proven effective in certain situations, it has not been widely used in police work. It is simply too complex. As the police profession matures, we will undoubtedly see more enthusiasm for and interest in the critical incident approach to performance evaluation.

Behaviorally Anchored Rating Scales. Behaviorally Anchored Rating Scales (BARS) are gaining popularity as performance measuring devices in police work. They focus on what employees should be doing rather than on their personal traits by relating specific performance to critical job responsibilities.

Each scale identifies specific on-the-job activities to be evaluated. There are sample statements describing (in behavioral terms) what is considered to be unacceptable, average and excellent performance in representative incidents. Supervisors look for and rate definite, observable and measurable job behavior related to these categories. They choose a numerical designation that best fits the performance level of the person being evaluated (Holt, 1990).

The behaviors (tasks or activities) being evaluated are incorporated into a matrix configuration using a continuum of performance measurement ranging from 0-10. The actual score is assigned by raters based on their professional judgment. This produces a multidimensional assessment of performance as that performance relates to critical tasks or activities.

Figure 7.6
Application of Bars to Police Work

BEHAVIORAL STATEMENT	Performance Level	
	___ 10	—EXCELLENT
	___ 9	
	___ 8	
	___ 7	
Is cognizant of the need for officer safety while carrying out professional duties (give specific example such as a domestic violence call or a traffic stop).	___ 6	
	___ 5	—AVERAGE
	___ 4	
	___ 3	
	___ 2	
	___ 1	
	___ 0	—UNACCEPTABLE

Behaviorally Anchored Rating Scales use a sufficient array of critical incidents and corresponding behaviors to determine the level of performance as displayed in a graphic rating scale format. In order to work effectively, it is essential to have a participatory environment in which behavioral statements (see Figure 7.6) are developed by consensus between police officers and managers who are thoroughly familiar with the actual behavior being evaluated.

While the BARS approach to performance evaluation is fairly complex, it elicits valuable information for input into the self-development and managerial decision-making processes. Complexity can be overcome through the adequate training of first-line supervisors and a cooperative spirit on the part of rank-and-file police officers. The effective use of BARS produces a "win-win" situation.

Management by Objectives. Management by Objectives (MBO) is viewed as a complete management and control system. It is a process designed to convert goals and objectives into specific programs. MBO identifies exactly who is to do what within a given time frame based on the allocation of existing resources. MBO is a novel approach to performance evaluation, however. Rather than focusing exclusively on past performance, the first-line supervisor and the employee get together to map out future goals and objectives (which are consistent with the organization's mission). They work together to develop goals and objectives, measures of achievement and mutually acceptable time frames. The next regularly scheduled performance review, based on the concept of MBO, is set aside to evaluate how well the employee has done in accomplishing specified objectives. Plunkett (1992) has identified a series of distinct steps he feels will make MBO work in just about any organizational setting. They are:

1. Setting mutually acceptable goals and objectives.

2. Identifying resources and necessary actions.

3. Prioritizing goals and objectives.

4. Setting precise timetables.

5. Evaluating the results.

Clarity and specificity are essential components of MBO. While MBO produces a precise measurement of accomplishment, it requires time and a great deal of planning.

The accuracy of a performance evaluation protocol based on MBO will ultimately depend on the individual rater's judgment, knowledge, training and ability to establish a positive, empathetic, collaborative and goal-oriented relationship. Sergeants must have the desire, competence and human skills to help working police officers formulate legitimate, realistic and measurable job-related performance objectives that can be accomplished during the formal evaluation period. When used properly, MBO cuts through ambiguity and wishful thinking to establish concrete benchmarks with which to assess each employee's accomplishments. All successful MBO performance evaluation programs are built on a foundation of cooperation, collaboration and trust. Whether or not an MBO performance evaluation protocol works in a particular police department will depend on the caliber of the supervisors who come up through the promotion process.

Irrespective of the method that is selected, police sergeants (as first-line supervisors) are in a strategic position to determine the success or failure of the

performance evaluation process. Through neglect or by design, they can sabotage everything. Success in achieving the goals and objectives of performance appraisal, on the other hand, is almost entirely dependent on their knowledge, maturity, specialized training and human skills. Their DECISIONS must reflect sound judgment and their ACTIONS must be firm, yet fair.

The Human Factor

The integrity of the performance assessment process is inexorably linked to the ability and skill of those who have been promoted to the rank of sergeant. It is nurtured by experience and reinforced through continuous training.

In order to become impartial evaluators, sergeants must first accept themselves as human beings who are fallible and are susceptible to various influences that can bias their judgment and skew their decisions. Acceptance of one's self as flawed is the first step on the road to objectivity.

In the jargon of personnel evaluation, those influences that distort perceptions and interfere with an objective assessment are known as **errors**. While the chance of error cannot be eliminated altogether, supervisors can be trained to recognize common errors and to devise strategies designed to mitigate their effect on performance appraisal. Police departments with a desire to make the performance assessment process work train raters to recognize and deal with these errors so that supervisors can avoid some of the common pitfalls (Iannone, 1994). Some of the most widespread rating errors are explored below.

The Error of Leniency

The error of leniency is probably the most common error in rating police personnel. It involves the human tendency to give people the benefit of the doubt and evaluate their on-the-job performance beyond what the circumstances warrant. Police sergeants succumb to exactly the same pressures that tempt all other supervisors to be lenient with subordinates: the desire to be popular, to avoid interpersonal conflicts, to shield one's ego from criticism and to protect those who are less talented and more vulnerable. Some sergeants believe that by giving negative performance appraisals (even to those officers who deserve them) they draw undue attention to themselves and showcase their own limitations as a first-line supervisor. To many, it is an unacceptable risk. In some cases, sergeants opt to be lenient in evaluating their immediate subordinates in a calculated effort to offset the leniency of other supervisors within the police department. This is their attempt to create a balance and ensure that their employees have a fair shot when it comes to advancement.

Regardless of its cause, the error of leniency (if unchecked) acts to undermine the objectivity of the performance assessment process and almost always has a debilitating effect on the organization itself. Supervisors lose their credi-

bility, morale suffers, and men and women are placed in positions for which they are unprepared. Good first-line supervisors simply do not allow personal considerations to cloud their judgment. They strive to ensure the integrity of the performance evaluation process by being impartial and fair in their evaluation of each and every subordinate.

The Error of Central Tendency

In a normal distribution, more people will be rated closer to the mean than to any other point on the evaluative scale. This becomes an error of central tendency only when it fails to reflect a truly objective appraisal of on-the-job performance and forces many employees into an artificial category labeled "average." Whether supervisors lack sufficient data for valid assessments, fear there will be repercussions or are merely lazy, central tendency is an escape. It offers them a way to avoid risks. Average evaluations are the safest and least controversial. Thus, supervisors are able to skirt justifying high and low evaluations. By taking the middle road, the sergeant avoids criticism from other supervisors and minimizes the chances of a confrontation during the evaluation interview.

Central tendency is most likely to rear its ugly head in situations where sergeants are unfamiliar with the person or persons being evaluated, there is a lack of verifiable performance data or there is some ambiguity in terms of policies, procedures, rules and regulations. Labeling everyone as average does a disservice to individual employees and the police organization. It penalizes competent, achievement-oriented subordinates and rewards marginal employees. Central tendency destroys the credibility of the evaluation process and plays havoc with employee morale. Sergeants must recognize the problem created by central tendency and be ready to deal with it. This knowledge and a commitment to regular, thorough and objective performance appraisal will help to safeguard the integrity of the evaluative process.

The Halo Effect

One of the most frequently committed errors is known as the halo effect. This means that the first-line supervisor permits just one outstanding (positive or negative) characteristic or critical incident to shape the overall rating which is given to the employee. Once the supervisor formulates a general impression that the subordinate's on-the-job performance is good or poor, all evaluative ratings are adjusted to reflect that particular judgment. In other words, the sergeant assigns similar values to all characteristics or traits irrespective of the police officer's actual on-the-job performance. In this situation, the evaluator uses selective perception to justify the initial assessment. The halo effect is the MBO's version of the self-fulfilling prophecy. The distortion caused by the halo effect is often compounded by the error of related traits and the error of over-

weighting (Iannone, 1994). The error of related traits occurs when the evaluator assumes that an employee who exhibits one strength will automatically possess others. The error of overweighting (or recency) is the tendency of a supervisor to be unduly influenced by a critical incident, either good or bad, involving the evaluatee near the end of the performance review period. Due to the dynamics involved, a recent critical incident can skew a performance evaluation to the point where it becomes meaningless. Formal performance appraisals are supposed to profile the whole person. Better supervisors guard against letting isolated traits or critical incidents dominate the analysis of performance.

The Error of Bias

One of the most important and widespread errors involves personal bias. Many supervisors have a tendency to rate those employees they know and really like much higher than can reasonably be justified by an objective assessment of performance. Factors such as race, sex, sexual preference, color, creed, lifestyle and physical appearance may be either intentionally or unintentionally imbued in the evaluation based on the first-line supervisor's norms, values, prejudices and operational stereotypes. It is human nature for supervisors to write much more favorable performance evaluations for those with whom they are compatible and to view those persons they dislike as being of little or no value to the organization. It is fairly easy for supervisors to fall into the trap of over-rating subordinates they helped select or currently supervise in elite or highly specialized units. There is a certain egoism involved in stating that "employees are good because they work for me" or "if they work for me, they must be good." These supervisors have forgotten a basic principle in personnel management; they are rating the person rather than on-the-job performance. This type of "personal politics" destroys the morale of truly competent employees and induces other supervisors to become more lenient when they evaluate their own personnel. Unless a police officer's social background and personality interfere with personal performance, they should not be factored into the appraisal process. While the sergeant may not like a subordinate, the evaluation must be fair and based on the analysis of objective data. First-line supervisors simply cannot allow personal biases and prejudices to cloud their judgment about the performance of an employee. Supervisors need to recognize and deal with their biases in order to keep them from subverting the performance assessment process.

The Contrast Error

This particular rating error, according to Trojanowicz (1980), arises from the tendency of some first-line supervisors to judge subordinates in terms of their own expectations and aspirations. Police officers who vicariously fulfill the personal needs of the sergeant are generally rated higher than others, irrespec-

tive of their actual performance on the job. They are valued by the supervisor for what they represent, not for what they accomplish or the skill required to accomplish it. This type of emotion-based evaluation is inherently subjective and self-serving. The contrast error forces the employee to guess what qualities or traits the supervisor is looking for and to curry favor (in the form of a positive appraisal) through gamesmanship or outright deception. First-line supervisors must learn to separate their own expectations and aspirations from those of the evaluation protocol. A valid and reliable performance assessment can only be derived from an analysis of what really exists rather than what supervisors would like to see. Subjective personnel appraisals increase anxiety and threaten to undermine the credibility of the evaluation process itself.

Sergeants are the human ingredient in performance appraisal. If they are knowledgeable and competent, the performance evaluation process will work. They hold the key to efficiency, effectiveness and productivity in police work.

The Validity and Reliability of Performance Appraisal

Performance assessments are a superfluous waste of time and energy unless appropriate steps are taken to make sure they are both **valid** and **reliable**. The objective is to develop a reasonably accurate profile that reflects the competency of personnel, their individual capabilities and their overall value to the police organization. This is an inordinately complex process that involves the use of an objective measuring instrument and the exercise of mature judgment by the first-line supervisor. Validity and reliability are critical variables in the success or failure of the performance review process.

A valid performance appraisal is an accurate measurement of the traits (graphic rating scale), applied problem-solving (critical incident) or goal acquisition (management by objectives) the evaluation process purports to measure. It zeroes in on the essential elements of the job and a limited number of important job-related behaviors. The appraisal itself is an assessment of the degree to which a very specific accomplishment is related to a clearly stated performance standard. If the measuring device is sound, essentially the same results will be achieved by any rater who uses it.

The employee appraisal process is considered to be reliable when it measures appropriate job-related performance accurately and consistently each time it is used. A reliable performance appraisal is one that is not biased by the idiosyncrasies (or errors) of the rater, manipulation by the evaluatee, flaws in the design of the measuring device or the constraints of time or place. Reliability relates to the degree of confidence one has that the supervisor, with the tools available, developed a realistic profile of the subordinate's on-the-job behavior.

Due to the nature of performance appraisal in complex criminal justice organizations, reliability is often difficult to achieve. No evaluative protocol is perfect. Performance ratings are developed, administered, scored and acted upon by people who exhibit prejudices and who, at times, exercise poor judg-

ment. While these problems are fairly serious, they are not insurmountable. The following actions may be needed:

1. Adoption of clear-cut policies, procedures, rules and regulations designed to govern the performance evaluation process.

2. Selection of a relatively simple yet valid performance appraisal instrument.

3. Training for supervisors in gathering and analyzing objective evaluative data.

4. Active participation by those being evaluated in all aspects of performance assessment.

5. A commitment by management to base appropriate personnel decisions on data derived from formal performance appraisals.

These measures will add to the reliability of the process and should help allay the anxiety of those police officers who are scheduled for a performance appraisal. A relevant, reliable and fair evaluation protocol is the keystone in a sound police personnel system.

The Evaluation Interview

Once the formal performance rating has been compiled, it (along with all recommendations for remediation) should be communicated to the employee as soon as possible. This is almost always done in what is known as an **evaluation** or **appraisal interview**. Here again, the sergeant is the lead actor in this drama.

If the evaluation interview is handled well, everyone benefits. The employee is molded into a more competent police officer; the sergeant gains self-confidence in the area of personnel development; and the police agency becomes more efficient, effective and productive. Mature human beings are able to deal with and accept criticism they view as deserved, constructive and fair. If, on the other hand, the interview is handled poorly, no one benefits. What started out as a creative way to motivate subordinates quickly degenerates into misunderstanding, distrust, resentment and open hostility. Under these circumstances, performance appraisal becomes a demotivating factor that can jeopardize the organizational health of the entire police department.

The performance appraisal interview is a forum for very positive face-to-face interaction between first-line supervisors and their subordinates. It is designed to facilitate collaborative problem-solving and mutual goal setting. Both parties share responsibility for making the process work. Sergeants need to be open, honest, helpful and supportive in dealing with employees. Police

---

Case Study

Sergeant Albert "Buster" Rosen

Sergeant Rosen, a very dedicated and aggressive perfectionist, has been in charge of the police department's Special Weapons and Tactics Unit for about two years. Almost all of the original team members have been reassigned. They have been replaced by young, aggressive and fiercely loyal white males who were handpicked by Sergeant Rosen. The new SWAT team has a macho image that has spread throughout the city.

Officer Amelio Sanchez, a veteran member of the SWAT team, was recently involved in a very questionable shooting incident that raised a great deal of public concern. He does not fit the mold and is not viewed as part of Sgt. Rosen's new breed.

While the previous SWAT commander rated Officer Sanchez above average to superior in all evaluative categories, he has not fared nearly as well with Sergeant Rosen. He is viewed as a laid-back, often cynical Hispanic who is too individualistic. The clash of personalities is obvious.

In the most recent performance evaluation, Sergeant Rosen rated Officer Sanchez from average to poor in all categories and has recommended that Sanchez be reassigned to another unit "for the good of the service."

Officer Sanchez has appealed the rating and has asked for a hearing before the Civil Service Commission. He claims that he has been the victim of discrimination and harassment. The Civil Service Commission has ordered Sergeant Rosen (and his supervisors) to show cause why the performance rating should stand.

As the principal actor in the performance evaluation process, what rater errors do you, a sergeant, suspect might be operating in this particular situation? Why is absolute objectivity almost impossible to achieve? How can you help protect the integrity of your performance appraisals? What can be done to make them more reliable? Why is the perception of fairness so critical to the success of the performance evaluation process?

---

officers, on the other hand, must be willing to cooperate with and take reasonable direction from their superiors. Sincerity, empathy and mutual respect are absolutely essential.

Statistically speaking, half of the employees fall below the median in terms of performance. Nonetheless, research shows that *average* employees estimate their own performance level at around the 75th percentile. Consequently, appraising and reporting on another person's performance (especially where there is a conflict in perception) becomes one of the most emotionally charged of all management activities (Robbins, 1989).

The purpose of the appraisal interview is to explore the employee's strengths and weaknesses in light of objective evaluative data. If their performance meets

or exceeds reasonable expectations, some positive reinforcement should be provided. Praise or a sincere "thank you" is appropriate. Other types of rewards may also be in order. If deficiencies or performance problems are identified, however, remedial action must be agreed upon and initiated. At this point, the appraisal interview is transformed into a vehicle for collaborative problem solving and mutual goal setting. The two parties must work cooperatively to formulate a strategy for improving the employee's on-the-job performance. The ultimate value of the interview will depend, then, on a police officer's ability to recognize the need for self-improvement and the sergeant's ability to stimulate that subordinate's desire to change.

A constructive performance assessment interview is designed to focus the subordinate's attention on the future rather than belaboring the past. According to management theorists like Chruden and Sherman (1976), first-line supervisors should:

1. Discuss actual performance in very specific terms and express their criticism in a helpful, tactful way.

2. Emphasize the strengths on which the employee can build as opposed to stressing only the weaknesses to be overcome.

3. Avoid suggestions involving only a cosmetic change in traits by promoting conformity through acceptable on-the-job behavior.

4. Concentrate on the opportunities for both personal growth and professional development that exist within the framework of the person's present position.

5. Limit expectations and specific plans for substantive change to a few important items that can be achieved within a reasonable period of time based on the expenditure of available resources.

The performance appraisal interview is a supervisor-employee activity that involves evaluating, teaching, coaching and counseling. Once again, this task is not nearly as simple as it might appear. In order to accomplish even these relatively modest objectives, the sergeant must be able to establish rapport, empathize and communicate effectively with subordinates. Sergeants must also possess the leadership skills necessary to motivate their personnel. Without natural talent, specialized training, acquired supervisory experience and leadership ability, sergeants are bound to fail. Under these conditions, performance appraisal is nothing more than a ritualistic exercise in futility.

While there is no single best way to handle the performance appraisal interview, there are a number of operational steps that can add structure to the process and help to ensure a positive outcome. These steps are discussed below.

STEP 1.   Exercise care in scheduling the formal performance appraisal interview. Choose a time and place that affords maximum privacy and is free of unwarranted interruption. Encourage meaningful interaction by allowing sufficient time for a full exploration of the evaluative data as well as the sergeant's report. Solicit input and relevant feedback from the evaluatee. Defuse anxiety and reduce defensiveness by using techniques designed to put the officer at ease and to stimulate a dialogue about performance problems and possible solutions to those problems. The environment in which the interview takes place is a critical variable in determining the overall value of the performance appraisal.

STEP 2.   Adequate preparation is absolutely essential. Both parties (supervisor/subordinate) should be ready and willing to review documentation, compare notes and reach a consensus concerning the employee's job-related performance. Thorough preparation and uninhibited participation are key elements in effective performance appraisal. Anything less tends to undermine the reliability of the subordinate's performance profile.

STEP 3.   Compare the police officer's accomplishments with specific objectives or targets. Use objective data derived from the appraisal instrument. Don't be vague or use generalizations. Be precise about what was expected and how close the employee came to actually meeting the goal. Specificity is an absolutely essential element in the performance assessment process.

STEP 4.   Give adequate credit (in terms of recognition and other forms of positive reinforcement) for what the police officer has, in fact, accomplished. Don't succumb to the temptation to take for granted those things that have been done and to zero in on the employee's deficiencies or problems. Give credit where credit is due; build upon the employee's strengths. Use the appraisal interview as a vehicle for growth and development, not as a forum for punishment.

STEP 5.   Carefully review those things that have not been accomplished by the subordinate during the review period. Emphasize exactly where improvement is required. Explore with the officer why on-the-job performance must be improved and just how it can be done. Encourage dialogue and develop a plan to ensure full participation. Mutual problem solving and collective goal setting represent other key elements in the performance evaluation process.

STEP 6.   Avoid making the assumption that the fault is all due to the subordinate. If both parties have contributed to the performance problem, admit it. Don't overemphasize the officer's mistakes, faults or weaknesses. Judge the police officer's performance, not personality. Never compare the subordinate to an ideal-type third person. Stick to a mutual examination of concrete data and facts in an effort to determine exactly what they mean to the police officer, the sergeant and the police department as a whole.

STEP 7.   Formulate and agree upon new objectives and goals to be achieved during the next evaluation period. Be very specific in terms of what and how much is to be accomplished in a particular period of time. Show how the new objectives and goals are directly related to what has or has not been accomplished during the current evaluation period. This sets the stage for an even more objective performance appraisal the next time around.

STEP 8.   Review what you, as a first-line supervisor, can do to help the officer achieve specific objectives and goals. Identify other resources that are available and explain how to access them. Play the role of the teacher, the coach and the counselor. Improvement in job performance is almost always a mutually dependent activity. Sharing the responsibility for personal and professional development brings about mutual respect, a shared sense of confidence and renewed enthusiasm, as well as a commitment to the job.

STEP 9.   Formulate (in conjunction with the employee) a plan to monitor remediation and reevaluate the situation as conditions change. The belief that there will be some type of follow-up is a powerful catalyst for change. It motivates police officers to improve their own on-the-job performance and places an affirmative responsibility on the sergeant to make sure that actual improvement takes place (Bittel and Newstrom, 1990).

The appraisal interview is critically important. From a human resource development perspective, it is the nexus between police department needs and improved employee performance. The goal of the sergeant should be to handle the interview in such a way that officers (with the exception of incompetents and malcontents) will return to their job with an enthusiastic attitude and a genuine desire to improve their own on-the-job performance.

Performance appraisals and evaluative interviews are meaningless exercises unless there is remediation and follow-up. Follow-up is the synergistic ingredient in the performance evaluation process.

Remediation

There are, as was previously noted, three basic elements in the formal per-formance-evaluation process; they are (1) the objective assessment, (2) the appraisal interview, and (3) remediation. **Remediation** refers to using available resources to correct a personnel problem or remedy a deficiency. While sergeants are almost always responsible for the assessment and normally conduct the appraisal interview, their role in remediation is often less direct.

If a deficiency or performance problem is relatively minor or fairly easy to correct, the sergeant is almost always authorized to deal with it directly. Due to the rank structure used in police work, sergeants resolve most performance-related problems informally and at their level (in the organization) based on their appraisal, teaching, coaching and counseling skills. They keep noise out of the system. As first-line supervisors, sergeants also are responsible for the maintenance/direction function. They continuously monitor each offi-cer's job-related performance in an effort to keep it on an even keel and to make sure it is consistent with the police department's mission, goals and objectives. Sergeants use the formal performance appraisal process to diagnose serious problems, communicate concern, plan for remediation, provide follow-up and schedule the more difficult cases for administrative intervention. The perfor-mance-review process is built on a medical model that has been adapted to police management.

In the event there is no improvement in the police officer's on-the-job per-formance, or if it continues to deteriorate, the sergeant has an obligation to take further action. The sergeant may be forced into recommending remediation through retraining, increasingly more severe disciplinary action or total separa-tion from police service.

Due to the nature of bureaucracy, more serious and persistent performance problems are handled in a much different manner. They are "kicked upstairs," so to speak, for remediation or resolution. Consequently, the sergeant's role shifts to that of a supporting actor. All major personnel decisions are made by superior officers and are made based on an organization-wide perspective. The sergeant gathers information for and makes recommendations to decisionmakers but no longer controls the evaluation process. Under these circumstances, the adminis-tration assumes responsibility for quality assurance within the police department.

Many of the more progressive police departments in the United States have initiated comprehensive employee assistance programs (EAPs) designed to help deviant, maladjusted or marginal personnel who still may be capable of making a substantive contribution to the organization. They also provide a variety of pos-itive support services like marital counseling, stress management programs and financial as well as preretirement planning. Specialized employee assistance pro-grams represent an investment in the department's human resources and a tacit recognition that first-line supervisors are not miracle workers. Sergeants are sim-ply not equipped to handle problems related to health, stress, alcoholism, drug addiction, domestic conflict, and so forth. Sergeants can be trained (using a thor-

ough performance evaluation) to formulate a preliminary diagnosis of the problem and to make an appropriate referral. The EAP movement is predicated on the assumption that it is better and often much more cost-effective to salvage employees through medical, psychological and social intervention than it is to apply negative sanctions or to separate them from the service. Therefore, sergeants play a pivotal role in the development of a police department's human resources.

Follow-Up

Follow-up by the supervisor completes the evaluation cycle, sets the stage for subsequent appraisals and provides momentum for the performance assessment process. Sergeants are expected to check on each subordinate's progress in meeting the mutually acceptable goals established during the performance-appraisal interview. This role-related task requires surveillance and the continuous examination of data derived from a variety of performance measurements. In order to fulfill this responsibility, the sergeant should:

1. Recognize and reward those police officers who are doing a good job.

2. Provide positive reinforcement for those police officers who are making a good-faith effort to change their behavior and improve their on-the-job performance.

3. Assist (through training, coaching, counseling and other referral services) those police officers who need help to improve their performance at work.

4. Recommend appropriate disciplinary action for individual police officers who won't change their behavior or work to improve their job-related performance.

Follow-up is a supervisory activity designed to motivate personnel and serve as a springboard to professional growth and development.

Without adequate follow-up, periodic performance appraisals become rather mundane, routine managerial tasks with little or no practical value. Police managers, sergeants and their subordinates merely attempt to project the impression that they care about the efficiency, effectiveness and productivity of human resources in police work. Perfunctory performance appraisal is used to disguise the discrepancy between the status quo and what could be; honest assessment motivates those in search of excellence. Appraisal should be a daily activity that is summarized periodically in a formal appraisal report and interview. All other things being equal, police officers who accept the inevitability of fair and continuous assessment will try to perform their best work at all times, not just during the formal evaluation period. (See Figure 7.7)

Figure 7.7
The Sergeant's Role in Performance Appraisal

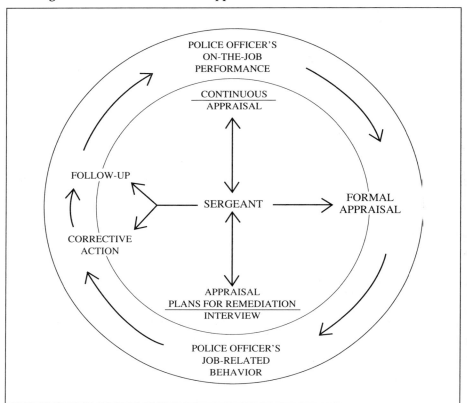

What's New on the Horizon?

While the Total Quality Management guru W. Edwards Deming called performance appraisals "management by fear" (Behn, 1994), they are not headed for extinction in modern police work. On the contrary, they are becoming much more help oriented and far less punitive. Based on the realization that rank-and-file police officers are the primary source of all productive gain, the philosophy stressed throughout this chapter is that supervisors must *lead* their subordinates to higher levels of performance by using natural forces within the work group as opposed to the formal authority vested in them by virtue of their position in the organization (Kennish, 1994). This is a quantum leap from the days when negative discipline reigned supreme and humane concern was the exception rather than the rule.

Two new trends which will have a definite impact on first-line police supervision are emerging at this time. The first deals with evaluating police officer performance under community-oriented policing. The second relates to subordinates evaluating their supervisor's performance. Both of these trends are the by-product of the new emphasis on participatory management in modern police work.

Performance Evaluation in Community-Oriented Policing

Community-oriented policing, regardless of its specific form, is essentially a program in which the police adopt organizational arrangements that focus on fear reduction and order maintenance activities through the involvement of citizens while using mutually acceptable problem-solving techniques (Gaines, Kappeler and Vaughn, 1994). It is an interactive process involving police officers and citizens working together collaboratively.

More and more municipal governments are experimenting with some form of community-oriented policing. It is designed to elicit different kinds of resources for use in the battle against crime. First-line police supervisors are expected to achieve total quality results (TQR) with human resources in the work group coupled with those in the community at large.

Community-oriented policing is based on the assumption that delegation of authority plus meaningful participation in decision making leads to empowerment. The empowerment of police personnel and members of the community is viewed as the bottom line in any effective law enforcement strategy (Whisenand and Rush, 1993).

Traditional performance evaluation methods are not, in and of themselves, sufficient to gauge the quality of officer performance in a community-oriented policing environment. Three other dimensions have been identified and must be integrated into the process. Performance evaluations are also used:

1. To convey reasonable expectations to police personnel concerning both the content and style of their behavior while reinforcing commitment to the department's mission, values, goals and objectives. This serves as a vehicle for socialization.

2. To document the types of problems and situations that officers encounter in the neighborhood and approaches they take in resolving them. This provides a data-based analysis of the types of resources and other managerial supports needed to deal with problems. It gives police officers an opportunity to have their individual efforts recognized.

3. To identify organizational factors that hinder performance enhancement or the solicitation of ideas for dealing with changing conditions. This gives the people doing the work a meaningful role in reshaping that work in order to improve departmental as well as individual performance.

The Houston Police Department embraced community-oriented policing as its new policing style in 1986. Known as Neighborhood Oriented Policing (NOP), it provides managers with a philosophical foundation and conceptual framework to direct the organization in a manner consistent with community needs. From an operational point of view, it encourages police officers to assume responsibility for managing the delivery of essential services in those geographical areas to which they are assigned.

A task force composed of police officers and first-line supervisors spent a considerable amount of time gathering, massaging and collating information. A second group, consisting of police volunteers, took the information gathered by the task force and developed a new performance evaluation protocol. This process and the resulting instrumentation sought to bridge existing roles and responsibilities with emerging ones based on the neighborhood policing philosophy.

Performance evaluations of patrol officers and their respective sergeants utilized six newly developed forms designed to elicit data and feedback. Each of the forms is described below:

1. **Patrol Officer's Bi-Annual Assessment Report.** This form is used by sergeants to evaluate police officer performance based on 22 specific criteria. In addition, space is provided for written comments regarding work assignments, work progress, overall and special recognition. The criteria reflect the department's expectations concerning police officer performance when it comes to Neighborhood Oriented Policing.

2. **Patrol Officer's Monthly Worksheet.** The form is designed as a tool to guide each officer's actions during a designated tour of duty. Police officers are given direct input into their own appraisal. This allows officers to identify the different types of projects or programs they have worked on during the evaluation period and report on progress they have made.

3. **Community Information Form.** Citizen-police officer interaction is implicit in all Neighborhood Oriented Policing strategies. This particular form, if the officer chooses to submit it, elicits information from citizens who worked on projects with specific officers. The information requested is very specific and provides sergeants with additional insight into what the officer was trying to accomplish and how the officer is going about doing it.

4. **Calls for Service—Citizen Feedback Form.** Like almost all police departments, the most frequent source of officer-citizen interaction is the call for service. The Calls for Service—Citizen Feedback form is designed to gather information on the quality as well as the nature of the contact. Citizens are asked a few questions by sergeants. The responses are made a matter of "record" and factored into the overall evaluation. Sergeants use the form at least once a month.

5. **Investigator Questionnaire.** All police officers are expected to conduct high-quality criminal investigations. Even though the information contained in an investigative report provides a critical database for case managers, this material was seldom reviewed by the officer's immediate supervisor. The function of the Investigator Questionnaire is to obtain information from investigative sergeants concerning an officer's knowledge and

quality of performance as these factors relate to both preliminary and follow-up investigations. The police officer determines whether or not to submit the form.

6. **Officer's Immediate Supervisor Assessment Form.** The officers are given an opportunity to evaluate their immediate supervisors in relation to different dimensions of supervisory work. While the feedback is fairly general in nature, the form must be completed and returned to the sergeant's superior. The information helps to identify significant trends in the relationship between the sergeant and subordinate personnel (Wycoff and Oettmeier, 1994).

Needless to say, the performance evaluation protocol described above represents a radical departure from past practice in law enforcement.

New approaches to police work generate a need for new performance evaluation strategies. Houston's evaluation protocol is experimental and undergoing continuous revision. One thing is certain; it has changed the traditional role of the police sergeant in the performance evaluation process. It also subjects first-line supervisors to performance evaluation by their subordinates.

Evaluating the Performance of Supervisors and Managers

In a related development, management theorists are placing more emphasis on employees evaluating the performance of their own supervisors and managers. The theorists link this to the popular participatory management and worker empowerment movements sweeping the country today.

While some mainstream academic, industrial and corporate entities see some value in having employees rate their supervisors (McGaney and Smith, 1993), the concept has been slow to develop in police work. In most police departments, performance evaluation is still considered the prerogative of management. The evolving participatory management and worker empowerment movements in law enforcement may alter the status quo, however.

Thomas Whetstone (1994) has outlined what should be evaluated in terms of beneficial supervisory traits as well as the pitfalls inherent in the evaluative process. Since much of a supervisor's or manager's work is not observed by subordinates, he argues that the appraisal of performance should focus primarily on leadership issues.

In order to provide superiors with meaningful feedback, police officers should have sufficient training to perform the evaluation. In Whetstone's opinion, the officers should use a standard forced-choice instrument designed to provide structure and guide the rater in evaluating those attributes the police department feels are most important.

While there are several commercially available upward feedback rating forms on the market, Whetstone believes that departments may be ahead in the game by creating their own. In doing so, they can target those traits that are most important to them (see Figure 7.8).

Figure 7.8
Supervisor Performance Rating Form

SUPERVISORY PERSONNEL RATING FORM

This form is to be completed by the employee and returned to the designated proctor. Deviation from procedure may invalidate this evaluation.

Supervisor Being Rated: _____

Evaluating Employee: _____

Proctor: _____

Using the graphic scales, rate the performance against the criteria listed. A **10** indicates total agreement or really outstanding performance; a **1** indicates total disagreement or unsatisfactory performance. Check the "not observed" (**NO**) column if you have not observed performance in that area or do not feel that you are qualified to rate in that area.

Leadership Skills   **NO**

1. Officers are encouraged to excel through the positive,
    professional attitude and action of this supervisor.   1 2 3 4 5 6 7 8 9 10
2. Creative ideas are elicited from officers to improve the
    overall effectiveness of the unit.   1 2 3 4 5 6 7 8 9 10
3. Department goals, needs, plans and information are
    communicated to subordinates.   1 2 3 4 5 6 7 8 9 10
4. Plans, projects and objectives are consistent with department
    needs, goals & resources.   1 2 3 4 5 6 7 8 9 10
5. **Overall Leadership Rating:**   1 2 3 4 5 6 7 8 9 10

Judgment and Decision-Making Skills

1. Makes decisions in a timely manner.   1 2 3 4 5 6 7 8 9 10
2. Demonstrates decisiveness when faced with options.   1 2 3 4 5 6 7 8 9 10
3. Decisions made are in conformance with departmental policies, procedures,
    rules, regulations and all applicable laws.   1 2 3 4 5 6 7 8 9 10
4. Personnel assignments reflect the appropriate utilization of human resources. 1 2 3 4 5 6 7 8 9 10
5. **Overall Judgment and Decision-making Rating:**   1 2 3 4 5 6 7 8 9 10

Directing Officers in Emergency, Unusual or Stressful Events

1. Supervisor is present as appropriate.   1 2 3 4 5 6 7 8 9 10
2. Situation is correctly analyzed, and appropriate actions are taken to
    control the situation.   1 2 3 4 5 6 7 8 9 10
3. Available resources are properly deployed.   1 2 3 4 5 6 7 8 9 10
4. **Overall Emergency and Stress Performance Rating:**   1 2 3 4 5 6 7 8 9 10

Application of Policies, Procedures, Rules and Regulations

1. Sets good example by adhering to established policies, procedures,
    rules & regulations.   1 2 3 4 5 6 7 8 9 10
2. Policies and directives are explained when necessary.   1 2 3 4 5 6 7 8 9 10
3. Violations are identified, and timely and appropriate corrective action is taken. 1 2 3 4 5 6 7 8 9 10
4. Rules are applied fairly and impartially to all subordinates. 1 2 3 4 5 6 7 8 9 10
5. Subordinates receive evaluation and counseling in an objective manner
    in line with established procedure along with constructive suggestions
    concerning how one's performance can be improved.   1 2 3 4 5 6 7 8 9 10
6. **Overall Application of Rules Rating:**   1 2 3 4 5 6 7 8 9 10

Training Ability and Communication Skills

1. In-service training needs are identified, and efforts are made
    to provide proper training.   1 2 3 4 5 6 7 8 9 10
2. Information given is relevant and timely.   1 2 3 4 5 6 7 8 9 10
3. Ideas are presented in a clear, concise and understandable way. 1 2 3 4 5 6 7 8 9 10
4. Presentations are very organized, logical and in compliance with current
    policies and standards.   1 2 3 4 5 6 7 8 9 10
5. **Overall Training/Communication Rating:**   1 2 3 4 5 6 7 8 9 10

Composite Supervisor Rating

Consider the above criteria as well as areas not specifically addressed
in this evaluation. Rate the supervisor in terms of his or her
overall performance as a supervisor.   1 2 3 4 5 6 7 8 9 10

Comments:

Feel free to use this section to explain any answers and/or address points not covered which you feel are significant. Attach additional sheets if necessary. Your interest and cooperation are sincerely appreciated.

Modified from: T.S. Whetstone, "Subordinates Evaluate Supervisory & Administrative Performance," *The Police Chief,* June 1994.

The notion of supervisor evaluations sounds good, although some police officers are reluctant to support this concept for fear of some type of retaliation by those who receive negative appraisals. This fear coupled with the "errors" discussed earlier in this chapter could have an adverse effect on the objectivity of the evaluation and produce morale problems. The success or failure of the upward feedback program is dependent on management's commitment to the concept as well as the safeguards built into the implementation process.

Whetstone argues that the police officers doing the evaluation should sign the rating form. This gives top management the opportunity when necessary to check with the evaluator on specific incidents used as the basis for the evaluation. He also recommends that the completed rating forms be turned in to a neutral evaluation proctor. In one pilot program it was found that officer confidence, candor and security increased when they were allowed to have meaningful input in the proctor selection process. Individual evaluations are held in total confidentiality with the contents integrated in such a way so as to produce a composite profile.

Upward feedback programs are designed to promote more positive interaction between employees, provide top management with a new source of information about individual on-the-job performance by all police personnel and aid in the career development of those who are involved in the process. Armed with knowledge (concerning their strengths and weaknesses), supervisors and administrators are in a position to adjust their leadership style to benefit subordinates, the police department and themselves. The ultimate goal is self-improvement.

Even though bureaucratic inertia is well entrenched in police work, changes are in the wind. The emerging emphasis on things like meaningful employee participation, total quality management, total quality results, community-oriented policing and empowerment make it a truly exciting time to be in law enforcement.

Summary

The success of any organization in accomplishing its mission, goals and objectives is, in large measure, dependent on the quality of its personnel. This is particularly true when it comes to law enforcement. Police work is labor-intensive and propelled by people power. According to human resource managers, personnel are the arms, legs and mind of the police service.

Personnel development is a contemporary management strategy designed to produce a more efficient, effective and productive work force through proper utilization of available human resources. A comprehensive and objective performance evaluation process is the keystone in personnel development. Police sergeants play a central role in all aspects of performance evaluation and personnel development.

The performance evaluation process consists of an objective assessment, the appraisal interview and remediation. Some type of follow-up completes the evaluative cycle and reactivates the entire process. Performance appraisal is an ongoing activity that works best when it is used on a daily basis. A valid, reli-

Case Study

Sergeant R.J. Lyons

Sergeant Lyons has been a municipal police officer for 15 years. He has held his present rank for a little over one year. As the junior sergeant, he was assigned the often unappreciated task of conducting performance reviews for three police officers. Fortunately, the administration had selected a valid rating instrument and had provided him with some training in the interpretation of evaluative data. As a result, he was able to develop a fairly accurate profile of each officer's strengths and weaknesses.

Now, based on department policy, Sergeant Lyons is required to meet with each officer in an appraisal interview. This is causing some anxiety. He is not really sure it is necessary and doesn't know exactly what to do. The other sergeants have not been very helpful. They avoid face-to-face evaluations whenever possible.

After considering his alternatives, Sergeant Lyons has decided to approach the appraisal interview as a vehicle for personnel development. He has enrolled in an intensive three-day seminar on police-performance evaluation at the regional police academy. The brochure described the course as "An Adventure in Human Resource Management."

As a seasoned first-line supervisor, what material would you expect to cover in this particular seminar? What is the purpose of the appraisal interview and how does it fit into the personnel evaluation process? What type of preparation is required? What skills do you feel Sergeant Lyons will need in order to be successful? How important is empathy? What would you do to make sure that the appraisal interview becomes a catalyst for positive change rather than simply a ritualistic exercise?

able, objective and error-free performance assessment provides management with a database for effective decisionmaking. Evaluation protocols, using graphic rating scales, critical incidents, goal acquisition and behaviorally anchored rating techniques objectify the evaluation process and help the evaluator zero in on truly significant performance as opposed to the subordinate's personality.

A work-centered performance evaluation process allows all of the participants (managers, supervisors and employees) to formulate some mutually acceptable goals, set realistic performance standards and determine what remediation (in terms of training, coaching, counseling and developmental experiences) the employee will need to help reach those objectives. The evaluation process helps to establish a plan designed to foster the police officer's personal growth and professional development.

There are some exciting developments on the horizon. One is finding an effective performance evaluation protocol adaptable to the total quality manage-

ment aspects of community-oriented policing. We are also more likely to see increased emphasis on police officers evaluating the performance of supervisors and administrators.

The effectiveness of the performance evaluation process will be determined to a large degree by talent, training and human skills of men and women promoted to the rank of sergeant. As first-line supervisors, they set the tone, manage, and safeguard the integrity of the evaluative process. They maintain the quality of the work force and determine the success or failure of the organization. This is an awesome responsibility.

Key Concepts

community-oriented policing	participation and empowerment
cycle of evaluation	performance appraisal
error	performance evaluation
evaluating supervisor performance	performance measures
evaluation interview	personnel and productivity
evaluative methods	personnel development
follow-up	remediation
frequency of evaluation	roles and responsibilities
goals and objectives	sources of error
institutional support	supervisor's lead role
objectivity, validity, reliability	

Discussion Topics and Questions

1. Why is performance appraisal now being emphasized by leading police management theorists?

2. What are some of the justifications for use of performance appraisals in police agencies?

3. Identify the components of the performance evaluation process. Why does the sergeant play such a critical role in performance appraisal?

4. Which of the evaluative methods described in the text do you favor? Why do you like this particular method as compared to the others?

5. To the best of your knowledge, what type of error influences you the most? What can you do to neutralize its influence?

6. How would you explain the difference between validity and reliability?

7. How would you, as a first-line supervisor, structure and conduct the evaluative interview to ensure that it will accomplish its purpose or purposes?

8. Why is follow-up such a critical element in the performance evaluation process?

9. What institutional resources are required to ensure that performance appraisals are done properly?

10. Should employees be given the opportunity to evaluate the performance of supervisors and other administrators? What basic principles did you consider in arriving at your conclusion?

11. What steps should be taken by top management to ensure that performance evaluation does not degenerate into "management by fear"?

For Further Reading

Bennett, Wayne W. and Karen M. Hess (1992). *Management and Supervision in Law Enforcement* 2nd ed. New York: West Publishing Company.

> Contains a comprehensive chapter dealing with police performance appraisals as well as excellent advice on how to make sure they withstand legal scrutiny if challenged in court.

Kappeler, Victor E. (1993). *Critical Issues in Police Civil Liability*. Prospect Heights, IL: Waveland Press, Inc.

> Discusses civil liability based on administrative negligence or deliberate indifference. Demonstrates the consequences of management's failure to properly monitor performance and effectively supervise police personnel.

Roberg, Roy R. and Jack Kuykendall (1990). *Police Organization and Management.* Pacific Grove, CA: Brooks/Cole Publishing Company.

> Explores performance appraisal in terms of evaluation categories, standards and measurements and evaluation problems (errors). Performance appraisal is viewed, in a sense, as a component of the career enhancement process.

References

Behn, Robert D. (1994). "Motivating Without Rewards: A Challenge to Public Managers." *Governing,* Vol. 7, No. 8.

Bittel, Lester R. and John W. Newstrom (1990). *What Every Supervisor Should Know*, 6th ed. New York: McGraw-Hill Book Company.

Chruden, Herbert J. and Arthur W. Sherman, Jr. (1976). *Personnel Management.* Cincinnati, OH: South-Western Publishing Company.

Fulmer, Robert M. (1988). *The New Management,* 4th ed. New York: Macmillan Publishing Co.

Gaines, Larry K., Victor E. Kappeler and Joseph B. Vaughn (1994). *Policing in America.* Cincinnati, OH: Anderson Publishing Co.

Gaines, Larry K., Mittie D. Southerland and John E. Angell (1991). *Police Administration.* New York: McGraw-Hill Book Company.

Hamblin, Ken (1994). "Why the Surprise at Crime Bill's Catch-22?" *The Denver Post,* Oct. 23: 3F.

Hilgert, Raymond L. and Theo Haimann (1991). *Supervision: Concepts and Practices of Management,* 5th ed. Cincinnati, OH: South-Western Publishing Company.

Holden, Richard W. (1994). *Modern Police Management,* 2nd ed. Englewood Cliffs, NJ: Prentice-Hall, Inc.

Holt, David H., (1990). *Management: Principles and Practices,* 2nd ed. Englewood Cliffs, NJ: Prentice-Hall, Inc.

Iannone, Nathan F. (1994). *Supervision of Police Personnel,* 5th ed. Englewood Cliffs, NJ: Prentice-Hall, Inc.

Kennish, John W. (1994). "Managing: Motivating With a Positive, Participatory Policy." *Security Management,* Vol. 38, No. 8.

Leonard, V.A. and Harry W. More (1993). *Police Organization and Management,* 8th ed. Westbury, NY: The Foundation Press, Inc.

McGaney, Robert and Scott Smith (1993). "When Workers Rate the Boss." *Training,* March.

Plunkett, Richard W. (1992). *Supervision: The Direction of People at Work,* 6th ed. Boston: Allyn and Bacon, Inc.

Robbins, Stephen P. (1989). *Organizational Behavior,* 4th ed. Englewood Cliffs, NJ: Prentice-Hall, Inc.

Steinmetz, Lawrence L. and H. Ralph Todd, Jr. (1992). *Supervision: First-Line Management,* 5th ed. Boston: Richard D. Irwin, Inc.

Swanson, Charles R., Leonard Territo and Robert W. Taylor (1993). *Police Administration,* 3rd ed. New York: Macmillan Publishing Co.

Trojanowicz, Robert G. (1980). *The Environment of the First-Line Police Supervisor.* Englewood Cliffs, NJ: Prentice-Hall, Inc.

United States Government (1973). *The Police.* Washington, DC: National Advisory Commission on Criminal Justice Standards and Goals.

U.S. Department of Justice (1994). *Sourcebook of Criminal Justice Statistics.* Washington, DC: Bureau of Justice Statistics.

Walsh, William F. and Edwin J. Donovan (1990). *The Supervision of Police Personnel: A Performance-Based Approach.* Dubuque, IA: Kendall/Hunt Publishing Company.

Whetstone, Thomas S. (1994). "Subordinates Evaluate Supervisory and Administrative Performance." *The Police Chief,* Vol. LXI, No. 6.

Whisenand, Paul M. and George E. Rush (1993). *Supervising Police Personnel,* 2nd ed. Englewood Cliffs, NJ: Prentice-Hall, Inc.

Wycoff, Mary Ann and Timothy N. Oettmeier (1994). *Evaluating Patrol Officer Performance Under Community Policing: The Houston Experience.* Washington, DC: National Institute of Justice.

Team-Building—

Maximizing the Group Process 8

Introductory Case Study

Sergeant Katie Cease

Katie Cease has just been promoted to sergeant, an advancement she has anticipated with considerable pride. She has been on the force for six years, during which time she has been assigned to patrol. She has now been assigned to the midnight shift and is scheduled to supervise a team of officers in the highest crime area of town.

Sergeant Cease is the first woman in the department to be promoted to the position of first-line supervisor, and the team of officers she will supervise all have more field experience than she does. She knows she will be supervising a group of officers who have worked together for many years and will probably be looked upon as an outsider.

For years the department has had a policy allowing officers to select their beat assignment based upon seniority. Thus, the officers she is to command have chosen this particular beat assignment in the high crime area because this is where the action is, and they want to be right in the middle of this fast-moving operation. Each of the officers on the team personify the "macho" image of the real tough cop. They play the part to the hilt even to the extent of not fully complying with departmental rules and regulations. In fact, rules are ignored if they interfere with a much sought-after bust.

The first month in her new position has been somewhat uneventful, as the team interacts with her to see the kind of supervisor she will be. No one has challenged her authority and from the events she has observed, all the officers are following departmental policy when making arrests and performing other police duties. At the end of their shift, the officers get together at a coffee shop near the police building, but she has never been asked to join the group. She feels she is viewed strictly as the supervisor and not part of the team. In subtle ways it is quite obvious to her that she is tolerated but not accepted.

The only conduct by the team not in compliance with departmental policy, that she has observed, occurs when the officers congregate at an all-night restaurant, even though departmental policy states that only two officers will

be present in any restaurant at the same time. On various occasions she has observed as many as four officers taking a break at the same time. The restaurant is centrally located, so the officers on break never fail to respond to incidents immediately. From everything she has been able to observe, no one (officer or citizen) has been placed in jeopardy even though a policy is being violated.

Sergeant Cease realizes she must speak to the officers about the violation of department policy, even though it has not impaired their performance. The chief has recently emphasized the need to comply with the policy in order to reduce the number of complaints from the public about the large number of officers in a restaurant at the same time.

If you were Sergeant Cease, would you enforce the policy? If so, how would you go about it? What norm (if any) is influencing the conduct of the members of the team?

When dealing with human behavior, as a supervisor in a police organization, it is of foremost importance to acquire an understanding and working knowledge of group dynamics. Generally speaking, everyone has been involved with different groups such as the family, church, school, clubs or the military. Some of these groups are highly structured and others are informal and loosely organized. Some have had a substantial impact on the individual while others have had a limited influence.

A supervisor can function more effectively when fully aware of group processes. It is impossible to ignore groups in a law enforcement agency. They are a significant and integral component of the organization. The interrelationships between groups within an organization can be exceedingly complex, and strongly influence effectiveness.

A group consists of two or more people who interact with and influence each other for a common purpose. Two factors are important to the definition of a group: (1) interaction, and (2) influence.

The interaction of group members can be either extensive or limited. It can be based upon a close interrelationship between two or more officers or (at the other extreme) it can be distant to the point where there is no face-to-face contact. Even if there is some degree of contact between members, it might turn out that body language will prove to be the most important variable in the group process.

Influence is the second component of our definition and its impact may range from limited to extensive. Influence is generated by such things as position power, rank, experience, reputation or expertise. Individuals seldom exhibit behavior not influenced by the group to which they belong. For many, individual success depends upon one's ability to get along within the group.

The Individual

Socialization into the police agency is the means by which rookies are transformed from civilian status to productive members of an operating agency. It is the means whereby the new employee is indoctrinated into (and acquires the values and norms of) the organization.

The police occupation, for the majority of officers, is not only demanding but requires a positive identification with the police task and fellow police officers. This can occur even to the point where there is a degree of paranoia and the job becomes one of "it's us or them." It is the thin blue line against the world.

The job itself socializes the officer because it is highly circumscribed by law. If that is not enough, there are always policies, rules and regulations tending to influence beliefs, attitudes, values and actual behavior. Additionally, the organizational structure designates a formal reporting relationship, groups individuals, and serves to facilitate communications (Johnson, 1994).

The new candidate for a police position interacts with the police social system from the point of initial contact when applying for a position through the socialization occurring throughout one's career. The new employee is expected to adjust to the organization: under no circumstances is the organization allowed to adjust to the individual.

The officer adapts to the police value system and this is the only acceptable conduct allowed. In other words, this obedience is the price that must be paid to become a member of the organization. The agency will generally require officers to acquire norms, values and specific behavior that emerge from (Tosi, 1976):

1. Organizational goals.

2. Approved means utilized to achieve goals.

3. Individual responsibility as defined by the agency.

4. Behavior patterns required as a part of performance.

5. Policy, rules and regulations that maintain the organization.

The police academy is a significant point in the new officer's career socialization process as this is where identity with the occupation is emphasized (Bahn, 1984). In the academy, conformity is emphasized throughout the process and new officers are molded in such a way as to become the visible expression of the ideal cop. It is somewhat of a cookie-cutter mentality in which the candidate is expected to dress appropriately, accept authority, never criticize the agency and become a member of the team. The expression of individuality is rejected. There is usually one best way to do things—the way it is taught at the academy.

Upon completion of the academy, the officer may be coached by a Field Training Officer (FTO) or at least by a senior officer; thus the socialization process continues and the norms of the agency are emphasized. At the same

time the peer value system comes into play. This, in some instances, is where new police officers are told "now that you are in the real world, this is how we actually do things rather than the way you were taught in the academy." Identification with the department, rather than with the community, serves to isolate the officer and reinforce police solidarity.

In recent years there seems to be less organization effectiveness in promoting and reinforcing a strong and viable police identity. Various reasons have been suggested to explain why the current recruits are not adjusting to the agency as they have in the past. First, it is seldom possible for every member to go along with all the group norms (Cohen, Fink, Gadon, Willits, and Josefowitz, 1992). Next, the average recruit today is older and, in many instances, has greater work experience and more education. Third, the standards for entry into the field have been modified by affirmative action, so the ethnic mix of some departments has changed drastically. Finally, the recruitment of women is altering a previously male-dominated occupation. Each factor contributes in varying degrees to the impact of the individual's socialization process and to the perceived weakening of the police identity.

Even though there is an indication that the identity of the individual to the department is not as strong as in the past, it is still an important factor because it is a means of building commitment and creating a feeling of loyalty to the department. Esprit de corps and high morale are by-products of the socialization process. Thus, the more committed the individual becomes to the agency, the sooner the possibility that he or she will become a full-fledged member of the organization.

The Individual and the Group

Within the context of the day-to-day work environment, the police officer will (in many instances) work alone. However, police departments are becoming increasingly aware of the benefits to be obtained from the use of groups of officers as team task forces or quality control circles.

In reality, the department is a social organization and by creating groups, a sense of belonging can develop, there is an attachment to the agency, and officers are provided a sense of stability. Groups do not automatically prove to be more effective than individuals when performing certain tasks. Everyone is aware of the cliche "too many cooks can spoil the broth." Thus, there are some situations in which the group approach to problem solving is best, and other instances where an individual effort will prove most effective.

It is readily apparent that some police tasks are most effectively accomplished by a joint response to the situation. A barricaded individual or a house-to-house search for a lost child are examples. It would be difficult to accomplish such tasks in any other way than a coordinated group effort.

In this approach to management, it is the primary responsibility of a supervisor to achieve results through people. It is impossible for a good supervisor to

perform all tasks without the assistance of others. Thus, interaction with others to obtain positive results is imperative. In this context the human being is important and the supervisor can have a positive influence on the individual and their work effectiveness as a part of a group. A positive leader excels in obtaining active individual involvement, bringing commitment to achieving both unit and departmental goals.

As the law enforcement function has become increasingly complex, the supervisor soon discovers a lack of knowledge in some areas; therefore, every decision may not prove to be sound. The interaction with other units such as tactical, traffic sections or the investigative division ordains the supervisor to be dependent upon their information and knowledge if goals are to be attained. Interaction is essential (especially if the decision impacts upon more than one unit of the organization) and both individual and group knowledge must be tapped if the best decision is to be made.

Unquestionably, some individuals have difficulty in adapting to groups due to their personality, the specific situation or even variables unknown to the supervisor. Nevertheless a reduction in conflict between the individual and the organization must constantly be the goal. When considering the relationship between the individual and the group, the supervisor should consider the following (Cartwright and Lippitt, 1957):

1. Groups, both formal and informal, will always exist within an organization.

2. Groups can become power centers that will have an important impact on the agency.

3. Groups can be both destructive and supportive.

4. An understanding of group dynamics will enhance the achievement of goals.

The individual is an essential part of the group. The more knowledge a supervisor accumulates about each member, the greater the opportunity for effective work with the group.

Role and Function of the Group

If a supervisor is to understand how an organization actually operates, it is essential to develop an acute awareness of how a group functions. This is especially critical for the first-line supervisor position. While a great deal of a sergeant's time is spent with individual officers, it must be kept in mind that those officers belong to one or more groups. When a supervisor understands the interaction between individuals and groups, it will (in all probability) lead to more effective problem solving (Gray, 1984).

When considering organizational behavior, groups can usually be described as either formal or informal.

Formal Groups

Formal work groups are those created and supported by the organization for the express purpose of fulfilling specific organizational needs or performing special tasks. These groups can be either temporary or permanent, depending upon the needs of the organization. A shift of officers under the supervision of a sergeant is an excellent example of a command group or team. Another example is a group created to function as a sting operation for purchasing stolen property. This undercover operation culminates with the arrest and prosecution of the accused.

The assignment of officers to a special traffic detail, for conducting a roadblock, in an effort to identify drivers who are impaired, is another example of a work group set up by the organization, and then dissolved after its task has been accomplished.

Another type of formal work group becoming increasingly common in law enforcement is the task force. It is usually a temporary group formed for achieving a specific objective or performing a definite task. In recent years, larger police departments have set up special task forces to investigate serial murders. In some instances, the task force has involved the coordinated efforts of more than one agency.

Narcotics task forces are being used increasingly in joint efforts, normally within a county, and usually are formed on a permanent basis. Temporary task forces have been utilized to deal with a wide range of problems including the development of policies or the creation of rules and regulations. In one instance, a task force consisting of nine members drawn from various units and levels of the organization was chaired by a lieutenant with the expressed purpose of determining when an officer should or should not wear a hat when in uniform.

Informal Groups

While the formal work groups are quite obvious to any new employee, it takes a while to identify **informal groups**. In many instances, these groups have never been sanctioned by the formal organization. It is also interesting to note that informal groups cut across organizational lines—rank is usually not important when forming an informal group membership. For example, an informal group can be composed of individuals who have a common interest, such as pistol shooting, where they get together for the pure enjoyment of the sport. This group is not sanctioned by the department.

Informal groups form quite naturally, according to personal preferences. A variety of personal relationships will be established by officers as they search for

a means of fulfilling their needs. Informal groups evolve as a result of the inability of the formal organization to meet all social or departmental officer requirements. Such groups can work to support or not to support the formal organization.

Workers become members of informal groups for varying reasons such as to improve working conditions, or they band together in an effort to obtain equipment to enhance job performance. In one department a group of officers worked together in an effort to set up a shift rotation system rather than the current system, based upon seniority. Some might argue then, that the majority of police unions have evolved from informal groups.

Informal groups, in many instances, also have proven to be most supportive of the formal organization. This is particularly noticeable when officers assist each other in performing tasks supposedly to be performed by another officer, or when they have shown there is a better way of doing something. One observer pointed out that in many instances, if it was not for such activities, the organization would undoubtedly perform less effectively.

Another informal group can be based solely upon social needs for friendship and interaction with others. Such a relationship can effectively support task accomplishment, reduce absenteeism and elevate job satisfaction. On the other hand, the social interaction between members of a group can occur to such an extent that it distracts them from getting work done. One of the most common examples is the coffee or smoke break, suddenly extending from a 15-minute break to 20 minutes and then half an hour.

There are some informal groups that control the rate of production. This seems to occur most often in such areas as the number of field interrogations performed by an officer or the number of traffic citations issued. Beware of those who work too hard or those whose production clearly exceeds the norm for a shift of officers constantly interacting. There is nothing wrong with competition, but one should never do anything to make another officer look bad. The group will bring pressure upon anyone who does not abide by the accepted code of behavior. Punishment of nonconforming officers usually takes the form of excluding them from after hours social events (Cohen, Fink, Gadon, Willits, and Josefowitz, 1992).

Informal groups can evolve into **cliques**—something a supervisor should be aware of. Cliques can easily lead to misunderstandings and hostility (Gastil, 1993). Cliques are generally described as one of three types: vertical, horizontal or random.

Vertical Cliques. This type of clique generally occurs in one unit of the police department such as patrol or investigation. The relationship is generally between the first-line supervisor and subordinate officers.

The supervisor in this type of clique does everything possible to assist and protect underlings. When it is necessary to demand something from an officer, the request is temporized as much as possible. When errors are made, they are disregarded or everything possible is done to minimize the problem. The goal

is to humanize the organization and reduce friction between the department and the officers.

This clique is not a one-way street. The officers also look out for the welfare of the first-line supervisor. If there is a threatening situation, the supervisor is made aware of the incident immediately. For example, when a manager of higher rank appears unannounced, the word is instantly relayed back to the supervisor.

Officers also apprise the sergeant of all situations that might cause trouble or generate waves, such as any type of occurrence to which the press will respond.

Horizontal Cliques. This type of clique differs from the vertical inasmuch as it cuts across departmental lines and will normally include a number of first-line supervisors. This clique will function either defensively or offensively depending upon the situation and the nature of the threat. If the threat is imminent, the clique will take an aggressive posture, but prefers to work defensively because of the bureaucratic nature of most police departments. The horizontal clique functions effectively under most circumstances because of the experience its members have acquired from working within the bureaucracy.

This clique functions most effectively when it is dealing with problems perceived as weakening someone's authority or creating some type of change, which is looked upon as being inimical to its members' welfare. New policies eroding operational authority are always suspect. This might include instituting new review procedures when making felony arrests and reducing the first-line supervisor's power. The expansion of controls from above is considered fair game in terms of the type of issue with which this clique should be concerned.

The horizontal clique generally assumes a defensive posture and only functions when the situation dictates that it must respond to ensure the status quo. It is generally more powerful than the vertical clique and it can be utilized effectively by a first-line supervisor when the issue is of general interest. This is especially true when it involves such issues as a reduction in authority, an expansion of review procedures, a significant reorganization or a reduction in force.

Random Cliques. This type of clique bears no similarity to the other two types of cliques. Rank, role and unit assignment have no bearing in terms of its membership. Officers become members for the primary purpose of exchanging information. There is no effort by its members to strive for a change in working conditions, just a basic desire to associate with other members of the department.

In most departments, members of this clique are not active members of either the horizontal or vertical cliques. The random clique proves to be important to the first-line supervisor because it is usually the primary source of rumors. It can be utilized to pass on information or as an information source. It serves a highly important function by intensifying social relationships within the department. The officers who get together at the end of the shift for a beer or a meal are an excellent illustration of a random clique.

Group Development Process

As a newly-organized group evolves, it passes through six **stages**: orientation, conflict and challenge, cohesion, delusion, disillusion and acceptance (Jewell and Reitz, 1981). In some instances the process can be rather fast, but in other situations the evolution from stage one to stage six might never occur. It all depends upon a number of variables including difficulty of the task, the maturity of the group, and the time and resources allocated to the group (See Figure 8.1).

The initial stage, *orientation*, can be most crucial to the group's success. Thus, the supervisor should do everything possible to properly prepare for the beginning meeting so as to ensure as many members as possible are fully aware of the ground rules. Questions such as who is the head of the group, what procedures are to be followed, and what the reason is for the existence of the group need to be answered to clarify ground rules. New members of a group want to know what is going on and what is expected of them.

Figure 8.1
Group Development Stages

Number	Stage
1	Orientation
2	Conflict and Challenge
3	Cohesion
4	Delusion
5	Disillusion
6	Acceptance

The *conflict and challenge* stage may occur almost immediately and is a result of the ambiguity arising in any group. It is normal to anticipate that the leader of the group will be challenged as procedures for conducting meetings are agreed upon.

Stage three is *cohesion* and occurs when each member of the group has received enough information to accept group objectives and the leadership as legitimate. If the problem to be considered and resolved by a group is controversial, or the group is highly polarized, cohesion might never occur. But if a great deal of care is taken when the composition of the group is decided, the potentiality for reaching stage three will be enhanced. Cohesiveness can be enhanced by creating a working relationship where employees feel their values and those of the organization are aligned (Kouzes and Posner, 1993).

Stage four, *delusion*, is the point where uncertainty enters the picture and members of the group become aware of the fact that everything is not moving smoothly and, in fact, the group has numerous interpersonal problems. In some instances, members will go along with the group even though they disagree with the way things are being handled. Others will take the position that it is of no use to fight it because they cannot change anything anyway.

Stage five, *disillusion*, concerns a process whereby members of the group fully accept their being on a treadmill and are going nowhere. There is a polarization between members who want to confront issues and others who resist the process. It is at this point that strong leadership must exert itself, issues should be clarified and differences resolved. The supervisor should do everything possible to see this stage is passed through with the least amount of disruption and divisive turmoil.

The last stage is *acceptance*. It is the point at which a newly-organized group interacts positively, as it strives to achieve its assigned goals.

Group Norms

As a group evolves from the interaction of its members, **group norms** come into play. Norms are the techniques members of a group develop as a way of controlling the behavior of others. As members interact, initial norms are developed specifying the way members should conduct themselves. Members of a group soon learn the difference between acceptable and unacceptable behavior.

A supervisor is constantly responding to group norms and must deal with the conduct generated by them. Undeniably, norms exert a strong influence over the conduct of individuals. If officers are to perform effectively they must have some common areas of agreement around which to organize their attitudes, values and perceptions. In the absence of norms, the guidance necessary for success is nonexistent.

Norms are unwritten, but in many instances are more influential than organizational rules and regulations. Norms strongly influence conduct because they are backed by the power of the group in terms of some type of sanction when the situation calls for it. They not only set forth the type of acceptable behavior, but include the group's value judgment as to what is permissible and whether something is right or wrong.

Norms come into existence because of social interaction of the members of the group. In most instances norms are not established by any formal process nor are they consciously decided. Norms provide continuity in the work environment, the predictability of behavior that leads to a feeling of well-being, and the carrying out of routine procedures without disruption. A realistic evaluation of the importance of the group should lead to an awareness by the supervisor of each member's importance and the fact that groups have a definite impact on the behavior of each and every member.

Law Enforcement Norms

The identification of the norms in any particular agency proves to be difficult because certain departments will have some of the operational norms listed below while other departments will have all these norms as well as others not identified here (see Figure 8.2).

Figure 8.2
Law Enforcement Norms

Loyalty
Secrecy
Danger
Deadly Force
Isolation
Performance

Loyalty. Most police departments have a quasi-military structure, and the chain of command mentality is strongly entrenched (Johnson, 1994). Consequently, police departments exact a strong degree of loyalty from each and every member including non-sworn personnel. Extensive rules and regulations serve to reinforce this norm and specific sanctions apply to those who deviate from the expected behavior. Under most circumstances, loyalty applies to the police at large and is not restricted to the department to which an individual belongs.

Secrecy. The socialization process within a police department makes it abundantly clear that the "Code of Secrecy" is operational at all times and under no circumstances will officers discuss police procedures with outsiders or tell them how they cope with the demands of the occupation. While departmental policy may control conduct, the norm of secrecy coupled with that of loyalty dictates that one officer will never inform on another officer. This is true even though it might involve brutality by an officer. The secrecy norm even extends to all police incidents, and one officer never "turns in" another for sloppy work or failure to perform duties.

Danger. From the initial day at the academy through the termination of supervision by a Field Training Officer (FTO), the dangers of police work are continually emphasized. This is done to such an extent that many officers perceive almost every situation as potentially dangerous. Danger is reinforced by the social interaction between officers and it can reach the point where officers view the majority of the public with some degree of suspicion. This suspicion tends to strengthen the kinship felt between police officers and the concept of "we and they." Policing occurs in a dangerous (or at the very least an apprehensive) working environment. In 1991, 71 police officers were killed in the United States, and during a 14-year period (1978-1991) 1,137 officers were killed (Maguire, Pastore, and Flanagan, 1993).

Deadly Force. The only agent of government routinely having the authority to use physical force against citizens is the police. Unfortunately, numerous lives are taken by the police as we become an increasingly violent society (Couper, 1994). In a recent year it was estimated that 600 suspects were killed

by the police and approximately 1,200 were wounded. Most police use of deadly force occurs at night in public locations within high-crime areas of big cities. These incidents often involve on-duty, uniformed officers firing at suspects in the crime-prone ages of 17-30 (More, 1992).

Isolation. Law enforcement, as an occupation, leads to isolation from the community. Many view the police as a necessary evil. When you need them they are never there and when you commit a traffic infraction or violate a minor ordinance they are always present. Officers soon determine their work usually is not appreciated and the public they are supposed to protect is uncaring. This leads officers to turn inward for recognition and support. In time, many officers limit their socialization to other officers and their families. The more they are rejected by the members of the community the more they turn to their job and the police social system. Isolation reinforces clannishness and occupational solidarity.

Performance. The police are no different than other working groups in the sense that they have working norms that officers accept. In most instances it is not a question of restricting productivity because the work load is usually dictated by the dispatcher. In large cities, the demand is such that calls for service of a nonemergency nature are "stacked" until an officer can respond. Within this context, officers can control the number of cases they handle by being exceedingly meticulous when completing reports. Officers know what other officers are doing, so norms affecting performance come into existence. At other times, officers on the midnight shift will find the work flow can be very slow; thus, patrol can become exceedingly monotonous. In this situation officers will take long meal breaks, numerous coffee breaks, sleep if the opportunity presents itself or leave their beat to socialize with other officers. In other instances officers will violate departmental policy and congregate at certain eating establishments. One officer will advise another as to what is acceptable and what is not acceptable in terms of personal and work performance. The more cohesive the group, the greater the possibility that productivity will be controlled by establishing tolerance levels (Cohen, Fink, Gadon, Willits, and Josefowitz, 1992).

Group Performance

A supervisor's attitude toward the group and its ability to perform is critical to its success and the attainment of departmental objectives. If working with a group is viewed as forcing one to conform and is a process whereby one loses identity or where the individual is never allowed to excel, then it is a group doomed to failure.

There is no doubt that problems must be faced and dealt with before a group can become effective, but it should be accepted as a challenge. This is best done by cultivating a positive attitude toward groups. They should be viewed as a tool for bringing collective judgment together for the purpose of solving problems.

Exceptional performance can occur when the group utilizes its resources effectively and each officer is motivated to achieve. Groups have the potential for greater productivity for several reasons, including allowing officers to specialize and utilize their own unique skills.

Groups serve as a vehicle for enhancing personal relationships because social needs are more easily satisfied. Furthermore, as a group develops and becomes more close-knit, members of the group will obtain status. As they become more productive, recognition will be received from the group.

Cohesiveness can be important to the group and is the result of the officer's desire to be a member of the group and the degree of commitment felt by group members. If individuals satisfy their needs in a group, the group becomes something the officers seek out so they can become members. A group generating a high degree of cohesiveness finds its members are more loyal, they readily identify with the group, accept group decisions and are more apt to conform to group norms. Group cohesiveness is really evident when everyone is aware of their team spirit. If a positive outcome is generated by cohesiveness, it is the development of a workplace officers find more friendly and pleasant.

When a group performs successfully by attaining its objectives it becomes more cohesive. When there is a degree of positive participation and a great deal of communication, coupled with acquiescence to norms, the group will prove to be more successful. For many reasons, cohesiveness is a positive factor for a supervisor to cultivate, but this is only true when the group's goals are compatible with organizational objectives. For example, if a group of officers violate the rights of defendants as a means of achieving an agreed upon arrest standard, then cohesiveness can create a problem for a supervisor rather than serving as a factor integrating and energizing a group.

Cohesive groups can become an additional problem to first-line supervisors because they have more power than any single officer. A group of managers in a medium-sized police department successfully destroyed the effectiveness of a team policing program by resisting it in every way they could, because they felt their power and authority was threatened.

Notwithstanding the negative aspects of cohesiveness, the positive aspects are such that the supervisor should work diligently to create a working environment fostering the development of cohesiveness. The more cohesive the group is, the more apt they are to be highly productive.

Building a Winning Team

When the behavior of effective supervisors who have demonstrated the capacity to change a random collection of officers into a productive work unit is analyzed, it is obvious they perceive their role as being one where they wear many different hats. This includes those of coach, facilitator, developer and team builder (Garfield, 1986).

Effective **team-building** involves more than learning a few interpersonal skills. Team-building is a complex process that does not just happen, it takes a great deal of leadership and team effort.

A group leader who has proven to be effective generally exhibits the following types of behavior (Hellriegel, Slocum and Woodman, 1983):

1. Ability to focus continuously on a goal.

2. Participates in the group and at the same time observes the activities of the group as a detached leader.

3. Acknowledges the need for assuming primary responsibility for controlling the relationships between the group and other units or individuals.

4. Facilitates group members in the assumption of leadership roles when the situation dictates, because of changing group needs.

Numerous factors influence the effectiveness of the group including such things as the size of the group and norms, goals and environment in which the group operates. In every instance strong leadership can overcome limitations imposed by any of these factors. The goal of a supervisor should be to create a climate wherein the officers supervised develop to the point where they truly function as a team. Team-building does not just occur, but is the result of hard work and a consideration of the behavior of both the members of the group and the leader.

Effective Relationships

When supervising a group, it is best to determine an actual personal relationship to that group. At first it may seem this is a waste of time, but some members of the group do not view the supervisor the anticipated way. In fact, one might be surprised to find some view the supervisor as highly competent while others view that person as mediocre, and not someone to write home about. Then there may be others who either dislike or even despise a supervisor. Some may view the same supervisor as warm and understanding and some (at the other extreme) cold and indifferent. Whatever the truth, it is best to attempt to determine an exact personal status with each of the team members.

A supervisor can do this by approaching those with whom there is a close relationship and asking for their opinion. This should give some idea as to the supervisor's standing standing with the group. Then the supervisor should sit down and talk with each member of the group, certainly in the most relaxed environment to be found.

The opening statement when talking with a member of the team might be something like: "Your help is needed in solving a team problem." The initial

reaction might not be everything anticipated, but it is an opening and then numerous questions can be asked to determine the personal working relationship with team members (see Figure 8.3).

Figure 8.3
Questions for Determining Effective Relationships

1.	How can the performance of the team be improved?
2.	Is there an adequate sharing of information?
3.	Are the goals of the team clear?
4.	Is everyone allowed to participate in the decision-making process?
5.	Does everyone feel like a member of the team?
6.	Are all possible skills utilized by the team?
7.	Are meetings informative?
8.	Can meetings be more productive? How?
9.	Is planning adequate?
10.	Is everyone on the team treated with respect?
11.	Does the team have adequate resources to accomplish its task?

It is important to ask questions dealing with problems and not personalities. Solutions are needed, or, at the very least, the identification of problem areas. Once the concerns of other members of the team are determined the supervisor should review his or her own opinion regarding the matter in an attempt to resolve a problem. This can prove to be difficult, but it must be done, and every effort should be made to really understand everyone on the team, especially those one might dislike.

Personal judgments about other officers should never be allowed to interfere with team efforts. As a supervisor it is imperative to make every effort to see that team members agree to working together (Rogers, 1986). A great deal of time and effort can be expended on resolving problems between members, but such effort can be better spent on goal attainment. Intergroup conflict can be devastating. It is best dealt with by a supervisor who becomes thoroughly knowledgeable about the needs of each team member and works to meet their needs and reduce conflict with organizational needs.

The development of positive personal relationships takes time; it cannot be done overnight. It can also be frustrating and one might never reach the stage needed to have a smooth-functioning team. But it is a goal worth striving for and the rewards will usually outweigh the disappointments. Every effort should be made to eventually have a team that is self-managed (Grossman and Doherty, 1994).

Size of the Team

The larger the team of officers, the more difficult it is to create a positive work environment leading to esprit de corps and a cohesive working unit (Gray, 1984). The smaller the size of the unit, the greater the potential for interaction between each member of the group. Also, group norms are more easily developed in a small group and have a greater impact on group activities.

There is no magic number where a group changes from small to large, but it would seem to be in the area of 10 members. This is evident particularly in patrol, where officers usually function independently. In a selection of departments from a nationwide survey, it was found the number of officers supervised by a sergeant ranged from 4.5 to 16.6 and the average team consisted of slightly more than eight members (Police Foundation, 1981).

The same study reflected that when departments had tactical units, the number of officers supervised by a sergeant ranged from 4.5 to 10.6 and the average team had slightly more than seven members. In the same study, out of 61 departments, it was found that 22 percent of the tactical units were supervised by a sergeant. The majority of departments serving cities with populations under 75,000 fell into this group (Police Foundation, 1981).

Group identity and team spirit are a reflection of the size of a team; consequently, it is recommended that teams be kept under 10 members whenever possible as a means of fostering cohesiveness within the group.

Interaction

One of the most difficult things for a supervisor to do, when assigned to patrol, is to create a sufficient number of times when officers can interact. In many departments this is limited to roll call, and can become a one-way communication process unless the sergeant makes a sincere effort to create an atmosphere fostering interaction.

When new policies are discussed, ample time should be allowed for determining their impact on operations or the conduct of employees. This necessitates a follow-up by the sergeant on a one-to-one basis when officers are supervised in the field. If the policy proves to be somewhat ambiguous or subject to varying interpretations it should be discussed not only at the next roll call meeting but (if there is sufficient need) at a special meeting of the team.

If adequate time cannot be found during working hours, the supervisor should hold meetings outside the job. This technique should be used sparingly and only when the situation dictates. The scheduling of officers' time should be such that there is adequate time for group interaction (Gray, 1984).

Case Study

Sergeant Ralph Dart

Newly promoted, Ralph Dart (a team supervisor) had been an agent for the last seven years. Previously he was in patrol. As an agent, he investigated crimes against persons; consequently, he was familiar with the work of the majority of the officers who were assigned to his team. He had either read their preliminary investigation reports or worked with them during the investigation of an offense.

Of the nine officers he was to supervise, each had been in patrol for a minimum of six years and each perceived him or herself as an accomplished officer, capable of handling any situation. Sergeant Dart heard through the grapevine the officers on his team viewed him as a good investigator, but they had serious doubts as to whether he would turn out to be a good supervisor.

Dart's predecessor was promoted to lieutenant and had a reputation of being an outstanding supervisor, always showing an intense interest in the welfare of the officers he supervised. He had been well liked by the officers on the team and they were as protective of him as he had been of them. Dart knows he is going to have a difficult time filling the shoes of his predecessor. He also knows he has a tough job cut out for himself if he is to gain the confidence of the members of his team.

Sergeant Dart knows he is faced with a difficult task and he has decided that, in order to establish an effective working relationship with the team, he has to do something immediately. He fully realizes there is not going to be the normal "honeymoon" period while he adjusts to the team and the members of the team adjust to him.

How would you go about resolving the problem faced by Sergeant Dart? What would you do initially and how would you follow this up?

Controversy and Conflict

Controversy within a group is inevitable and should be handled openly. When a disagreement occurs it should be discussed with all members of the team in a forthright manner. Keep in mind that disagreements are a normal consequence of the interaction between team members. Above all discuss issues, not personalities. This allows team members to deal with facts, and reduces the nature and degree of emotional response.

A supervisor should endeavor to respectfully treat every member's opinion. Try to never show favoritism toward any particular member's opinions over those of others. In other words, a supervisor should be as impartial and fair as possible.

One should work diligently to spot potential problems and personality clashes before they occur by being aware of everything happening and dealing with

undercurrents. A good way to do this is to constantly interact with every team member and, above all, LISTEN. There is a lot more to be learned this way than can ever be learned from communication that can easily become one-way rather than two-way (Rogers, 1986).

If conflict has occurred, or is possible, one should deal with it immediately—do not wait. Conflict can lead to the creation of factions within a team as well as misunderstanding, a reduction in cooperation and destruction of team morale.

A supervisor should identify and (if at all possible) eliminate conflict before it occurs. The best strategy is to encourage controversy and discourage discord.

Team Goals

A first-line supervisor should set a clear-cut sense of direction for the team. There should be no doubt concerning where they are going and how they are going to achieve objectives. Priorities must be established and there should be no room for misinterpretations. Each and every member of the team should know specifically what is expected of them and what their responsibilities will include. Above all every goal should be truly meaningful (Cox and Hoover, 1992).

Whenever possible, one should stress what has to be accomplished in terms facilitating measurability and, above all, the objectives should be achievable. If there are risks involved, or if it is questionable that goals can be achieved, this must be communicated and allowances specified. An example would be the setting forth of a team objective as follows (Leonard and More, 1993):

> Objective: Decrease the incidence of resisting arrest during the next calendar year by 15 percent.
>
> Means:
>
> 1. Implement a 25-hour training session (one-half hour twice a week) to be held from January 1st through June 30th.
> 2. Implement a training course that emphasizes physical fitness/ self-defense.
> 3. Implement a training program that addresses the psychology of arrest.
>
> Measures:
>
> 1. Percent decrease in charges of resisting arrest.
> 2. Decrease in the number of officers injured when making an arrest.
> 3. Decrease in citizen complaints.

The supervisor can facilitate goal attainment by ensuring that all necessary information is shared. There is no room for secretiveness or hidden agendas. When there is openness and issues are discussed candidly, the framework is laid

for the development of a cohesive group. When everyone knows what is going on and they are privy to all the information needed to do their work, it reinforces team spirit (Tarkenton, 1986).

Group Problem Solving

In recent years, the police field has turned to the group as one process to be utilized effectively in solving problems. The group is commonly known as a **task force** and is distinguished from other groups because it is usually temporary in nature and focuses its attention on one subject or problem. The task force has been especially useful in dealing with problems impacting on the whole department such as a policy for the use of roadblocks in an emergency or the selection of a new handgun.

It is widely accepted that groups can be highly productive when it is necessary to generate many ideas, recall information accurately or evaluate uncertain situations (Hellriegel, Slocum and Woodman, 1983). The role of the supervisor is to maximize the advantages inherent in group decisionmaking, so the best possible decision is reached.

Another advantage of a task force is the greater likelihood of the final solution being implemented because of the involvement of a cross section of the department (Bellman, 1992). The involvement of individuals in the task force from various units throughout the department enhances the awareness of how others function. This leads to better coordination as the members work to achieve organizational goals (see Figure 8.4).

Figure 8.4
Advantages of a Task Force

1. Decisionmaking improved.
2. Greater acceptance of the decision.
3. Coordination improved.
4. Problems viewed from a broader perspective.
5. Power shared.

Task forces can serve as vehicles for training employees as they learn how to work with others and arrive at a decision based upon consensus. This process is in sharp contrast to many police situations where the officer makes a decision, usually independent of immediate supervision. The officer is expected to command the situation. Such group interaction forces its members to think of broader issues and their implication to the whole agency. Finally, the task force serves as a vehicle for power sharing. Members have the opportunity to express their

opinion and they become a part of the decision-making process. Just the establishment of the task force reduces the power of the individual who has authorized its existence.

There are, of course, disadvantages that may occur when a task force is created. A supervisor should review these carefully and try to avoid them. An individual can come to a task force assignment with a complaint and defend this position at all costs, never giving the slightest consideration to alternative solutions. Such an individual can serve as a disrupting influence, so the supervisor must demonstrate strong leadership skills by structuring the meetings in such a way that all sides of an issue are discussed.

Another situation that works to a supervisor's disadvantage occurs when one individual exerts an exceptional amount of influence on the team, to the point where the total decision-making process is impaired or disrupted. In some instances, individuals who have a higher rank, or have a great deal of expertise in an area under consideration, influence the process excessively (Davidson, 1986).

From time to time a task force will have a member who dominates every meeting. This domination usually does not stem from rank, expertise or bias, but from the personality of the individual. It can be due to the individual's charisma, but is more apt to be based upon exceptional interpersonal skills the person has developed. One technique useful to a supervisor faced with dealing with such an individual is to encourage others to express their opinions by directing specific questions to them, and asking other members to summarize issues and positions. If techniques such as this do not work, it will be necessary for the supervisor to meet privately with the disruptive member and firmly establish ground rules for subsequent meetings.

When a task force makes a recommendation, it is based upon the judgment of the group. Consequently, task force members usually take the position that they are not individually responsible for the final decision. There is little a supervisor can do about this particular disadvantage but to accept it as an inherent disadvantage (see Figure 8.5).

Figure 8.5
Disadvantages of a Task Force

1. Bias of members can be intensified.
2. Excessive influence of individuals with rank or expertise.
3. Domination by a member of the group.
4. Diffused responsibility.
5. Cost in terms of time and money.

Finally, it is necessary to consider the cost of including officers in the decision-making process. In one law enforcement agency, the cost per hour for a patrol officer, including all benefits, is $30. Just stop and think how fast that can

add up with a task force of nine officers plus the sergeant in charge of the task force, whose cost is $45 per hour. The cost then for each hour of meeting will be $315. In summation, a task force taking ten hours to reach a decision will cost $3,150. If the meetings are held during working hours there has been a loss of 100 man hours of work that could have been devoted to other police tasks.

Undoubtedly, task forces can contribute to the effective management of an agency, but each time they are established, consideration should be given to the expenses involved. The benefits should outweigh the costs.

Conducting a Meeting

An important function with which a supervisor must immediately become acquainted is conducting effective meetings. Meetings are viewed by many as an exercise in futility and a total waste of time. Clearly some meetings are unproductive and costly in terms of time and money.

Supervisors can learn skills to utilize a task force in such a way that problems can be resolved and solutions recommended. It is a team leader's function to perform as a facilitator. Every effort should be made to draw out the best in people and create a working environment maximizing problem solving (Tarkenton, 1986).

A supervisor should start out on the right foot by clearly establishing ground rules at the initial meeting. Information should be set forth as to how often meetings will be held. Subsequently, the nature of the problem should be identified, and the authority set forth. It is also best to state the various subjects not included within the authority of the task force, such as grievances or personnel matters. If the group is merely to present a recommendation (rather than make a final decision), the facts should be set forth so misunderstandings concerning the reasons for forming the task force are eliminated.

After the above issues have been clarified, it is necessary to outline specific rules to utilize in governing each session. The group should participate in this process reaching conclusions regarding such basic issues as: (1) Starting the meeting on time; (2) Closing the meeting on time; (3) Members will not be interrupted when they are presenting their views; (4) Ideas will not be criticized; (5) Agendas will be prepared and given to each member before the meeting; and (6) Members will be treated as equals regardless of rank or seniority. The extensiveness of these ground rules depends upon the composition of the group and the nature of the problem to be resolved (Tarkenton, 1986).

It cannot be emphasized too strongly that the above rules are decided upon by the group, not imposed by the leader. Consensus is important and greatly facilitates the decision-making process inasmuch as members have a greater commitment to rules when they have been involved in their development.

While experts vary in their judgment concerning conducting the meeting, it would seem at the very least, a leader should (Watson, 1992):

1.   State the problem in a straightforward manner without any indication of a solution.

2.   Provide all necessary data and information pertinent to the problem under consideration.

3.   Encourage the presentation of all ideas.

4.   Never ask leading questions.

5.   Never make specific recommendations including a solution to the problem.

6.   Ask questions to stimulate discussion.

7.   Summarize and clarify.

8.   Set the time and date for the next meeting.

9.   Close each meeting on a positive note.

One of the most difficult problems for a meeting leader is to deal fairly and justly with every member. The leader must control those attempting to dominate meetings (especially those who talk just for the sake of talking) and whose verbosity exceeds their knowledge. One way to do this is to set a time limit for each presentation or set up a rotation system for presentations.

A definite barrier to effective group communication can easily occur if members will not enter into the discussion because they are unwilling to oppose the opinion of someone with higher rank, or if they are uncertain their judgment will be accepted. The reason for noncommunication is unimportant; however, the situation must be controlled, preferably by structuring every meeting to ensure the maximum participation by everyone. When a group member seems reluctant to state opinions, specific questions can be asked to stimulate that person's participation.

Those who might attempt to dominate the meeting can be scheduled as the last participants. The same might be done for those who have rank or seniority. It is essential for the overall group working environment to exude positiveness and straightforwardness so members feel free to express ideas even though they might conflict with the opinion of others (Gray, 1984).

Another potential inhibiting factor for the leader is *groupthink*. This is a deliberating style that can be used by members when consensus is more important than arriving at the best solution. Generally, discussion is limited to reviewing a limited number of alternatives while the consequences of the decision are ignored. Another groupthink characteristic is the extensive amount of time spent justifying the decision.

Groupthink can be effectively handled by selecting someone in the group to be the devil's advocate, to seriously question the solution. The position of criti-

cal evaluator should be rotated within the membership. Having the group identify and review the weaknesses of the solution one by one might be helpful. Finally, the leader can bring in experts to present their position.

With imagination and ingenuity, a group leader can maximize the positive aspects of group decisionmaking and negate the objectionable. Excellent decisions can be made by groups so the leader should strive for consensus, as this provides a basis of support for a decision.

Summary

Groups are a significant and integral part of a law enforcement agency. Unquestionably, they can either help or hinder the functions of the department. For purposes of this discussion a group has been defined as two or more people who interact with and influence each other for a common purpose.

A new officer interacts with the police social system from the time the initial application is filed until retirement. The department expects each officer to acquire the norms, values and behavior compatible with organizational goals and policy.

Within a police department, both formal and informal groups will always exist. They can become power centers within the organization. Groups can be either destructive or supportive, but properly managed, they will contribute to the achievement of departmental goals.

Formal work groups are created for the specific purpose of performing special tasks varying from such groupings as the Investigative Unit to a Sting Unit. In recent years, task forces have come into existence. They are usually temporary and created to perform a single task such as developing a plan for a departmental reorganization or investigating a case involving a serial murderer.

Informal groups are formed because of the natural human desire of most officers to interact with each other. They can either support or detract from the attainment of organizational goals, and can evolve into cliques such as vertical, horizontal or random.

A newly-organized group will normally pass through the following six stages: orientation, conflict and challenge, cohesion, delusion, disillusion, and acceptance. The speed with which a group passes through these stages depends upon a number of variables including the difficulty of the task, the maturity of the members of the group, and the time and resources allocated to them.

Norms peculiar to law enforcement include loyalty, secrecy, danger, isolation and performance. These norms and their intensity will vary from agency to agency, and may even be nonexistent in some departments. Cohesiveness is a very desirable trait that can be cultivated, so a supervisor should work diligently to create a working environment fostering its development. The more cohesive the group, the more likely it is to be highly productive.

In building a winning team, a supervisor should assume the role of coach, facilitator, developer and team builder. Tasks to be performed by a supervisor include developing effective relationships, limiting the size of the team to under 11

members, creating time for positive interaction with each member, constructively handling controversy and conflict, and carefully identifying team goals.

Group problem solving in law enforcement has been facilitated by the development of temporary task forces to resolve special issues or problems. The advantages of a task force definitely outweigh the disadvantages in contributing to effective management.

There are definite skills a supervisor can learn in order to improve the quality of decisions made in team meetings. With imagination and ingenuity, a group leader can maximize the positive aspects of group decisionmaking while negating the undesirable.

Case Study

Sergeant Chet Johnston

Sergeant Chet Johnston had been a first-line supervisor assigned to patrol for a period of four years. He is one of five sergeants who have just completed a 40-hour training course on team policing. Having finished his BS degree, majoring in administration of justice, he feels well prepared, from a training viewpoint, to be a party to the implementation of team policing.

Sergeant Johnston has been transferred to the swing shift and has nine officers on the team (seven men and two women) whose field experience ranges from one year to 12 years, with an average length of six years. Four of the newer officers have college degrees, while the remainder have completed high school.

When reviewing the list of officers to assign to the team, Chet noted he has worked with all but three of the officers, so he already knows of several existing potential problems. One problem concerns Officer Clyde Chase, who has 12 years of experience and has failed to pass the sergeant's test twice. Consequently, Chase has become a sour and recalcitrant person. He expresses, without hesitation or reservation, that management "has it in for him." He points out to everyone who will listen that he is the best street cop in the department.

Sergeant Johnston feels Chase will (in all probability) prove to be a problem by opposing the concept of team policing and disrupting team meetings.

Two of the officers are rather new, so they are still hesitant to enter into discussions or take a position on anything controversial. One thing Johnston hopes to do is to ensure that the two new members of the team do not come under Chase's influence. He feels he might be able to do this by working closely with them.

Sergeant Johnston is preparing for the first scheduled meeting of the team. It is set for the following Tuesday at 2:00 p.m. (before the start of the shift), and the officers will be paid overtime.

If you were Johnston what would you do to prepare for the meeting? How would you open the meeting? What would you do to control Officer Chase? What would you do to maximize the participation of all the officers?

Key Concepts

cliques
formal groups
group norms
group performance
group problem solving
importance of the individual
individual and the group

informal groups
role of the group
stages of group development
task force
team-building
team meetings

Discussion Topics and Questions

1. Who is more important in decisionmaking: the individual or the group? Why?

2. What should a supervisor be concerned about when dealing with groups?

3. Compare vertical and horizontal cliques.

4. How can a supervisor work effectively with the informal group?

5. How should a supervisor deal with controversy and conflict?

6. What is groupthink?

For Further Reading

Cohen, Allan R., Stephen L. Fink, Herman Gadon, Robin D. Willits and Natasha Josefowitz (1992). *Effective Behavior in Organizations*, 5th ed., Homewood, IL: Richard D. Irwin, Inc.

> Presents an excellent discussion of the work group, cohesiveness in groups, differentiation in groups and methods for developing group effectiveness. Of particular interest is a discussion of values and norms. Finally, there is a detailed discussion of how to maximize intergroup cooperation.

Couper, David C. (1994). "Seven Seeds for Policing." *FBI Law Enforcement Bulletin*, Vol. 63, No. 3.

> This article briefly reviews seven factors influencing contemporary law enforcement. These include, leadership, knowledge, creativity, problem solving, diversity, control of force and community policing. All these have a relationship to team-building.

Gastil, John (1993). *Democracy in Small Groups: Participation, Decision Making and Communication*. Philadelphia: New Society Publishers.

> This book presents a good discussion of the meaning of democracy with a special emphasis on democracy in small groups. A chapter on this subject discusses group power, inclusiveness, commitment, relationships, deliberation and listening. There are a number of small group exercises concerning issues central to small group democracy.

Watson, Jane (1992). *The Minute Taker's Handbook*. North Vancouver, British Columbia: International Self-Counsel Press Ltd.

> Presents a detailed discussion of the role of a meeting leader. Lists 20 things that the leader should do in order to conduct a successful meeting. Emphasizes the need for the meeting leader to understand the responsibilities of the position as well as identifying procedures that must be followed if the goals of a meeting are to be attained.

References

Bahn, Charles (1984). "Police Socialization in the Eighties: Strains in the Forging of an Occupational Identity." *Journal of Police Science and Administration*, 12, 4.

Bellman, Geoffery M. (1992). *Getting Things Done When You Are Not in Charge*. San Francisco: Berrett-Koehler Publishers, Inc.

Cartwright, D. and R. Lippitt (1957). "Group Dynamics and the Individual." *International Journal of Group Psychotherapy*, 7.

Cohen, Allan R., Stephen L. Fink, Herman Gadon, Robin D. Willits and Natasha Josefowitz (1992). *Effective Behavior in Organizations*, 5th ed. Homewood, IL: Richard D. Irwin, Inc.

Couper, David C. (1994). "Seven Seeds for Policing." *FBI Law Enforcement Bulletin*, Vol. 63, No. 3.

Cox, Danny and John Hoover (1992). *Leadership When the Heat's On*. New York: McGraw-Hill Book Company.

Davidson, Jeffrey P. (1986). *Checklist Management*. New York: Practicum Press.

Garfield, Charles (1986). *Peak Performers*. New York: William Morrow and Company.

Gastil, John (1993). *Democracy in Small Groups: Participation, Decision Making and Communications*. Philadelphia: New Society Publishers.

Gray, Jerry L. (1984). *Supervision*. Belmont, CA: Kent Publishing Company.

Grossman, Ira and Jack Doherty (1994). "On Troubled Waters: Promotion and Advancement in the 1990s." *FBI Law Enforcement Bulletin*, Vol. 63, No. 4.

Hellriegel, Don, John W. Slocum, Jr. and Richard W. Woodman (1983). *Organizational Behavior*, 3rd ed. St. Paul, MN: West Publishing Company.

Jewell, L.N. and H.J. Reitz (1981). *Group Effectiveness in Organizations*. Glenview, IL: Scott Foresman.

Johnson, Robert A. (1994). "Police Organizational Design and Structure." *FBI Law Enforcement Bulletin*, Vol. 63, No. 6.

Kouzes, James M. and Barry Z. Posner (1993). *Credibility: How Leaders Gain and Lose It, Why People Demand It*. San Francisco: Jossey-Bass Publishers.

Leonard, V. A. and Harry W. More (1993). *Police Organization and Management*, 8th ed. Westbury, NY: The Foundation Press.

Maguire, Kathleen, Ann L. Pastore and Timonthy J. Flanagan (eds.) (1993). *Sourcebook of Criminal Justice Statistics 1992*. Washington, DC: U.S. Department of Justice, Bureau of Justice Statistics.

More, Harry W. (1992). *Special Topics in Policing*. Cincinnati, OH: Anderson Publishing Co.

Police Foundation (1981). *Survey of Police Operational Administrative Practices—1981*. Washington, DC: Police Executive Research Forum.

Rogers, Henry C. (1986). *The One-Hat Solution*. New York: St. Martin's Press.

Tarkenton, Fran (1986). *How to Motivate People*. New York: Harper and Row.

Tosi, Henry L. (1976). *Readings in Management: Contingencies, Structure and Process*. Chicago: St. Clair Press.

Watson, Jane (1992). *The Minute Taker's Handbook*. North Vancouver, British Columbia: International Self-Counsel Press Ltd.

Change—

Coping with Organizational Life

9

Introductory Case Study

Sergeant Mike Stroub

Sergeant Stroub has been a patrol supervisor for 10 years in the Middleville Police Department. Recently, Stroub was fortunate enough to be transferred to the day shift because of his seniority. Traditionally, once officers become supervisors in the patrol division they remain there, are honored to serve only the one division and never have to serve in other divisions or units of the department.

The patrol unit is viewed as the outstanding unit in the department and is credited with always performing at a maximum level. Other units are regarded as being supportive of the patrol function but seldom receive budgetary and personnel priority. This concept is so ingrained in the department, the officers compete to get into patrol. In fact, there is a waiting list of investigators who want to return to patrol. The normal policy is to assign new officers to patrol, and then transfer them to support units. The best officers are retained, and assigned to the midnight shift where the majority of the real crimes occur and there is a lot of action.

A newly appointed chief of police has decided on a policy of rotation and is desirous of making the majority of the officers generalists. It is the chief's position that excessive specialization stifles initiative. With this in mind, a general order has been issued establishing a rotation policy limiting an officer's service to five years in each major unit of the department. As one might suspect, the initial reaction by the officers is disbelief, and then real shock. It is perceived as a policy that will destroy the effectiveness of the patrol division. Rumors and complaints abound.

In the locker room and at meal breaks the new policy is discussed repeatedly. The policy is viewed as threatening and is resented because it was implemented by executive fiat. Some of the officers are talking about a slowdown, to force the chief to reconsider the policy. In fact, the blue flu has already occurred on the midnight shift when five officers called in sick. Management's concern is that the resistance to the policy will reduce the effectiveness of the department.

Sergeant Stroub is personally opposed to the new policy, but is refraining from voicing his personal opinion to management or to the line officers. He had no input to the policy decision and feels strongly that it will make patrol less effective. Until now, he viewed the department positively and realized he has always enjoyed coming to work. Now his whole world is shaken and he does not know what to do. As a supervisor, he knows that he is a part of management and responsible for implementing the new policy. On the other hand he believes the new policy will destroy the effectiveness of the patrol unit where he has worked hard to create a real team atmosphere. He is very proud of all the things the officers under his supervision have accomplished during the last seven years.

If you were Sergeant Stroub what would you do? Would you side with management or the line officers? You are number two on the promotions list for lieutenant, and anticipate pinning on the bars within the next six months.

Change is an inevitable manifestation of organizational life. It cannot be disregarded. It is a reality of the working environment in which policing is done. One does not have to work long in an agency to realize that very little is static. The names and places may change, but the dynamics of the situation exemplify anything but the status quo.

While change might make one uncomfortable, it is certain to occur. In fact, it is vital to the positive growth of a law enforcement agency. As a bureaucratic institution, the police usually respond to change rather than initiating it.

It is necessary to realize that while change is seldom fostered by the police, they are certainly reactors to it. Change must not only be met, but anticipated whenever possible and accepted (Garfield, 1986). While other managers have the privilege of being somewhat distant from the reality of operational change, it is the first-line supervisor who must deal with it on a day-to-day basis.

A careful observer of the functions performed by a line supervisor will immediately acknowledge that practically everything pertinent to everyday police operations is concerned with the implementation of change. This can range from breaking in a new officer to implementing a totally new procedure. For example, it was not too many years ago that a bag of white powder found at an intersection was just kicked over to the gutter, but now it is treated as a hazardous materials spill and the intersection is closed, pending the arrival of experts and the identification of the unknown substance.

The ability to deal with change requires the application of numerous skills discussed throughout this text including communication, motivation, team building and leadership.

Factors Fostering Change

Change does not occur in a vacuum nor is it static. Change is synergistic and cumulative, often being called for in one area because it occurred in another. For example, in recent years numerous county or city jails have become so overcrowded the convicted offenders have been released before their due date because of a court order. An indirect impact has been the implementation of a new policy, in some departments, where minor offenders are cited rather than being booked. While a supervisor might feel that in a particular instance the accused would (in all probability) benefit from incarceration and society would be protected, it cannot be done because of conditions beyond the control of any first-line supervisor or the department.

Change places exceptional demand upon supervisors and includes factors ranging from changing **social values** to the increasing power of police unions.

Social Values

Not only are organizations changing but so are individuals. Change is a continual process that at times can be gradual, but sometimes is rapid. Change can be supported or resisted. The more bureaucratic the department, the more it will resist change. The larger the department, the more likely the barrier to change.

The majority of first-line supervisors are selected from their own department, hence they normally have a somewhat narrow view of the variety of ways the same task can be accomplished. The manager's view is usually predicated on a maze of rules and regulations they have been responsible for developing and implementing. Thus, management's view can easily become one stating "this is the way that it will be done because it has always been done that way."

It is more than a marriage of convenience; it is a deep commitment to the status quo. A strict interpretation of rules and regulations is a must. First-line supervisors generally have a value system that differs from line personnel. Generally, they are at least five to 10 years older and their organizational attitudes are very well set (Washo, 1984).

The image of a good police officer has changed because of necessity. No longer is the primary criteria for selection based on "give me someone with a lot of strength and muscle." Today's image is as diverse as the culture in many of our communities. Officers come in all shapes and sizes, not just those who are 6 feet tall and perceived as being able to handle themselves in a barroom brawl.

Today's officer is apt to be better educated, more intelligent, emotionally stable and more compassionate than many of those in positions of higher authority. Rigorous selection criteria based on an array of examinations and tests ranging from psychiatric to polygraph, result in the selection of candidates who are well qualified.

The younger officers are more likely to be dissatisfied with departmental policies requiring them to go by the book at all times regardless of circumstances. Many of these officers perceive absolute conformity as stifling initiative, but soon find that implementing discretion can only result in being "written up."

Today's line officer is more apt to have been raised in a lenient family setting and is less likely to have spent time in the military. These two factors, coupled with less rigid schooling, have resulted in many officers never having experienced a no-nonsense leadership style demanding unquestioned obedience and absolute compliance with orders. It has been shocking and decidedly unsettling to many young officers to be treated as a mere cog in the wheel and to have their opinions ignored.

The line officer of today has needs and expectations not being met by a police department that is exceedingly bureaucratic and structured along traditional military lines. The values and attitudes of line officers are different from those in earlier generations. Supervisors cannot live in the past or yearn for the "good old days" when those supervised were more pliable, willing to accept authority and take orders without question.

Supervisors must adjust to situations they find undesirable. When values differ greatly between those being supervised and those doing the supervision conflict is inevitable. Line officers have demonstrated their frustration by defying management in different ways, including marching in front of city hall in opposition to working conditions.

One of the main targets of officers has been oppressive and exceedingly detailed departmental policies. Often these conditions make officers feel like they are just a social security number, are powerless and are treated with such indifference they feel like a nonentity.

Police Unions

One result of the changing values of line officers has been the increasing support of labor unions. It has been estimated that 73 percent of the nation's police officers are represented by some form of association or union (More, 1992). It does not take a new officer long to realize there is strength in numbers and a police union is a way to fight for better working conditions or to have a say in the management of the organization.

Police officers have willingly accepted union leadership when it has led to the opportunity to participate in decisions affecting their future, provide for some semblance of economic security and challenge the autocratic power of police managers. **Collective bargaining**, a process whereby the department and the union negotiate a formal written agreement over wages, hours and working conditions, is legal in about half of the country and has become a means of clarifying management rights. Some of the primary interests of police employee organizations are to get some voice in policymaking, and to improve benefits including salaries, overtime, compensation time, pensions, paid holidays, health insurance and tuition reimbursement (Guyot, 1991).

Police unions have viewed collective bargaining as the best means of checking or stalemating the abuse of power by police managers. Unions have been successful in altering rules and regulations, and it is quite common for unions to bargain for the right to review new policies before their implementation.

Active support of police unions is increasing daily because officers view administration as far apart from line officers and nonsupportive. In many instances unions battle for the control of the police department and influence the appointment of a new chief of police (Bouza, 1990). There are certainly departments that do not fit this description, but enough exist to bring into question the relationship between line officers and managers.

It does not take an officer long to learn it is necessary to safely cover all personal actions. In many instances, bureaucratic restrictions serve to protect the top-level supervisors to the detriment of line officers. Another issue in collective bargaining involves the first-line supervisors and whether they should be considered a part of management or labor. The answer is self-evident because a sergeant is a manager and an integral part of the management team. Under no circumstances should a supervisor be a part of a line bargaining unit.

The Law

The law conditions and reconditions the functions performed by the police. "All you have to do is wait for the next session of the U.S. Supreme Court and you will have to change the way you enforce the law" is a common complaint of many officers.

Other problems are the ambiguity and vagueness of the law. The language of some statutes is so unclear it must be interpreted by the courts, but this is usually done after the fact, not before. The officer on the street is continually faced with the problem of enforcing the law and then accepting the consequences if the decision is questioned.

Other laws are obsolete and outmoded but are still on the books. In practice, the police are expected to enforce all laws; however, there are many unenforced and routinely disregarded. Occasionally the police receive criticism because they do not enforce a law. This usually occurs with sumptuary laws involving gambling. In one case where the police department was not enforcing the law, bingo games were being sponsored as a means of raising funds for charity by several churches and such organizations as the Elks. Before the issue receded from the front page of the newspaper it was necessary to change the state statute on gambling to exempt bingo.

Actually, it would seem the United States has become a society inundated by laws. The policy seems to be that if there is something we do not like, then we must pass a law against it. At the focal point of this landslide of laws one finds the members of patrol units. Undoubtedly, there are too many criminal laws. There are too many purely personal activities involving law violations that should not be within the purview of the law.

This is obviously true in the area of victimless crimes where, in general, enforcement is limited, but the police must deal with it as a continuing issue when working the streets. Political pressure can alter enforcement of victimless crimes overnight as a specific crime becomes a headline and the mayor's office becomes unglued. It seems strange for an officer to ignore a minor drug violation or sexual offense one day, and be expected to enforce the violation to the fullest extent of the law the next day. It is the ambiguity of the whole process that is of concern to the officer, since the process is nonpredictable and such changes are not only frustrating, but difficult to handle.

Positive Aspects of Change

The first-line supervisor deals with the reality of change from two perspectives. First, the sergeant is usually the one who interprets new policies, becoming immediately placed in the position of being the spokesperson for management. On the other hand, supervisors are concerned because the primary work group dealing with those new policies on a continuing basis is comprised of line officers. It is their concerns that must be dealt with if the squad of officers is to operate effectively. It surprises new officers to find out that the main person to consult for advice on these matters is the immediate supervisor, not top managers. Beyond an occasional roll call session, the other superiors in the department are seldom seen except for major emergencies.

The sergeant whose supervisory style exemplifies objectivity, fairness, and a demonstration of concern for subordinate welfare will soon find that not all change is resisted. Not many organizations accept change as readily as law enforcement agencies. The police are subject to continual change from external agencies and their greatest displeasure would seem to be with the failure of police managers to adapt to changing times.

The average police officer takes the position that the police department fails to provide an environment satisfying important personnel needs. It is the quality of work life that takes priority in satisfying the need system of officers. The job is viewed as dominant and the positive feelings generated by the job lead to an increased job satisfaction.

One study found, when examining the actual police job, that the most important characteristic (as perceived by the employees) was the feeling that the job was important and yielded a feeling of accomplishment. **Job satisfaction** differs for each employee, but studies seem to confirm that key elements include (Albrecht, 1981):

1.	Accomplishment	7.	Management
2.	Accountability	8.	Relationships
3.	Advancement	9.	Resources
4.	Challenge	10.	Supervision
5.	Comfort	11.	Workload
6.	Compensation		

The supervisor must work with these variables and identify those important to each individual, then strive to achieve selected departmental goals by optimizing worker needs and reducing undesirable side effects.

When the variables listed above are recognized and handled with dispatch, there is less likelihood of negative reaction to change. Unfortunately, this particular negativism will always overshadow the positive aspects because it seems bad news is always of greater interest than good news. Officers are not, by nature, anti-change in their approach to new situations, but they can be ground down to the point where they become negative in their outlook toward life and the job. If this is allowed to happen, police management has lost its chance to tap its most important resource: its employees.

Officers are certainly adaptable to change and will accept it readily when involved in the decision-making process. If supervisors accept this premise, they can then proceed to determine reasons for resistance when it occurs (Harvey, 1990).

Accepting Change

The reasons for acceding to change vary considerably, but at least include the following (Gray, 1984):

1. *Choice.* This is an important feature of change. If individuals are knowledgeable about the consequences of the change, a decision to accept is more apt to occur because it is something they want to do, not something they have been forced to accept.

2. *Improvement.* If a change improves working conditions, it becomes immediately acceptable to most officers. For instance, after having driven a squad car for more than 100,000 miles, it is a great feeling to get behind the wheel of a new vehicle. The same concept applies to working conditions when, for example, a city has finally adopted computer-aided dispatching, allowing the officer to respond more readily.

3. *Informed.* It is reassuring to know all pertinent facts right from the start. It is most disconcerting when a decision has been made affecting the way officers are required to operate, but this was discovered after the fact. With today's means of communicating, there is every reason for management to keep its employees fully informed. In fact, it can be suggested, in the majority of instances, that too much information will prove to be helpful rather than detrimental. When one is aware of all operations it reduces anxiety.

4. *A Need Is Satisfied.* If an officer has a need fulfilled by a change, there is less reason to anticipate resistance to the change. Each

person has needs that the job can fulfill. This can vary from something providing greater self-esteem to improved job satisfaction. It is believed that when the majority of officer needs are met by management, there will be a decrease in absenteeism and turnover. In addition, it is theorized there will be fewer accidents and increased production.

5. *Planned.* When it is perceived a change is necessary, it is important to plan for it rather than to react to it. Planned change acknowledges that officers will be affected and any alteration of policy or procedures can impact positively or negatively. When, for example, computers are introduced into patrol cars they affect not only the officers but the total department including records, dispatching and even the deployment of personnel.

With the changing composition of many police departments, it is essential to plan for social changes. The introduction of women into patrol units, preferential selection of employees who are bilingual and the promotion of officers to obtain racial balance are all programs requiring careful planning for implementation. Such programs must be monitored carefully and adjusted when necessary (see Figure 9.1).

Figure 9.1
Reasons for Accepting Change

Choice
Improvement
Informed
A Need is Satisfied
Planned

When fully aware of the reasons officers accept change, the first-line supervisor is in a better position to deal with the variables supporting rather than impeding change.

Resistance to Change

A clear understanding of the reasons officers resist change will allow a supervisor the opportunity to deal with **resistance**. When a change is viewed as threatening, it will be resisted by most employees. If the change is immaterial or of no consequence it will, in all probability, not be resisted. If in fact, the change proves to be supportive or helpful, it will most likely be welcomed by everyone.

Resistance takes many forms and can range from just ignoring something, to open resistance (De Meuse and McDaris, 1994). In one police agency involved in a pay dispute, most of the officers left the state so they would not be

served a court order requiring their return to work. In another instance, officers enforced traffic regulations to the maximum, causing a public outcry when the resulting traffic jams created havoc in the downtown area. Figure 9.2 lists some of the reasons change is resisted.

Figure 9.2
Resistance to Change

Economic Reasons
Ambiguity Created
Relationships Restricted
Habits Altered
Discretion Restricted or Eliminated
Unpopular Decisions
Cultural Reasons

Economic Reasons

Money (in terms of salaries and fringe benefits) is a key issue for most police officers. This is especially noticed when income is below what is considered par. If the officers know the neighboring agencies have higher pay levels, they are more apt to engage in activities adverse to the department.

If the city moves to reduce or eliminate overtime pay, it can be a definite threat to an officer's welfare. In agencies allowing overtime to become an integral part of the payroll, an elimination or reduction will have an immediate and negative impact on the lifestyle of each officer. The same thing can occur when city councils reduce fringe benefits, such as dental, medical or retirement, that have become an integral part of a pay package.

Money weighs heavily in officers' decisions to resist change. If any part of a pay package is threatened, it is difficult to imagine that it would not be met with collective resistance.

Increasingly this has been done through associations or unions. Like other occupations, officers have found a united response will generally produce results when compared to individual efforts to right a perceived monetary wrong.

Ambiguity Created

Frequently the effects of change are unknown, so officers are more apt to oppose it when there is doubt as to the possible consequence. The greater the ambiguity, the greater the potential for resistance (Holton and Holton, 1992). Most officers soon learn that one positive value of numerous rules and regulations is the tendency to create stability and reduce uncertainty. When things are done "by the book," each officer is provided with guidance, increasing the prob-

ability that the outcome is known and predictable. Change, especially when it is extensive, can disturb or disrupt established procedures and generate resistance.

If a specific change is looked upon as creating uncertainty (even though there is no evidence to support this conclusion) it will make most officers anxious about the new change (Hellriegel, Slocum and Woodman, 1983).

If a proposed change is slight or viewed with some degree of indifference, officers will be more apt to accept it, especially if they perceive the change as being somewhat beneficial. Though, again, there is no evidence to support such a position.

Relationships Restricted

With the exception of certain shifts or areas of a community, it has become increasingly common for officers to work alone. The result is social relationships between officers become of utmost importance. Generally, officers will go to great efforts to socialize with fellow officers by taking meals together, taking breaks at locations where other officers gather, getting together at the end of a shift or engaging in off-duty activities together.

Efforts by management to restrict or limit social interaction are generally resisted by most officers. Group norms determine behavior and can be the most difficult source of resistance for managers to control. Patrol officers are usually isolated from the community so they turn to each other for support. The result is the development of a police subculture where common occupational values come into existence. Officers readily share job coping techniques in an effort to deal with policies impacting negatively on social relationships.

A change in organizational structure may be resisted if it revises or alters working relationships between officers. An example is a department where officers have traditionally had the responsibility of coordinating certain types of investigations with neighboring beat officers when the circumstance dictated. A new policy provided that investigators would now be responsible for coordinating such investigations. An immediate and vociferous resistance scuttled what management perceived as a needed reform.

Habits Altered

Individual resistance to change can stem from something as simple as habit (Tichy and Devanna, 1990). Officers become comfortable doing something a certain way, prefer to keep things the way they are and see no reason to change. This is especially true if the officers receive satisfaction from an established habit (Kirby, 1989).

If officers are required to learn new skills to perform their job, but it is not viewed as an improvement over the way they are currently doing it, resistance will occur. There is comfort in doing things in a familiar way. The greater the

chance of change altering an established habit, the greater the possibility that it will be resisted. Change causes losses and people resist, in many instances, because of the loss not the actual change itself (Bridges, 1991).

Discretion Restricted or Eliminated

In many instances, management will take steps to clearly spell out authority, responsibility and accountability in an effort to circumscribe and limit the power of line officers. In most instances, predictability becomes a means to an end and discretion is viewed as a necessary evil that must be controlled under all circumstances. The bureaucracy must prevail and must never be subjected to criticism. Reporting procedures are carefully spelled out and rules and regulations abound.

The greater the control of discretion, the greater the amount of power taken away from the line officer. The street cops will generally feel excessive control limits their ability to perform effectively. Managers (especially those at the top) are perceived as bureaucrats who have lost touch with street reality and have forsaken line personnel. The freedom to act when confronted with uncertainty is viewed by many officers as paramount to providing the public with quality police services to enhance their safety.

Unpopular Decisions

All managers must, at some time, make an unpopular decision, and this is certainly true of first-line supervisors. Certain decisions seem to be of more concern than others and it is important to know what managerial decisions might cause dissent and how one might work to obtain compliance when it is known in advance that a decision will be unpopular.

Just as important is the need to determine what action employees will take when an unpopular decision is first announced. One study determined these three situations as definitely unpopular managerial decisions: actions dealing with discipline, changes in work schedules and changes impacting on salary (Malik and Wexley, 1986).

Compliance-gaining techniques vary depending upon the situation but, generally speaking, the most effective technique is to give officers adequate justification for the decision. Next (in terms of reducing resistance) is the technique of obtaining input from officers before issuing what is known to be an unpopular decision.

It should be noted that, in general, the more highly educated the officers and the greater their longevity, the more apt they are to want some justification of, or input into, the decision-making process. It is also important to note that the majority of officers will not take overt actions when responding to unpopular decisions. The decision is either accepted without dissent because management is perceived as having the authority to make it, or the resistance increases proportional to decision unpopularity.

Cultural Reasons

The typical culture of a police organization is such that it develops certain values and long-time members feel the way their organization approaches problems is the only way it should be done. Attitudes and values support the customary way of doing things (Cohen, Fink, Gadon, Willits and Josefowitz, 1992). To conceive of other ways of doing something is usually perceived as wasteful so it is resisted. Organizational culture reinforces the need to do something the way it has always been done. It has worked for many years so why change. Law enforcement has traditionally been an agency demanding conformity making the culture of the organization unreceptive to change (Tichy and Devanna, 1990).

The Nature of Resistance

Resistance to change can, at times, be totally *rational* and have no emotional basis whatsoever. When first challenged with a proposed or actual change, officers have, in some instances, become immediately aware a new procedure will create more problems than it will resolve. This form of resistance should be viewed as something to enhance the change process because it causes an in-depth analysis of the problem. A first-line supervisor should carefully analyze a change situation to see if there might be a real basis for rational resistance. When identified as such, the resulting conflict can be utilized to alter the change so it can be supported by line personnel as well as management.

For example, officers in one agency resisted a new procedure for booking youthful offenders in juvenile hall because, while it simplified the booking process for probation personnel, it doubled the time police officers had to devote to their booking process. In this instance the proposed procedures were altered to the satisfaction of both agencies and all personnel.

Emotional resistance to change presents the supervisor with an entirely different problem. In some instances the problem seems to be with the first-line supervisor, who may view a proposed change as beneficial to everyone involved, but officers view it differently.

The perception of change is usually individual and not collective so it is essential for a supervisor to try to understand how others view the change (Gray, 1984). In one department, a change in radio procedures received negative reactions because it was believed by line personnel that dispatchers were given too much authority. An analysis of the resulting conflict determined the resistance was emotionally based because officers felt it limited their control of emergency situations and was the first of efforts to restrict their authority. It was the position of management however that the proposed change would enhance officer security.

Supervisors must distinguish between rational and emotional resistance if organizational change is to be accomplished. If a supervisor makes a serious effort to distinguish between the two types of resistance, then it can be handled to the benefit of all concerned. In some instances, providing officers with more

Case Study

Sergeant Don Stewart

Sergeant Don Stewart has been a member of the Midvale Police Department for eight years and has held his position of patrol supervisor for two years. During the last year, a national union has made serious efforts to unionize the police department. The union has held numerous informational meetings with the approval of the mayor and city manager.

Union organizers stress the need for presenting a united front in order to improve wages and working conditions. During the last five months, union organizers have bombarded members of the department with flyers and letters extolling the virtues of union membership. A picnic was held on Labor Day with all members and their families invited. Union officials from the national office and police officers who were active in unions in other cities gave speeches in support of unionization.

The efforts to unionize the department are massive and their views contrast sharply with city officials and the Chief of Police who take a completely neutral position. In fact, the chief has asked other police managers not to oppose or support the union efforts to organize.

Most of the officers are in full support of union efforts while a few expressed concern for affiliating with a national union with a reputation for supporting violent strikes as well as allegedly having connections to organized crime. The officers who are opposed feel that if unionization is necessary it should be done by affiliating with some professional police association.

The department has the reputation of paying the lowest salaries in the area. Officers enter the department for a few years of experience, then leave for greener pastures. The administration is viewed as essentially authoritarian and in support of this leadership style. Rules and regulations abound. Other than for the most minor type of arrests, supervisory approval is necessary.

Sergeant Stewart is not considered by the chief to be part of management, so his perception of the union situation is different. He has developed an allegiance to his officers and feels he, in all probability, has a great deal to gain and not much to lose by supporting the union. The vote for unionization is scheduled for the coming month and Stewart has decided not only to vote for unionization, but to campaign vigorously for its approval.

Stewart is especially concerned with the continuing loss of personnel because of low salaries and what he perceives as the over-supervision of line personnel. He has found the new officers are bright, well-educated and highly motivated, but they feel stifled and do not have enough freedom to perform effectively.

What is the real issue in this case? Working conditions, the prospects of unionization or management style? What change factors are at work? If you were Sergeant Stewart, would you support and work for the new union? Why?

information might serve to resolve the problem and in other situations the supervisor may need to deal directly with each officer in an effort to determine the reason for resistance.

Working for Change

Resistance must be identified before it can be properly handled with successful solutions to the problems it causes. These solutions for resistance might be as simple as providing those in opposition with more information or, at the other extreme, involving personnel in the decision-making process.

It has become increasingly common to be involved almost constantly in some type of change process. In some instances the consequences of change are readily identifiable as having the potential for limited impact. In other situations it can be interpreted as being potentially harmful, and lastly there might be no way of determining what will happen when a change occurs.

If several changes are occurring at the same time, the problem of dealing with resistance can become exceedingly complex. It is usually necessary then for those who are working for change to use more than one strategy when making an effort to overcome resistance to change.

If the supervisor is a real part of management (and not apart from it), there is a greater potential for being involved in the planning that precedes change. If not, the first-line supervisor will be at a definite disadvantage. Dealing with conflict occurs after the fact and limits the alternatives the supervisor can use.

Whatever the realities of the situation, there are definite techniques a supervisor can utilize when attempting to defuse situations that can develop into resistance to change. There are always forces supporting the school of philosophy believing no change is good change. On the other hand, change can occur that is just change for the sake of changing. It is somewhat like managers who have to be in the forefront, always involved in implementing the latest fad whether it works or not.

The first-line supervisor is not in a position to resolve every occurrence resulting in resistance, or utilize any one or more techniques successfully in every instance. In other words there is no proven method that will successfully sell change, but some techniques have proven to be more successful than others. Some of the methods of fostering change are discussed below.

Being Knowledgeable

Ignorance might be bliss, but is out of place when a supervisor is striving to develop a strategy for selling change. Change seldom occurs without some stimulation from management, so supervisors must take the view that change must be sold. Before someone can be convinced that a change should occur, it is necessary to gather and assimilate all the available facts regarding any proposal. It

is real work to become knowledgeable about a proposed change and it takes time to acquire information. This is especially pertinent when change drastically alters the current habits of officers or their social relationships.

Human behavior is complex, so a supervisor should develop more than one strategy for change. The advantages and disadvantages of each alternative should be reviewed; the strategy with greatest promise should be selected. In one instance, a sergeant (who had the complete support of management) considered several alternatives and finally decided the greatest resistance would come from three informal leaders within the department. Meeting with them on an individual basis to explain the change before presenting the new proposal at roll call was felt to be the strategy to enhance its implementation.

Involvement

The potential for creating a positive environment that will be more receptive to a proposed change is enhanced by involving those who will be most affected by it. This is not to suggest this will always succeed, but experience has shown the advantages of this technique outweigh the disadvantages.

Those involved in the change process are in a position to use facts to combat rumors and erroneous information. Another important feature is the reduction or elimination of anxiety as officers become less concerned about pending change (Gray, 1984).

Involvement serves to reduce resistance because the unknown becomes the known. When the decision is made to involve personnel in the change process it is imperative for management to totally support the implementation of such a program. Lip service or the tactic of manipulation will, in short order, weaken or destroy future efforts of involving personnel in the decision-making process.

Participation is time consuming, so the rewards should exceed the costs. This brings up the question of when, during a decision-making process, affected employees should be involved. There is no simple answer, but in general it has been found that participation can be maximized if management has done its homework efficiently and gathered all the data needed to initiate a positive participation process.

In many instances, it will be essential to initially spell out that participation will be limited to the specific topic under consideration. This sets the limits allowing for a freer exchange of ideas and it will keep the decision-making process on target.

As involvement becomes a part of the leadership style, the supervisor may find some subordinates feel most comfortable when not involved in the decision-making process, but of utmost importance to them is their having been given an opportunity to be involved if they so desire.

Communication

Without communication, a proposal to implement a new policy or any other type of change will, in all probability, have a limited opportunity of succeeding. In most instances, keeping channels of communication open will provide a supervisor with information to be utilized when working at "selling" change (Garfield, 1986).

Even over-communication will generally prove to be beneficial, although it can create unnecessary employee anxiety. This will be especially pertinent if the information involves a change in working conditions. While it can be argued that waiting until more information can be obtained would upset a number of employees, it is still a judgment call. The evidence would seem to support the importance of communication as much as possible and as soon as possible (Gray, 1984).

When officers know management has made every effort to maintain and foster open communication, it will result in a reduction of resistance and provide them with greater prospects of implementing change. Efforts to restrict the flow of information can only enhance resistance and reinforce the informal organization. In such a situation, the grapevine will soon prevail and rumors will abound.

Utilizing the Influence of Informal Leaders

As previously indicated, a normal by-product of groups is the development of **informal leaders.** Officers who fulfill this role usually can be easily identified. Normally one officer in a group will be the social leader and another officer will be looked upon as the group leader. The more the supervisor knows about each of the informal leaders in terms of their concerns, objectives and personal styles, the better the chance of influencing those individuals (Cohen and Bradford, 1991).

Informal leaders are a vital resource to be utilized in the change process. In almost all instances they should be integrated into the team or group as soon as possible so they will be a part of the change process and not apart from it.

Circumstances will dictate whether or not a first-line supervisor should include formal leaders in the change process. When it is evident that informal leaders are influential, they should be involved; otherwise, supervisors may be totally unaware of individuals (or situations) possibly playing an important part in resistance to change.

Involved informal leaders who are committed to the proposed change can, in most instances, reduce employee resistance and facilitate implementation. Informal leaders can provide information to the decision-making process (that would otherwise be unavailable), thus allowing those involved an opportunity to meet this resistance head-on.

Informal leaders have influence that should be used, not ignored. It must be kept in mind that informal leaders should never be manipulated when being integrated into the decision-making process.

Mandated Change

It is inevitable a supervisor will eventually meet a situation where every effort has been made to involve officers in the change process, but they are not successful. Possibly change occurs without consultation or involvement because of inadequate time to prepare for the change. This is a fact of managerial life and there is no easy solution when such a situation occurs.

It is imperative for a supervisor to be open and candid with everyone concerned and carefully explain the reasons for the change decision. Obviously such a straightforward approach is an effort to deal with the anticipated or actual resistance rationally. Such an appeal will fall on deaf ears if resistance is emotionally based.

At this point the supervisor must make every effort to emphasize the positive aspects of the change, explaining the way it can help each officer. Everything the supervisor does will bring a reaction of some sort from the officers, so the sergeant (supervisor) should strive to remain a reliable source of information and a steadying influence during the initial stages of a change.

It is the supervisor's responsibility to shield subordinates as much as possible from the anxiety created by change and this can be done by showing the officers a genuine concern for their welfare. In other words, a supervisor must have a caring attitude (Tarkenton, 1984). Officers will generally respond positively to their supervisor's efforts to stabilize a situation and show sound judgment based on common sense. If officers respond even slightly to such efforts, the supervisor has started to lay a foundation, hopefully leading to a reduction or elimination of resistance.

Summary

Change is an inevitable reality and is becoming an increasingly important part of the police officer's working life.

Change places an exceptional demand upon supervisors. Change factors to be dealt with include: social values, the law and police unions. None of the three dominate the change process. In different agencies, one of the three factors may prove to be central to change issues, while in other departments it may be of limited impact.

The first-line supervisor is deeply involved in the change process, functioning as primary interpreter of new policies, and serving as the focal point of relationships with line personnel.

Changes come into existence as the result of careful planning, taking into consideration the consequences of their implementation. Reasons for the acceptance of change include officers having a choice, improving working conditions, employees being fully informed and a need is being satisfied.

Officers will normally resist change when it involves such things as a negative economic impact, a lack of stability, altered social relationships, a change in habits, restricted or eliminated discretion or a fundamentally unpopular decision.

Case Study

Sergeant Terri Block

Sergeant Terri Block has recently completed a three-year assignment with the Crime Prevention Unit where her primary responsibility was to develop neighborhood watch programs throughout the city. During the assignment, she was instrumental in setting up 24 programs and initiating a monthly newsletter so participants would be kept up to date.

Before that assignment, she had been in the patrol division for two years. Her new assignment is as a patrol supervisor on the swing shift. She is one of the first women to have been assigned to patrol. Since her initial assignment, it has become more common to assign other women to patrol. In fact, the general feeling within the department is that women have proven they can function effectively when assigned to patrol.

The entire department has just completed a training course in organizational development. Sergeant Block's first assignment is to head a task force for the express purpose of defining the exact responsibilities of officers investigating burglaries of commercial establishments.

The current policy provides for minimum patrol officer involvement when investigating commercial burglaries. It actually means that patrol protects the crime scene, and burglary investigators handle everything else. The mandate Sergeant Block received is to develop a policy requiring patrol to complete a comprehensive preliminary investigation with specific attention paid to solvability factors.

The task force is to consist of three patrol officers and three burglary investigators. A key problem Sergeant Block immediately notices is that patrol and investigation have functioned for years as almost separate departments and real coordination and cooperation is almost nonexistent.

Another problem is that organizational development is new to the department and her task force is the first to be organized. She has been advised by the lieutenant and the captain that there is "a lot riding" on the success of her task force.

Sergeant Block is interested in becoming as knowledgeable as possible about the working relationship between patrol and investigations. If you were Sergeant Block, how would you go about this? She also knows that she wants to maximize participation by the total task force. How can this be done? Sergeant Block is anticipating considerable resistance. What resistance do you think she can anticipate and how should she deal with it?

Resistance to change can be either rational or emotional. The former type of resistance can be dealt with objectively while the latter requires the supervisor to expend a great deal of effort in attempting to resolve a problem that defies a solution.

When a supervisor does everything possible to gather all the facts relating to any proposed change, they are utilizing the best tool they have to combat resistance. The supervisor can use information to deal objectively with resistance to change. In most instances, this resistance can be lessened by involving officers in the change process.

Other means of overcoming resistance include developing skills to communicate effectively and utilizing the influence of informal leaders as vital resources in effectuating change.

Key Concepts

collective bargaining   need satisfaction
informal leaders   resistance to change
involvement   social values
job satisfaction

Discussion Topics and Questions

1. Why is change an inevitable consequence of organizational life?

2. Describe the social values found in many police departments.

3. Why do police officers join unions?

4. What are the advantages of planning change?

5. How can a supervisor utilize the influence of informal leaders?

6. How should a supervisor deal with mandated change?

For Further Reading

Bellman, Geoffery M. (1992). *Getting Things Done When You Are Not in Charge*. San Francisco: Berrett-Koehler Publishers, Inc..

Presents powerful insights on leadership, teamwork, empowerment, organizational politics and organizational change. Encourages the reader to take the initiative for positive change and discover personal meaning in work. Shows how to be more effective in enlisting key players in change.

Bridges, William (1991). *Managing Transitions: Making the Most of Change*. Reading. MA: Addison-Wesley Publishing.

> This book helps the reader to understand the difficulties encountered when one tr_es to get people to change the way they do things. Presents ways to deal with change both organizationally and personally. Discusses tactics that can be used when managing change.

Cohen, Allan R. and David L. Bradford (1991). *Influence Without Authority*. New York: John Wiley and Sons, Inc.

> A highly readable book dealing with how to create change in contemporary organizations. Points out how every member in the organization is a potential ally during the change process. Presents techniques that can be used to overcome interpersonal and interdepartmental barriers.

Kouzes, James M. and Barry Z. Posner (1993). *Credibility: How Leaders Gain and Lose It, Why People Demand It*. San Francisco: Jossey-Bass Publishers.

> Identifies characteristics of effective leaders with an emphasis on credibility. Reveals six specific disciplines and related practices that strengthen a leader's capacity for developing and sustaining credibility. Illustrates ways to resolve conflict on the basis of principles not positions.

References

Albrecht, Karl L. (1981). *Executive Tune-Up*. Englewood Cliffs, NJ: Prentice-Hall, Inc.

Bouza, Anthony, V. (1990). *The Police Mystique: An Insider's Look at Cops, Crime, and the Criminal Justice System*. New York: Plenum Press.

Bridges, William (1991). *Managing Transitions: Making the Most of Change*. Reading, MA: Addison-Wesley Publishing Co.

Cohen, Allan R. and David L. Bradford (1991). *Influence Without Authority*. New York: John Wiley & Sons, Inc.

Cohen, Allan R., Stephen L. Fink, Herman Gadon, Robin D. Willits and Natashe Josefowitz (1992). *Effective Behavior in Organizations*, 5th ed. Homewood, IL: Richard D. Irwin, Inc.

De Meuse, Kenneth P. and Kevin K. McDaris (1994). "An Exercise in Managing Change." *Training and Development*, Vol. 48, No. 2.

Garfield, Charles (1986). *Peak Performers*. New York: William Morrow and Company, Inc.

Guyot, Dorothy (1991). *Policing as Though People Matter*. Philadelphia: Temple University Press.

Gray, Jerry L. (1984). *Supervision*. Belmont, CA: Wadsworth Publishing Co.

Harvey, Thomas R. (1990). *Checklist for Change: A Pragmatic Approach to Creating and Controlling Change*. Boston, Ally and Bacon, Inc.

Hellriegel, Don, John W. Slocum and Richard W. Woodman (1983). *Organizational Behavior*. St. Paul, MN: West Publishing Company.

Holton, Bill and Cher Holton (1992). *The Manager's Short Course*. New York: John Wiley and Sons, Inc.

Kirby, Tess (1989). *The Can-do Manager: How to Get Your Employees to Take Risks, Take Action, and Get Things Done*. New York: AMACOM.

Malik, S.D. and Kenneth N. Wexley (1986). "Improving the Owner/Manager's Handling of Subordinates Resistance to Unpopular Decisions." *Journal of Small Business Management*.

More, Harry W. (1992). *Special Topics in Policing.* Cincinnati, OH: Anderson Publishing Co.

Tarkenton, Fran (1984). *Playing to Win.* New York: Harper and Row.

Tichy, Noel M. and Mary Anne Devanna (1990). *The Transformational Leader.* New York: John Wiley and Sons, Inc.

Washo, Brad D. (1984). "Effecting Planned Change Within a Police Department." *The Police Chief,* Vol. LIV, No. 9.

Supervising the Difficult Employee—

Special Considerations

10

Introductory Case Study

Officer Ralph Carter

Officer Ralph Carter has been an employee of the Stratford Police Department for 16 years. During that time, he has served most of his career in patrol. Previously, he served on task forces and special details in other divisions for short periods. Officer Carter is 41 years of age, and he is the oldest line officer in the agency. He is a member of the local National Guard Military Police Company and holds the rank of Master Sergeant. He spent nine months on active duty during Desert Storm, and during off-duty hours, he spends considerable time performing guard duties. Officer Carter has never taken a promotion examination. He tells everyone he is very happy in patrol and does not want to become a supervisor.

Younger officers look up to him as a "real" police officer and seek his advice. He has served as a Field Training Officer for many years and trained many of the officers on the swing shift which is his current assignment. In fact, Officer Carter prefers the swing shift because it has the most "action." He responds readily to backup calls, and other officers appreciate his supportive behavior. The department does not have a union, and Officer Carter serves as the informal intermediator between management and line personnel. His personality and knowledge of police work serve as a calming influence on others. He has a good sense of humor and is well liked. He constantly engages in practical jokes, and other officers reciprocate.

His wife divorced him, causing considerable suffering and pain. During the last year, he has become more than a social drinker and is on the verge of becoming a problem drinker. During the last two months, he has been late for work many times and takes other days off after calling in sick.

As Carter's supervisor, what things would you do to deal with his current behavior? How would you deal with the drinking problem? What would you do about his taking too many sick days and reporting to work late? What type of records would you keep? What departmental resources would you use?

Contemporary supervisors must set the tone, change the paradigms and create a foundation that results in a truly supportive working environment. There is a need to change supervisory values and beliefs. They should be built upon, or replaced with, new ones (Zook, 1994). This changing role presents not only a challenge to each supervisor, but the concomitant possibility of creating apprehension and anxiety caused by the change. It demands the application of new skills and the modification of traditional guidelines and creeds. Imaginative leadership will be the key if consistent quality performance is to be required of every employee. The supervisor plays a crucial role in managing a contemporary productive workplace. There is need for a new accountability within police organizations which strains the traditional way of dealing with employees. A transformation is necessary as organizations change, the work force becomes increasingly diversified and communities demand improved police services at lesser costs. The first-line supervisor is the key if the new organization is to become a learning organization.

The quality of a psychological work environment should be such that employees feel at ease and new patterns of thinking are accepted. It is where officers are encouraged to improve themselves and where new ways of thinking about problem-solving occur (Zook, 1994). In a positive working environment, supervisors tailor the supervisory techniques they use to fit the competence level of each employee. Some employees will need closer supervision than others. Some will respond to one motivational technique, and others to something else.

Employees should be part of the decision-making process and responsible for results. This makes officers accountable and allows them the freedom to "buy into" the situation. This results in the actual implementation of accountability (Cottringer, 1994). As an officer assumes responsibility and completes operations successfully, supervisors can increase officer responsibility. All of this leads to an improved quality of life in the work place.

In recent years, **value statements** have set the tone for many organizations. Typical of these are those expressed by the Alexandria Police Department as it relates to the members of the organization (see Figure 10.1). Values are the basis for the beliefs and actions taken by the department. The values guide the work and decisions of the department. They represent ideals and are the foundation for the policies, goals and operations that affect employees. They are nonnegotiable and are never ignored for the sake of expediency or personal preference. Such values constantly remind supervisors and managers of the factors contributing to a positive working environment (Samarra, 1992).

Employees as Individuals

Unfortunately, there are many rocks in the roadway impeding progress as change occurs. One of these is the **problem employee**. Dealing with problem employees occurs more often than most supervisors would like. We do not live in a perfect world, and employees are not perfect. Notably, the Declaration of

Figure 10.1
Alexandria Police Department Values

OURSELVES

We are capable, caring people who are doing important and satisfying work for the citizens of Alexandria.

Therefore:

We respect, care about, trust, and support each other.
We enjoy our work and take pride in our accomplishments.
We are disciplined and reliable.
We keep our perspective and sense of humor.
We balance our professional and personal lives.
We consult those who will be affected by our decisions.
We have a positive, "can-do" attitude.
We cultivate our best characteristics: initiative, enthusiasm, creativity, patience, competence, and judgment.

Source: Charles E. Samarra, 1992, *Alexandria Police: These are our Values,* Alexandria, VA., Alexandria Police Department.

Independence states ". . . all men are created equal." Such is not the case. Everyone is not equal, as is clearly evident in our society and the work place. Some employees are more productive than others. Some are more analytical than others. Some have special skills that others do not have—such as writing, verbal or physical. Others are more effective working with young people, and yet others with older people. Some officers function most effectively on "undercover" assignments, and others would never be selected for such a task.

Each officer is a distinctive person with an individualistic personality, definite needs and a personally unique lifestyle.

A supervisor also functions as a singular individual with experiences, needs and drives that may or may not be similar to those supervised (Harvey, 1990). This presents a real challenge, especially if the value systems are in conflict. The police field is in a state of flux, and diversity is increasingly common in the workplace. As the working environment has undergone change, the role of the first-line supervisor has become increasingly important. The supervisor must develop subordinate skills and provide a supportive climate in which the common purposes of the organization become achievable (Kouzes, 1993). This presents the supervisor with a dilemma. When an employee becomes difficult to work with, tasks are not accomplished or work is done with indifference, a supervisor must take corrective action. In some situations, unsuitable behavior can impair the effectiveness of the officer, and in other cases unacceptable behavior can impact negatively on other organizational members. Inappropriate behavior can occur at any stage of an officer's employment ranging from newly appointed individuals to those who are biding their time until retirement.

Types of Employees

One expert found three types of individuals in organizations: **ascendant**, **indifferent** and **ambivalent**. The number of employees in each group vary from agency to agency, and this grouping of employees seems to be what supervisors actually find in an organization (Leonard and More, 1993). We must acknowledge it is not easy to categorize employees because of our limited knowledge of why people behave the way they do. Human beings are very complex and, individuals can and do change depending upon needs, aspirations, attitudes and beliefs. With a change in departmental policies, some officers have shifted from one class to another. In other instances, officers who are either ascendant or ambivalent have "burned out" because of excessive stress. These generalized groupings can be used by the supervisor for viewing employee conduct that is similar to other employees. Also, the supervisor must treat employees on an individual basis (Steinmetz and Todd, 1992).

Ascendant

There are few *ascendant* officers within an organization compared to the other two groupings. In fact, if a supervisor had to manage a squad of ascendants, it would, in all likelihood, prove to be disastrous for both the supervisor and the officers. The ascendant is a workaholic, an "organizational man" or someone on the fast track. This group of employees is work-oriented and perceives the job as being uppermost in life (More and Wegener, 1992). They are success driven and exhibit a high energy level. They focus on their assignment as well as the needs of the department and are self starters. Recognition and promotion are the name of the game, and everything else is secondary. Ascendants believe in themselves and know that they can produce. They especially accept the challenge of the unknown and relish working on difficult assignments. They are loners and feel they are the only ones who accomplish a task with dispatch and effectiveness.

Ascendants are usually intolerant of others who fail to work rapidly and effectively. They usually take the position that if something is to be done, they would rather do it themselves. Goal orientation dominates their work style, and they ardently support the values and mission of the department. Ascendants actively seek advancement and do everything possible to make themselves eligible for promotion. They volunteer, whenever possible, for special assignments, attend as many training programs as possible and vigorously pursue advanced academic degrees. Their allegiance is usually to the profession rather than the department, and they actively pursue openings in other agencies. Others with similar views attract them, and they use information obtained from others to enhance their own position. Figure 10.2 lists the attitudes that each of these groups has toward work.

Supervisors usually work well with ascendants. This is because, unless they become excessively exuberant, they require little supervision. Since they are achievers, supervisors turn to them when time constraints are such that immediate completion of a project is essential. This is done with the full knowledge that the task accomplishment will occur swiftly and correctly. Ascendants readily accept and follow departmental rules and require limited supervision. This allows supervisors to spend more time with subordinates in the other groups (Steinmetz and Todd, 1992).

Indifferent

Some police departments have more *indifferents* than they would like to have, but usually, most agencies have to deal with few such officers. They perform their duties at what they perceive as an acceptable level which proves to be minimal. It does not take them long to determine what is an acceptable performance level and never exceed that level. They make sure they never do so little that discipline, reprimand or termination might occur. Their primary motivation is to earn enough money so they can concentrate on their family or nondepartmental activities. Indifferents have a strong affiliative drive and get along with most everyone (Steinmetz and Greenridge, 1976). The department becomes just a place of work for this type of employee. Such an individual never volunteers or seeks promotion. The desirable operating mode is maintaining existing conditions and change is definitely undesirable. If change is personally inimical, the indifferent seeks protection from the work group or the union. This type of individual strengthens informal work groups and views peers as a primary support element. They will socialize with other officers and are prone to violate departmental rules. Even though policy might prohibit officers from leaving their beat, they will leave the beat and join other officers at eating establishments. When the union wants cooperation from officers during negotiations, these officers are ones who will respond. They will enforce the letter of the law or engage in a slow-down. Then for some miraculous reason, they will get the "blue flu" when appropriate.

When working with this group, supervisors find that motivational efforts have a short life span, and close supervision is the only way to insure the completion of tasks within a reasonable time. Indifferents, by their performance, require the supervisor to constantly document their activities. This is done to insure compliance with departmental policy and their functioning at an acceptable work level. They are really "good old boys" but can prove to be a headache for a supervisor. These individuals just slide by, seldom create waves and escape by daydreaming. They function at such a borderline that discipline can only occur after an extensive paper trail. One needs to expend an exceptional amount of effort documenting an unacceptable performance level. Officers in this group have decided the pace at which they will work even if the work level is less than acceptable. Even at a slow pace, these employees accomplish considerable work (Steinmetz and Todd, 1992).

Ambivalent

Most officers in a police organization are *ambivalent*. They are often imaginative and intelligent. They spend considerable time becoming knowledgeable about critical areas such as the use of deadly force, narcotics and dangerous drugs. They also concentrate on such areas as surveillance, crime prevention, juvenile delinquency or problem solving. Upon mastering a technique or procedure, they search for more interesting work. To the ambivalent, the routine task becomes boring quickly, and it is usually put off. Procrastination becomes the marching order.

If the frustration level becomes excessive, these officers will become anxious about their work and become less decisive in their decisionmaking. As a result, poorer decisions will be made. Resistance to new rules is quite common and becomes a typical behavior pattern. Additionally, they will, over time, become less committed to the department. If work is dull and exceedingly routine, this type of employee will become less productive. Many employees in this group do not aspire to higher ranks because of a general distrust of management. In fact, many officers in this group become antagonistic toward high levels of management. If appropriate, they will actively oppose policy changes that they perceive as detrimental (Leonard and More, 1993).

A challenging assignment is what this type of individual needs if performance is to remain high. The supervisor must spend considerable time finding new assignments, identifying new responsibilities and recognizing resolvable problems to motivate and challenge these employees. Similar to the ascerdant, ambivalents respond to praise and commendation for work well done. They readily participate in professional development programs and supervisors can recommend them for training as a motivational technique. They covet promotions at least to the level of first-line supervisor or promotion within rank. Sergeants can use this desire to increase their involvement, improve work habits and change behavior (Steinmetz and Todd, 1992).

Supervisory expectations are critical to subordinate performance. No matter what group an employee might fall into, it is essential for the supervisor to express and act in such a way that every employee knows the acceptable level of job performance. High expectations are an essential ingredient of positive performance. The reason for this is that research supports the motivational aspects of the Pygmalion effect. Most employees in an organization perform as one expects them to perform. If a supervisor conveys to an officer that a task will probably not be completed up to standards, there is every reason to believe the employee will respond accordingly. If one expects poor performance, that will be the result. If one expresses high expectations, the results are more likely to be positive (Steinmetz and Todd, 1992). A supervisor should never conduct themselves in such a way that negative expectations are part of the message received by those supervised.

As a supervisor, you will have to deal with a wide range of employee behavior. Like most supervisors, you will do your best to deal with officers fairly and

Figure 10.2
Officer Attitudes Toward Work

Ascendent

High achievement orientation
Identifies with the department
Strong work orientation
Works effectively under pressure
Receptive to feedback from superiors
Readily accepts rules and regulations
Failure can be overcome by hard work

Indifferent

Work at a minimal level
Resists motivational efforts
Promotion not sought
Gravitates toward off-the-job satisfaction
Reluctant to accept change
Identifies with the work group and police union
Will not seek added responsibilities

Ambivalent

Does not like to make decisions
Seeks approval and recognition
Superior work performer if the tasks are challenging
Often creative and intelligent
Most likely to challenge departmental policies
Receptive to change
Tends to rise to a supervisory position

competently when assessing their behavior. A simple way to rate yourself is to identify the most troublesome employee supervised. It should be someone you feel a little uncomfortable with and someone to whom you have difficulty giving negative feedback. List beliefs, attitudes and behavior of that individual that cause you difficulty. The goal is to describe what it is about the employee that distinguishes that employee from others. Next, create a second list that describes an employee with whom you are most comfortable. List that officer's behavior, characteristics, attitudes and beliefs (Holton and Holton, 1992).

Compare the descriptions, and you will find that if you are like most supervisors, you are much more similar to the officer with whom you are comfortable. All of us are more comfortable around people who have similar beliefs, attitudes and behaviors. You will judge those who are different from you more severely. You might want to use this information to rate how you deal with those being supervised.

Problem Employees

Supervisors spend a considerable amount of their time dealing with conflict created by officers. These officers behave in a way that is not acceptable to the organization. One study pointed out that about 70 percent of behavior problems involve the organization itself, the immediate supervisor and the employee (Bennett and Hess, 1992). In many instances, the conflict impacts negatively on performance. When managing personnel, you must consider a minimum of three variables: the supervisor, the officer and the individual's performance. Too often one of these variables is no longer part of the equation.

The failure to perform effectively is conditioned by other variables. Each feature must be given careful consideration as modified by the situation. Performance problems require a supervisor to analyze the situation carefully and spend the time necessary to resolve the problem (Kottler, 1994).

Problem behavior seldom evolves from a personality conflict between a supervisor and an officer. Most often, it is the result of the failure of one of the involved parties to accept tenets, behaviors and views other than their own (Steinmetz and Todd, 1992). Whatever the cause of conflict, the supervisor must deal with conduct that is inimical to the organization. If unacceptable behavior occurs, the supervisor must respond. If ignored, it can, in many instances, impact negatively on other employees and the organization itself (Bennett and Hess, 1992). Problem employees can usually be placed under one of the following headings: erudites, tyrannizers, defeatists, manipulators, or indecisives. These categories are not mutually exclusive, and they provide the supervisor with a typology of subordinates that can be useful when dealing with conflict (see Figure 10.3).

Figure 10.3
Problem Employees

Erudites Tyrannizers Defeatists Manipulators Indecisives

Erudites

Erudites are seldom at a loss for an opinion on just about every possible problem. This is especially true if they have just completed a college course or a specialized training program. Officers in this group are seldom at a loss for words and pride themselves in their command of language. The more loquacious they can be, the better they like it. They see themselves as intellectuals, learned

and in a class by themselves. Their tolerance level is somewhat low, and the acceptance of others usually comes with reluctance. This is especially true when there is a difference of opinion. They respect order and work comfortably within departmental regulations. These officers use their expertise as a power base for influencing decisions.

Supervisors can deal with this type of employee by using their own expertise especially when facing the unknown or complex problem solving. The supervisor should assimilate the knowledge of erudites in such a way that others do not take offense. The erudite should never be allowed to take over the leadership position. As a supervisor, you should acknowledge their contribution with appropriate praise.

Tyrannizers

Tyrannizers are control-oriented and do not respect others. These officers respond explosively and do everything possible to intimidate anyone who stands in their way. If one resists their ideas, the reaction of the tyrannizer is immediate. Denunciations and even personal attack are used to maintain their position. Domination of the situation is the goal, and open warfare is the game. This type of officer wants to win and will not hesitate to use coercion or create a climate of fear. They also will use threats to get their way. Their technique of choice is that of overwhelming the opposition. They follow the principle of always attacking to keep those they oppose off balance. This behavior allows them to gain control over others.

Supervisors must deal with this type of behavior by responding at the same level. The supervisor should maintain control and rebuff aggressive behavior. It requires an authoritarian response, and the supervisor must convert a lose-lose situation to one that is win-lose. The rejection of aggressive behavior is essential. Supervisors should use every tool at their disposal. Confrontation is essential, and it should be done privately and as often as necessary.

Defeatists

Defeatists are those who resist every new idea. Change is something to be skeptical of, and they find real enjoyment in performing a cynical role. These officers never say anything good about anyone or anything. They are chronic "bitchers." They never have solutions, feel comfortable as a disrupter and are rigid (CareerTrack, 1995). The name of the game is no one wins, and everyone is a loser. Defeatists complain about administrators, politicians, citizens, the Supreme Court and prosecuting attorneys. New policies are repudiated out of hand, and new programs viewed as worthless.

The way to deal with this type of employee is to confront them over an issue by asking for specifics, not generalities. Make them explain their position. Ask

penetrating questions and address the core of the issue. When rules are in dispute, get a copy of the document and discuss it in depth. Everything possible should be done to clarify the situation and deal with a specific problem. It is not the place of the supervisor to try and change the personality of the defeatist.

Manipulators

There are a few officers who fall into this group. **Manipulators** are fundamentally unethical and have no difficulty doing everything needed to gain an advantage. Half-truths and innuendos are acceptable and part of the arsenal used to maintain or enhance one's position. Knowledge is power, and the manipulators gather and impart information that will lead to an advantageous position. They enjoy dividing and conquering and, when possible, play one person against another or officers against managers. Manipulators are masters of deceit and strive to create conflict and an atmosphere where they win and others lose. Supervisors must investigate every action taken by a manipulator, then provide feedback to reduce or neutralize the impact of this type of officer. The supervisor must learn to pass judgment based on facts and objectively refute the manipulator.

Indecisives

Indecisives are impervious to either praise or punishment. Officers in this group will work diligently to avoid making a decision and are experts at procrastination. Their position is to delay until tomorrow what can be done today. They hide their attitudes and beliefs. They suppress their feelings and remain as neutral as possible. This makes it very difficult for the supervisor to judge their response. One never knows whether they support or disapprove of a decision. By never expressing support or rejection of anything, they become experts at neutrality. If indecisives do not respond negatively or positively, they are protected from others who pass judgment.

Supervisors must try to determine why the indecisive is stonewalling. What is the real reason they refuse to make a decision? One must listen carefully, then ask specific questions directed toward clarification and illumination. Ask the indecisive officers to simplify their response, and do not allow them to use platitudes, vagueness or a nondefinitive posture. The supervisor should respond with specificity and decisiveness to every dubious answer.

The Marginal Performer

When officers perform marginally, they become a real problem for a supervisor and can consume inordinate supervisory time. A minimally performing officer does just enough to get by with the intent of avoiding reprimand or dis-

Case Study

Officer Charles Chang

Officer Charles Chang was the first officer of Chinese descent appointed to the Greenvale Police Department. He is 25 years old, married and has two children. He is a graduate of a local university with a degree in political science. He was one of the top graduates of the police academy, and upon graduation, he was assigned to the swing shift in the patrol division. After finishing his probationary period, he was assigned to a patrol beat whose constituency was primarily Chinese with a mixture of blacks and Latinos. He speaks the Mandarin dialect fluently. He enjoys the respect of neighborhood leaders. He serves as an interpreter as needed and occasionally helps officers on nearby beats.

Officer Chang received outstanding performance ratings during the initial three years, but his last rating was only satisfactory. This is his second year of law school, and his total personification has been directed to the demands of higher education. His major concern is advancing his education and completing law school as soon as possible. He has expressed to his peers that his career goal is to become a prosecuting attorney. Police work provides him funds needed to support his family and pursue his educational goals.

Since entering law school, Chang's job performance has deteriorated to the point of becoming marginal. His response to calls for service has been less than desired. His enforcement of traffic laws has dropped substantially, and he conducted very few field interviews (FIs) during the last year. His coffee and meal breaks have become study periods, and the miles he has driven have dropped considerably. The sergeant assumes that Chang has been parking his vehicle, rather than patrolling, and hitting the books. The department has a policy of supporting officers who pursue higher education, and Chang's schedule allows him to attend night law school.

As Chang's immediate supervisor, how would you deal with the marginal performance of this officer? Would you try to determine whether he is studying on the job? Would you meet with him about his performance? What would you do about his issuance of fewer traffic citations, conducting fewer field interviews (FIs) and responding slowly to calls for service? Would you give any consideration to his considerable influence with the Chinese community?

cipline. The **marginal performer** knows all of the work norms and consistently performs just below the acceptable level. Report writing takes longer than expected, fewer traffic citations are issued and field interviews (FIs) may be conducted but with reduced frequency. Coffee and meal breaks are either taken more frequently, or the time of each break is extended. In some instances, they accept the challenge of finding ways to barely get by. These officers take the position that there is no reason they should work any harder than necessary. Just getting by seems to be a badge of honor.

Some marginal performers are habitually late and absent themselves from duty as much as possible. They believe sick leave is a right, not a privilege. They never volunteer for any assignment and if selected, beg off. Their general demeanor is such that they always look busy and highly involved, but such is not the case. They commit acts of commission as well as omission. Their complacency extends to every aspect of the job, and their primary interests are external to the department. Their overall behavior is passive, and they have a short-time perspective.

The marginal performer readily accepts a subordinate position and strives to never "rock the boat." Promotions are of little consequence. Opposition to change is part of an overall resistance format. They point out that there is nothing wrong with the way we are doing things now. If the proposed change is important enough, they will vigorously oppose the change, but this is usually done through the informal structure of the department.

Beyond the problems generated by their supervisor, the police organization is seen as the real culprit. Top brass are viewed as being out of step with reality. Hiding behind their desks, marginal performers see policy makers performing in a vacuum. Blaming management for their problems is a means that the marginal employee uses to excuse themselves from personal responsibility. They believe that if the supervisor and the "brass" are the sources of the problem, there is little they can do to correct the situation.

Marginal employees seldom have clearly defined short- or long- range goals, and if this is true, the supervisor should sit down with the employee and formally set goals. A plan should be agreed to that will help the employee to achieve the goals. The supervisor should ensure that the goals are compatible with departmental mission/value statements. If there is a question of formal authority, the supervisor should review what makes up the mutual working relationship. All employees must understand their status and place within the organization. The supervisor's task is to place responsibility where it belongs. Job descriptions should be reevaluated, and the supervisor should review those tasks that are the employee's responsibility (Brown, 1992).

The supervisor should praise marginal employees when they have performed effectively and should keep in mind the need for giving feedback as soon as possible after the completion of a task or assignment. The supervisor should express confidence in the employee and should voice the need for the employee to maintain acceptable performance standards and a positive attitude. The employee should be told about promotional opportunities and should be encouraged to attend special training programs as a means of improving his or her performance. The officer should be made aware of the importance of volunteering for new assignments. Hopefully, all of these will increase the officer's potentiality for promotion.

The supervisor should strive to deal with the employee on a positive level displaying enthusiasm and a positive attitude (Davidson, 1986). The employee should have every opportunity to improve performance and become a viable member of the organization. When performance exceeds recognized standards,

the officer should be given better assignments. They should be supported for promotion and, at the very least, praised for a job well done. If the employee fails to follow performance standards, this fact should be documented and corrective action taken. See Chapter 11 for a discussion of internal discipline.

Work Stressors

Organizational stress can have an effect not only on the organization but the individual. From an organizational view, the supervisor can see productivity slip and morale decline. They can also see the completion of tasks delayed, greater use of sick leave and other signs of employee discontent. Figure 10.4 lists a number of personal and organizational effects of **work stressors**. For the individual, stress can result in numerous problems ranging from alcohol abuse to suicide.

The police culture and working environment have a definite impact on police officers, and this interaction can result in an acute interruption of psychological or behavioral homeostasis. These reactions or disruptions, if prolonged, are thought to lead to a variety of illnesses. The most commonly researched of these job-stress-related illnesses have been hypertension, coronary

Figure 10.4
Personal and Organizational Effects of Work Stressors

Personal	
Alcohol abuse	Anxiety
Drug abuse	Psychosomatic diseases
Emotional instability	Eating disorders
Lack of self-control	Boredom
Fatigue	Mental illness
Marital Problems	Suicide
Depression	Health breakdowns
Insomnia	Irresponsibility
Insecurity	Violence
Frustration	
Organizational	
Accidents	Unpreparedness
Reduced productivity	Lack of creativity
High turnover	Increased sick leave
Increased errors	Premature retirement
Absenteeism	Job dissatisfaction
Damage and waste	Poor decisions
Antagonistic group action	

Adapted from: Lawrence R. Murphy and Theodore F. Schoenborn, Editors, 1987, *Stress Management in Work Settings.* Washington, DC, Government Printing Office.

heart disease, alcoholism and mental illness. Additionally, unrelieved stress can cause chronic headaches and gastric ulcers. Also, job stress can lead to severe depression, alcohol or drug abuse, aggression, marital problems and suicide. Other stressors endemic to police work include boredom, danger, shift work, lack of public support, unfavorable court decisions, unfair administrative policies and poor supervision (More and Wegener, 1992).

Everyone is impacted by stress to one degree or another; in some instances, it is positive and in others negative. Of concern to the supervisor are the negative consequences of stress, which can affect officers' alertness, physical stamina and their ability to work effectively (Goolkasian, Geddes and DeJong, 1985). Stress can also lead to excessive absenteeism, disability or early retirement. Stress can be costly to an organization. For example, in one state, the courts have ruled that coronary heart disease is occupationally related.

Task Stressors

Task stressors are wide-ranging and include role conflict and ambiguity, control over work, use of excessive force, danger, boredom and shift work. All of these complicate not only the officer's personal life but also the officer's organizational life.

Danger. The possibility of an officer being seriously injured or killed when on duty is somewhat remote, but these events do occur. Unfortunately, attacks against the police are happening with increased frequency. When emergency calls come over the radio, the officer usually responds, and energy is mobilized to deal with the contingency. In 1992, there were 62 officers killed in the line of duty. The situations in which these killings occurred were: disturbance calls, arrest situations involving robberies in progress and traffic pursuits/stops. It also included investigating suspicious persons/circumstances and ambush situations. Additionally, 66 officers were accidentally killed—the majority in automobile accidents. During the same year, 81,252 officers were assaulted and 36.5 percent of those were injured (Maguire and Pastore, 1994). In recent years, soft body armor has been worn by more and more police officers, and it has saved numerous lives. Over a 20-year period ending in 1992, there were 1,448 officers "saved" from assaults and accidents. Of these, the top three circumstances were traffic pursuits/stops, investigating suspicious persons and drug-related matters (Geller and Scott, 1992).

Boredom. One major stressor unique to part of the operational role of law enforcement is boredom. Patrolling a beat in a low-crime area can prove to be less than challenging. Time can pass very slowly during the wee hours of the morning with little to do. Dealing with the same inebriate, time after time, presents little challenge. The same applies to those who are mentally ill or live on the street. Officers soon find when enforcing traffic laws that in a short time

they have heard every excuse possible for failure to comply with the law. On the other hand, an emergency can arise where an officer must shift gears and respond to stressful and traumatic events. Confronting an armed suspect, entering a dark building, viewing a victim of a drive-by shooting and comforting an abused child are all emotionally traumatizing events that can take their toll (Phillips and Schwartz, 1992).

Role Conflict and Ambiguity. These two factors are significant sources of stress for law enforcement personnel and the police organization. This is especially true with the move toward community policing and the emphasis on resolving community problems. How does this new approach balance out against the more traditional role of control of crime? What is more important— responding to calls for service or working with a neighborhood community to reduce the sales of narcotics? These competing demands can result in role pressures that, in turn, cause conflict. The greater the conflict, the greater the potential for the creation of negative stress.

Role ambiguity occurs when there is a lack of clarity about the way tasks should be carried out. This is especially true when managers create policy that leaves line personnel hanging out to dry. This happens, for example, when a new policy is written so broadly that it defies interpretation, such as a use of force policy where the phrase "use force necessary and appropriate for the situation" is used. Such a statement, without amplification, is open to conflicting interpretations (More and Wegener, 1992).

Ambiguity is rather broad and includes the lack of clarity about objectives associated with the work role, expectations concerning the work role, and the scope and responsibilities of the job (Murphy and Schoenborn, 1987). Employees experiencing role ambiguity and conflict experience low self-confidence, higher job related tension and lower job satisfaction.

Control Over Work. Recent evidence suggests that the amount of work is not as critical to the health of a worker as the control the worker has over the work pace and related work processes. In departments engaging in community policing, it is anticipated that the officer will have more control over the tasks they have to perform. Hence, it is hoped there will be a reduction in stressors. One study found that workers with a high work load and low control have an increased risk of coronary heart disease, higher blood pressure and smoke more than employees in jobs without these characteristics.

Shift Work. An additional job demand affecting the health of workers is shift work. There is evidence that night and rotating shifts can lead to gastrointestinal disorders, emotional disturbances and an increased risk of on-the-job injury. There is a disruption of biological rhythms that result in biochemical and physiological disturbances. The shift worker becomes sleep-deprived for two reasons: (1) sleeping during the day conflicts with the biological clock that says it is day time, and (2) numerous interruptions occurring during a normal day

(Mahowald, 1994). The average day-shift worker gets eight hours more sleep weekly than the typical night-shift worker. Cumulative sleep-deprivation causes the night-shift worker to be sleepier while on the job.

In a study of scheduling shift changes, the researcher recommended that shifts be changed in a clockwise direction. It was also suggested that officers spend three weeks on each shift and limit their work time to either a four- or five-day week. When comparing officers who worked under the new system to the old, it was determined that (Law Enforcement News, 1989):

1. The frequency of poor sleep decreased four-fold.

2. There was a decline of 25 percent in incidents of falling asleep on the night shift.

3. Officers had 40 percent fewer on-duty automobile accidents per mile compared to the previous two years.

4. When officers experienced sleep deprivation, they used alcohol and sleeping pills less often.

Shift work causes officers to have impaired judgment, insight and reasoning; and as a consequence, it can create supervisory problems (Mahowald, 1994). Shift work is an essential ingredient of police work, and the supervisor should strive to create a working environment that provides for optimal functioning.

Use of Excessive Force. Civilian deaths caused by the police ranged from 297 to 424 annually for the 10-year period ending in 1990. In the last year of this period there were 385 justifiable killings of felony suspects. Of the latter, 179 involved a felon attacking a police officer and 89 felons were killed in the commission of a crime. These data reflect only the information voluntarily reported to the FBI. Historically, the primary data on justifiable homicides has been collected by the Public Health Service (U.S. Department of Health and Human Services, 1988). This data was taken from death certificates submitted by coroners and medical examiners. These data reflect that in 1986 there were 247 reported civilian deaths by legal intervention. This is in contrast to the FBI data that listed 301 justifiable killings. Researchers feel that neither figure is a true representation and suggest that death certificates are probably underreported by approximately 50 percent.

Actually, police shootings are infrequent, and only one officer in 60 has killed someone during a 15-year period (Fyfe, 1982). In a study of the Los Angeles Police Department, it was determined that a significant number of officers repeatedly misused force and persistently ignored written policies. An Assistant Chief of the department pointed out that the department had failed miserably to hold supervisors accountable when excessive force was used under their command (Independent Commission of the LAPD, 1991).

Officers who have been involved in excessive use of force situations can have severe legal, physical and emotional problems. In one study, respondents to a survey indicated that involvement in a shooting incident was the most dangerous and traumatic experience that an officer could face during a career. Post-shooting traumatic responses include a wide range of stressful reactions, and these are set forth in Figure 10.5.

Figure 10.5
Post-Shooting Traumatic Responses

1. Guilt
2. Anxiety
3. Fear
4. Nightmares
5. Flashbacks
6. Social withdrawal
7. Impaired memory
8. Inability to sleep
9. Sensory distortion
10. Grasping for life
11. Crying
12. A heightened sense of danger
13. Sorrow over depriving a person of life
14. Family problems
15. Alcohol abuse
16. Fear they will be fired, criminally charged or sued in civil court

Sources: Harold E. Russell and Allan Biegel, 1990, *Understanding Human Behavior for Effective Police Work,* Third Edition, New York, Basic Books; Roger M. Solomon and James M. Horn, 1986, "Post Shooting Traumatic Reactions: A Pilot Study," in James T. Reese and Harvey A. Goldstein, editors, 1986, *Psychological Services For Law Enforcement,* Washington, DC, Federal Bureau of Investigation; and Bill Clede, 1994, "Stress Insidious or Traumatic is Treatable," *Law and Order,* Vol. 42, No. 6, 68-77.

Without question an officer involved in a shooting is seldom prepared to cope with such a traumatic event, and the same is true of the officer's family, fellow officers and supervisors. The supervisor should ensure that an officer involved in a shooting is referred to available employee assistance programs. In one survey, it was found that 79 percent of police psychologists counseled officers charged with excessive force (Scrivner, 1994).

Personal Problems

Information can come to the attention of the supervisor that might possibly require an intervention on the part of the supervisor. In some instances, the supervisor intervenes directly, and in other cases, an officer asks for help. Of all management levels, the close contact the supervisor has with line personnel will

usually result in their becoming aware of inadequate or deteriorating work performance before other managers. In some situations, the supervisor can function as a counselor, and in other instances the officer should be referred to appropriate employee assistance programs. Symptoms of stress can result in a wide variety of maladies, and those that have been studied and found important to law enforcement are discussed below.

Suicide

Earlier studies conducted from the 1930s thorough the 1960s concluded that the police had a high **suicide** rate. These earlier studies included officers from such diverse police departments as San Francisco, Chicago and New York. In a Wyoming study, it was determined that the suicide rate for officers was the second highest among occupational groups studied. In Tennessee, a report published in 1975 found that police officers had the third highest suicide rate among occupational groups. In a study of Chicago police officers, it was found that 60 percent of the suicides were linked to alcoholism (Wagner and Brzeczek, 1983).

From 1950 to 1967, the suicide rate of officers in the New York City Police Department averaged 22 per 100,000 (Friedman, 1967), and in 1994 there were 29 per 100,000 annually (Law Enforcement News, October 1994). This contrasts with the general population rate of 12.2 per 100,000. In 1991, the suicide rate for white males was 21.7 per 100,000, and for white females it was 5.2 per 100,000. During the same year, the suicide rate for black males was 12.1, and for black females it was 1.9. In 1991 there were 24,769 suicides in this nation (Statistical Abstract of the U.S., 1994). Hence, suicide is more prevalent in the white male population, and the same is true for the police field.

Nationally, some 300 officers committed suicide in 1994, compared to 137 who were killed in the line of duty by weapons or other causes (Hays, 1994). In the 10 years before 1995, 64 New York City Police officers killed themselves, and during the same period, 20 officers were killed in the line of duty. One of the suicides in 1994 was an officer who had been implicated in the "Dirty 30" drug-corruption scandal. This case involved more than two dozen New York City Police officers who had been arrested. In another instance, a 30-year-old officer killed himself after being charged with drunken driving and leaving the scene of the accident. In a study issued in 1994, the New York City Police Foundation concluded the fundamental reasons officers kill themselves are because of personal problems, substance abuse and despondency. The study further stated suicide was not from job-related stress, as many would believe (Law Enforcement News, October 1994). There is no single reason for the suicide of police officers, but it is happening with such frequency that supervisors should not overlook the possibility of such an occurrence.

Alcohol Abuse

Studies by the federal government point out that one in 10 adults in the United States have a drinking problem. In 1992, the adult population used 37.4 gallons of **alcohol** per capita. A 1990 study showed that of those 26 years of age and older, 5.51 percent had five or more drinks in a single day during the two weeks before the study (Statistical Abstract of the U.S., 1994). Additionally, in 1989 there were 374,437 adults in alcohol treatment programs. It has also been estimated that 200,000 individuals die annually of alcohol-caused diseases (Autry, 1994). One estimate puts the number of alcoholics at 10 million, including individuals from every occupation and age level. Many use alcohol as a drug of choice to reduce discomfort and provide for a degree of pleasure. It has been suggested that stress may be involved in the decision to use alcohol (Violanti, Marshall and Howe, 1985). Whatever the reason for the consumption of alcohol, it can become a serious supervisory problem.

Alcohol as a drug of choice is extolled in advertisements suggesting that it leads to happiness and enjoyment. Based on advertising, one can hardly imagine having a party without alcoholic refreshments (Campbell and Graham, 1988). Police officers in many agencies find a subculture that supports heavy drinking (Farmer, 1990). Within the police field, the practice of "hoisting a few" is common and has become known as "choir practice." When officers drink to deal with problems, it can lead to a wide range of inimical job behaviors.

In one of its pamphlets, Alcoholics Anonymous has defined alcoholism as follows:

> Whether or not you are an alcoholic is not determined by where you drink, when you started drinking, how long you have been drinking, . . . what, or even how much. The true test is the answer to this question: What has alcohol done to you? If it has affected your relationships; if it has influenced the way you schedule your days; if it has affected your health, . . . if you are in any way preoccupied with alcohol—then the likelihood is that you have a problem.

As far back as 1955, the Chicago Police Department organized officers to help other officers with a drinking problem. Another early program was the police stress program of the Boston Police Department. It initially focused on police officers with drinking problems and in later years, expanded to include a wide range of stress-related difficulties (Goolkasian, Geddes and DeJong, 1985). Today, it is quite common to find departments that have their own counseling program for alcoholics or refer officers to other agencies or organizations (Alpert and Dunham, 1992). Treatment has proven to be effective as indicated by a program in the Philadelphia Police Department. Officers had a 38 percent reduction in sick days and a 62 percent annual reduction in injury days (Campbell and Graham, 1988).

Divorce

The incidence of **divorce** has increased considerably over the years. In 1970, the divorce rate was 4.3 million in the United States, and this increased to 16.7 million by 1993. Whatever the divorce rate, most observers agree that police work is especially demanding. Officers can really get involved in their work and bring their problems home. Consequently, police work tends to become a 24-hour-a-day involvement which can strain the best of relationships. Shift changes are especially difficult for all family members. It seems to some police officers that one is on a constant shift merry-go-round wherein one hardly gets accustomed to a shift and it is time to change. It interrupts the social life of the officer and his or her spouse. In many instances, officers socialize only with other officers and their spouses.

Early research reflected a high divorce rate. In three communities, the percentage of divorced officers ranged from 17 to 33.3 percent. This was in contrast to a 1983 study showing a divorce rate of 5 percent in the Los Angeles Police Department. Training programs for spouses describing the nature and problems in police work, support groups and counseling have all contributed to stronger police families (Alpert and Dunham, 1992).

Spousal Concerns About Danger

Spouses are also placed in the position of being constantly concerned about the physical well-being of officers. Our society is becoming increasingly violent and, correspondingly, police work increasingly dangerous. In 1982, there were 55,775 assaults on law enforcement officers, and this increased to 81,252 in 1992. During the same years, the percentage of those personally injured increased from 16.4 percent to 25.5 (Maguire and Pastor, 1994). If other officers in the department are injured or killed, the spouse reacts by becoming increasingly concerned about her loved one. Peer counseling, spousal groups and police psychologists have been especially effective in dealing with this problem.

Early Warning Systems

The **early warning system** has been instituted in several departments as a means of monitoring officer conduct and alerting managers to inappropriate behavior. The development of these programs is still in its infancy. There is a clear-cut impetus and need for developing a system that deals with certain traits or behavior patterns. This system usually utilizes information based on the behaviors of officers who have been fired for disciplinary reasons and then identifies officers who have been recognized as having similar problems.

Using computer software, the department tracks and records incidents as they occur. It is a non-disciplinary management system and "flags" officers at risk. Behavioral activities are utilized to establish a pattern even though a single activity may, in and of itself, prove to be of limited consequence. When combined with other activities, it may indicate a behavioral pattern that needs to be reviewed by management (Oliver, 1994). It allows managers to intervene before the occurrence of serious misconduct that could get officers arrested, fired or sued (Law Enforcement News, 1994).

Factors considered relevant vary considerably. One set of factors used to assess an officer's propensity to misuse force is listed in Figure 10.6. In Chicago, information used to identify behavior problems included such variables as race, sex, age, education, marital status and frequency of sick days. It also includes traffic accidents and lost weapons or badges. This list of traits was derived from the analysis of information about 200 terminated officers (Law Enforcement News, 1994). Of the police officers who were fired, a majority of the problems identified extended back over a number of years. Treated as isolated incidents, they were not serious enough to warrant disciplinary action (Ehrenhalt, 1994).

Figure 10.6
Factors Used to Assess an Officer's Propensity to Use Force

1. Complaints
2. Discipline records
3. Commendations and evaluations
4. Assignments, including partners and supervisors
5. Rate of disorderly conduct charges filed against arrestees
6. Rate of charges against arrestees for resisting or assaulting the officer
7. Shooting incidents
8. Incidents resulting in injury

Source: William A. Geller and Michael Scott, 1992, *Deadly Force: What We Know.* Washington, DC, Police Executive Research Forum.

Another list of elements, prepared by Will Oliver (Oliver, 1994), includes:

1. Loss of equipment
2. Vehicular accidents
3. Injured on duty reports
4. Discharge of firearms
   A. Accidental
   B. Duty related
5. Excessive use of force reports
6. Sick leave in excess of five days

7. A pattern of using sick leave of one or two days over a long period of time

8. Complaints

9. Reprimands

10. Disciplinary action

11. Pursuits

12. Resisting arrest reports

13. Performance reports

14. Financial difficulties

15. Frequent transfers

The early warning system should be monitored by supervisors or higher ranking management personnel. Those conducting such a review should remember that the process, at this point, is nondisciplinary. Database information should be analyzed in an attempt to discover the source of a problem. The goal is to intervene and prevent behavior from becoming a disciplinary problem. This is done by tailoring a response to the identified behavior. The response can include (Oliver, 1994):

1. Counseling

2. Training

3. Referral to departmental resources such as an employee assistance program

4. Psychological examination

5. Physical examination

6. Urinalysis

The response is predicated on a discussion with the officer during which the problem(s) is identified and treatment strategies determined. The desire is to get the officer back into the departmental "mainstream." It is nondisciplinary, and the officer has the right to refuse participation (Law Enforcement News, September 1994). In one department, treatment strategies are referred to the chief for approval before the implementation of corrective action. It is essential to monitor an officer's progress on a quarterly basis to see that treatment strategies are effective (Oliver, 1994).

Employee Assistance Programs

The majority of organizations recognize that it is very costly to keep nonproductive employees who have personal or behavioral problems. On the other hand, managers know that it is costly to lose well-trained, experienced officers. Consequently, agencies have created programs to provide structured assistance

to employees. These programs have been a part of businesses for many years and, more recently, a part of public administration. One part of these programs, employee counseling, has been a fixture in law enforcement for a long time. In 1990, approximately 77 percent of municipal police agencies had a policy about this activity (Reaves, 1992). During the last decade, a wide range of assistance activities have been incorporated into what is called **Employee Assistance Programs** (EAPs). Comprehensive programs use in-house and external specialists when providing assistance to employees. Employees are offered the same kind of assistance that is given to those who have physical illnesses (Plunkett, 1992). Today EAPs cover a wide range of services to help employees deal with emotional, family, psychological, financial and retirement matters. Figure 10.7 lists some of the problems addressed by an employee assistance program.

Figure 10.7
Problems that Can Be Dealt with by an Employee Assistance Program

Alcohol and drug abuse	Job stress
Anxiety	Legal problems
Career development	Marital problems
Compulsive gambling	Monetary problems
Depression	Nutrition
Disciplinary action	Police shootings
Divorce	Retirement planning
Eating disorders	Smoking
Exercise	Spouse abuse
Grief	Termination
Job burnout	Weight Control

Sources: John G. Stratton (1987). "Employee Assistance Programs—A Profitable Approach for Employees and Organization," in Harry W. More and Peter C. Unsinger (eds.). *Police Managerial Use of Psychology and Psychologists.* Springfield, IL., Charles C Thomas; and James M. Jenks and Brian L. P. Zevnik (1993). *Employee Benefits: Plain and Simple.* New York: Collier Books.

Critical Incident Stress Management

Extreme violence and trauma do not occur on a daily basis in the lives of a majority of police officers. When they do occur, they can leave numerous psychological scars. It is not just the taking of a life. It can be involvement in a shoot-out or assisting at a disaster such as an earthquake, tornado or flood. Other incidents that can cause significant emotional response include vehicular and airplane crashes. Continued exposure to violence can result in **Post Traumatic Stress Disorder** (PTSD), a psychological condition that is caused by one's inability to successfully manage an emotional response triggered by severe trauma (Paradise, 1991).

The symptoms of PTSD generally include (Phillips and Schwartz, 1992):

1. When exposed to places and situations resembling the initial traumatic event, the officer re-experiences the traumatic event. The officer can have nightmares, flashbacks or hallucinations.

2. Continual avoidance of any thought about the traumatic event.

3. A sense of detachment from others, including family members.

4. Insomnia.

5. Spontaneous outbursts of anger.

6. Preoccupation with thoughts of death or dying.

7. Inability to concentrate.

If any of the above symptoms persist for more than one month, an officer is probably suffering from PTSD. Daily pressure of police work can take a toll on officers as they are repeatedly exposed to critical incidents. These officers will have marital problems, become chronically irritable and abuse alcohol or drugs. They can also suffer from depression, use excessive force or develop ulcers (Clede, 1994). All of these can impair the officers' usefulness not only to themselves but to the agency.

Intervention early enough after a critical incident or the identification of an officer who is having problems similar to those listed above can help eliminate the propensity for the development of full-blown symptoms of PTSD (Paradise, 1992).

As soon as possible after a critical incident, officers should participate in a debriefing session. Typical of these programs is the one utilized by the Drug Enforcement Agency (DEA). This organization requires agents involved in a shooting to attend a briefing session within 48 hours. During this session, it is stressed that the officer is human, and although a reaction may not have occurred yet, it can occur. Information about PTSD is discussed. As trauma occurs, the DEA utilizes Trauma Teams composed of trained agents who provide nonclinical supportive intervention (Paradise, 1992).

Peer Counseling

One of the first programs in **peer counseling** was started by the Boston Police Department. Its initial program was limited to officers with alcohol problems. Peer counselors should have several years of "street experience" in order to enjoy the trust and respect of fellow officers. One's credibility rating is high when one has been there. Peer counselors can truly empathize with fellow officers who are experiencing problems created by the unique demands of police

work. Officers trust other police officers, and if non-police personnel are used, they have to attain credibility.

Officers are reluctant to seek help and admit that they have stress-related problems with which they are not coping (Shearer, 1993). Professional psychologists have been used to train police peer counselors, serve as consultants and function as referral sources (Stratton, 1987). Peer counselors have been highly successful in dealing with such problems as alcoholism, drug abuse, terminal illness, deaths, on-the-job injuries and retirement. The real advantage of peer counseling is that it provides officers and members of their family with an opportunity to confidentially discuss personal and professional problems (Janik, 1995). Peers are equals, readily available and have a greater ease of interaction than professionals. Some peer counseling programs are quite well-developed as illustrated by the Fort Worth Police Department program. It has a ratio of one peer to every 60 officers, allowing for an immediate response to critical incidents including mass casualty situations (Greenstone, Dunn, and Leviton, 1995).

Summary

Supervisors must set the tone, change the paradigms and create a foundation resulting in a truly supportive working environment. This can be done by drawing employees into the decision-making process and making them responsible for results. In recent years, the tone of many police organizations has been set by creating departmental value statements. Values become the basis for the beliefs and actions that are taken by each officer.

Dealing with problem employees occurs more often than one would like. When an employee becomes difficult to work with, tasks are not accomplished or work is done with indifference, a supervisor must take corrective action. In some situations, unsuitable behavior can impair the effectiveness of the officer, and in other cases, it can impair the effectiveness of other organizational members. Problem employees can usually be placed in one of the following categories: erudites, tyrannizers, defeatists, manipulators, or indecisives.

One expert found three types of individuals in organizations: ascendent, indifferent and ambivalent. The number of employees in each group varies from agency to agency, but these are what supervisors actually find in an organization. These generalized categories can be utilized by supervisors as a means of viewing employee conduct.

Marginal performers are a real problem for supervisors and can consume considerable supervisory time. Such employees should be given every opportunity to improve their performance. They should be praised when work performance improves. They should be monitored, and when they perform inadequately, corrective action should be taken.

The police culture and working environment have a definite impact on police officers, and this interaction can result in an acute interruption of psychological or behavioral homeostasis. These reactions or disruptions, if prolonged, are thought to lead to a variety of illnesses.

Specific task stressors in law enforcement are wide-ranging and include role conflict and ambiguity. It also includes the use of excessive force, danger, boredom and shift work. All of these complicate not only the officer's personal life but their organizational life as well.

In some situations the supervisor can function as a counselor, and in other instances, the officer should be referred to an appropriate employee assistance program. Symptoms of stress can result in a wide variety of maladies, and those that have been studied and found important to law enforcement are suicide, alcohol abuse, spousal concerns about danger and divorce.

The early warning system has been instituted in several departments to monitor officer conduct and alert managers to inappropriate behavior. This system utilizes information based on the behavior of officers who have been terminated for disciplinary reasons. Using this data, it then identifies currently employed officers who may have similar problems.

Employee assistance programs offer the same type of assistance that is given to those who have a physical illness. Comprehensive programs use in-house and external specialists when providing assistance to employees. Today EAPs cover a wide range of services to help employees deal with emotional, psychological, family, financial and retirement matters.

Case Study

Officer Roberta Stone

Officer Roberta Stone, an employee of the department for three years, has served in the patrol division all of that time. She graduated from the local college where she majored in psychology. She completed the police academy without difficulty and her Field Training Officer (FTO) passed her with flying colors. She was the first one in her family to obtain a college degree, and every family member opposed her entry into law enforcement. She initially became interested in police work after completing an internship in her local department. This sparked her interest in a law enforcement career, and immediately after graduation from college, she entered the police academy.

She was not the first woman assigned to patrol, but she is the only female currently in that assignment. Four other women are sworn officers and serve in other divisions out of a total of 47 officers. She is 25 years old, single and enrolled as a part-time student in the local university. She is pursuing a graduate degree in business management and taking two classes each semester. She is assigned to the night shift at her request so she can attend evening graduate classes.

Male officers have accepted her as an equal in the patrol shift to which she is assigned. She works in a one-person patrol car assigned to a beat that contains a mixture of residential and commercial units. The majority of her shift is spent responding to calls for service. The bulk of these involve family dis-

putes, drunkenness and burglary. During her three years of service, she has received two commendations for preliminary investigations conducted in armed robbery cases. She has developed numerous sources of information on her beat and readily shares information with other officers and detectives.

Two months ago she engaged in a pursuit involving an armed robbery suspect during which her vehicle went out of control and the car was totaled. She was not seriously injured but underwent physical therapy for back pains. She was on sick leave for four days. Recently she dropped her 9mm pistol, and it accidentally discharged. Additionally, this month she took two sick days stating that she had the flu. The two days she was off coincided with the days she was scheduled for finals at the local university. Last week, she filed an excessive use of force report that involved subduing a suspect who was throwing large stones at passing vehicles. She and a back-up officer were able to resolve this problem and place the suspect under arrest even though the subject threw stones at each of them, and she was struck twice. She took two days off on sick leave after this incident.

Because you are Roberta Stone's immediate supervisor a computer printout has been sent to you listing all of the above events. You have been requested to respond to the lieutenant regarding what should be done. These items are listed as part of the department's early warning system. Keep in mind that it is a nondisciplinary situation. What would you do? What would you include in the response? Why?

Key Concepts

alcohol	indifferent employees
ambivalent employees	manipulators
ascendant employees	marginal performers
critical incident stress management	peer counseling
departmental values	post traumatic stress disorder
defeatists	problem employees
divorce	suicide
early warning systems	task stressors
employee assistance programs	tyrannizers
erudites	value statements
indecisives	work stressors

Discussion Topics and Questions

1. Why is it important to create departmental values?

2. What is the difference between ascendant and indifferent employees?

3. Discuss the types of problem employees.

4.   What are some of the organizational effects of work stressors?

5.   Discuss the behavior of marginal employees.

6.   Why are manipulators difficult to supervise?

For Further Reading

Geller, William A. and Michael S. Scott (1992). *Deadly Force: What We Know.* Washington, DC: Police Executive Research Forum.

> A definitive study of the use of force by American police. Includes an excellent chapter on shooting control strategies to encompass policy development, enforcement and personnel practices. Of special interest is the section that discusses the delicate balance of supporting officers while holding them to high standards of conduct.

Greenstone, James L., J. Michael Dunn and Sharon C. Leviton (1995). "Fort Worth's Departmental Peer Counseling Program." *The Police Chief,* Vol. LXII, No. 1.

> Since its inception, the peer counseling team has grown from six counselors to 25. The authors point out that all peer counselors serve without compensation and are available 24 hours a day. All are volunteers and are carefully screened, tested, evaluated and trained prior to appointment. Counselors provide crisis intervention services and critical incident stress management in the form of debriefings and defusing.

Mahowald, Mark W. (1994). "Sleep Disorders and Their Effect on Law Enforcement." *The Police Chief,* Vol. LXI, No. 6.

> Sleep requirements appear to be determined by heredity rather than personality factors. The same seems to be true for one's biological clock. The author discusses shift work pointing out the well-documented impairment of such functions as judgment, insight and reasoning. He lists rules of thumb that can be used to deal with shift work.

Oliver, Will (1994). "The Early Warning System." *Law and Order,* Vol. 42, No. 9.

> Describes the emerging concept of an early warning system. Emphasizes that it is a nondisciplinary management system used to identify potential problem officers. It describes a computer database which tracks individual officers based on reportable elements of behavior. The article describes behaviors utilized ranging from the discharge of a firearm to motor vehicle damage.

References

Alpert, Geoffrey P. and Roger G. Dunham (1992). *Policing Urban America,* 2nd ed. Prospect Heights, IL: Waveland Press, Inc.

Autry, James A. (1994). *Life and Work.* New York: William Morrow and Company, Inc.

Bennett, Wayne W. and Karen M. Hess (1992). *Management and Supervision in Law Enforcement.* St. Paul: West Publishing Company.

Brown, Michael F. (1992). "The Sergeant's Role in a Modern Law Enforcement Agency." *The Police Chief,* Vol. LIX, No. 5.

Campbell, Drusilla and Marilyn Graham (1988). *Drugs and Alcohol in the Workplace.* New York: Facts on File Publications.

CareerTrack (1995). *How to Overcome Negativity in the Workplace.* Boulder, CO: CareerTrack.

Clede, Bill (1994). "Stress: Insidious or Traumatic is Treatable." *Law and Order,* Vol. 42, No. 6.

Cottringer, William (1994). "Managing: Creating Quality Work Environments." *Security Management,* Vol. 38, No. 6.

Ehrenhalt, Alan (1994). "Cops, Computers and the Concept of Character." *Governing,* Vol. 91, No. 10.

Farmer, R. (1990). "Clinical and Managerial Implications of Stress Research on the Police." *Journal of Police Science and Administration,* Vol. 17, No. 4.

Friedman, P. (1967). "Suicide Among Police." In E. Schneidman (ed.) *Essays in Self-destruction.* New York: Science.

Fyfe, James J. (1982). *Readings on Use of Deadly Force.* Washington, DC: Police Foundation.

Geller, William A. and Michael S. Scott (1992). *Deadly Force: What We Know.* Washington, DC: Police Executive Research Forum.

Goldstein, Harvey A. (1986). *Psychological Services for Law Enforcement.* Washington, DC: Federal Bureau of Investigation.

Goolkasian, Gail A., Ronald W. Geddes and William DeJong (1985). *Coping With Police Stress.* Washington, DC: National Institute of Justice.

Greenstone, James L., J. Michael Dunn and Sharon C. Leviton (1995). "Fort Worth's Departmental Peer Counseling Program." *The Police Chief,* Vol. LXII, No. 1.

Harvey, Thomas R. (1990). *Checklist for Change.* Boston: Allyn and Bacon, Inc.

Hays, Tom (1994). "Suicide Continues to Stalk the Police Beat." *The Washington Post,* Dec. 31.

Holton, Bill and Cher Holton (1992). *The Manager's Short Course.* New York: John Wiley and Sons, Inc.

Independent Commission on the Los Angeles Police Department (1991). *Report of the Independent Commission on the Los Angeles Police Department.* Los Angeles: Independent Commission on the Los Angeles Police Department.

Janik, James (1995). "Who Needs Peer Support?" *The Police Chief,* Vol. LXII, No. 1.

Jenks, James M. and Brian L. P. Zevnik (1993). *Employee Benefits: Plain and Simple.* New York: Collier Books.

Kottler, Jeffrey (1994). "Beyond Blame: Resolving Conflict at Work." *Hemispheres.* Chicago: Pace Communications, Inc.

Kouzes, James M. and Barry Z. Posner (1993). *Credibility: How Leaders Gain and Lose It, Why People Demand It.* San Francisco: Jossey-Boss Publishers.

Law Enforcement News (1989). "Police Study in Philadelphia Finds Benefits in Revised Shifts." Oct. 15, Vol. XV, No. 300.

Law Enforcement News (1994). "Artificial Intelligence Tackles a Very Real Problem—Police Misconduct Control." Sept. 30, Vol. XX, No. 408.

Law Enforcement News (1994). "NYPD Officials Grope For Answers to Record-tying Binge of Cop Suicides." Oct. 31, Vol. XX, No. 410.

Leonard, V.A. and Harry W. More (1993). *Police Organization and Management,* 8th ed. Westbury, NY: The Foundation Press, Inc.

Maguire Kathleen and Ann L. Pastore (eds.) (1994). *Sourcebook of Criminal Justice Statistics—1993*. Washington, DC: Bureau of Justice Statistics.

Mahowald, Mark W. (1994). "Sleep Disorders and their Effect on Law Enforcement." *The Police Chief,* Vol. LXI, No. 6.

More, Harry W. and W. Fred Wegener (1992). *Behavioral Police Management.* New York: Macmillan Publishing Co.

Murphy, Lawrence R. and Theodore F. Schoenborn (eds.) (1987). *Stress Management in Work Settings.* Washington, DC: Department of Health and Human Services.

Oliver, Will (1994). "The Early Warning System." *Law and Order,* Vol. 42, No. 9.

Paradise, Paul R. (1992). "The DEA Trauma Team." *Law and Order,* Vol. 39, No. 6.

Phillips, Wayne and Gene Schwartz (1992). "Post-traumatic Stress." *Sheriff,* Vol. 44, No.2.

Plunkett, W. Richard (1992). *Supervision: The Direction of People at Work,* 6th ed. Boston, Allyn and Bacon, Inc.

Reaves, Brian A. (1992). *Law Enforcement Management and Administrative Statistics, 1990: Data for Individual State and Local Agencies with 100 or More Officers.* Washington, DC: Bureau of Justice Statistics.

Russell, Harold E. and Allan Biegel (1990). *Understanding Human Behavior for Effective Police Work,* 3rd ed. New York: Basic Books.

Samarra, Charles (1992). *Alexandria Police: These are our Values.* Alexandria, VA: Alexandria Police Department.

Scrivner, Ellen M. (1994). *Controlling Police Use of Excessive Force: The Role of the Police Psychologist.* Washington, DC: National Institute of Justice.

Shearer, Robert W. (1993). "Police Officer Stress: New Approaches for Handling Tension." *The Police Chief,* Vol. LX, No.8.

Solomon, Roger M. and James M. Horn (1986). "Post-Shooting Traumatic Reactions: A Pilot Study." In James T. Reese and Harvey A. Goldstein (eds.). *Psychological Services for Law Enforcement.* Washington, DC: Federal Bureau of Investigation.

Statistical Abstract of the United States (1994). *Statistical Abstract of the United States,* 114th ed. Lanham, MD: Bernard Press.

Steinmetz, Lawrence L. and Charles D. Greenridge (1976). "Realities that Shape Managerial Style: Participative Philosophy Won't Always Work." In *Participative Management: Concepts, Theory and Implementation.* Atlanta, GA: Georgia State University.

Steinmetz, Lawrence L. and H. Ralph Todd, Jr. (1992). *Supervision: First Line Management,* 5th ed. Homewood, IL: Richard D. Irwin, Inc.

Stratton, John G. (1987). "Employee Assistance Programs—A Profitable Approach for Employees and Organizations." In Harry W. More and Peter C. Unsinger (eds.) *Police Managerial Use of Psychology and Psychologists.* Springfield, IL: Charles C Thomas, Publisher.

U.S. Department of Health and Human Services (1988). *Vital Statistics of the United States 1986* (Vol. II, Mortality). Hyattsburg, MD: Public Health Service.

Violanti, John M., James R. Marshall and Barbara Howe (1985). "Stress, Coping, and Alcohol Use: The Police Connection." *Journal of Police Science and Administration,* Vol. 13, No.2.

Wagner, M. and R. Brzeczek (1983). "Alcoholism and Suicide: A Fatal Connection." *FBI Law Enforcement Bulletin,* Vol. 52, No. 10.

Zook, Frank B. (1994). "Deming's Ideas to Live By: Not Just Empty Buzzwords." *Pennsylvania Business Central,* Vol. 3, No. 9.

Internal Discipline—
A System of Accountability

11

Introductory Case Study

Sergeant Kenneth J. Horton

Sergeant Kenneth J. "Kenny" Horton, second in command of a very small suburban police department, received information from an anonymous source indicating that two veteran police officers had been stopping teenage motorists without the required "probable cause" in order to search their vehicles for drugs, alcoholic beverages and other forms of contraband. The officers have made several arrests subsequent to these illegal searches. They have, according to the source, filed false reports and given perjured testimony designed to cover up their professional misconduct and justify their unlawful actions.

Sergeant Horton is reluctant to deal with this situation. The accused officers are his friends as well as his colleagues. He also knows the department has been under considerable pressure to get tough on teenage alcohol consumption.

After a week of soul searching, Sergeant Horton has decided not to act on the complaint. He has convinced himself that anonymous complaints lack merit and that he may do more harm than good by pursuing the matter. In addition, he is now willing to accept the idea that it may be necessary to violate some individual rights in order to protect and serve the society at large.

Do the ends justify the means in a democratic society? If you were in Sergeant Horton's shoes, how would you have processed this particular complaint? What steps should have been taken to ensure accountability in this situation? Is inaction a legitimate alternative? Who is ultimately responsible for setting the moral tone for the organization and its members?

Police Work

Police work is an incredibly complex human enterprise. The assigned mission of the American police establishment is to serve and protect the community. While the "law enforcer" image has been made popular by the mass media, it is inaccurate and far too simplistic. According to one expert (Newman, 1986), general assignment police personnel spend no more than 10 to 15 percent of their on-duty time actually enforcing the criminal law. Most of their time is spent keeping the peace and providing essential nonpolice services. In carrying out their mission, police departments are expected to:

1. Protect life and property.

2. Resolve interpersonal conflict and preserve the peace.

3. Maintain social order.

4. Prevent crime by proactive patrol and other measures.

5. Repress crime through effective law enforcement.

6. Create and perpetuate a sense of security.

7. Identify and apprehend those who have broken the law.

8. Regulate various types of noncriminal behavior.

9. Recognize and deal with police/public safety hazards.

10. Facilitate the movement of people and motor vehicles.

11. Provide essential emergency services.

12. Help those individuals who cannot care for themselves.

13. Safeguard legal and constitutional rights of citizens.

The job is complex; it lacks clear-cut boundaries and is frequently underrated, unappreciated and unpleasant. Even though policing is a rewarding career, it is often dull, monotonous, dirty and dangerous.

Police officers work at the critical pressure point where law, human tragedy and society's expectations (for safety and a sense of security) come together. The police represent the fine line that separates freedom from chaos and legitimate social control from tyranny. American police officers are inundated with complexity and buffeted about by change, ambiguity, stress and radically different demands coming from various segments of the community. While they also come from the community, police officers are isolated from it in terms of their

awesome power, formal authority, occupational role and distinct subcultural orientation. American police personnel exercise virtually unlimited discretion in low-visibility transactions with all sorts of people. They are constantly being bombarded with reality as they grapple with uncontrolled passion, brutality and the evil side of human nature. Men and women who wear the badge see crime, predatory violence, human degradation, insanity, corruption and bizarre behavior on a daily basis. They are often confronted with grisly reminders of man's inhumanity and mortality. Mark Baker (1985) has observed that police officers are a composite of their unique experiences and a reflection of the people they police. Many police officers perceive themselves as society's garbage men.

Due to their broad discretionary power, the inordinately complex nature of their work and the type of clientele with whom they interact, police officers are particularly vulnerable to corruption and other forms of police deviance. **Police deviance** describes activities which are inconsistent with the officer's legal authority, organizational authority or standards of ethical conduct. Corruption usually refers to the sale of legitimate authority for personal gain. Police occupational deviance includes not only corruption but the unlawful use of force, mistreatment of prisoners, discrimination, illegal search and seizure, perjury, planting of evidence and other forms of misconduct that are committed under the color of police authority (Barker and Carter, 1991). **Occupational deviance** can, for the purpose of analysis, be broken down into three general categories:

1.   **Nonfeasance**. Failure to take appropriate action as required by law or department policy.

2.   **Misfeasance**. Performing a required and lawful task in an unacceptable, inappropriate or unprofessional manner.

3.   **Malfeasance**. Wrongdoing or illegal conduct that is dependent on or related to the misuse of legitimate authority.

Police deviance is a persistent and inescapable reality that serves to spotlight incompetence and the seedy side of human nature.

Police personnel work in a complex, hazard-prone environment and, like all other human beings, have feet of clay. Some make errors, fail to perform assigned duties, abuse authority, misuse discretion, commit illegal acts and engage in behavior "unbecoming an officer." Police administrators and first-line supervisors (i.e., sergeants) are responsible for policing the police.

No one can say with certainty just how much corruption, crime and other forms of deviance there is in law enforcement because those who participate in it often have the power and know-how to cover it up. In addition, most police departments are simply not equipped to keep score. According to many of those who study this phenomenon, the nature of police crime, corruption and occupational deviance makes it impossible to quantify. Consequently, when we try to estimate the extent of the problem, we are forced to deal with general impressions and isolated bits of information.

Due to the nature of their job, the clientele with whom they interact and the wide variety of temptations they face every day, police officers represent a population at risk in terms of illegal and other forms of inappropriate behavior. They find themselves with ample opportunity to commit crimes and to benefit from the largess of those who seek to influence them. There are police officers who sell their professional soul for power, money, sex and drugs. They mortgage the public interest for their own personal gain. Incompetent and corrupt police officers are a plague on the land.

Police administrators are finally beginning to acknowledge that crime, corruption and other forms of occupational deviance may be endemic to policing and accept the idea that varying types of less than lawful behavior exist in all police agencies (Kappeler, Sluder and Alpert, 1994). Many now realize that corruption may be the oldest and most persistent problem in American policing (Walker, 1992). Policing the police is a paramount issue and a growing concern for all police managers.

Researchers have identified five basic problems in urban policing that they regard as institutional preconditions for police crime, corruption and occupational deviance:

1. **Wide Discretion**. Discretion does not, in itself, make illegal police behavior inevitable, but it enables policemen to conceal their poor decisions and improper conduct. If it is used inappropriately, discretion fosters the belief that justice is a matter of personal judgment that should be auctioned to the highest bidder.

2. **Low Managerial Visibility**. Police officers, as a general rule, work on their own or with a single partner. Due to the nature of police work, supervisors rarely observe line officers as they provide services, conduct investigations, make arrests, enforce criminal laws or use discretion. Institutional controls on the use of police discretion are very weak (and almost always after the fact). Officers prefer to be left alone to do the job. Sergeants, on the other hand, often adopt the attitude that what they don't know won't hurt them.

3. **Low Public Visibility**. If police supervisors have little knowledge about the on-the-job behavior of their immediate subordinates, the public has even less. When they see the police in action, they rarely know what is going on. Low public visibility, like low managerial visibility, gives police officers the opportunity to conceal poor decisions, corruption and criminal behavior.

4. **Peer Group Secrecy**. The person most likely to see a blue-coat criminal or corrupt cop at work is another cop. In many, if not most cases, they do little or nothing about the illegal behavior. The socialization process in the police department may promote illegal behavior or encourage other officers to passively accept

the crime and corruption of their colleagues. Loyalty, brotherhood, a garrison mentality and the *blue curtain* help to protect
those who have become morally bankrupt.

5.   **Managerial Secrecy**. Most police supervisors come from the
ranks. They have been socialized by the system and have used it
to enhance their status. They are reluctant to investigate and discipline police officers for criminal behavior unless they are forced
into it. Even today proactive strategies against police crime and
corruption (accessible complaint procedure, active investigation,
imposition of effective sanctions and an ongoing effort to stop
wrongdoing before it starts) are not being used in all police
departments. Police administrators often want to keep the problem within the department. Police supervisors are not immune
from the effects of the "garrison mentality" (Johnston, 1982).

Low visibility coupled with a vast amount of discretion creates an environment
within which police crime, corruption and occupational deviance germinate and
flourish. Discretion, secrecy and the lack of supervision are three important factors which lead to police deviance.

The most effective means to fight deviance and corruption within the police
department is to build a strong supervisory structure in which sergeants have
both the authority and the skills needed to regulate the behavior of their subordinates. Supervisors and managers must make an up-front and proactive commitment to integrity. They must do everything they can to prevent deviance and
corruption in the department. They must also be willing to do whatever it takes
to separate undesirables from the police service.

While there is no doubt that individual police officers must be held accountable for unacceptable on-the-job performance or inappropriate behavior, police
managers must establish realistic ethical and professional standards by which to
judge their employees. The organizational response to occupational deviance
should be tempered with an understanding of human nature and some appreciation for the milieu within which police work takes place.

Americans have traditionally had a love/hate relationship with the police
establishment. While the police are generally acknowledged to be an essential element in the glue that holds our pluralistic society together, they are (at the same
time) viewed with a great deal of suspicion. Power, authority, discretion and the
potential for abuse are indigenous to the police role. Trust in and fear of authority
are deeply rooted in the American psyche and are wrapped in the persona of the
individual police officer. We often cast police officers as superheroes who:

> . . . are expected to be knights errant, fearless in the face of danger,
> incorruptible in the midst of corruption, cool and knowledgeable in the
> determination of constitutional questions over which learned judges
> may reflect and wrangle and divide. They are supposed to be tough on
> criminals but tender regarding rights of individuals, minority groups,

and the innocent generally. They are asked to be incessantly courteous, kind and cheerful, and to be ready to lay down their lives at any moment if need be in the defense of law and order (Smith, 1965).

No police officer can reasonably be expected to play each and every one of these roles simultaneously. There is far too much ambiguity; there are too many contradictions. It appears that the pathway to professional police work may have been booby-trapped with good intentions.

When police officers act appropriately and in accordance with the law, they are treated with deference and respect. If, on the other hand, an officer's job-related behavior falls short of culturally prescribed or group-shared expectations, there is likely to be a collective sense of betrayal. Under these particular circumstances, even petty violations tend to elicit very strong reactions from the community. Conflicting perceptions are formed and are used to vilify the police as a group, and to scapegoat individual officers for the transgressions of their peers. The misconduct of one police officer frequently casts suspicion on the entire department, and police managers soon discover that the integrity of the police force cannot be restored by simply punishing the offending officer. This discipline is usually viewed as being merely cosmetic. A managerial commitment to continuous monitoring (for accountability) is by far superior to an occasional witch hunt. It represents a genuine good-faith reaffirmation of the community's control over the police.

Strong internal discipline and a commitment to accountability are required in order to safeguard the organizational health of the police department. The integrity of police work and those who serve as police officers can only be maintained if there is an efficient, effective and responsive discipline system. Public confidence will be restored and strengthened if there is a proactive effort to protect all citizens from police deviance. This can be accomplished by revising inadequate policies and procedures and correcting or separating from police service those individuals who have been found guilty of serious professional misconduct.

Controlling the Police

Police officers are government officials with a special duty to serve and protect the community. They are responsible for public safety and security. The concept of **responsibility** encompasses such notions as *professional ethics*, *answerability* and *accountability* (Gaines, Kappeler and Vaughn, 1994). While these are very noble ideals, they often degenerate into empty rhetoric. Ethical ambiguity permits the police to operate in a vacuum. Left uncontrolled, police officers may pursue their own ends by whatever means they so choose. Under these circumstances, deviance (legal, moral and ethical) often becomes the rule rather than the exception. Police occupational deviance represents an insidious threat to the democratic process.

The National Commission on Law Observance and Enforcement (1931), The President's Commission on Law Enforcement and the Administration of Justice (1967), The National Advisory Committee on Criminal Justice Standards and Goals (1973) and the American Bar Association's Task Force on the Urban Police Function (1973) came to the conclusion that public control over the police is a national imperative. In the words of the American Bar Association:

> Since a principal function of police is the safeguarding of democratic processes, if police fail to conform their conduct to the requirements of law, they subvert the democratic process and frustrate the achievement of a principal police function. It is for this reason that high priority must be given for ensuring that the police are made fully accountable to the police administrator and to the public for their actions.

Ethics, answerability and accountability are essential ingredients in police professionalism and have, as guiding principles, been incorporated into a new Police Code of Conduct (see Figure 11.1). It is the police manager's job to develop and implement the policies, procedures, rules and regulations needed to translate ethics theory into practice. First-line supervisors, on the other hand, are the operating engineers who make sure the internal discipline apparatus works properly.

Occupational deviance will occur in virtually all police departments over time. Allegations of personal and professional misconduct are commonplace. They are, in fact, an occupational hazard. As long as police officers are empowered to restrict the activities of people, intervene when they commit criminal acts and engage in authoritative control over their behavior in ways causing inconvenience or resentment, complaints can be expected. It is imperative, then, that every police department establish a fair and impartial mechanism designed to deal with these complaints. This will help ensure the integrity of the police department and the law enforcement process.

The chief executive officer of the police agency is ultimately responsible for the discipline and control of all subordinate personnel. In order to fulfill this responsibility, the chief should formulate policies, procedures, rules and regulations that define occupational deviance and specify how complaints against police officers are to be received, processed and adjudicated.

Policing the police is a volatile issue in contemporary American society. Good intentions are simply not enough to placate the community. Police administrators must now demonstrate, through policy statements and deeds, that they are willing to ferret out and deal decisively with all types of police misconduct. Anything less will fan the fires of social discontent and could rekindle the spark of violent civil disobedience that was so prevalent in the late 1960s and early 1970s. This phenomenon manifested itself again during the Lozano incident in Miami (1989) and throughout the Rodney King affair (1991) in Los Angeles.

Figure 11.1
1989 Police Code of Conduct

All law enforcement officers must be fully aware of the ethical responsibilities of their position and must strive constantly to live up to the highest possible standards of professional policing.

The International Association of Chiefs of Police believes it important that police officers have clear advice and counsel available to assist them in performing their duties consistent with these standards, and has adopted the following ethical mandates as guidelines to meet these ends.

Primary Responsibilities of a Police Officer

A police officer acts as an official representative of government who is required and trusted to work within the law. The officer's powers and duties are conferred by statute. The fundamental duties of a police officer include serving the community, safeguarding lives and property, protecting the innocent, keeping the peace and ensuring the rights of all to liberty, equality and justice.

Performance of the Duties of a Police Officer

A police officer shall perform all duties impartially, without favor or affection or ill will and without regard to status, sex, race, religion, political belief or aspiration. All citizens will be treated equally with courtesy, consideration and dignity.

Officers will never allow personal feelings, animosities or friendships to influence official conduct. Laws will be enforced appropriately and courteously and, in carrying out their responsibilities, officers will strive to obtain maximum cooperation from the public. They will conduct themselves in appearance and deportment in such a manner as to inspire confidence and respect for the position of public trust they hold.

Discretion

A police officer will use responsibly the discretion vested in the position and exercise it within the law. The principle of reasonableness will guide the officer's determinations and the officer will consider all surrounding circumstances in determining whether any legal action shall be taken.

Consistent and wise use of discretion, based on professional policing competence, will do much to preserve good relationships and retain the confidence of the public. There can be difficulty in choosing between conflicting courses of action. It is important to remember that a timely word of advice rather than arrest—which may be correct in appropriate circumstances—can be a more effective means of achieving a desired end.

Use of Force

A police officer will never employ unnecessary force or violence and will use only such force in the discharge of duty as is reasonable in all circumstances.

The use of force should only be used with the greatest restraint and only after discussion, negotiation and persuasion have been found to be inappropriate or ineffective. While the use of force is occasionally unavoidable, every police officer will refrain from applying the unnecessary infliction of pain or suffering and will never engage in cruel, degrading or inhuman treatment of any person.

Confidentiality

Whatever a police officer sees, hears or learns of that is of a confidential nature, will be kept secret unless the performance of duty or legal provision requires otherwise.

Members of the public have a right to security and privacy, and information obtained about them must not be improperly divulged.

Integrity

A police officer will not engage in acts of corruption or bribery, nor will an officer condone such acts by other police officers.

The public demands that the integrity of police officers be above reproach. Police officers must, therefore, avoid any conduct that might compromise integrity and thus undercut the public confidence in a law enforcement agency. Officers will refuse to accept any gifts, presents, subscriptions, favors, gratuities or promises that could be interpreted as seeking to cause the officer to refrain from performing official responsibilities honestly and within the law. Police officers must not receive private or special advantage from their official status. Respect from the public cannot be bought; it can only be earned and cultivated.

Cooperation with Other Officers and Agencies

Police officers will cooperate with all legally authorized agencies and their representatives in the pursuit of justice.

An officer or agency may be one among many organizations that may provide law enforcement services to a jurisdiction. It is imperative that a police officer assist colleagues fully and completely with respect and consideration at all times.

Personal/Professional Capabilities

Police officers will be responsible for their own standard of professional performance and will take every reasonable opportunity to enhance and improve their level of knowledge and competence.

Through study and experience, a police officer can acquire the high level of knowledge and competence that is essential for the efficient and effective performance of duty. The acquisition of knowledge is a never-ending process of personal and professional development that should be pursued constantly.

Private Life

Police officers will behave in a manner that does not bring discredit to their agencies or themselves.

A police officer's character and conduct while off duty must always be exemplary, thus maintaining a position of respect in the community in which he or she lives and serves. The officer's personal behavior must be beyond reproach.

Source: *The Police Chief*, January, 1990, p. 18.

Personnel Complaint Investigation Policy

A forthright policy that defines, prohibits and encourages the reporting of occupational deviance is in the public interest and represents yet another step on the road to accountability. Policies of this nature serve as a guide to thinking and decisionmaking within the police department. They reflect the purpose and philosophy of the organization and help convey that purpose and philosophy to all members. Policy creates realistic parameters that control the use of discretion in complex criminal justice organizations. The control of discretion is absolutely essential if the department is to:

1. Protect individual citizens from police misconduct.

2. Build community confidence in the police department.

3. Protect the integrity and reputation of the entire police force.

4. Protect the accused employee from unfounded and/or malicious allegations of occupational deviance.

5. Guarantee equal protection of the law and administrative due process to those accused of misbehavior.

In order to accomplish these critically important objectives, police managers must make a commitment to investigate all substantive complaints that are lodged against their personnel. In addition, they must become **proactive** in the search for police deviance. It is no longer sufficient to merely react to complaints initiated by those outside the organization (Leonard and More, 1993).

Police officers must understand policies, procedures, rules and regulations if they are to conform with them. Consequently, they should be written clearly and concisely and distributed to those expected to obey them. According to the National Advisory Commission on Criminal Justice Standards and Goals (1973):

> Every police agency immediately should formalize policies, procedures, and rules in written form for the administration of internal discipline. The internal discipline system should be based on essential fairness, but not bound by formal procedures and proceedings such as are used in criminal trials.
>
> 1. Each police agency immediately should establish formal written procedures for the administration of internal discipline and an appropriate summary of those procedures should be made public.
>
> 2. The chief executive of every police agency should have ultimate responsibility for the administration of internal discipline.

3. Every employee at the time of employment should be given writ-
    ten rules for conduct and appearance. They should be stated in
    brief, understandable language. In addition to other rules that may
    be drafted with assistance from employee participants, one pro-
    hibiting a general classification of misconduct, traditionally
    known as "conduct unbecoming an officer," should be included.
    This rule would prohibit conduct that may tend to reflect unfa-
    vorably upon the employee or the agency.

4. The policies, procedures, and rules governing employee conduct
    and the administration of discipline should be strengthened by
    incorporating them in training programs and promotional exam-
    inations, and by encouraging employee participation in the disci-
    pline system.

While the police department's personnel complaint investigation policy cannot,
and indeed should not, be written to cover every possible contingency, it is a
valuable administrative tool that establishes a regularized approach to defining,
detecting and dealing with various forms of police misconduct. The written policy statement must be carefully crafted to strike a synergistic balance between
managerial control, community expectations, professional ethics and the discretionary flexibility needed to perform complex police work on the streets (see
Figure 11.2). Ill-conceived, hastily prepared and overly rigid policy statements
are inherently counterproductive and tend to aggravate the problems they were
designed to resolve.

Figure 11.2
The Synergistic Balance

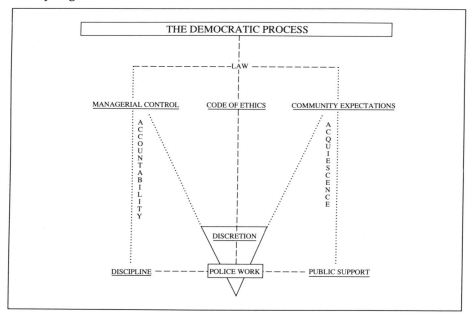

Dealing with Police Occupational Deviance

As previously noted, the chief executive officer of the police department is responsible for the discipline and control of agency personnel. In medium- to large-sized police departments, occupational deviance occurs frequently enough to justify the creation of a specialized internal affairs unit. In small departments, the chief or chief's designee (often a patrol sergeant) conducts internal investigations. Most of the nation's municipal police agencies are small. More than 80 percent of them have fewer than 20 sworn officers (Adams, 1990). Consequently, sergeants often take center stage in dealing with occupational deviance at the local level.

The procedures (or specific guidelines for action) involved in conducting internal personnel complaint investigations will differ somewhat depending on the origin, nature and seriousness of the allegation. If, during the normal course of supervision, the sergeant observes a minor infraction, the situation should ordinarily be discussed with the employee, an on-the-spot warning may be issued and the incident is recorded for future reference or follow-up to determine what effect the intervention had on that individual officer. The procedures to be followed by a supervisor confronted with a serious complaint of misconduct coming from inside or outside the police department, however, will be more structured and much more formal. The seven basic steps involved in the investigation of serious personnel complaints are as follows:

1. The nature and extent of the alleged police occupational deviance must be determined.

2. An internal investigation must be conducted to ascertain the merit of the complaint and the extent to which the accused police officer is culpable if the allegation is, in fact, sustained.

3. Logical conclusions must be drawn based on the evidence that is uncovered during the investigation.

4. Alternative courses of action must be evaluated and converted into recommendations concerning an appropriate disposition of the case.

5. If corrective disciplinary measures are required, they must be administered in an impartial, firm, fair and timely manner.

6. Precautions must be taken to ensure administrative due process and equal protection under the law for those who are accused of serious misconduct.

7. Supervisors must do a follow-up in order to assess the positive and/or negative effects of any disciplinary action that has been taken.

Department-specific policies, procedures, rules and regulations will determine the investigative protocol to be used in all police misconduct cases.

Personnel Complaints

A **personnel complaint** is a formal accusation alleging that a particular employee is guilty of legal, moral or professional misconduct. These complaints run the gamut from trivial to extremely serious. Trivial complaints should be filtered out immediately and disposed of through appropriate administrative action. Substantive personnel complaints, on the other hand, should be plugged into the internal investigations process and dealt with in a very straightforward manner. If there is any doubt as to how a specific complaint ought to be classified in terms of its validity or seriousness, it should be targeted for a thorough internal investigation. While discretion may be the better part of valor, the zealous pursuit of integrity is a prerequisite for police professionalism.

The misconduct complaints lodged against police officers come from two sources. *Internal complaints* originate within the organization. They are initiated by first-line supervisors or command officers who have witnessed occupational deviance first-hand and choose to deal with it. Unfortunately, some police managers tacitly condone less than professional conduct rather than create bad publicity or risk employee hostility by aggressively pursuing cases of police misconduct. Internal personnel complaints also come from police officers who, based on their particular job in the department or their personal interaction with other employees, know or have good reason to believe that another employee is guilty of misconduct. Mark Baker (1985) has noted that good cops often are more outraged by the misdeeds of their colleagues than the general public, simply because these officers know that their reputation and character are being maligned just because the "bad cops" wear the same uniform.

External complaints, on the other hand, emanate from outside the police department. These complaints come from lawyers, elected officials, pressure groups, relatives and others who (for whatever reason) have chosen to focus their attention on (real or imagined) police misconduct. Most of the complaints lodged against municipal police personnel come from external sources.

Due to the nature of their job, the power they wield and the milieu within which they work, police officers are often targeted for criticism or allegations of wrongdoing. Some of these accusations are justifiable and serve as indicators of real occupational deviance or personal misconduct and others are not. Unless personnel complaints are obviously frivolous, they should be given credence until they are disproven through the investigatory process. Sergeants must also be concerned with due process. Perceptions are not always accurate and complainants are not always truthful. In addition, there are those (criminals, political activists and mentally ill individuals) who are inclined to fabricate stories designed to discredit the police or the whole criminal justice system. They will do anything to achieve their own personal, political or social goals. The end jus-

tifies the means (distortion, lies and false accusations). Sergeants often walk a tightrope between fact and fiction. They are the guardians of integrity and represent the bulwark of professional responsibility. Receiving, investigating and resolving personnel complaints tests the mettle of the men and women who are first-line supervisors in complex criminal justice organizations. It is the inglorious part of the job that many sergeants avoid.

Personnel complaints are a fact of life in modern police work. They are a permanent part of the occupational landscape and will not disappear just because they are cloaked in a "blue veil of secrecy." While most personnel complaints prove to be unfounded (Alpert and Dunham, 1992), they still provide first-line supervisors and police managers with invaluable feedback. Complaints, whether they are substantiated or not, increase awareness of both real and potential problems, help sharpen problem-solving skills and provide yet another basis for the evaluation of the department's human resources. Consequently, every precaution must be taken to guard against artificial barriers that hinder or discourage the filing of legitimate personnel complaints. Without complaints, problems that could be resolved fester and poison the whole system. Inaction almost always makes the problem worse. Problems that are hidden or ignored are like a virulent cancer. As the malignancy spreads, it eats away at the integrity of the police department and undermines community confidence in the police establishment. From a practical as well as a theoretical point of view, internal and external "whistle-blowing" should not be considered negative. In fact, it is one of the checks and balances built into the democratic process. The most effective way to prevent abuse of police power (occupational deviance) is through vigilance and use of prompt disciplinary action when abuse is found.

Processing Personnel Complaints

Even though an overwhelming majority of the misconduct complaints filed against police personnel are proven to be unfounded, most police organization and management theorists agree that all substantive complaints (from whatever the source) should be accepted and thoroughly investigated. This type of openness is the natural enemy of arbitrariness and an ally in the battle against occupational deviance (Kappeler, Sluder and Alpert, 1994). The National Advisory Commission on Criminal Justice Standards and Goals (1973) recommends that:

> Every police agency immediately should implement procedures to facilitate the making of a complaint alleging employee misconduct, whether that complaint is initiated internally or externally.

> 1. The making of a complaint should not be accompanied by fear of reprisal or harassment. Every person making a complaint should receive verification that the complaint is being processed by the police agency. This receipt should contain a general description of the investigative process and appeal provisions.

2. Every police agency, on a continuing basis, should inform the public of its complaint reception and investigation procedures.

3. All persons who file a complaint should be notified of its final disposition; personal discussion regarding this disposition should be encouraged.

4. Every police agency should develop procedures that will ensure that all complaints, whether from an internal or external source, are permanently and chronologically recorded in a central record. The procedure should ensure that the agency's chief executive or his assistant is made fully aware of every complaint without delay.

5. Complete records of complaint reception, investigation and adjudication should be maintained. Statistical summaries based on these records should also be published for all police personnel and should be available to the public.

Filing a complaint alleging police misconduct should be a quick and simple process. The public has a right to present reasonable grievances and to have them properly investigated. By ignoring negative feedback from the citizens, police supervisors and managers improperly insulate themselves from those whom they are sworn to protect and serve (Kappeler, Sluder and Alpert, 1994).

Sergeants and command officers often share responsibility for receiving and processing personnel complaints in the nation's small police departments. They deal primarily with three types of complaints:

1. **Primary Complaints.** Complaints that are received directly from the alleged victim of the police misconduct.

2. **Secondary Complaints.** Complaints from persons who, while not victims themselves, complain about police misconduct on behalf of others.

3. **Anonymous Complaints.** Complaints of police occupational deviance coming from an unidentified source.

Complaints from anonymous sources must be handled with the greatest care and utmost discretion because of the impact they might have on the morale of the employees involved. No police supervisor or manager, however, can afford to discount the validity of a personnel complaint solely because it comes from an unidentified source. Each complaint must be judged on its own merit.

Nathan Iannone (1994) has pointed out that some of the most serious and bizarre cases of police misconduct have been brought to light by anonymous information. Once it is determined that a personnel complaint is not merely frivolous, it is preferable to deal openly and honestly with it in the public arena. Openness serves as an antidote to suspicion and distrust.

Figure 11.3
Personnel Incident Report

Commendable Action [ ]   Censurable Conduct [ ]

              Personnel Investigation_____ - _____

Officer(s) _____   Rank _____

            _____

Complainant _____   Telephone: Home _____

Address _____   Office _____

Incident: Date ___/___/___   Time: _____ Hours   Unknown [ ]

        Location_____

Summary of incident: Department Complaint # (if any)_____

Witness No. 1 _____   Telephone: Home _____

Address _____   Office _____

Witness No. 2 _____   Telephone: Home_____

Address _____   Office _____

Violations(s): Section _____   Major _____   Minor _____

              Section _____   Major _____   Minor _____

              Section _____   Major _____   Minor _____

Assigned Investigating Officer _____

Date _____

In order to initiate a formal inquiry, the complaint should be summarized on a personnel incident report form (see Figure 11.3), assigned an administrative control number and processed according to department policies, procedures, rules and regulations. The person filing the complaint should be given a copy of the report form as a receipt. This is tangible evidence that the personnel complaint is being taken seriously and that the police department is making a sincere effort to monitor the legal, moral and professional conduct of its employees.

It is in the best interests of the police service that all incidents of serious misconduct be discovered. Unless the public is convinced that the police department is truly receptive to complaints, it will not actively participate in this critically important process.

Personnel Complaint Investigations

There are more than 17,000 law enforcement agencies in the United States. While some of them (like Chicago, Los Angeles and New York) are huge bureaucracies, most police departments are small and not very sophisticated in terms of their organization/management structure. Under these circumstances, specialization is usually the exception rather than the rule. As generalist administrators in small organizations, sergeants play a variety of different and, at times, unconventional roles. Consequently, it is very difficult to describe, with precision, the part sergeants play in personnel complaint investigations.

Sergeants are usually the most visible and often the most approachable members of the police department's management team. They interact with police officers and civilians from all walks of life on a regular basis. Since they represent the first link in the chain of command, it is likely that many, if not most, of the allegations of personal or professional misconduct will be channeled through them to their superiors. Dealing with the corrupt side of human nature (inside and outside of the department) goes with the territory. Streetwise supervisors know the score. As one sergeant put it, every cop has had a bad day (a hangover, a domestic squabble, a screw-up at work or disagreement with the boss) and has taken it out on the people the officer has sworn to protect and serve. The officer may be rude, insulting, intimidating or downright criminal in dealing with others.

According to Mark Baker (1985), many cops give in to temptation and misuse their discretionary power to gratify their own ego by tormenting a civilian like a cat tormenting a mouse. As one cynical police officer said, in any department five percent of the officers are hard working and honest in all situations. They never do anything wrong. Five percent are always on the other side of the continuum. They have character flaws and would be ordinary criminals if they had not become police officers. The remaining 90 percent tend to go whichever way peer pressure goes. While this might be a gross overstatement, sergeants have an ethical obligation as well as a functional obligation to accept, investigate and resolve all legitimate allegations of personal or professional misconduct lodged against their subordinates.

Sergeants, as first-line supervisors, are almost always given the power to receive and process personnel complaints. Based on the authority inherent in their rank, they monitor employee performance and serve as departmental disciplinarians. In minor cases involving police deviance they bring charges, investigate, adjudicate and (where appropriate) punish their subordinates. Summary action of this type is normally subject to administrative review and must be con-

Case Study

Sergeant Oliver Samuelson

Ted Gardner, a probationary officer with eight months of service, is assigned to the center city patrol district. He has been doing a good job and has earned an excellent performance rating. Officer Gardner is, however, beginning to have problems relating to members of his own platoon. They see Gardner as a show off whose overzealousness causes them problems on the street. Several of the officers have lodged unofficial complaints with Sergeant Oliver Samuelson, the shift supervisor. The sergeant has taken the complaints under advisement and has indicated that he will take "appropriate action" if the complaints are valid.

While he was providing backup on a domestic disturbance call, Sergeant Samuelson noted that Ted Gardner was acting in an officious manner and that he was being verbally abusive to an intoxicated male who was being ordered out of the house. Gardner's language (filled with profanities) was offensive as well as threatening. As far as the sergeant was concerned, Ted Gardner's behavior was unacceptable. It violated professional standards and department policy. It was conduct unbecoming an officer.

The intoxicated male agreed to leave the house. He was picked up by his brother and transported to another location. The female complainant was advised to keep the doors locked and to consult an attorney. No further action was taken.

Sergeant Samuelson has decided, based on an evaluation of Ted Gardner's previous performance and his clean disciplinary record, to classify the incident as minor misconduct and to deal with it informally. He is convinced that a warning, counseling and follow-up will resolve the problem. Do you agree with the sergeant? What would you do to ensure the success of the intervention? How would you want this matter to be handled if you were Ted Gardner? Is the sergeant fulfilling his responsibility as a first-line supervisor?

sistent with departmental policy, civil service regulations, collective bargaining agreements and the law. In large police departments, specialization rather than rank determines who will conduct the investigation of serious personnel complaints. Corruption and other forms of serious occupational deviance are usually investigated by a special internal affairs unit. Internal affairs units report directly to the chief executive officer. In smaller departments, sergeants normally work in tandem with command officers and are frequently called upon to help investigate serious allegations of police misconduct.

Investigating alleged police misconduct requires a great deal of skill. In order to be effective, the investigator (a sergeant, an internal affairs officer or police manager) must be specifically trained for the task and given constant

guidance and administrative support. Since the internal investigation process must be swift, certain, fair and lawful, only the most competent employees should be selected and trained to conduct personnel investigations. Few of the small police departments provide any, let alone sufficient, training for those involved in personnel complaint investigations. The National Advisory Commission on Criminal Justice Standards and Goals (1973) considered this problem and recommends that:

> Every police agency immediately should ensure that internal discipline complaint investigations are performed with the greatest possible skill. The investigative effort expended on all internal discipline complaints should be at least equal to the effort expended in the investigation of felony crimes where a suspect is known.

> 1. All personnel assigned to investigate internal discipline complaints should be given specific training in this task and should be provided with written investigative procedures.

> 2. Every police agency should establish formal procedures for investigating minor internal misconduct allegations. These procedures should be designed to ensure swift, fair and efficient correction of minor disciplinary problems.

> 3. Every investigator of internal discipline complaints should conduct investigations in a manner that best reveals the facts while preserving the dignity of all persons and maintaining the confidential nature of the investigation.

> 4. Every police agency should provide, at the time of employment, and again, prior to the specific investigation, all its employees with a written statement of their duties and rights when they are the subject of an internal discipline investigation.

> 5. Every police chief executive should have legal authority during an internal discipline investigation to relieve police employees from their duties when it is in the best interests of the public and the police agency. A police employee normally should be relieved from duty whenever under investigation for a crime, corruption, or serious misconduct, or when the proof is evident and the presumption is great, or when that person is physically or mentally unable to perform duties satisfactorily.

> 6. Investigators should use all available investigative tools that can reasonably be used to determine the facts and secure necessary evidence during an internal discipline investigation. The polygraph should be administered to employees only at the express approval of the police chief executive.

7. All internal discipline investigations should be concluded 30 days from the date the complaint is made unless an extension is granted by the chief executive of the agency. The complainant and the accused employee should be notified of any delay.

These are minimal considerations designed to give substance to the internal investigations process. The benign neglect of police occupational deviance is no longer acceptable.

Once a formal personnel complaint is plugged into the internal investigations process, official fact-finding begins. The tools and techniques used to investigate police misconduct should not differ substantially from those employed in other types of investigations. The investigator must approach each and every complaint objectively and should avoid drawing any conclusions concerning the merits of the case until all the evidence has been collected and analyzed. In keeping with the principles of investigation, the investigator simply cannot afford to be charged with adjudicating the matter. Neither whitewashing nor lynching are in the best interests of the police department.

The first step in a personnel investigation is to interview the complainant. Where accusations have been raised anonymously or by second parties, every effort should be made to contact the victim or whistle-blower directly. All other things being equal, direct evidence is the best evidence. The function of the interview is to:

1. Gather additional information concerning the personnel complaint.

2. Identify witnesses and investigative leads related to the alleged police misconduct.

3. Assess the complainant's credibility.

4. Determine the merits of the accusation.

5. Ascertain, if possible, the complainant's motive or motives for making the allegation.

The interview is a primary source of investigative data and as such, its importance should not be underestimated.

Preparation is the key to conducting a successful investigative interview. The person assigned to conduct the internal investigation should carefully review the personnel incident report (filed by the complainant) in order to become familiar with the case and to make a preliminary determination as to the specific department policies, procedures, rules and regulations that may have been violated by the accused. In addition, the investigator should develop a complainant profile. The profile should, based on a thorough records check, indicate whether or not the complainant has had previous encounters with the police, the nature of those incidents and that individual's proclivity to file misconduct complaints against police

personnel. Armed with this type of information, the internal investigator is in a position to more accurately assess the validity of the individual's complaint.

The interview itself must be handled discreetly and conducted in a skillful manner. Sergeants or other internal personnel complaint investigators should not editorialize or reveal information that can be misconstrued by the complainant. The interviewer should be careful not to:

1. Commit the police department to a particular course of action regarding the internal investigation, disposition of the complaint or discipline to be imposed.

2. Indicate personal professional opinion concerning the merit of the allegation, the culpability of the accused officer or the officer's behavior in similar situations.

3. Prejudge the validity of the complaint or formulate subjective conclusions as to the complainant's veracity.

The interview gives direction to and provides a foundation for the internal investigation. It is, therefore, a critically important component in the personnel complaint investigation process.

Information acquired during the investigative interview should be reduced to writing as soon as possible. The official written account of the interview must be clear, concise, accurate and factual. It may (depending on the nature, seriousness and complexity of the police deviance) be advisable to have the interview transcribed or tape-recorded. This is standard operating procedure in those cases involving criminality, corruption, serious misconduct and vicarious civil liability. As a general rule, the scope of the investigative interview and the precision with which the information is recorded should be proportionate to the severity of the alleged misconduct (Redlich, 1994). It should also be noted that what started out as fact-finding might well become documentary evidence in a subsequent criminal trial. In some states it is illegal to make false reports to law enforcement authorities. According to the Pennsylvania Crimes Code (1993):

False Reports to Law Enforcement Authorities

(a) Falsely Incriminating Another. A person who knowingly gives false information to any law enforcement officer with the intent to implicate another commits a misdemeanor of the second degree.

(b) Fictitious Reports. A person commits a misdemeanor of the third degree if he:

(1) reports to law enforcement authorities an offense or other incident within their concern, knowing that it did not occur; or

(2) pretends to furnish such authorities with information relating to an offense or incident when he knows he has no information relating to such offense or incident.

While recent court decisions have given sergeants and other internal personnel complaint investigators some leeway in dealing with police misconduct, they are still constrained by the due process provisions contained in administrative law, civil service regulations and collective bargaining agreements. The rules governing procedural due process almost always require that those police officers accused of serious misconduct be informed of their (civil law and contract) rights, notified as to the specific nature of the allegation and advised when they are under investigation. Notice must be timely and in sufficient detail to permit the accused officer to prepare an adequate defense.

If the allegation of police deviance constitutes a violation of the criminal law as well as a breach of agency policies, procedures, rules and regulations, the officer involved should (with a few exceptions arising from one's personal role as a government official) be allowed to exercise those constitutional rights accorded to all other citizens in the United States of America. Consequently, first-line supervisors and other internal personnel complaint investigators must familiarize themselves with administrative and constitutional rules governing procedural due process in complex criminal justice organizations. Procedural due process protects innocent police officers and insures that those who are guilty of legal, moral and professional misconduct are treated fairly as they are brought before the bar of justice.

Roger Dunham and Geoffrey Alpert (1989) argue that the use of administrative discipline should not be viewed as a substitute for or an impediment to criminal prosecution when serious police deviance is discovered. While justice can often be served by the administration of internal discipline, police managers must not resist or avoid criminal prosecutions. The police service must not treat those employees who break the law differently from other criminal offenders within the community.

Once the complainant has been interviewed and it is determined that there may be some substance to the accusation, the internal investigation should be expedited. Delays hamper the inquiry, reduce employee morale and erode public confidence in the police force. If first-line supervisors and police managers fail to put their house in order, someone from the outside (i.e., an interest group or civilian review board) will try to do it for them.

Some type of immediate intervention might be required in cases involving crime, corruption and other kinds of serious misconduct. In the absence of departmental policy to the contrary, the sergeant should attempt to defuse the situation. Police officers who are temporarily unable to function due to alcohol or drug abuse should be relieved of duty and taken home by the supervisor. Appropriate disciplinary action can be taken at a later time. Officers who are suspected of corruption or serious misconduct and pose a threat to the integrity of the department should, based on the authority of a command officer who has reviewed the evidence, be suspended from duty pending a thorough internal investigation. Any officer engaged in felonious crimes involving violence, moral turpitude or theft should be suspended from the department, arrested and booked. The decision to arrest a police officer must be approved by the chief

executive officer of the department. Immediate and radical action of this type is usually unnecessary. Most criminal complaints against police officers may be processed normally through the district attorney's office.

Police officers, as a condition of employment, are required to cooperate with supervisors and others within the department who are investigating them for alleged legal, moral or professional misconduct which is directly related to the performance of their assigned duties. Administrative law and recent court decisions give internal personnel investigators a great deal of latitude in dealing with police employees suspected of serious misconduct. The failure to cooperate subjects them to further disciplinary action and possible separation from the police service.

Legislatures and courts have generally supported the right of government agencies to protect themselves (and the public) against unethical or criminal employees. In many jurisdictions, supervisors and other personnel complaint investigators have been given the authority to:

1. Access the accused officer's personnel file, performance evaluations, merit ratings, attendance records and other relevant information.

2. Deny the accused officer's request for legal representation during the investigatory interview.

3. Obtain a verbatim transcript or tape recording of the investigatory interview.

4. Search, with or without a warrant, those areas in the workplace where there is no reasonable expectation of privacy.

5. Require the accused officer to participate in a properly constituted and representative lineup.

6. Order the accused officer to take a polygraph examination (unless such an order is specifically prohibited by a collective bargaining agreement or state law).

7. Demand the accused officer submit to physical testing (blood, urine, breath, etc.) designed to yield tangible evidence that can be used in disciplinary hearings.

This authority must be carefully regulated and should be codified in department-specific policies, procedures, rules and regulations. According to Nathan Iannone (1994), the law is clear; almost any "reasonable" order to an employee is enforceable administratively. The courts have been reluctant to interfere in employer/employee relations unless the employer's directives are arbitrary, capricious or breach the procedural due process requirements in established administrative law, civil service regulations or labor contracts.

After all the relevant evidence has been gathered and evaluated, the sergeant, internal affairs officer or police manager must attempt to reconstruct reality in such a way as to prove or disprove the allegation. The findings should be integrated into a comprehensive investigative report (keyed to who, what, where, when, why and how) and used to formulate a recommendation concerning the best disposition of the case (see Figure 11.4). All of the material should be forwarded to the chief executive officer of the police department for appropriate administrative action.

Figure 11.4
Personnel Incident Final Report

Final Report Censurable Conduct   Personnel Investigation ___-___

Summary of Findings

Attachments: Complainant Statement [ ], Witness Statement [ ], Officer
Statement [ ], Other [ ] (explain) _____
Recommendation: Unfounded [ ], Exonerated [ ], Not Sustained [ ],
Sustained [ ]
(State Section # charged)

Recommended Disciplinary Action (Refer to Manual Section 5-055/000)

                    Investigator _____
                    Division Commander _____
Final Disposition:
Concur [ ]   Do not concur [ ]
Reason _____
_____
_____
_____
_____

Final Disposition:
_____
_____
_____
_____

Date_____ Chief of Police_____

The Adjudication of Personnel Complaints

The chief executive officer of the police department is responsible for the **adjudication** (or final disposition) of all internal discipline complaints. The person who conducted the investigation and prepared the investigative report, however, should have laid the foundation for the adjudication. If everything works properly, the chief executive's decisions should flow logically from the investigation, conclusions and recommendations made by the internal complaint investigator. Steps must be taken to ensure the assumption of responsibility and to safeguard the integrity of the decision-making process. According to the National Advisory Commission on Criminal Justice Standards and Goals (1973):

> Every police agency immediately should ensure that provisions are established to allow the police chief executive ultimate authority in the adjudication of internal discipline complaints, subject only to appeal through the courts or established civil service bodies, and review by responsible legal and governmental entities (see Figure 11.5).

1. A complaint disposition should be classified as *sustained, not sustained, exonerated, unfounded or misconduct not based on the original complaint.*

2. Adjudication and, if warranted, disciplinary action should be based partially on recommendations of the involved employee's immediate supervisor. The penalty should be at least a suspension up to six months or, in severe cases, removal from duty.

3. An administrative fact-finding trial board should be available to all police agencies to assist in the adjudication phase. It should be activated when necessary in the interests of the police agency, the public, or the accused employee, and should be available at the direction of the chief executive or upon the request of any employee who is to be penalized in any manner that exceeds verbal or written reprimand. The chief executive of the agency should review the recommendations of the trial board and decide on the penalty.

4. The accused employee should be entitled to representation equal to that afforded the person representing the agency in the trial board proceeding.

5. Police employees should be allowed to appeal a chief executive's decision. The police agency should not provide the resources or fund the appeal.

6. The chief executive of every police agency should establish written policy on the retention of internal discipline investigation reports. Only the reports of sustained and, if appealed, investi-

Figure 11.5
Statement of Charges

Civil Service [ ]   Non-Civil Service [ ]

Employee _____ I.D. # _____

Position Classification _____

Personnel Investigation # _____ Dept. Complaint # _____

Date of this Statement _____

Person Making Personnel Complaint _____

Police Department Manual of Policy and Procedures—Section(s) Violated:

_____

Personnel Rule(s) Violated (if applicable):

_____

Section Description:

Synopsis of Incident:

Findings:

Disciplinary Action Taken:

_____

I have read and understand the charges filed against me and have received a copy of said charges. I also understand that I may appeal this finding within seven (7) calendar days from the date shown below to either the Civil Service Commission or the Department Personnel Officer depending upon my status as indicated on this form.

_____

Employee Signature   Date

_____

Officer Serving Charges   Date

gations that are upheld should become part of the accused employee's personnel folder. All disciplinary investigations should be kept confidential.

7. Administrative adjudication of internal discipline complaints involving a violation of law should neither depend on nor curtail criminal prosecution. Regardless of the administrative adjudication, every police agency should refer all complaints that involve violation of law to the prosecuting agency for the decision to prosecute criminally. Police employees should not be treated differently from other members of the community in cases involving violations of law. The complainant, witnesses and accused employee should be encouraged to participate in the process that leads to a final disposition, even though that decision rests squarely on the shoulders of the police chief executive.

With reference to the classification of personnel complaint dispositions, the following general categories may be used to reflect adjudicatory findings.

1. **Sustained** indicates, based on the facts obtained, that the accused committed all or part of the alleged police misconduct.

2. **Not Sustained** means that the investigation produced insufficient evidence to prove or disprove the allegation and that the matter is being resolved in favor of the employee.

3. **Exonerated** denotes that the alleged act or omission occurred, but was, in fact, legal, proper and necessary.

4. **Unfounded** is used when the alleged police misconduct did not occur and the complaint was false.

5. **Misconduct Not Based On Original Complaint** means that, while there was misconduct on the part of the police officer, it was separate and distinct from that alleged in the original complaint.

While most police departments use four categories, the five-category system (including Misconduct Not Based On Original Complaint) discussed above is superior because it gives the chief executive officer more latitude and flexibility.

In the event that someone other than the employee's immediate first-line supervisor conducted the internal personnel complaint investigation and prepared the comprehensive investigative report, the chief executive officer should contact the sergeant before making a final disposition in the case. All other things being equal, the sergeant is in the best overall position to assess the accused officer's job performance, professional conduct and value as a human resource. The sergeant's input must be carefully evaluated in terms of its objectivity and consistency and should be considered a major factor in determining the final disposition and selecting the appropriate disciplinary action.

When an internal discipline complaint is sustained, the chief of police must select the most appropriate remedy available. Corrective measures may include reassignment, retraining, psychological counseling or participation in a multi-purpose employee assistance program. The most frequently used sanctions in serious misconduct cases, however, are separation from the police service, suspension, and loss of time in lieu of suspension.

If a serious personnel complaint is sustained by the evidence and the loss of time, a suspension or a dismissal is considered to be an appropriate sanction, emphasis during the investigation should be placed on procedural **due process**. The courts will reverse on appeal, and the police department may be civilly liable if accused officers are arbitrarily denied procedural due process. Nathan Iannone (1994) suggests that the safest way to avoid reversal and civil liability in cases involving serious legal, moral or professional misconduct is to adhere to the minimum requirements of procedural due process as outlined by the U.S. Supreme Court in the 1972 case of *Morrissey v. Brewer*:

1. Written notice of the specific charge or charges filed against the officer.

2. Disclosure of the evidence that will be used against the officer during the disciplinary hearing.

3. The opportunity to appear in person and to present witnesses and evidence.

4. The right to confront and cross-examine adverse witnesses (unless the hearing board specifically finds good cause for not allowing the confrontation).

5. An impartial hearing before a "neutral and detached" administrative body.

6. A written statement by that body concerning the evidence it relied upon and the reasons for its action.

7. Administrative and/or judicial review of adverse dispositions.

These provisions are representative of the average American's concern for fairness and procedural due process in labor/management relations and should be incorporated into department policies, procedures, rules and regulations.

Many police departments have adopted some form of **trial board** system. These trial boards are designed to help the police chief executive make sound decisions in internal discipline cases. They provide for a diversity of opinion and allow more direct participation in the adjudication of police misconduct cases by those who conducted the internal complaint investigation.

Under ideal circumstances, the administrative trial board should consist of five police officers coming from within the department. Four of the members should

be appointed by the chief and one by the accused officer. Trial boards should not have any investigative authority and should handle only serious cases of police misconduct assigned to them by the chief of police or cases (regardless of their seriousness) in which accused officers specifically request a disciplinary hearing.

Trial boards are administrative proceedings in which a "neutral and detached" body hears the evidence and oral arguments and, based on them, renders a decision concerning the appropriate action to be taken on a personnel complaint. Members of the trial board are expected to use rational, objective and analytical reasoning in reaching that decision. The board is responsible for determining fact and making a recommendation to the chief executive.

Trial boards are quasi-judicial entities. Their hearings must be governed by the principle of fundamental fairness and need not comply with strict courtroom protocol. The board should, however, have a presiding officer who understands the adjudication process and is familiar with parliamentary procedures. Decisions (usually determined by majority vote) should be based on "a preponderance of evidence" and not "proof beyond a reasonable doubt." The rules of criminal procedure are simply not germane to administrative decisionmaking. According to Larry K. Gaines and his colleagues (1991), the trial board should conclude its deliberations with a formal recommendation accompanied by a written summary of the evidence it relied on and the rationale behind its recommendation.

The recommendation of the trial board, however, is purely advisory. It is up to the police chief executive to institute proper corrective action. If the chief habitually ignores or modifies the trial board's suggestions, this noble experiment in what Mary Parker Follett (Fox and Urwick, 1977) or Stephen Covey (1992) might refer to as "participatory management" is bound to fail. Under these circumstances, the police are denied the right to police themselves and lose the key element needed to achieve professional status (Walker, 1992).

Unless it is carefully monitored and managed, the trial board apparatus can become defective and function as an impediment to good discipline. Instead of an objective "peer review" process, it may become self-serving by shifting to a cover-up modality situated in the morass of procedural due process. The Los Angeles Police Department has been criticized in this regard. Additionally, in Pittsburgh the trial board system got so bad that the city had to seek state legislative relief to correct the problem. The union contract and state law which created the original system made it virtually impossible for police administrators to exercise management's right to discipline officers even in cases of serious occupational deviance.

In most police departments, only those internal personnel complaint investigations that are sustained are placed in the employee's personnel file. It is standard operating procedure in some agencies to remove investigative reports from personnel files after what is considered to be a reasonable length of time (from two to five years) if no other complaints are sustained. Keeping unproven and possibly false personnel complaints on file is a dangerous practice because they are subject to subpoena in subsequent civil litigation against the officer and/or the police department. Since the introduction of this evidence could prejudice a

jury, the benefit of keeping it must be weighed against the risk of incurring greater civil liability. In addition, it is totally inappropriate for police managers to use unsubstantiated allegations of police misconduct as a negative factor in performance evaluation or promotion considerations. Superfluous paperwork of this type should be disposed of on a regular basis.

The prompt adjudication of serious personnel complaints gives police chiefs an opportunity to make it clear, through the imposition of firm and fair disciplinary action, that they will not tolerate serious employee misconduct. In addition, when serious personnel complaints are not sustained, it allows them to go on record in support of the legal, moral and professional conduct exhibited by the vast majority of the nation's police personnel.

The Civilian Review Movement

Many police departments have flirted with the concept of civilian control since the late 1950s. Direct review of police behavior is as popular with critics of the police as it is unpopular with police officers themselves. Most traditional civilian review boards, like those established in New York, Philadelphia, Detroit and Kansas City, were created in response to specific police-community relations problems. They were organized so that complaints about police occupational deviance could be channeled through a formally structured committee of citizens who would examine complaints and recommend remedial action. Unfortunately, the civilian review process did not resolve problems, and in many situations made them worse. Consequently, most of the traditional civilian review boards have been abandoned. Since police misconduct has not disappeared and the internal investigations process does not always work as well as it should, other alternatives are now being explored.

The renewed interest in civilian oversight of government activity in the mid-1980s has produced a second generation of review strategies with interests far broader than law enforcement. The "accountability" movement is based on the fact that unless government is receptive and agrees to deal with citizen complaints there will be more than the usual amount of fear and distrust. The ombudsman and the independent review panel are examples of this renewed emphasis on accountability. The ombudsman, or "citizen advocate," is a government official who acts as a grievance commissioner with the authority to investigate all complaints of administrative abuse. The ombudsman has discretion in determining which cases to probe. While ombudsmen usually have no power to discipline or prosecute government employees, they usher in openness, raise issues and marshal public sentiment. The advantage of the ombudsman approach to accountability is that it does not single out one particular agency (like the police) but covers all government agencies (Johnson, Misner and Brown, 1981).

Some political subdivisions are, on the other hand, establishing independent review panels to deal with citizen complaints. The panels accept complaints, conduct fact-finding inquiries and make remedial recommendations to appro-

priate authorities. While some independent review panels have a great deal of authority, others are very limited in scope. The review process ensures that all public employees are to be treated in the same way regardless of their job classification. Many police officers and public employee unions oppose outside review in any form. Only time will tell if independent review will be any more successful than the first generation civilian review boards and which model, if any, will survive (Alpert and Dunham, 1992).

Forecasting and Dealing with Potential Disciplinary Problems

One approach to forecasting and dealing with potential disciplinary problems now being used in progressive police departments is known as the **Early Warning System** (EWS). The EWS is programmed, either manually or by computer, to keep track of all personnel complaints lodged with the department whether they are substantiated or not. The program tracks complaints in terms of type, seriousness, location and other important variables. After a specified number of complaints have been filed against a particular officer, the proverbial red flag is raised and the officer's entire file is reviewed to assess potential problems. Even a number of unsubstantiated or relatively minor complaints, for example, trigger the review and interview process built into the Early Warning System.

The sole function of the EWS is to alert internal affairs personnel and first-line supervisors that there may be potential disciplinary problems on the horizon. Since EWS is a diagnostic tool, it need not be cloaked in the same procedural due process as an internal investigation or a formal disciplinary action.

The interview is a critical component in the EWS process. After meeting with the officer, it may become apparent that the concerns are unfounded. The officer might be assigned to a high crime area and has been tough on both crime and alleged criminals. Complaints against the officer may be an orchestrated attempt to have the officer transferred from the area so that the criminal element can return to its old habits.

The same interview could produce a different result, however. Internal affairs personnel or the sergeant might realize that the officer's on-the-job behavior is being adversely affected by problems at home, alcohol abuse, emotional stress or other factors. As a result, the investigator or sergeant (based on impetus from the EWS) can advise police managers that the officer is in need of help before the problem gets too serious. Help may come in the form of coaching, counseling, professional care or referral to the department's **Employee Assistance Program**.

The point is, the Early Warning System is diagnostic and help-oriented rather than punitive. It is part of the Total Quality Management commitment to personnel development within the police department (Alpert and Dunham, 1992).

Discipline and the Employee Assistance Movement

Many progressive police administrators now realize that formal disciplinary action which, like that described above, is designed primarily to punish marginal employees or to separate them from police service may, in today's rights-oriented environment, be objectionable and even counterproductive. Collective bargaining agreements and civil service regulations often stress intervention and remediation rather than termination of employment. Consequently, employee assistance programs have sprung up all over the country. These employee assistance programs offer a wide range of diagnostic, counseling and other remedial services to police officers whose on-the-job performance is being adversely affected by physical, psychological or social problems. Employee assistance programs are based on the assumption that it is more humane to treat (and hopefully to resolve) an employee's problems rather than to terminate that employee. It is also considered more cost-effective to invest in existing human resources than it is to recruit, screen, hire, orient and train new employees.

Employee assistance programs give police managers the opportunity to use *intervention* and *remediation* strategies to keep discipline problems from developing. Sergeants, as first-line supervisors, are expected to know their personnel well enough to spot personal problems that could have a negative impact on performance. They act as referral agents. In some cases, police officers are given a choice. Participation in the employee assistance program is strictly voluntary. At other times it is mandatory and stipulated as a condition of continued employment.

The employee assistance program may also be incorporated into the department's disciplinary process. Under these circumstances, officers being disciplined are required (by trial board or chief of police) to participate in counseling or other forms of remedial treatment in lieu of demotion, suspension or termination. These negative sanctions will, as in the case of probation, be held in abeyance, or not imposed at all, if the officer makes an honest effort to change behavior. Employee assistance programs substitute intervention and treatment for punishment when remediation is in the best interest of the police department. Sergeants monitor the on-the-job performance of the officer during and after treatment. They must be willing to make an objective appraisal. Those officers who do not respond to the treatment provided through the employee assistance program must (based on the recommendation of their supervisor) be considered for termination. This is an awesome responsibility.

Summary

Police work is a complex occupation with the inherent potential for personal misconduct and occupational deviance. The situation is complicated by the fact that many of the clients do not want the service and resent those who exercise control over their lives. Police work is performed in an emotion-charged environment, booby-trapped with all kinds of temptation. Officers also wield vast amounts of discretion with little or no direct supervision. We expect mere

mortals to exhibit the perfection of an automaton and become angry when they fail to meet those expectations.

A personnel complaint is a formal accusation that a particular employee is guilty of some type of legal, moral or professional misconduct. These complaints come from internal and external sources. The complaints run the gamut from abusive language to major forms of "blue-coat" crime. Most are minor and are handled by the sergeant in a summary manner. Others are more serious. They require a much more thorough investigation. First-line supervisors, acting as the chief's designees, conduct internal investigations in many of the nation's small police departments. They are less directly involved in the disposition of serious misconduct complaints in larger police departments with internal affairs units.

The purpose of an internal investigation is to determine if the allegation is valid and to assess the police officer's culpability in the matter. The disciplinary process, itself, can be broken down into four very distinct phases: (1) Complaint Reception, (2) Complaint Investigation, (3) Complaint Adjudication, and (4) Disciplinary Action. Quasi-judicial trial boards are unique entities created to hear testimony, evaluate evidence and make a recommendation concerning an appropriate disposition in serious misconduct cases. Emphasis is placed on neutrality, objectivity and procedural due process.

The imposition of punishment in the form of negative sanctions is designed to produce conformity (with police department policies, procedures, rules and regulations), change the officer's future behavior, safeguard the integrity of the police establishment and earn respect from the community. In order to accomplish these goals, internal discipline must be firm, fair, swift, timely and consistent. Maintaining effective discipline takes time, effort and a great deal of energy. The quality of discipline is inexorably linked to the human skills of and ethical tone set by sergeants, commanders and police executives.

Internal discipline, if used properly, is a positive force that meets the needs of the department, the accused officer and the community. Effective internal discipline systems almost always have the following characteristics:

1. They are proactive rather than being merely reactive.

2. They are firm, fair, impartial and compassionate.

3. Emphasis is placed on equity and procedural due process.

4. They are open and easily accessible to the public.

5. The inquiry and sanctions imposed are proportionate to the seriousness of the police misconduct.

6. Employees are allowed to participate in all phases.

7. They are perceived by everyone involved as a vehicle for personnel development rather than simply being a means of punitive coercion.

8.   They promote professionalism and collegiality through participatory management.

9.   The police chief executive sets the moral tone for the department and exercises ultimate control over all disciplinary action.

In an effort to minimize the need for formal disciplinary action in cases involving noncriminal and less serious police deviance, many departments are experimenting with Early Warning Systems and Employee Assistance Programs. The objective is to deal with the real needs of personnel rather than to dispose of them through the disciplinary process. Investment in human resources is an essential element when it comes to Total Quality Management.

If the police are to attain and maintain professional status, they must work hard to translate the abstract concept of accountability into concrete reality through self-discipline. It is in the public interest for the police to police themselves. Unless they do, someone else will try to do it. Their world will be invaded by an army of lawyers, litigants and political activists demanding civilian review of police actions. The police hold their destiny in their own hands.

Case Study

Sergeant Zachary Taylor

Sergeant Zachary Taylor is the senior noncommissioned officer in a fairly large township police department. He has been designated as the "internal affairs officer" by the chief of police. Sergeant Taylor has also been asked to develop formal policies, procedures, rules and regulations to govern the internal personnel complaint investigation process. He has been able to incorporate most of the recommendations made by the National Advisory Commission on Criminal Justice Standards and Goals (for receiving, classifying, investigating and adjudicating complaints).

The chief of police is reluctant to go along with the creation of a trial board system, however. He feels that it will limit his managerial prerogatives and reduce his control over personnel.

The sergeant has scheduled a meeting with the chief. He plans to make a case for the trial board system based on (1) the value of participatory management, and (2) the need for procedural due process in the imposition of disciplinary action in complex criminal justice organizations. Sergeant Taylor is convinced that participation and fundamental fairness are essential to the development of esprit de corps in a police agency.

Sergeant Taylor needs your assistance. He will explain the conceptual foundation of the trial board approach and would like you to explore the technical aspects (size, composition, operations protocol, due process safeguards and recommendatory function) of the trial board system. You are to prepare a memorandum outlining your presentation. What, based on current theory and practice, would you recommend to the chief of police? What resources will be needed in order to implement the trial board system? Will the chief's role as the ultimate disciplinarian change under the new system? Will the chief executive officer lose control of present personnel?

Key Concepts

adjudication
complaint receipt
disciplinary action
dispositions
due process
early warning system
employee assistance programs
executive leadership
fairness
internal discipline

occupational deviance
participation
personnel complaints
police deviance
police misconduct
proactive policy
professionalism
responsibility
supervisor's role
trial boards

Discussion Topics and Questions

1. What is the assigned mission of the American police establishment? Why, based on their strategic role in our society, are they so vulnerable to personnel complaints?

2. How do corruption and other forms of legalistic police deviance differ from moral and/or professional misconduct?

3. Policies are a guide to thinking within an organization. Why is a proactive personnel complaint investigation policy in the public interest? What are the implications for police professionalism?

4. Who is ultimately responsible for leadership and control of the internal disciplinary system? How do the public, police officers and the police department benefit from an easily accessible and open forum for the resolution of personnel complaints?

5. Most misconduct complaints are minor, not serious. Where do personnel complaints come from? What are the three basic types of external complaints that sergeants, internal affairs officers and police managers deal with most of the time?

6. What techniques would you, as a sergeant, use to interview and investigate an employee accused of serious misconduct? What investigative tools are available to you? Why do you have more latitude in a personnel investigation than you would have in a criminal case?

7. What is the function of an administrative trial board? How are they usually structured? How do they arrive at a decision? What are their options in terms of classifying findings and recommending disciplinary action?

8. Why is procedural due process so very important when it comes to the imposition of disciplinary action? Are the due process standards spelled out in *Morrissey v. Brewer* adequate to protect those personnel accused of occupational deviance? Where would you look to find out your due process rights as a member of the police department?

9. Why is it so difficult to state, with precision, exactly what role sergeants play in the administration of internal discipline? Can anything be done to reduce this role conflict?

10. What is the Early Warning System (EWS)? How does it differ from the disciplinary process? What should its relationship be to the department's Employee Assistance Program?

For Further Reading

Gaines, Larry K., Mittie D. Southerland and John E. Angell (1991). *Police Administration*. New York: McGraw-Hill Book Company.

> An excellent chapter on operational accountability and control. Emphasis is placed on initiating and investigating complaints related to police misconduct. Outlines specific procedures applicable to the internal investigation process.

Roberg, Roy R. and Jack Kuykendall (1993). *Police and Society*. Belmont, CA: Wadsworth Publishing Co.

> Details police behavior and discretion with special attention to occupational deviance, professional misconduct and illegal acts or omissions. The authors also discuss a systemic theory of police corruption.

Skolnick, Jerome H. and Thomas C. Gray (1975). *Police in America*. Boston: Education Associates/Little, Brown and Company.

> Classic study of police corruption and "blue-coat" crime. It sets the tone for much of the work that has followed. The book provides a comprehensive framework for the exploration of a very complex social phenomenon.

Swanson, Charles R., Leonard Territo and Robert Taylor (1993). *Police Administration*, 3rd ed. New York: Macmillan Publishing Co.

> Contemporary review of the internal discipline process based on both procedural and substantive due process.

References

Adams, Thomas F. (1990). *Police Field Operations*, 2nd ed. Englewood Cliffs, NJ: Prentice-Hall, Inc.

Alpert, Geoffrey P. and Roger G. Dunham (1992). *Policing Urban America*, 2nd ed. Prospect Heights, IL: Waveland Press, Inc.

American Bar Association (1973). *Standards Related to the Urban Police Function*. Chicago: American Bar Association.

Baker, Mark (1985). *Cops: Their Lives in their Own Words*. New York: Pocket Books/Simon & Schuster, Inc.

Barker, T. and D.L. Carter (1991). *Police Deviance*, 2nd ed. Cincinnati: Anderson Publishing Co.

Commonwealth of Pennsylvania (1993). *Crimes Code*. Longwood, FL: Gould Publications.

Covey, Stephen R. (1992). *Principle-Centered Leadership*. New York: Simon and Schuster, Inc.

Dunham, Roger G. and Geoffrey P. Alpert (1989). *Critical Issues in Policing*. Prospect Heights, IL: Waveland Press, Inc.

Fox, Elliott and L. Urwick (eds.) (1977). *Dynamic Administration: The Collected Papers of Mary Parker Follett,* 2nd ed. New York: Hippocrene Books, Inc.

Gaines, Larry K., Victor E. Kappeler and Joseph B. Vaughn (1994). *Policing in America*. Cincinnati: Anderson Publishing Co.

Gaines, Larry K., Mittie D. Southerland and John E. Angell (1991). *Police Administration*. New York: McGraw-Hill Book Company.

Iannone, Nathan F. (1994). *Supervision of Police Personnel*, 5th ed. Englewood Cliffs, NJ: Prentice-Hall, Inc.

Johnson, Thomas A., Gordon E. Misner and Lee P. Brown (1981). *The Police and Society*. Englewood Cliffs, NJ: Prentice-Hall, Inc.

Johnston, Michael (1982). *Political Corruption and Public Policy in America*. Monterey, CA: Brooks-Cole Publishing Company.

Kappeler, Victor E., Richard D. Sluder and Geoffrey P. Alpert (1994). *Forces of Deviance: Understanding the Dark Side of Policing*. Prospect Heights, IL: Waveland Press, Inc.

Leonard, V.A. and Harry W. More (1993). *Police Organization and Management*, 8th ed. Westbury, NY: The Foundation Press, Inc.

National Advisory Commission on Criminal Justice Standards and Goals (1973). *The Police* Washington, DC: The U.S. Government Printing Office.

Newman, Donald J. (1986). *Introduction to Criminal Justice*. New York: Random House.

Redlich, James W. (1994). "Disciplinary Interrogations: Which Warnings Apply? And When?" *The Police Chief*, Vol. LXI, No. 6.

Smith, Ralph Lee (1965). *The Tarnished Badge*. New York: Thomas Y. Crowell Company.

Walker, Samuel (1992). *The Police in America*, 2nd ed. New York: McGraw-Hill Book Publishers

Labor Relations—

Problem Solving through Constructive Conflict

12

Introductory Case Study

Sergeant Brent A. Bosworth

Sergeant Brent Bosworth is a competent first-line supervisor in a medium-sized, non-union police department. He sees himself as a leader and a member of the department's management team. Sergeant Bosworth is an excellent communicator who understands the importance of group dynamics. He has worked very hard to establish both personal and professional rapport with his subordinates based on mutual respect and trust. Members of Sergeant Bosworth's squad have developed a genuine esprit de corps.

A local lodge of the Fraternal Order of Police wants to unionize the department and has successfully petitioned the State Labor Relations Board (SLRB) to hold a union representation election as authorized by the new public employees' collective bargaining act. The SLRB staff is in the process of determining the final configuration of the proposed bargaining unit. There is some question as to whether or not sergeants should be members of the bargaining unit. The police chief executive wants sergeants excluded from the bargaining unit based on their status as first-line managers. The union has argued that sergeants are not managers per se and that they should be included in the proposed bargaining unit. Sergeant Bosworth has been asked for input and has agreed to testify at a unit-determination hearing.

Since he wants to have meaningful input into the process, as well as to be a good witness, Sergeant Bosworth has decided to research the basic issues involved in unit determination. He plans to use this data in a position paper focusing on the role of the sergeant in labor relations.

Why is past practice not necessarily a reliable guide to bargaining unit determination in police work? If you were Sergeant Bosworth, what types of data would you be looking for? What are the best sources of the data?

Sowing the Seeds of Unionism

European-style unionism never caught on in the United States. As a matter of fact, labor unions were banned in this country until the mid-1930s. It took the economic upheaval of the Great Depression to change public policy concerning collective bargaining. The legalization of collective bargaining ushered this country into a new and radically different era.

The Wagner Act was signed into law by Franklin D. Roosevelt in 1935. Officially known as the National Labor Relations Act, it permitted workers in private industry to form labor unions and actually encouraged them to bargain with their employers concerning "wages, hours and working conditions." While the National Labor Relations Act is often referred to as organized labor's Magna Charta, it was never intended to cover everyone in the work force. Government employees were, for example, specifically excluded from participation in the collective bargaining process.

After the initial surge of organizing activity in traditional blue collar industries, union membership stabilized and then began to decline. In 1945, union membership reached an all-time high of 35.5 percent of the work force (Foulkes and Livernash, 1989). By the late 1970s, fewer than one-fourth of the nation's workers were still unionized (Dressler, 1979). It is now estimated that only 16.1 percent of all American workers are represented by unions (The World Almanac, 1993). The face of organized labor has changed and the future of the labor movement is uncertain.

Public employees at all levels of government resented the fact that they were systematically excluded from collective bargaining and rejected this prohibition as a totally unwarranted intrusion on their First Amendment right to freedom of association. As their influence and purchasing power lagged behind that of other workers, they became much more militant in their demands for equality under the law (Stahl, 1983). Union organizers seized on this widespread discontent. It gave them a chance to fan the fire of collectivism among government employees. Unionism was actively promoted as a viable alternative to the managerial despotism of the past. By working together, public employees and unions delivered a classic one-two punch, and the legal barriers to collective bargaining in the public sector slowly began to erode.

The Boston police strike of 1919, viewed by many unionists as one of the most important events in American police history, was the cause célèbre that gave the nation its first real exposure to labor problems in municipal government. The basic issue involved the right of the police, as public employees, to form a union and to affiliate with the American Federation of Labor. The strike shocked the national conscience and solidified political opposition to all forms of collective bargaining. The response was both swift and decisive. The Boston police had to be kept in their place irrespective of the cost. According to Jay Shafritz et al. (1986), it was political power and not strict rationality that determined the rules of play and the winner of the game. While the unionization of public employees is now legal in most states, there is a distinct undercurrent of anti-union sentiment that can be traced directly to the Boston police strike of 1919.

In 1919, Boston police officers earned $1,400 a year and had not received a pay raise in nearly 20 years. They worked an average of 87 hours per week under deplorable conditions. The cost of living had skyrocketed (by 86 percent) and promotions were based solely on political considerations. The situation was truly grim. Morale hit an all-time low. When the police officers' demand for a $200-a-year pay raise was rejected, they voted to convert their social club into a bona fide labor union and join the American Federation of Labor. The city's police commissioner reacted immediately. He suspended the leaders of the new organization. Tension mounted. All attempts at mediation failed and a strike seemed to be inevitable. On September 9, 1919, 1,117 Boston police officers went on strike in the first publicly proclaimed "job action" against a municipal government in the United States. Only 427 policemen remained on the job (Walker, 1992).

Violence, disorder and crime erupted as Boston reverted to a Hobbesian "state of nature." Looting was commonplace. Lawlessness and mob action became the rule rather than the exception. Declaring a state of emergency, the mayor asked the governor to help restore law and order in the city. On the third day of the strike, more than 7,000 fully armed members of the State Militia took control of the city. In defending the state's action, Governor Calvin Coolidge made the famous statement that now serves as a rallying cry against unionism in the public sector; he said, "There is no right to strike against the public safety by anybody, anywhere, at any time." All of the strikers were fired and anti-union sentiment spread like wildfire throughout the nation.

While the Boston police strike failed to achieve its objectives, it sent reverberations coursing through the American political establishment. Maintaining control over public employees became a national obsession. State legislatures, in what amounted to a knee-jerk reaction, enacted very repressive legislation prohibiting the unionization of state and local government employees. The courts, responding to social and political pressure to maintain the status quo, consistently ruled that public employees per se had absolutely no statutory or constitutional right to organize for the purpose of collective bargaining with their employers. In most states it was illegal for any governmental unit to engage in collective bargaining with its employees. The gerrymandering of public employees out of the National Labor Relations Act was by no means accidental. The die was cast in Boston. Public employees were to be excluded from the collective bargaining process for the next 40 years.

Public sector labor-management relations deteriorated during World War II. Poor pay, rampant inflation and a generalized sense of exploitation took its toll on police morale. Perceiving strength in numbers, the police flirted with unionism once again. Beginning in 1943, these unions (while they had absolutely no legal standing) experienced some limited success in negotiating with their employers. The informal collective bargaining process seemed to be working. Within a few years, however, these fledgling unions were crushed by even more restrictive legislation, unfavorable court decisions, firm opposition from police administrators and the refusal of local politicians to alter the existing balance of power in any way vis-à-vis meaningful collective bargaining with their employees. No one was willing to compromise. The battle lines were drawn.

Government employees did not give up on the idea of collective bargaining. They formed union-like professional associations and continued to push for substantive changes in the law. These groups lobbied legislators, agitated for social change and, on occasion, took illegal job actions to press their demands. As the number of state and local government employees mushroomed, these groups flexed their muscles and were able to exercise more clout in the political arena. Everything seemed to come together in 1959. In that year, Wisconsin became the first state in the nation to grant public employees a limited right to bargain with their employers concerning typical union items like wages, hours and working conditions. Wisconsin's public employees were specifically prohibited from using the strike as a tool for impasse resolution. Public employees found the door open and were prepared to seize the opportunity to solve their problems through constructive conflict.

Things have changed dramatically since 1959. More than 80 percent of the states have now adopted legislation that permits public employees to participate in the collective bargaining process. In some states, public employees (with the exception of fire and police personnel) are allowed to strike. Ohio's 1984 public bargaining law is a classic example. It gives all employees except public safety personnel the right to strike (after a mandatory 10-day advance notice). By 1985, 24 states had opted to provide public employees with some type of arbitration as an alternative to a strike. Figure 12.1 is an analysis of Pennsylvania's Act 111. While compulsory binding arbitration was initially intended only for those involved in critical services, there has been some movement to broaden the scope of coverage to include other types of public employees as well (Swanson, Territo and Taylor, 1993).

Figure 12.1
Public Employee Act

In May 1968, Governor Raymond Shaffer appointed a commission to review the Pennsylvania Public Employee Act of 1947. The commission was to be known as the Heckman Commission, taking the name of its chairman, Leon E. Heckman. Governor Shaffer directed this commission to "review the whole area of public relations dealing with public employees and public employers and to make recommendations to him for the establishment of orderly, fair and workable procedures governing those relations; including legislation, if the commission deems it appropriate."

After several intensive months of review, the commission stated that the Public Employee Act of 1947 had at least three (3) major weaknesses in its basic structure.

[a] The act does not require public employers to bargain collectively with their employees. This has led to a near breakdown in communication where the public employer has not chosen to recognize the right of its employees to bargain collectively. This inability to bargain collectively has created more ill will and led to more friction and strikes than any other cause.

Figure 12.1, *continued*

[b] The act forbids any and all strikes by public employees. Twenty (20) years of experience has taught us that such a policy is unreasonable and unenforceable, particularly when coupled with ineffective or nonexistent collective bargaining. It is based upon a philosophy that one may not strike against the sovereign. But, today's sovereign is engaged not only in government, but in a great variety of other activities. The consequences of a strike by a policeman are very different from those of a gardener in a public park.

[c] The mandatory penalties of the 1947 Act are self-defeating. By forbidding a public employer to give normal pay increases for three (3) years to one who has struck and has been reemployed, simply reduces the value of such position to that employee and drives him to seek other work.

The commission made the following recommendations:

[A] The Public Employee Act of 1947 should be replaced by an entirely new law governing relationships between public employees and employer.

(1) The commission forged a single statute for all public instrumentalities and their employees in order to insure a uniform policy for all agencies of government.

[B] The new law should recognize the right of all public employees, including police and firemen, to bargain collectively subject to enumerated safeguards.

(1) The bargaining unit should be determined in each instance by the Pennsylvania Labor Relations Board pursuant to statutory guidelines.

(2) The bargaining agent should be determined only by elections supervised by the Labor Board.

(3) Bargaining should be permitted with respect to wages, hours and conditions of employment, appropriately qualified by a recognition of existing laws dealing with aspects of the same subject matter and by a carefully defined reservation of managerial rights.

(4) Employees should be protected from an obligation to become members of an employee organization as a condition of employment, but the right to collect dues from members of the employee organization should be recognized as a bargainable issue under appropriate safeguards.

[C] The law should require both parties to bargain in good faith through the following steps:

(1) Face-to-face collective bargaining between the parties, the final agreement to be reduced to writing and signed by representatives of all parties.

(2) The utilization of the State mediation service in the event collective bargaining is not successful without it.

Figure 12.1, *continued*

(3) Fact-finding, recommendations and publication thereof by a tribunal of three experienced arbitrators appointed by the Labor Board.

(4) In disputes involving policemen and firemen, if collective bargaining and mediation do not resolve the dispute, mandatory binding arbitration.

[D] Except for Policemen and Firemen, a limited right to strike should be recognized, subject to these safeguards:

(1) No strike should be permitted for any reason whatsoever until all of the collective bargaining procedures outlined above have been fully complied with.

(2) No strike should be permitted to begin or continue where health, safety or welfare of the general public is in danger.

(3) Unlawful strikes should be subject to injunctions and violations thereof enforced by penalties that will be effective against the bargaining agent or individual employee(s) or both.

The Heckman Commission favored a single statute for all public instrumentalities, but Pennsylvania now has two laws providing for collective bargaining for public employees. These two laws are indeed a strange contrast, particularly because they were passed by essentially the same legislature and signed by the same Governor.

Act 111 of June 24, 1968, as a result of a constitutional change in 1967, provided for collective bargaining of policemen and firemen of public jurisdiction in the Commonwealth. It designates binding arbitration for impasses in lieu of the right to strike. Act 111 was rushed through the legislative process in four days without staff work, publicity or public hearings.

It took a little over two years to complete Public Employee Relations Act 195 from Commission to operation. Members of the Commission wrote the act, public hearings were held, interest and viewpoints of opposing parties were solicited and the Act received wide publicity. As passed by the General Assembly, Act 195 permits strikes by those public employees in nonsafety categories such as teachers, health care providers, social services personnel, and so forth. Act 195 is completely silent on the salient issue of binding arbitration.

While Act 111 has been modified somewhat, its basic thrust remains unchanged. Pennsylvania labor law encourages collective bargaining between local governments and certified employee organizations authorized to represent police personnel. Act 111 has served as the prototype for collective bargaining statutes throughout the United States.

According to O. Glenn Stahl (1983), most state and local government employees are now represented by labor unions. The American Federation of State, County and Municipal Employees (AFSCME) is one of the largest and most powerful unions in America. AFSCME has more than 3,000 locals and

more than 1,280,000 members. It is affiliated with the American Federation of Labor and Congress of Industrial Organizations (AFL-CIO). In addition to AFSCME, there are scores of smaller labor organizations (like the American Federation of Teachers, Fraternal Order of Police, International Association of Fire Fighters, Service Employees International Union, etc.) that are engaged in collective bargaining on behalf of public employees. Independent and unaffiliated local unions have sprung up to represent the unique interests of specialized government personnel. Teachers, fire fighters and municipal police officers are the most heavily unionized groups in the public sector.

The public sector is a natural habitat for labor unions. They serve two masters by providing gains for workers and political support for legislators as well as government managers. Given this situation, it is conceivable that the upper limit of public sector unionization may reach nearly 100 percent at some time in the future (Bellante and Porter, 1992).

The dramatic rise of membership in police unions can, in large measure, be attributed to one or more of the following factors:

1. Job dissatisfaction (especially with regard to wages and working conditions).

2. The perception that other public employees are improving their lot through the collective bargaining process.

3. A deep-seated belief that the public is unsympathetic or even hostile to the personal and professional needs of police officers.

4. An influx of younger police officers who hold a far less traditional view of authority and bureaucratic regimentation.

5. A strong recruiting effort by organized labor to make up for a decline in membership caused by the shift from an industrial to a service-based economy.

Nearly three-fourths of all American police officers are dues-paying members of labor unions today (Cole, 1992).

Many of the existing police unions evolved from social or fraternal organizations. Local police benevolent associations and the national Fraternal Order of Police are excellent examples of this phenomenon. Due to the decentralization of municipal government (with more than 17,000 separate police departments), unions were forced to focus on local issues, not national concerns. Consequently, there is no national labor organization that can legitimately claim to represent the interests of all police personnel in the United States. Hervey Juris and Peter Feuille (1973) argue very convincingly that it is the local character of the employment relationship that helps explain why the relatively centralized national police organizations have not attracted large numbers of rank-and-file police officers as members.

While they do not represent the interests of all police officers, national labor organizations like the American Federation of State, County and Municipal Employees (AFSCME), Fraternal Order of Police (FOP), International Brotherhood of Police Officers (IBPO), International Conference of Police Associations (ICPA), International Union of Police Associations (IUPA) and the Teamsters wield a substantial amount of political power and have the ability to influence public policy making at all levels of government. Unionism and collective bargaining have now become permanent fixtures in public-sector labor relations.

Unionism and collective bargaining by police officers represent what Sam Walker has referred to as **"the hidden revolution"** in contemporary police administration. According to Walker (1992), there has been a fundamental shift in the balance of power as far as management and labor are concerned. Unilateral decisionmaking by supervisors and managers is a thing of the past. Participatory, bilateral management is a *fait accompli*. Collective bargaining is a vehicle for problem solving through constructive conflict.

One of the most important issues in labor relations relates to the scope of bargaining. What should or should not be determined at the bargaining table? Management has not, for a variety of reasons, been particularly successful in limiting the scope of negotiations. An analysis of various police collective bargaining agreements shows that most of them do not have the strongest management rights clauses. This would suggest that police administrators have been less than vigorous in preserving their prerogatives. They have failed to regulate the input of organized labor in the decision-making process (Rynecki, Cairns and Carnes, 1984). Consequently, police unions have had a profound influence on matters such as:

1.   Salaries, supplemental pay and benefits

2.   Hours and working conditions

3.   Manpower allocations

4.   Job assignments

5.   Occupational safety

6.   Discipline and procedural due process

7.   Evaluation and promotion procedures

8.   Resource allocation

9.   Law enforcement policy

10.   Police-community relations

11.   Training and professional development

Balanced power is the key to success in collective bargaining. In some unionized departments, however, there is an unhealthy shift of administrative power from the chief executive officer to the union. This is unfortunate. An organization needs someone to take charge and give it a sense of direction. The leader must have the managerial skill and legitimate authority to keep the organization operating as a goal-oriented system of coordinated and cooperative effort. The function of the police executive (Barnard, 1976) is to mobilize the human and economic resources necessary to accomplish the police department's mission, goals and objectives.

Many first-line supervisors, managers, elected officials and police theorists have not come to grips with unionism. They do not fully appreciate the magnitude of the hidden revolution that has taken place in this country over the last 25 years. Many practitioners seem content to muddle their way through life and are unconcerned with the legacy they will leave to the next generation of managers. Some police theorists, on the other hand, are in a state of denial. Some new textbooks on police management and supervision fail to mention labor relations, unions, collective bargaining or contract administration. This ignorance and denial could transform the hidden revolution into degenerative conflict between organized labor and management.

Management Rights

Management rights refers to those decisions governing the conditions of employment over which management claims to have exclusive jurisdiction. Since almost every management right can and has been challenged by unions, the ultimate determination will depend on the relative bargaining power of the two sides. Union concessions and cooperation have a price tag. Under these circumstances, time-honored management rights are often negotiable.

There are two basic ways to approach the management rights issue. One is the *reserved rights concept*. The other is referred to as the *designated rights concept*. They are based on different sets of assumptions. The reserved rights approach presumes that management authority is supreme in all matters except those it has expressly conceded in the collective bargaining agreement or where its authority is restricted by law. Consequently, little or nothing is said about management rights in the contract. The designated rights approach, on the other hand, is specifically intended to clarify and reinforce the rights claimed by management. A management rights clause is made part of the bargaining agreement in an effort to reduce confusion and misunderstanding. A strong management rights clause sets very clear boundaries designed to help both parties understand the ground rules for future negotiations (Chruden and Sherman, 1984).

The lack of attention to the issue of management rights has had a far reaching effect on police organization and management. In a national survey of police administrators, almost 50 percent of the respondents stated that their managerial prerogatives related to improving the police service had been "lost" as the result of collective bargaining (Sapp, Carter and Stephens, 1990).

Understanding Labor Relations

Collective bargaining is built on the assumption that a certain amount of **controlled conflict** is healthy. It promotes organizational growth and development. If police officers are going to benefit fully from their association with one another (in labor unions), they and their managers should be willing to differ, to push self-interests and to accept the idea that there is inherent value in conflict. If employees and managers do not oppose each other enough, their relationships tend to become static or counterproductive. If they oppose each other too much, conflict may get out of hand and could upset even routine operations in the police department. Here again, balance is the key to success in labor relations. Mutually acceptable collective bargaining procedures and sound judgments help to ensure that differences and conflict will remain within reasonable limits. Integrity, good will and procedural regularity are absolutely essential elements in an ethical collective bargaining process. While tension may be a catalyst for mutual problem solving and coordinated action, there is nothing to be gained from the intraorganizational conflict created by petty feuding, maliciousness or self-destructive behavior. Management prerogatives, employee rights and organization needs might best be viewed as a three-legged stool. If one of the legs is weakened, the stool will collapse. No matter how strong the other legs are, they cannot, in and of themselves, keep the stool in an upright position. When the stool collapses, the community is the loser. It is the community that ends up paying (in higher taxes and fewer services) when the collective bargaining process breaks down (Ewing, 1983).

As peripheral members of the management team, sergeants interact most directly with those line personnel who do the actual work of the police department. They deal with unionized employees on a daily basis. In order to do their job properly, sergeants need to have a fairly comprehensive understanding of human behavior, work, workers, unions and the collective bargaining process. In addition, they must prepare themselves for a unique role in labor contract administration.

Selecting a Bargaining Agent

Police officers, as public employees, are not covered by the federal National Labor Relations Act of 1935. More than 80 percent of the states have, as was noted before, passed enabling legislation specifically authorizing collective bargaining by public employees subject to their jurisdiction. No two bargaining statutes are exactly the same. Some public employee bargaining laws are fairly permissive (even allowing strikes under certain circumstances) while others are more detailed, specific and much more restrictive. In most states, the State Labor Relations Board (SLRB) administers the law and regulates the collective bargaining process. Almost all administrative and regulatory decisions made by these boards are reviewable in the courts.

An employee, a group of employees, a union or an employer can petition the SLRB for a representation election. The purpose of the election is to determine if the employees desire to select an **exclusive bargaining agent**. In most cases, a petition must be supported by a show of interest on the part of a specified percentage of the work force. The federal standard of 30 percent has been adopted in a large number of states.

Once a petition for a representation election has been accepted, it is up to the SLRB to determine (based on job descriptions) who should and should not be in the proposed bargaining unit. In determining the exact composition of the unit, the SLRB looks for a commonality of interest based on things such as:

1. The similarity of duties, skills, wages and working conditions.

2. The pertinent collective bargaining history of those involved.

3. The nature and extent of union organization that is already in place.

4. The employees' wishes in the matter (when they are not inconsistent with other factors).

5. The appropriateness of the proposed unit in relation to the organizational structure of the department.

Unions should represent employees whose jobs are similar and who also share a common interest. Unfortunately, labor relations theory is not always translated into practice. Bargaining unit determination in law enforcement has been a mixed bag. In Pittsburgh, for example, the FOP represents all police officers up to the rank of captain. In Toledo and Detroit, the union represents only those employees at the rank of police officer. Toledo has a separate Command Officers' Association that represents sergeants, lieutenants and captains. Civilian personnel are often represented by AFSCME. It is not uncommon for a local government to deal with three or four separate unions representing employees in the same police department.

From a practical point of view, it is far better for management personnel to be in the same bargaining unit with other managers who have similar duties, responsibilities and interests. This is also true when it comes to sergeants. They are much more likely to support management initiatives and function as effective first-line managers if they consider themselves to be a real part of the management team (Ayres and Coble, 1987). There has, unfortunately, been little consistency in this area and many existing bargaining unit configurations simply cannot be justified in logical terms.

Assuming there are no problems in determining the composition of the proposed bargaining unit and that no other group has been certified as the exclusive bargaining agent for the employees, the SLRB is obligated by law to conduct a representation election. If everyone agrees, the staff of the SLRB will

conduct what is called a consent election. In the event there is any disagreement, an election will be authorized after a formal hearing has been held and an official finding is made by the Board. The time and date of the election will be set in an effort to ensure that most of the eligible employees on all shifts will have the opportunity to vote. All parties to the election are expected to adhere to the pre-election campaign guidelines set by the SLRB. Both labor and management have the right to appoint a number of observers to act as poll watchers, checkers, challengers and tabulators. Everything must be done to ensure the fairness of the election and the validity of each ballot.

If no objections are filed or if those that are filed are rejected, the Board has the legal authority to certify the results. There are two basic types of certification:

1. ***Certification of Representation.*** Attesting to the fact that a majority of those in the bargaining unit voted for the union.

2. ***Certification of Election Results.*** Attesting to the fact that the employees in the bargaining unit voted against union representation.

Certification of Representation makes the union the sole bargaining agent for all members of the bargaining unit. It also gives the union authority to enter into legally binding negotiations with the state or local government (Anderson, 1975).

A certified police union is a force to be reckoned with. It is, by law, the exclusive bargaining agent for ALL members of the bargaining unit, whether they belong to the union or not. Management is not permitted to negotiate directly with individual police officers or other groups within the police department. There are other benefits to certification as well. For example:

1. The employer (state or local government) must bargain in good faith with a certified union and usually is required to meet and discuss items of mutual concern on a timely basis.

2. The employer (state or local government) is obligated to seek a collective bargaining agreement or contract with the certified union representing bargaining unit employees.

3. Certified unions may be authorized to file policy grievances, to strike or (if strikes are prohibited) to seek binding arbitration in an effort to enforce the collective bargaining agreement depending on how the public employee bargaining law is written.

4. Rival unions are not allowed to engage in striking or picketing for recognition under the collective bargaining statute if there is a certified labor organization already in place.

5. Even if the parties cannot reach a collective bargaining agreement, rival unions are normally prohibited from filing a petition for a new representation election within 12 months of the original certification election.

6. An existing contract (for a definite term of up to three years) is
    usually considered a bar to a new election while it is in force.

In the event that (a specified percentage of all) union members become dissatisfied with its performance, they can petition for "decertification" of the
union as their collective bargaining agent. A petition for an election to decerti-
fy a union can be filed by another union, a group of disaffected members or an
individual member of the bargaining unit. If, after review, the SLRB accepts the
petition, it has an obligation to conduct a fair and impartial decertification election. While decertification efforts are usually unsuccessful, the process serves as
a check and balance. It helps to ensure that the union's leadership continues to
be responsive to the needs of its members (Myers and Twomey, 1975).

Most state public employee bargaining laws ban certain unfair labor practices.
The prohibition against unfair labor practices is designed to keep labor and man-
agement co-equal for purposes of collective bargaining. According to Sloane and
Witney (1991), it is usually considered an unfair labor practice for *management* to:

1. Interfere with, restrain or coerce employees in the exercise of
    their rights to organize, bargain collectively and participate in
    other activities for their mutual aid or protection.

2. Dominate or interfere with the formation or administration of
    any labor union or contribute financial or other support to it.

3. Encourage or discourage membership in any labor union organi-
    zation by discrimination with regard to hiring or tenure or con-
    ditions of employment (with the exception of a valid union-secu-
    rity agreement).

4. Discharge or otherwise discriminate against an employee
    because he or she filed unfair labor practice charges against the
    employer.

5. Refuse to bargain collectively and in good faith with the bar-
    gaining agent of employees.

It is, on the other hand, considered to be an unfair labor practice when *unions* do
any of the following:

1. Restrain or coerce employees in exercising their rights under
    the law.

2. Restrain or coerce an employer in the selection of a bargaining
    agent or grievance representative.

3. Cause or attempt to cause an employer to discriminate against an
    employee based on the person's membership or nonmembership
    in a labor organization.

4. Refuse to bargain collectively and in good faith with an employer if the union has been designated as a bargaining agent by a majority of the employees.

There is an assumption that collective bargaining is the product of independence and strength. The strong are inclined to bargain. The weak cave in. Weakness undermines the bargaining process.

Once the ground rules have been accepted and the union is in place, collective bargaining is set to begin. The initial bargaining session is a prelude to participatory management in police work.

Collective Bargaining

Collective bargaining is the process by which a labor contract is negotiated and enforced between the employees' exclusive bargaining agent (the union) and the state or local government responsible for operation of the police department. Labor and management have a mutual obligation to meet at reasonable times and to confer in good faith with respect to wages, hours and other terms and conditions of employment. While there is an affirmative duty to bargain, neither side is required to accept a proposal or make a concession. Most labor negotiations do, however, result in a formal written agreement that both sides can live with until the next regularly scheduled round of contract talks (Bittel and Newstrom, 1990).

The Bargaining Team

One of the first steps in the actual bargaining process is for each side (union and management) to select a competent negotiating team. This is an extremely important and, at times, difficult task. Most bargaining teams are fairly small. They normally consist of a chief negotiator, a recording secretary and three or four members who have conducted research in areas of special interest to management or the union. The knowledge, skill and dedication of the negotiators will determine the quality of the collective bargaining agreement and sets the moral or ethical tone for all future labor relations. Selectivity is a prerequisite for success.

While there are no hard-and-fast rules concerning the composition of the union's bargaining team, there are a few general principles that should be kept in mind. The union president (or a designee) almost always serves, along with other members of the bargaining unit, as part of the core team. The chief negotiator, who is usually not a police officer, leads the team and coordinates the bargaining effort. By bringing in an outside labor relations specialist as its chief negotiator, the union strengthens its position vis-à-vis management and gains practical advantages from that person's experience, expertise and objectivity. The chemistry of the team usually determines the quality of the contract.

The chief of police, on the other hand, seldom, if ever, serves as an official member of the management bargaining team. The chief's designee (or designees) represents the department's interest during the negotiations. This is an attempt to separate the politics of negotiation from the science of contract administration (Wilson and McLaren, 1977). Other department heads (legal, personnel, finance, etc.) are often pressed into service as members of the core team. In most jurisdictions, the director of labor relations serves as chief negotiator for the state or local government. Here again, the composition of the team and the way members of the team work together become critical factors in the outcome of the negotiations.

A major problem in many jurisdictions is that either police management has no representation at the bargaining table or its representation is inadequate to deal with the task at hand. Civilian managers normally represent the municipality. While these people may know a great deal about public administration and the budgetary process, they often know little or nothing about the needs of police managers. Consequently, they frequently bargain away management rights for concessions in the economic package. This leaves police managers who are accountable for achieving the department's mission, goals and objectives without the necessary authority to do the job (Ayres and Coble, 1987).

Once the bargaining teams have been formed, they must try to reach a consensus on the appropriate scope of the bargaining. In other words, what issues are to be discussed? While it is in management's interest to limit the scope of collective bargaining, organized labor normally wants everything placed on the table for discussion.

Scope of the Bargaining

Most public employee bargaining laws are patterned after federal statutes and, as such, attempt to identify those subjects that are either appropriate or inappropriate for collective bargaining. There are three types of bargaining proposals that merit further attention:

1. **Mandatory Subjects**. These are subjects (like disability pay, occupational safety and minimum staffing requirements) that clearly fall within the category of wages, hours and other terms and conditions of employment.

2. **Voluntary Subjects**. These are topics (like health club memberships, volume discounts based on group purchases, and new benefits for retirees) that clearly fall outside the mandatory category but are placed on the table for voluntary consideration and agreement. The other party is not required to bargain on them or to agree to include them in the new contract.

3. **Illegal Subjects**. These are subjects (like union shop agreements, binding arbitration and the right to strike) that have been specifically prohibited by the public employee bargaining law.

Negotiating the first contract requires a great deal of preparation and skill. The issues related to the mandatory subjects of **wages, hours and conditions of employment** become mind-boggling in complex criminal justice organizations.

While both the union and management want to negotiate a contract that gives them the greatest control over decisionmaking, parameters must be established to give some focus to the collective bargaining process. "Rights and responsibility" clauses are usually built in as an integral component of the collective bargaining agreement. These clauses are specifically designed to limit the scope of bargaining and delineate the areas of mutual concern.

According to the Police Executive Research Forum (1978), the goal of management is to obtain contract language that gives it the maximum discretion and flexibility in running the police department. The power that management retains is ordinarily spelled out in a **management rights clause**. A strong management rights clause gives the police administration a great deal of control over the operation of the department. A weak management rights clause gives away too much power. The National League of Cities (Rynecki, Cairns and Carnes, 1984) has recommended that a management rights clause be inserted into all municipal collective bargaining agreements. Such a clause could be stated as follows:

> It is agreed that the department possesses all of the rights, powers, privileges and authority it had prior to the execution of this agreement. Nothing in this agreement shall be construed to limit the department or the operation of the police enterprise, except as it may have been specifically relinquished or modified herein by an express provision of the collective bargaining agreement itself.

In simple terms, this contract language states that management retains certain rights that may not be challenged by the union no matter how infrequently they are used (Thibault, Lynch and McBride, 1990).

Cal Swank and James Conser (1983) argue that a strong management rights clause is probably the most important part of any contract or negotiation with an employee organization. A strong management rights clause and a mutually acceptable no-strike impasse resolution process are essential components of an effective management strategy. A good management rights clause should contain, but not be limited to, the following items:

1. Determining occupational qualifications and hiring human resources.

2. Directing the work force through formulation of departmental policies, procedures, rules and regulations.

3. Establishing work schedules and regulating overtime in a manner that is most advantageous to the employer.

4. Determining the method, process and manner used to perform police work.

5. Disciplining, suspending, demoting and discharging police personnel for reasonable and just cause.

6. Relieving and/or laying off police officers due to a lack of work, lack of funding or for disciplinary reasons.

7. Assigning, transferring and promoting police officers to positions within the department.

8. Consolidating and reorganizing the operations of the police department.

9. Taking action in emergency situations to insure proper operation of the police department.

While the enumeration of management rights may prove to be a stumbling block in negotiations, specificity is critically important. Managers need to know what is expected of them. They must be free to exercise legitimate authority.

Management rights clauses are usually negotiated in tandem with an employee responsibility clause. The first **union responsibility clause** in Detroit was very specific. According to the contract between the City of Detroit and the Detroit Police Officers Association (1973):

1. Recognizing the crucial role of law enforcement in the preservation of the public health, safety, and welfare of a free society, the union agrees that it will take all reasonable steps to cause the employees covered by this agreement, individually and collectively, to perform all police duties, rendering loyal and efficient service to the very best of their ability.

2. The union, therefore, agrees that there shall be no interruption of these services for any cause whatsoever by the employees it represents; nor shall they absent themselves from their work or abstain, in whole or in part, from the full, faithful, and proper performance of all the duties of their employment.

3. The union further agrees that it shall not encourage any strikes, sit-downs, stay-ins, slow-downs, stoppages of work, malingering, or any acts that interfere in any manner or to any degree with the continuity of police services.

Management rights and union responsibility become the starting point for all future negotiations.

The rights and responsibilities discussed above are fairly easy to understand. They are also subject to change. Management's right to make policy, for example, can be weakened or lost entirely as the result of negotiation, arbitration awards, court challenges or substantive changes in the collective bargaining statute. The only inherent rights of management are those that labor does not bargain away from it (Bouza, 1990). Unions, on the other hand, have been known to abdicate their responsibility to the public when they try to win policy concessions from their employers through intimidation rather than constructive conflict. It takes a great deal of time and effort on the part of labor and management to make the collective bargaining process work the way it was designed to work.

The Bargaining Table

The basic purpose of bargaining is to reach a mutually acceptable agreement on the issues raised at the table. The first meeting is ordinarily devoted to establishing the bargaining authority of each team, determining the ground rules for the negotiations and adopting a schedule. If the parties have not previously distributed their formal proposals, they may be distributed and clarified at this time. This gives the other side some indication as to why particular proposals are being made, how much thought has gone into them and the amount of support they have. The first session almost always sets the tone for subsequent meetings and may, in the long run, determine the success or failure of the collective bargaining process.

Labor contract negotiations take on the characteristics of a poker game in which each side attempts to determine the opponent's hand without revealing its own (Chruden and Sherman, 1984). The parties try to avoid disclosing the relative importance they attach to each proposal. They do not want to pay a higher price than is necessary to achieve those proposals that are of the greatest importance to them. Proposals can generally be divided into four basic categories:

1. *Non-negotiable*. Those the team feels it must have.

2. *Negotiable*. Those the team would like to have, but on which it is willing to compromise.

3. *Trade-off*. Those the team should submit for trading purposes.

4. *Expendable*. Those the team is willing to give up.

All proposals should be realistic. Unrealistic proposals serve only to aggravate the opponent and can, if taken seriously, create an impasse. It has been noted that unrealistic bargaining proposals have a nasty way of becoming real issues.

In order for a bargaining issue to be resolved satisfactorily, the point at which an agreement is possible must fall within limits that both the union team and the management team are willing to concede. This is called the zone of

acceptance. In some situations, proposals made by one party to the negotiations clearly exceed the tolerance limit of the other party. If this is the case, the solution is outside the zone of acceptance. If the party refuses to modify its demands enough (through compromises or trade-offs) to bring them within the zone of acceptance or if the opposing party will not extend its tolerance limit (based on some other form of compensation) to accommodate those demands, an impasse will result. The key to successful collective bargaining is to ascertain the parameters of the opponent's zone of acceptance and to compromise in such a way that all proposals fall within those parameters. This requires a great deal of skill.

The proposals submitted by each side must, regardless of the importance attached to them, be dealt with at the table if there is to be a collective bargaining agreement. Once a particular issue, clause or proposal is placed on the table, the other team is obligated to respond to it. There are four basic responses:

1. Accepted.

2. Accepted with minor modification.

3. Rejected.

4. Rejected with counter proposal.

An opponent cannot reject an issue, clause or proposal without an explanation. This would not be considered **bargaining in good faith**. A reason for the rejection must be given and that reason must, in and of itself, be reasonable. Having been informed of the opposing team's position, the bargaining begins. And as noted above, the bargaining process involves a great deal of give and take. It is designed to move the opposing teams closer to a mutually acceptable middle ground somewhere within the tolerance limits of both labor and management. From this perspective, collective bargaining is an applied art rather than an exact science.

Union Goals

The union always enters the collective bargaining process with a preset agenda. It wants to share power with the chief police executive through bilateral negotiations and to have a meaningful say in the day-to-day operation of the police department. Anything less is unacceptable and would be considered a sell out by the membership. The union bargaining team's big-ticket items usually fall into seven basic categories:

1. Wages and working conditions.

2. Union security measures.

3. Impasse resolution techniques.

4. Meet-and-discuss provisions.

5. Grievance procedures.

6. Procedural due process.

7. Job security and seniority.

Two additional bargaining categories have emerged as priority items for police officers in recent contract negotiations. One deals with issues surrounding officer safety in terms of personnel deployment, workplace security and equipment. The other focus is on adequate insurance coverage and the maintenance of fully paid health care benefits for those officers who have been injured on or retire from the job.

Concern about wages, hours and other terms and conditions of employment are traditional items that serve as a catalyst for unionization. A recent study indicated that 96.5 percent of the officers surveyed were primarily concerned about their compensation (Leonard and More, 1993). Union security measures, impasse resolution techniques and "meet-and-discuss" mechanisms are specifically designed to insure the stability of the union; whereas the grievance procedure, due process, job security and seniority deal with the non-economic issues that are considered most important to the membership.

Union bargaining teams place a high priority on negotiating very strong union security measures. These measures, such as dues checkoff, maintenance of membership and compulsory participation, give unions stability and enhance their clout in dealing with management. Basic **union security measures** can be summarized as follows:

1. *Dues Checkoff*. Management agrees to deduct union dues directly from the pay of its employees and to deliver the funds to the union on a regularly scheduled basis.

2. *Maintenance of Membership.* Management agrees that voluntary membership in a union cannot (as a condition of continued employment) be terminated by an employee while the negotiated contract is still in force.

3. *Compulsory Participation.* Management agrees that newly hired employees will, as a condition of employment, join the union (union shop) or pay a "service fee" in the form of union dues to the employee organization (agency shop).

Whether or not union or agency shop agreements can be negotiated as part of a labor contract depends on the state's collective bargaining statute. In many southern and western states with so-called "right-to-work" statutes on the books, most union security measures are outlawed. It is a different story in the northeastern states, however. The Pennsylvania General Assembly narrowly defeated

a very comprehensive agency shop bill for public employees during its 1987 legislative session. The agency shop bill was endorsed by Governor Robert Casey in 1987 and enacted into law as Act 84 of 1988.

There are trying times when, due to the nature of the collective bargaining process, negotiations will become deadlocked and something must be done to resolve the impasse if there is to be a mutually acceptable accord. The best way to prevent police strikes (and other job actions) is to provide for some combination of methods which will diffuse conflict and help implement the **impasse resolution** process (Holden, 1994). The most common impasse resolution techniques used in police work today (mediation, fact-finding, final best offer arbitration and binding arbitration) have been borrowed from private sector labor relations. Impasse resolution techniques are generally categorized as being either "non-binding" or "binding" and may best be described in the following manner:

1. ***Mediation.*** Mediation is a non-binding impasse resolution technique in which an authoritative third party attempts to help the disputants reach a mutually acceptable agreement. Mediators facilitate communication and clarify issues. Their value lies in their ability to review the dispute from an objective perspective, inject fresh ideas into the negotiations, recommend solutions and, when it is appropriate, extricate the parties from difficult or untenable positions. Professional mediation services are available from various state and federal agencies. While mediation is certainly not a panacea, the evidence suggests that it worked in more than 50 percent of the documented cases.

2. ***Fact-Finding.*** Fact-finding is a non-binding impasse resolution technique in which a fact-finder or panel of fact-finders gathers, interprets and assigns relative weight to data related to an issue in dispute. The process involves quasi-judicial hearings, compilation of an investigative report and formulation of very specific recommendations for resolving the impasse. An old study found that 89 percent of the disputes submitted to fact-finding were resolved (Stern, 1967). More recent data suggests that a success rate of 60 to 70 percent would probably be more accurate.

3. ***Final Best Offer Arbitration.*** Best offer arbitration is a binding impasse resolution technique in which each side submits a "final" offer to the arbitrator chosen to decide the issue. The arbitrator has absolutely no power to compromise and must select one or the other of the final offers submitted by the two parties. It is up to the arbitrator to choose the offer that is, on the whole, the most reasonable and fair. This plan encourages all parties to make concessions because the arbitrator's "award" is most likely to go to the party that has moved closest to a reasonable middle-ground position.

4. ***Binding Arbitration.*** Binding arbitration is an impasse resolution technique in which the disputants elect (voluntary) or are required (compulsory) to submit impasses to a neutral and mutually acceptable third party who is empowered to decide the issue. The decision is legally binding and enforceable in the courts. Most collective bargaining agreements now require that certain, if not all, labor disputes be submitted to binding arbitration for resolution (Myers and Twomey, 1975). A cadre of qualified and experienced arbitrators is available from the American Arbitration Association.

The most popular approach to impasse resolution in police work appears to be binding arbitration. The power that makes the arbitration binding may be found in the collective bargaining agreement, state law, a local ordinance, jurisdictional policy and court decisions (Sapp and Carter, 1991)

Whether or not these impasse resolution techniques work will depend, in large measure, on the importance of the issue, intensity of the conflict and good-faith bargaining of the disputants. Although some elected government officials attempt to renege on arbitration awards and openly challenge the legitimacy of the arbitration process as an unlawful encroachment on their legislative or administrative power, the courts have generally upheld the use of binding arbitration in the public sector. Many state and local governments have been forced, through the judicial process, to fund expensive, as well as very unpopular, police arbitration awards.

Communication is the lifeblood of the collective bargaining process and is an absolutely essential ingredient in successful conflict management. Regularly scheduled (and contractually mandated) meet-and-discuss sessions are designed to bring union representatives and managers together in an effort to promote communication, resolve issues and guarantee joint administration of the contract. Meet-and-discuss sessions provide a vehicle for participatory management in complex criminal justice organizations.

Dealing with Grievances

A **grievance** is a complaint arising out of the interpretation, application or compliance with provisions of a collective bargaining agreement. Grievance procedures and due process safeguards are built into virtually every labor contract. A multi-step grievance process is the norm in police work. In most cases:

1. There is a specific time limit within which a grievance must be filed once the police officer becomes aware that there is, or appears to be, a violation of the contract.

2. The officer is expected to discuss the alleged grievance informally with the immediate supervisor in an effort to resolve the problem.

3. If the grievance cannot be resolved informally and the employee wishes to pursue it further, a formal grievance is filed with the appropriate command officer.

4. The command officer processes the formal grievance and holds hearings at which the employee (and the union) present oral and written statements.

5. The command officer, based on the evidence, determines the merit of the grievance and notifies the grievant of the decision.

6. If the grievance is not resolved satisfactorily at the command level, it is sent to the chief executive officer for a final in-house disposition.

7. In many states (depending on the language of the public employee bargaining statute), an unresolved grievance goes to the political executive, Civil Service Commission, State Labor Relations Board or an arbitrator for final disposition.

If the grievant and the police union are dissatisfied with the final disposition of the grievance, they may (under most state laws) go to court for judicial review or injunctive relief. Winning the grievance is very important to both of them. A victory in each individual case is considered a victory for the union and the organized labor movement as a whole.

Procedural due process is near and dear to the heart of every unionist. It has long been the rallying cry for union activism in police departments. Unions and their members want to protect themselves from the arbitrary and capricious behavior of their employers. From their perspective, a "police officers' bill of rights" and due process standards for discipline are indispensable in a good contract. Procedural due process is considered sacrosanct and non-negotiable by virtually all rank-and-file police officers.

According to the Bureau of National Affairs, more than 90 percent of all union contracts emphasize the importance of worker seniority. Police work is no exception. In some cases, seniority has (based on negotiated collective bargaining agreements) become an overriding factor in the promotion, scheduling and assignment of personnel. In Pittsburgh, Pennsylvania, for example, police officers select their shifts, patrol zones and partners based on the seniority principle (Contract Between the City of Pittsburgh and the Fraternal Order of Police, 1992). The city can bypass a uniformed police officer for an open vehicle assignment on a particular shift only if it, in good faith, believes that because of incompatibility, the officer will not be effective in that assignment on that shift. Under these circumstances, it is not uncommon to find two rookie police officers patrolling high crime areas together on a midnight shift. While seniority should be considered, it is often antithetical to merit and often unduly limits management's ability to use its human resources in an efficient, effective and productive manner.

Impasse Resolution through Job Actions

Most police union goals are attained at the bargaining table or through very skillful political manipulation. Police unions have usually been able to deliver the goods to their members with a minimum amount of hassle. Tangling with the union is often considered to be political suicide. Consequently, most unions have been content to walk softly and carry a big stick.

When a police union is unable to obtain its goals through constructive conflict in collective bargaining and all of the normal impasse resolution techniques have failed, it may be forced to use a coercive strategy. While union leaders tend to oppose the tactical use of job actions, they know that job actions (whether they are legal or not) are a necessary part of the bargaining process. Without job actions to back them up, police unions feel they may lack the wherewithal to pressure the employer into making necessary concessions. A job action is, and should always be, the impasse resolution of last resort.

A job action is defined as a calculated disruption in normally assigned duties. The term can be used to describe any of several different types of activities that police officers engage in to show their dissatisfaction with a particular person, event, condition or situation. A job action can also be used in an effort to influence the deliberations of policy makers. Job actions send out a clear signal that there has been an unhealthy escalation in conflict and that the collective bargaining process has broken down.

Even though almost all states legally prohibit job actions by police personnel, the law has not proven to be an effective deterrent to poor labor relations. In 1979 alone, there were 52 police strikes throughout the nation (U.S. Department of Labor, 1981). While there have actually been fewer job actions by police personnel in the 1980s and 1990s, no one should be lulled into a false sense of security. The Johnstown, Pennsylvania police strike of 1987 is a clear demonstration that union members will, if they feel it is necessary, seek to resolve a bargaining impasse through some type of job action. Due to public safety considerations (directly related to the strike), the Pennsylvania State Police assumed jurisdiction over and provided law enforcement services for the third-class city of more than 37,000. Prohibition of police walkouts without a viable alternative to resolve a labor-management impasse is, in reality, no prohibition at all.

Job actions short of actual strikes or other work stoppages are much more common in today's labor relations environment. In New York City, where police officers were protesting an impasse in contract negotiations, the union—the Police Benevolent Association—tacitly supported a well-orchestrated work slowdown to demonstrate its displeasure with city government. As a result, the number of traffic tickets and summonses issued by 21,000 rank- and-file police personnel declined by more than 60 percent. This resulted in $1.5 million in lost revenue that the cash-starved city could ill afford to lose. Needless to say, the conflict was resolved rather quickly and in favor of the police. No one should underestimate the power of organized labor (Swanson, Territo and Taylor, 1993).

Case Study

Sergeant Sidney Sleighton

Sidney Sleighton is a sergeant in the patrol division of an urban police department. Police personnel are unionized. They are currently represented by the International Brotherhood of Teamsters. Conflict between the union and management has been anything but constructive. The grievance rate is very high and union members have participated in several very disruptive job actions during the past year.

Sergeant Sleighton, based on a unit determination ruling made by the State Labor Relations Board, is allowed to be an active member of the union. As such, he has been appointed to the union's team that will be negotiating a new CBA (collective bargaining agreement). He is looking forward to the challenge.

A strategy planning meeting was held to prepare for the upcoming contract negotiations. Sergeant Sleighton made two suggestions during the first session. He recommended that they hire an outside labor relations specialist as their chief negotiator and that they should seek a final best offer arbitration clause in the new collective bargaining agreement. Action on these recommendations was tabled until the next regularly scheduled meeting. The sergeant was asked to prepare a fully developed proposal for review by the team and submission to the union's executive committee.

After a thorough review of the sergeant's proposal, the bargaining team voted unanimously to recommend it to the union's executive committee. The executive committee, in turn, put the proposal on its agenda for discussion. Sergeant Sleighton has been asked to attend the next executive committee meeting in order to explain the merits of the proposal.

Put yourself in Sergeant Sleighton's shoes. How would you justify your proposal? Explain what you expect the union will gain by hiring an outside labor relations specialist as the chief negotiator and by bargaining for a final best offer arbitration award clause.

There are four basic types of job actions used in law enforcement. Charles Swanson and his colleagues (1993) describe these job actions in the following way:

1. **No-Confidence Votes.** In a no-confidence vote, rank-and-file union members formally signal their dissatisfaction with administrative policies or an administrator through a public and often highly publicized statement which, while it has no legal standing, can lead to the person's removal, resignation or early retirement. Even though no-confidence votes have played an important role in the departure of some police chief executives, like the removal of Robert Digrazia in Montgomery County, Maryland, and the retirement of Harold Bastrup in Anaheim,

California, they have not always accomplished the union's goal and have, in fact, been interpreted as a positive sign that needed reforms are taking place.

2. **Work Slowdowns**. In work slowdowns, while the police continue to provide all essential law enforcement services, police officers use less initiative and do their work at a measured pace so that each unit of work takes longer to complete. This causes a steep drop in productivity. Work begins to accumulate and benefits (in terms of public safety, a sense of security and revenues generated) are reduced. Pressure increases as more and more people perceive the loss in benefits and take affirmative action to reestablish the normal state of affairs. The effectiveness of the slowdown has been demonstrated in writing traffic tickets (California Highway Patrol), conducting criminal investigations (Phoenix, Arizona) and making arrests (Long Beach, California).

3. **Work Speedups**. In work speedups, there is an intentional acceleration in one or more types of police services designed to create anxiety and disruption through calculated overproduction. Speedups produce social stress and usually precipitate demands for acquiescence to the union. Work speedups have been used very successfully in New York City (transit authority smoking and littering violations), Chicago (moving violation "ticket blizzards") and Holyoke, Massachusetts (parking tickets). Speedups alter the normal pace of life and generate public demands for a return to the status quo.

4. **Work Stoppage**. Work stoppages involve the total withholding of production in one or more areas of service. The ultimate work stoppage (the strike) represents the total withholding of all services by union members. Described in picturesque terms like "blue flu" and the "bluebonic plague," mass resignations, "sick outs" and strikes have been used to protest economic conditions, judicial leniency, inadequate safety measures, staffing patterns, and so forth. While police strikes are illegal in almost all states, they usually accomplish their overall objective and few, if any, result in reprisals against the strikers or their union.

Job actions are one of the most controversial aspects in police unionism. While they may achieve the union's objectives, they also create anxiety, fear, resentment and a debilitating sense of betrayal within the community.

While it is fairly easy to overemphasize the negative aspect of job actions, the relations between police unions and management are normally constructive. Despite all the attention they receive, job actions are relatively infrequent events. The elimination of federal revenue sharing, erosion in state and local tax revenues and an unstable national economy have caused unions to reassess their demands. Most union effort is now designed to avoid cutbacks (retrenchment) or

reductions in existing benefits (givebacks), strengthen job security clauses in existing collective bargaining agreements and gain more input into the policy formulation process. Labor-management conflict is more and more symbolic and is played out on the bargaining table. Unions are attempting to achieve their objectives through accommodation and cooperation with management.

Union-Management Relations

V.A. Leonard and Harry More (1993) contend that unionization of the police can usually be traced back to the inadequacies of management. In most of the cases where unionization has occurred, officers had been frustrated by intolerable working conditions and were unable to obtain corrective action from indifferent state or local government officials. Trying to identify the impetus for unionization and to demonstrate that unions (based on inherent conservatism) generally have a negative effect on the development of professionalism may be counterproductive. Most of the nation's more than 800,000 sworn police officers (U.S. Department of Justice, 1993) are union members. Police administrators and elected officials have little or no choice except to work with the representatives of their employees. Trying to recapture the past through anti-union activity is a little like closing a barn door after the horses have been allowed to leave. The National Commission of Criminal Justice Standards and Goals (1973) came to the conclusion that the nation's police chief executives should recognize that police employees have a legal right, subject to certain reasonable limitations, to engage in activities protected by the First Amendment. They should acknowledge the right of their employees to join (or not join) employee organizations that represent their employment interests and give appropriate recognition to these organizations.

The Commission went on to emphasize the importance of the collective bargaining process in contemporary American society. In fact, it made the following specific recommendation in Standard 18.3:

> Every police agency and all police employees should be allowed, by 1975, to engage in collective negotiations in arriving at terms and conditions of employment that will maintain police service effectiveness and insure equitable representation for both parties.
>
> 1. Legislation enacted by states to provide for collective negotiations between police agencies and public employees should give equal protection for both parties and should include:
>
>   a. Provisions for local jurisdictions to enact specific rules for the collective negotiation process.
>   b. Procedures to prevent either party from circumventing the collective negotiation process.
>   c. Provisions for police agency retention of certain unrestricted management rights to insure proper direction and control in delivering police services.

    d.   Provisions to prohibit police employees from participating in any concerted work stoppage or job action.

    e.   Procedures that require adherence to the collective negotiation legislation by all parties.

2.   Every police chief should ensure that he or his personally designated representative is present during all collective bargaining negotiations involving the police agency, and that he is allowed to protect the interests of the community, the police agency, and all police employees.

3.   Every police agency should insure that all police employees receive training necessary to maintain effective management-employee relations. This training should include:

    a.   Sufficient information to provide all employees with a general knowledge of the management-employee relations process.

    b.   Specific instructions to persons who represent the police agency in the collective negotiation process.

    c.   Specific instructions to enable all supervisory police employees to perform their duties under a collective negotiation agreement.

4.   Every police chief executive should encourage employee organizations to provide training to enable their representatives to represent members in the negotiation process adequately.

5.   Every police chief executive should establish administrative procedures to facilitate the police agency's operation under any collective negotiation agreement.

6.   Every police chief executive should recognize that in the collective negotiation process the problems of unit determination, area-wide negotiation, and impasse procedures are largely unresolved and that little guidance is currently available in these essential areas.

The Commission took the position that job actions of any type should be illegal. It urged police executives to consider initiation of internal disciplinary action against any sworn police officer involved in a "concerted job action or work stoppage."

    The Commonwealth of Pennsylvania could be described as avant-garde when it comes to promoting positive labor-management relations through the collective bargaining process. Pennsylvania's Collective Bargaining and Compulsory Arbitration Act for Police and Fire (Act 111) was enacted into law in 1968. It authorizes collective bargaining by police officers and fire fighters and imposes binding arbitration as the final means of impasse resolution. An employee organization with more than 50 percent of the department's sworn personnel may be certified as the exclusive bargaining agent for all rank-and-

file officers. The union helps to formulate, implement and administer a collective bargaining agreement. In the event there is an impasse, a three-person arbitration panel is appointed. Management chooses one member, labor another, and the third is selected by mutual agreement. If the parties cannot decide on a mutually acceptable third member, an arbitrator must be chosen from a roster of names provided by the American Arbitration Association. The panel studies the issues and makes a final award that is binding on all parties. Act 111 has worked well most of the time.

Contract Administration

Signing a contract guarantees the continuation of the collective bargaining relationship for the duration of the agreement. One of the most important aspects of contract administration involves dissemination of information to all members of the department concerning the policies, programs, equipment and resources that are to be affected by the new agreement. It also requires labor and management to reach a consensus concerning the nature and extent of the participatory management to be allowed within the police department.

A police labor contract is a living document that is applied to a variety of very different issues in an ever-changing socioeconomic environment. In order to make it work, the parties must be prepared to spend a great deal of time and effort interpreting contract language, working out the bugs, making necessary adjustments, resolving problems through the formal grievance process and reaching ethical compromises that promote the interests of the employee, the department and the community at large.

Role of the Sergeant in Collective Bargaining

In small police departments, sergeants may be considered to be managers and assigned to play a significant role in the collective bargaining process. In most situations, however, the sergeant's role is limited to contract implementation or administration.

Sergeants, as first-line supervisors in police departments, are responsible for both people and production. They occupy an often ambiguous position between management and labor. Based on prevailing police organization/management theory, sergeants represent labor to management and management to labor. They are expected to identify minor problems and to deal with them before they become major issues. Sergeants have an obligation to help their subordinates as well as to apprise their superiors of potential problems. The police sergeant is a linchpin in effective labor relations. Even perfect labor relations policies will fail unless they are translated into practice by the sergeant (Walsh and Donovan, 1990). This is challenging and demands very specific skills.

The importance of sergeants in labor relations is underscored by their role in recommending or taking disciplinary action against their subordinates. Despite the many different types of issues that can or are actually grieved, nearly 90 percent of those taken to arbitration involve discipline against sworn police personnel. Since sergeants are departmental disciplinarians, they (and their actions) often become the focus of personnel as well as policy grievances. One study of arbitrated grievances disclosed that the officers involved were assigned to the uniformed patrol division in 84 percent of the cases and that the union won the arbitration award in more than 75 percent of the grievances (Lavan and Carley, 1985). Sergeants also play a very important role in resolving grievances. They are normally the first representative of management authorized to receive and settle grievances. Most truly effective grievance procedures formalize the sergeant's role by requiring grievants to seek an informal resolution of the case before it can be taken to the command level for a review and disposition. This emphasis on the sergeant corresponds to the principle that the best management decisions come from those who are directly involved in or are most familiar with the situation under review.

The sergeant's position is often very frustrating and is complicated by the conflicting demands made by fellow police officers and management. If management pushes too hard, sergeants may be forced to align themselves with labor. Under these circumstances, police managers become their own enemy and sergeants revert to the role of a promoted patrol officer. Ineffective supervision reduces productivity and has a deleterious influence on the overall quality of police service.

Unions have had both positive and negative effects on modern-day police work. On the plus side, they help shield police personnel from inept, autocratic and morally bankrupt managers and supervisors. They have, on the other hand, also been known to protect less than competent police officers, to make the taking of appropriate disciplinary action very difficult and to block the reforms needed to professionalize police service. Ineffective sergeants use the specter of unionization as an excuse to avoid the legitimate process of observing on-the-job performance, collecting information, documenting deviant behavior and knowing departmental policies, procedures, rules and regulations well enough to carry out their job-related supervisor responsibilities. It is much easier to blame the union (the union steward or grievance committee) than to acknowledge one's own shortcomings as a first-line supervisor.

Inadequate supervisory personnel react to crisis situations. They lack the skills required to manage them. Poor supervisors have not, as a general rule, formulated a workable set of principles to guide their actions. They are neither thorough or consistent and do only what is absolutely essential to guarantee their survival. Poor supervisors are usually not conscientious enough to put in the hard work that is required to represent their supervisees to management or to carry out those management responsibilities assigned to them by their superiors (Trojanowicz, 1980). Poor first-line supervision coupled with dynamic unionism creates an unhealthy climate for constructive conflict. It sets the stage for a dramatic deterioration in public sector labor relations.

Sergeants, if they are going to be good first-line supervisors, need to understand contemporary labor relations and to appreciate the value of constructive conflict in the collective bargaining process. They also need to develop a sound working relationship with the local union president (or "shop steward" in larger organizations). While sergeants and union representatives may be adversaries under certain circumstances, they should not be enemies. The sergeant should keep in mind that the union representative is an employee and a "worker." That person has been selected by peers to do an important job and is often given "released time" by the police department to see that the contract is implemented and administered fairly. The union representative has a legal responsibility and an absolute ethical obligation to fight for the contractual rights of all bargaining unit employees covered by the collective bargaining agreement. This symbolic conflict, no matter how intense it becomes, should never be allowed to degenerate into destructive personal animosity.

Competent first-line supervisors accept the fact that the union exists and, since they are powerless to change the situation, opt for constructive coexistence with, rather than open hostility to, the union representative. Figure 12.2 sets forth the labor relations duties of the police sergeants and their counterpart, the union president or shop steward. Based on a comparative analysis of their duties, it is clear there are far more similarities than there are differences.

Sergeants play a pivotal role in contract implementation and contract administration. Once again, the success or failure of the police department's labor relations effort will depend on the intelligence, knowledge, skill and dedication of the men and women who are selected to serve as first-line supervisors in these complex criminal justice organizations.

Many sergeants have experienced role conflict. They find it very difficult to perform well in all the roles assigned to them by virtue of their rank. Some are frustrated because they are not treated as managers or as patrol officers. They feel that they have little or no meaningful input into departmental policy and do not see themselves as part of the management team. On the other hand, management expects them to maintain a social as well as professional distance from their subordinates who do the actual work of the organization in order to preserve their objectivity and authority. This causes a dilemma for sergeants. Due to this role conflict and sense of frustration, sergeants in larger police departments have been forming their own labor unions.

Sergeants often bemoan the fact that they find themselves "in the middle" between labor and management. Some use this ambiguity as a rationale for inactivity and perpetuation of the status quo. Others see it as an opportunity for personal growth and development. They strive to carve out a niche in which they can satisfy their professional needs while making a meaningful contribution to law enforcement.

In healthy police organizations, sergeants are assimilated into the management team. Progressive managers know that police departments function much like military units. Commanders give orders. Sergeants, as first-line supervisors, see that rank-and-file police officers carry them out. Successful police work

Figure 12.2

Labor Relations Roles Played by the Police Sergeant and the Union Representative

SERGEANT	UNION REPRESENTATIVE
1. Accept collective bargaining.	1. Accept collective bargaining.
2. Know the contract.	2. Know the contract.
3. Enforce the agreement.	3. Enforce the agreement.
4. Look out for the welfare of all subordinates.	4. Look out for the welfare of all constituents.
5. Be a spokesperson for both management and employees.	5. Be a spokesperson for both union and constituents.
6. Settle grievances fairly (in line with management's interpretation of the contract).	6. Settle grievances fairly (in line with the union's interpretation of the contract).
7. Keep abreast of grievance solutions and changes in contract interpretation.	7. Keep abreast of grievance solutions and changes in contract interpretation.
8. Be firm, fair and impartial when dealing with the union.	8. Be firm, fair and impartial when dealing with management.
9. Maintain a good working relationship with the steward.	9. Maintain a good working relationship with the sergeant.
10. Keep the union representative informed of management decisions and sources of trouble.	10. Keep the sergeant informed as to the union's position and sources of trouble.
11. Protect management rights.	11. Protect labor rights.

Modified from: W. Richard Plunkett, *Supervision: The Direction of People at Work*, 6th ed. Boston: Allyn and Bacon (1992).

requires communication, cooperation and coordination. Under ideal conditions, sergeants facilitate communication, elicit voluntary cooperation and provide absolutely essential coordination. In other words, they energize and guide personnel in an effort to accomplish the organization's mission, goals and objectives. Sergeants are expected to be advocates, leaders, problem solvers, disciplinarians, labor relations specialists and contract administrators. They play a demanding role that requires a great deal of knowledge and interpersonal skill.

Most newly promoted sergeants are ill-equipped to handle the multidimensional role thrust upon them. Promoted largely on the basis of political affiliation or some paper and pencil test, they are given little or no training in supervision and are allowed to fend for themselves in an often hostile environment. New sergeants adopt survival strategies keyed to dangers they face. Some cave in to union demands and become "promoted patrol officers" who use the extra income to salve their conscience. Others attach their star to management and exude a hard-line, anti-union bias. Based on current legal and philosophical support for public sector collective bargaining, neither approach is productive. Both will lead to a sense of frustration and failure.

The occupational landscape has changed dramatically and so has the role of the sergeant in a paramilitary police organization. In order to fulfill this new role, sergeants must shed their paranoia and unshackle themselves from the past. They must learn to establish empathetic, goal-oriented relationships with their subordinates. Gamesmanship must be replaced with an honest, open and participative approach to the resolution of common problems. Sergeants must be prepared themselves to face tough issues. They cannot afford to let contract disputes or grievances go unattended. Unresolved issues fester. They destroy unity of purpose and undermine the common interest. Tomorrow's first-line supervisor must understand the human dynamics involved in collective bargaining, have the ability to motivate subordinates and be capable of forging a consensus about what needs to be accomplished and how it is to be done. Leadership will be the prerequisite for successful supervision in the future.

If sergeants are going to perform managerial duties related to supervision, discipline, evaluation and labor relations, we can no longer afford to debate the issue of their status within the police department. While they are supervisors, they are also involved in directing, planning, leading, controlling and coaching the activities of others. These are management functions (Steinmetz and Todd, 1992). Consequently, police sergeants are de facto managers and should be considered part of the department's management team.

Interest-Based Bargaining Process

As collective bargaining has become institutionalized in modern police work, there are signs that a subtle shift in its emphasis is beginning to take place. Since both management and unions desire to enhance rather than destroy their relationship, they are beginning to look for a process which minimizes confrontation and facilitates open and candid discussion of what are perceived as mutually significant issues. The movement away from **traditional (position-based) negotiations** to **innovative (win-win) negotiations** is buoyed when two strong institutions (union and management) respect each other and decide to work together cooperatively in an effort to achieve their mutual interests whenever possible. This interest-based bargaining approach may well become the rule rather than the exception in the future.

The win-win negotiation concept was originally developed by the United States Department of Labor and used to reach collective bargaining agreements with its own personnel. The focus is on mutual interests rather than preconceived positions.

With reference to the negotiation sessions themselves, there are two absolutely critical objectives:

1. Dynamic interaction among team members unencumbered by formal environmental arrangements or occupational status considerations.

2. Open and candid discussion of mutual interests or concerns with respect to a particular issue.

Once the salient issue or issues have been identified, the parties working together collectively as a team develop a variety of alternatives designed to deal with them and satisfy their mutual interests. All team members are encouraged to participate actively in this brainstorming process. The alternatives or options are recorded without evaluation or judgment. Team members take turns serving as facilitators and recorders. Information is shared openly to ensure that everyone is actively involved in the negotiations.

After the alternatives have been developed, the team members formulate a set of standards or criteria for use in evaluating the overall acceptability of the options. They use brainstorming techniques to compile an initial list of criteria and pare it down through candid discussion (designed to eliminate duplicative, vague or unmeasurable standards) until there is a genuine consensus. A final list of decision-making criteria might well include the following:

1. Legality

2. Constituent Acceptability

3. Effectiveness

4. Efficiency

5. Workability

6. Cost Effectiveness

7. Adequacy of Representation

These standards are then applied through open discussion designed to determine those options upon which members can reach agreement. Once the best option is selected, union and management negotiators work together to draft contract language and a brief history of the bargaining process. The proposed agreement is forwarded to management and the union for final review and adoption.

As the collaborative relationship between management and unions matures to the degree discussed above, more police departments are likely to engage in interest-based bargaining. It is the collegial alternative to traditional position bargaining designed to empower both parties as they jointly seek to achieve consensus on items of mutual interest. The differences in the two processes are reflected in Figure 12.3.

Figure 12.3
Two Types of Bargaining Strategies

BARGAINING PROCESS	
Traditional Negotiations	**Interest-Based Negotiations**
Positions developed separately by each side.	Emphasis on issues of mutual importance to both sides.
Arguments made in an adversarial environment.	Mutual interests are discussed candidly in a collegial atmosphere.
Power/competition determines who wins or who loses.	Joint development of mutually acceptable options.
Eventual outcome: WIN-LOSE LOSE-LOSE	Consensus concerning criteria to be used when evaluating the proposed options.
	Selection of the best option designed to satisfy the mutual interests of both sides.
	Collaborative development of contract language for the collective bargaining agreement.
	Sign-off by both management and the union.
	Eventual outcome: WIN-WIN

Modified from L.K. Goodwin, "Win-Win Negotiations: A Model for Cooperative Labor Relations," *The Public Manager*, Vol. 10, Summer 1993.

While there is no way to predict whether or not interest-based bargaining will become a widespread phenomenon in modern police work, it has the potential to revolutionize the way we currently approach labor relations. Success or failure will be determined by *key factors* such as those listed below:

1. **Commitment to the Process.** Management and labor must be committed to bringing about a cultural change whereby they listen to each other, understand each other's needs and interests, and seek collaborative solutions designed to strengthen each side in pursuit of the department's mission, goals and objectives.

2. **Information Sharing and Trust.** Meaningful interaction and absolute candor are essential to building mutual trust. Neither side should be surprised by the other, and privileged or private conversations must remain confidential.

3. **Model Behavior.** At all stages of the negotiations and during day-to-day contract administration, police managers and union leaders need to model collaborative behavior. Leaders on both sides must set the tone and exhibit those behaviors that are expected from all other members of the organization.

4. **Time to Prepare.** Members of the bargaining team must have a sense of trust in and commitment to the process so that they are willing to take risks, share vital information and model collaborative behavior. It takes time to create an interactive environment based on rapport and trust between the key players. From a practical point of view, most of the spadework must be done before anyone sits down at the bargaining table.

5. **Isolate the Problems.** Management and the union need to understand and accept the fact that some of their people simply will not buy interest-based bargaining in lieu of the traditional collective bargaining process. Managers and union leaders need to isolate these individuals, if possible, and concentrate on the vast majority of their constituents who prefer the cooperative model of labor relations

6. **Contract is Only Paper.** The key to success in interest-based bargaining is understanding that the conclusion of the negotiations represents nothing more than the beginning of a long-term partnership between management and the union to implement the contract and market this new collaborative approach to labor relations in the public sector. Traditional perspectives and organizational culture cannot be changed by issuing a new contract to everyone. Both sides must work together to develop a strategy for change over the life of the current collective bargaining agreement and beyond (Goodwin, 1993).

Summary

Police officers have experimented with unionism since the early 1900s. The Boston police strike of 1919 created an anti-union backlash that prompted Congress to exclude all public employees from the 1935 National Labor Relations Act. While the U.S. government was promoting unionization in the private sector, state governments steadfastly refused to sanction collective bargaining by public employees until 1959. Wisconsin became the first state to grant public employees the limited right to organize and bargain collectively with their employers concerning wages, hours and working conditions. Since that time, most of the states have enacted public employee bargaining laws and many states even allow public employees, with the exception of public safety personnel, to strike. More than half of the states have authorized binding arbitration in lieu of the strike. Fire fighters, police officers and teachers are heavily unionized. There has been a "hidden revolution" during which more than 75 percent of the police have decided to join unions.

Collective bargaining is a form of participatory management in which labor and management share power through constructive conflict. It is based on the assumption that bilateral decision making by coequals is in the public interest. There is an expectation that good-faith negotiations will produce a binding agreement that both parties can accept. Initial contract negotiations almost always focus on bargainable issues like wages, working conditions, management rights, employee responsibilities, impasse resolution, union security, grievance procedures, due process safeguards, seniority and job security. Almost all contract negotiations produce a mutually acceptable collective bargaining agreement.

Sergeants play a variety of different roles in labor relations. Some sergeants serve as negotiators. Whether they end up negotiating for labor or management will depend on how the state law is written. In most cases, however, the sergeant's role is restricted to contract implementation or administration. As department disciplinarians, sergeants (and their actions) are often the target of a grievance. More than 90 percent of all arbitrations involve grievances dealing with discipline. Sergeants also play a vital role in the resolution of grievances. Most formal grievance procedures require that the first-line supervisor be given an opportunity to resolve the problem before it is sent to the command level for disposition.

Sergeants are lead actors in labor relations. They are expected to look out for the welfare of their subordinates, enforce the collective bargaining agreement, recommend or take disciplinary action and work with union representatives to ensure smooth operation of the police department. Many sergeants have experienced role conflicts and frustration. Every effort should be made to clarify their status within the police department. Since sergeants perform a variety of management functions, they should be classified as managers and made full-fledged members of the management team.

As labor relations continue to mature in law enforcement, police managers and unions must be willing to embrace changes in the collective bargaining process. Interest-based negotiations may well represent the wave of the future. While we are unwilling to view interest-based negotiations as a panacea, this approach seems well suited for the 21st century.

Case Study

Sergeant Edward M. Bratton

Sergeant Ed Bratton has been a police officer for 16 years. He works for a medium-sized county police department on the Eastern Seaboard. The sergeant was recently assigned to a newly created position as administrative assistant to Chief Brady Tyler. As the police department's new human resources management specialist, he is responsible for the labor relations program.

In an effort to improve the department's efficiency, effectiveness and productivity through better union-management relations, Sergeant Bratton has designed a staff development program for newly promoted "first-line managers."* The program consists of four one-week seminars focusing on supervision, discipline, collective bargaining and contract administration. The seminars give each participant an opportunity to translate labor-management theory into practice.

According to Sergeant Bratton's view of management, sergeants play the pivotal role in contract administration. Their co-star, so to speak, is the union president or representative. Unless they work together to achieve the department's mission, goals and objectives, poor labor relations may lower morale and reduce overall productivity. Constructive conflict is learned, rather than natural, behavior. It is management's job to demonstrate the value of cooperative interaction.

Part of the seminar on contract administration deals with how to develop a positive (and cooperative) relationship with the union president or the representative. There is an emphasis on human communication, mutual problem-solving techniques and participatory management.

Sergeant Bratton is scheduled to meet with Chief Tyler sometime next week in order to brief him on the staff development project. He expects the chief of police to authorize implementation of the new training program.

---

*The state's Labor Relations Board classifies sergeants as "managers" with "supervisory responsibilities."

It is obvious that the staff development program is very important to Sergeant Bratton. The contract administration seminar is probably the most controversial part of the package. If you were the sergeant, how would you approach this topic? What can be done to avoid miscommunication? Would it help to develop a chart comparing the role of the sergeant vis-à-vis the union president or representative in contract administration? What should be included?

Key Concepts

balance through constructive conflict
bargaining in good faith
choosing a bargaining agent
compulsory binding arbitration
exclusive bargaining agent
grievance
impasse resolution techniques
management rights/union responsibility
negotiating a CBA or contract
noneconomic issues

participatory management by contracts
role conflict and its impact on morale
scope of bargaining
sergeants as contract administrators
sergeants as disciplinarians
"traditional" vs. "innovative" bargaining
unionism—the hidden revolution
union security measures
wages, hours and conditions of employment

Discussion Topics and Questions

1. Trace the historical development of police unionism in the United States and explain why Sam Walker refers to it as America's "hidden revolution." Do you agree? Why?

2. Discuss the process by which a union is certified as the exclusive collective bargaining agent for a particular group or class of employees. Describe the union's role in negotiating, implementing and executing a contract. What type of noneconomic issues will normally be given the highest priority during negotiations for the first contract?

3. Compare and contrast the role of the chief of police with that of the union president during negotiation of a collective bargaining agreement.

4. Identify, compare and contrast the major impasse resolution techniques used in police work. Which one is preferred by most police unions? Why?

5. Municipal police officers are almost always prohibited by law from taking job actions against their employers. What is a job action? What types of job actions have the police used in the past to resolve labor disputes? Give specific examples.

6. All police union contracts emphasize the grievance procedure and require extensive due process safeguards for those who may be subjected to disciplinary action. Describe a typical, multiple-step police grievance procedure. Why, in your opinion, are the police so concerned about procedural due process?

7. Compare the labor relations roles played by sergeants with those of the union representative (or shop steward). What are their objectives? Emphasize similarities as well as differences.

8. What is interest-based bargaining? How does it differ from the traditional collective bargaining process? Would the new approach have a positive or negative effect on labor relations in your department? Explain why.

For Further Reading

Gaines Larry K., Mittie D. Southerland and John E. Angell (1991). *Police Administration*. New York: McGraw-Hill Book Company.

> Very well researched and written chapter on police labor relations. Shows a great deal of insight into the dynamics of the collective bargaining process in relation to public sector labor negotiations.

More, Harry W. and W. Fred Wegener (1992). *Behavioral Police Management*. New York: Macmillan Publishing Co.

> Discusses unionism and its impact on police work. It explores managerial rights in relation to the successful negotiation of a meaningful collective bargaining agreement.

Whisenand, Paul and R. Fred Ferguson (1989). *The Managing of Police Organizations*, 3rd ed. Englewood Cliffs, NJ: Prentice-Hall, Inc.

> Excellent review of police labor-management relations with an emphasis on the managerial role of sergeants and the examination of the 15 commonly accepted "responsibilities of management."

References

Anderson, Howard J. (1975). *Primer of Labor Relations*. Washington, DC: The Bureau of National Affairs, Inc.

Ayres, Richard M. and Paul R. Coble (1987). *Safeguarding Management's Rights*. Dubuque, IA: Kendall/Hunt Publishing Company.

Barnard, Chester I. (1976). *The Functions of the Executive*. Cambridge, MA: Harvard University Press.

Bellante, Don and Philip K. Porter (1992). "Agency Costs, Property Rights, and the Evolution of Labor Unions." *Journal of Labor Research*, Vol. 11, No. 3.

Bittel, Lester R. and John W. Newstrom (1990). *What Every Supervisor Should Know*, 6th ed. New York: McGraw-Hill Book Company.

Bouza, Anthony V. (1990). *The Police Mystique*. New York: Plenum Press.

Chruden, Herbert J. and Arthur W. Sherman, Jr. (1984). *Managing Human Resources*, 7th ed. Cincinnati, OH: South-Western Publishing Company.

Cole, George F. (1992). *The American System of Criminal Justice*, 6th ed. Pacific Grove, CA: Brooks-Cole Publishing Company, Inc.

Commonwealth of Pennsylvania, Revised Statutes (1987). *Act 111 of 1968*, "Compulsory Collective Bargaining and Contract Arbitration for Police and Fire." Harrisburg, PA.

Contract between the City of Detroit and the Detroit Police Officers' Association (1973).

Contract between the City of Pittsburgh and the Fraternal Order of Police (1992).

Dressler, Gary (1979). *Management Fundamentals*. Reston, VA: Reston Publishing Company.

Ewing, David W. (1983). *Do It My Way or You're Fired*. New York: John Wiley and Sons, Inc.

Foulkes, Fred and E. Robert Livernash (1989). *Human Resources Management*, 2nd ed. Englewood Cliffs, NJ: Prentice-Hall, Inc.

Goodwin, Larry K. (1993). "Win-Win Negotiations: A Model for Cooperative Labor Relations." *The Public Manager*, Vol. 10, No. 2.

Holden, Richard N. (1994). *Modern Police Management*. Englewood Cliffs, NJ: Prentice-Hall, Inc.

Juris, Hervey A. and Peter Feuille (1973). *Police Unionism*. Lexington, MA: Lexington Books.

Lavan, Helen and Cameron Carley (1985). "Analysis of Arbitrated Employee Grievance Cases in Police Departments." *Journal of Collective Negotiation in the Public Sector*, Vol. 14, No. 3.

Leonard, V.A. and Harry W. More (1993). *Police Organization and Management*, 8th ed. Westbury, NY: The Foundation Press.

Myers, A. Howard and David P. Twomey (1975). *Labor Law and Legislation*. Cincinnati, OH: South-Western Publishing Company.

National Advisory Commission on Criminal Justice Standards and Goals, U.S. Department of Justice (1973). *The Police*. Washington, DC: U.S. Government Printing Office.

Plunkett, W. Richard (1992). *Supervision: The Direction of People at Work*, 6th ed. Boston: Allyn and Bacon, Inc.

Police Executive Research Forum (1978). *Police Collective Bargaining Agreements: A National Management Survey*. Washington, D.C.

Rynecki, Steven, Douglas A. Cairns and Donald J. Carnes (1984). *Police Collective Bargaining Agreements*. Washington, DC: National League of Cities.

Sapp, Allen D. and David L. Carter (1991). "Conflict and Conflict Resolution in Police Collective Bargaining." *The Police Forum*, Vol. 1, No. 1.

Sapp, Allen D., David L. Carter and Darrell W. Stephens (1990). *Police Labor Relations: Critical Findings*. Washington DC: Police Executive Research Forum.

Shafritz, Jay M., et al. (1986). *Personnel Management in Government*, 3rd ed. New York: Marcel Dekker, Inc.

Sloane, Arthur A. and Fred Witney (1991). *Labor Relations*, 7th ed. Englewood Cliffs, NJ: Prentice-Hall, Inc.

Stahl, O. Glenn (1983). *Public Personnel Administration*. New York: Harper and Row.

Steinmetz, Lawrence L. and H. Ralph Todd, Jr. (1992). *Supervision: First-Line Management*, 5th ed. Boston: Richard D. Irwin, Inc.

Stern, James L. (1967). "The Wisconsin Public Employee Fact-Finding Procedure." *Industrial Labor Relations Review*, 20 (Oct.).

Swank, Calvin J. and James A. Conser (1983). *The Police Personnel System*. New York: John Wiley and Sons, Inc.

Swanson, Charles R., Leonard Territo and Robert W. Taylor (1993). *Police Administration*, 3rd ed. New York: Macmillan Publishing.

Thibault, Edward A., Lawrence M. Lynch and R. Bruce McBride (1990). *Pro-Active Police Management*, 2nd ed. Englewood Cliffs, NJ: Prentice-Hall, Inc.

Trojanowicz, Robert C. (1980). *The Environment of the First-Line Police Supervisor*. Englewood Cliffs, NJ: Prentice-Hall, Inc.

U.S. Department of Justice, Bureau of Justice Statistics (1993). *Sourcebook of Criminal Justice Statistics*. Washington, DC: U.S. Government Printing Office.

U.S. Department of Labor, Bureau of Labor Statistics (1981). *Work Stoppage in Government, 1979*. Washington, DC: U.S. Government Printing Office.

Walker, Samuel (1992). *The Police in America*, 2nd ed. New York: McGraw-Hill Book Company.

Walsh, William F. and Edwin J. Donovan (1990). *The Supervision of Police Personnel: A Performance Based Approach*. Dubuque, IA: Kendall/Hunt Publishing Company.

Wilson, O.W. and Roy C. McLaren (1977). *Police Administration*. New York: McGraw-Hill Book Company.

World Almanac, The (1993). Pittsburgh: The Pittsburgh Press (and Pharos Books).

Supervising Minorities—

Respecting Individual and Cultural Differences

13

Introductory Case Study

Sergeant Orvid A. Halstead

Sergeant Orvid Halstead is a shift supervisor in a small city located in the Southwest. He is a college graduate who has been in law enforcement for near-ly 15 years. The sergeant is white and is considered to be "a good old boy." He is, nonetheless, a dedicated professional who tries to be open, honest and fair in dealing with all his subordinates.

Eva Estrada, the department's only female police officer, has just been transferred from the juvenile bureau to the patrol division. She has been assigned to Sergeant Halstead's unit and will report for duty immediately fol-lowing a two-week vacation. He must now decide how to redeploy existing per-sonnel. Since Officer Estrada will be the first woman ever assigned to general patrol duties in the city, the sergeant is somewhat concerned about the recep-tion she is likely to receive from her colleagues and the community at large. Sergeant Halstead is determined to make the transition as smooth as possible.

Several of the policemen assigned to the unit have made snide, sexist remarks to Sergeant Halstead. He has a feeling that his men plan to shun Officer Estrada when she reports for duty. The sergeant has concluded that the situation could get out of hand unless he deals with it in a very direct manner. Consequently, he has scheduled a shift meeting. He has apprised his lieutenant of the situation and the general purpose of the meeting.

The sergeant has gone to great lengths to prepare for the shift meeting. He has checked Officer Estrada's most recent performance appraisal and has spoken with her previous supervisor. Based on this data, there is no doubt in his mind that she is a competent police officer who can do the job. Sergeant Halstead has also reviewed the 1964 Civil Rights Act, the 1972 Equal Employment Opportunity Act and the department's EEO/AA plan. In addi-tion, he has familiarized himself with several studies that clearly indicate that carefully selected and well-trained female officers can be as effective as care-fully selected and well-trained male police officers.

During the shift meeting, Sergeant Halstead thoroughly explained the reason for his concern and asked for input from his officers. He gave Officer Estrada his unqualified endorsement. He also reviewed the law and provided them with an overview of the research data. The sergeant made it clear that he and his superiors were committed to equal employment opportunity and anticipated their cooperation. During the question-and-answer period, he encouraged his officers to explore their feelings and to deal with their prejudices. Sergeant Halstead guaranteed them that every subordinate would be judged by the same standards and that all police personnel would be treated equitably and fairly regardless of their race, religion, sex or national origin.

How would you, as a sergeant, handle a situation like this? Do you think that Sergeant Halstead went overboard in his preparation? Should Officer Estrada have attended the meeting since it dealt with her well-being? Do you think the sergeant accomplished his objective?

Coming to Grips with the Past

Until fairly recently, police work could easily have been described as a bastion for politically conservative white males. Police sergeants supervised other white men, like themselves, who came primarily from the working class. The typical police officer was a high school graduate with some military experience who had worked in blue-collar or lower-level white-collar occupations before joining the police department. Most of these men were attracted to police work for its job security and masculine camaraderie. In many areas of the country, a succession of ethnic groups (like the Irish, Italians and Jews) controlled police departments and used them as stepping stones to higher socioeconomic status.

Applicants who met the minimum qualifications were allowed to take a civil service examination, demonstrate their physical prowess in an agility test and spar with inquisitors on an oral board. If the applicant passed a background investigation, his final score was calculated and placed in its proper order on the certified list of candidates. Candidates with the highest score were evaluated by the chief of police (based on the "rule of three") and an appointment was made. Appointment as a probationary patrolman offered young men a career with job security, prestige, a chance to exercise authority and a little bit of glamour. It represented a rite of passage and an induction into the "old boy network."

Newly sworn rookie police officers were issued a uniform, a badge, a service revolver and other symbols of their new status. They were normally given a few words of advice, such as "Use your common sense," or "When you're in doubt, ask!" and put to work with little or no formal training. In most departments, police academy training (if there was any training) came later. Rookie police officers learned on the job from the old-timers who served as their mentors. The new men internalized the norms and values of their teachers. They

quickly learned that in order to get ahead in the bureaucratic world they had to play smart politics and work the system. If they learned well enough, promotions came along at fairly regular intervals (Broderick, 1987).

Police ranks were filled by men recruited not necessarily because of their capability or potential but because of their ability to fit into the police mold. They were hired to maintain the status quo, not to rock the boat. Rookie police officers were taught that criminals, liberals, civil rights activists and feminists were all part of a diabolical conspiracy to undermine law and order. Cynicism and a unique occupational paranoia became part of the police culture. Perplexed and disillusioned by rapid sociopolitical change, all but the most resilient retreated to the security of the womb (the police society), which the late William H. Parker called the "shell of Minorityism" (Turner, 1968). The police considered themselves to be outsiders who functioned as an instrument of civil society and resented it when that role was challenged as being racist.

Police work has changed over the past 30 years and so has the composition of the work force. Sergeants are now called on to supervise more minority, female and other nontraditional police employees. In order to do the job properly, they must respect the individual and cultural differences of their subordinates. The same holds true for the nontraditional employees who are going to be hired and promoted in far greater numbers in the future.

Women have been disadvantaged and discriminated against based on the cultural myth that police work is man's work. The opposition to blacks, Hispanics and other racial minorities is simply the result of bigotry. The police establishment has always resisted the assimilation of these nontraditional employees because it would mean sharing the power associated with the police function. This problem is exacerbated by the mentality of many white males. They have a deep-seated belief that they have a calling and are ordained to control the police profession (Holden, 1986). Their lock on power is self-evident.

In only a few major cities in the United States does the percentage of non-whites in blue approximate the proportion of non-whites in the overall community. National surveys reveal that the percentage of black and Hispanic officers, previously reported to be about 50 percent in some of America's 50 largest cities, has been increasing steadily and that there has been a significant increase in a number of metropolitan areas (Walker, 1992). As political power begins to shift toward minorities in some of the nation's cities, we can anticipate even more emphasis on black and Hispanic employment. Even the selection of black or Hispanic mayors may not precipitate radical changes in the composition of police departments, however. Political power is a crucial factor. In many large cities, the police are able to muster the political power needed to protect their turf from encroachment by those considered "outsiders," even if those outsiders are elected officials (Cole, 1995).

The importance of attracting women and minority officers cannot be overestimated. It is not the question of providing them with economically desirable government jobs that is important. Effective policing is the issue. It is very difficult for minorities who feel discriminated against to view law enforcement as

being responsive to their needs, unbiased and generally interested in justice if they do not see members of their group represented on the department's personnel roster. According to George Cole (1995), the ethnic character of American society makes it absolutely essential that participants in administration of criminal justice reflect the character of all the community.

Discrimination based on race and sex has been and continues to be a persistent human relations problem in our pluralistic society. It was, in fact, institutionalized by law (de jure) and through customary interpersonal relationships (de facto) until the mid-1960s. Propelled by deep-seated **prejudices**, discrimination permeated virtually every facet of American life. White Anglo Saxon Protestant (WASP) values set the moral tone and ensured that almost all substantive political power remained in the hands of white males. Municipal police departments (as instruments of the white political establishment) were composed of white males whose major function was to "protect and serve" the white community while preserving the status quo. The constitutional guarantees of due process and equal protection of law contained in the Bill of Rights and the anti-slavery amendments took a back seat to reality. The Constitution became little more than an abstract statement of human values unrelated to the treatment of racial minorities and women.

According to Gary Johns (1988), "prejudgment" is normal human behavior. People make all sorts of judgments based on previously acquired knowledge and past experience so as to bring some order into their lives. The mind assimilates as much as it can and then arranges the information in categories by which it prejudges a person or event. This saves time and effort. Such a mechanism, however, tends at times to produce irrational as opposed to rational categories. This is where prejudice, stereotyping and discrimination come in. These terms can be defined as follows:

1. **Prejudice.** Prejudice is a negative attitude toward a particular group considered to be different and inferior. The opinion is based partially on observation and partially on ignorance, ethnocentrism and xenophobia. These erroneous generalizations are applied to all members of the group regardless of individual differences.

2. **Stereotype.** Stereotypes are standardized mental images held by members of one group regarding the characteristics or traits of another group. A stereotype is a set of group-shared and generally negative attitudes based on tradition, limited interaction or ignorance that assigns similar undesirable attributes to all members of the out group.

3. **Discrimination.** Discrimination refers to the negative and unfavorable treatment of people based on their membership in a minority group. Discriminatory practices involve an act or omission that disadvantages one person vis-à-vis another in order to satisfy some prejudice.

Prejudice, stereotyping and discrimination against minority groups are normally by-products of uncontrolled ethnocentrism or xenophobia. A minority group is one that has subordinate status and is the object of discrimination. Ethnocentrism is the natural tendency of human beings to view their own culture and customs as right and superior and to judge all others by those standards (Zastrow and Bowker, 1984). Xenophobia, on the other hand, refers to the irrational fear or hatred of strangers and other foreigners. Minorities, especially racial minorities, are often viewed as strangers in their own land.

Prodded into action by racial unrest, social activism, anti-segregation rulings (such as *Brown v. Board of Education*), Kennedy's Camelot, and the Johnson administration's desire to create a discrimination-free "Great Society," Congress reassessed its stand on the need for civil rights legislation to protect blacks and other minorities. One of the most important antidiscrimination bills in American history was enacted into law in 1964. The **Civil Rights Act of 1964** prohibited discrimination based on national origin, ethnic group, sex, creed, age or race. According to Title VII of the Act (Public Law 92-261, Section 703):

> It shall be an unlawful employment practice for an employer (1) to fail or refuse to hire, or discharge any individual or otherwise to discriminate against any individual with respect to his compensation, terms, conditions, or privileges of employment, because of such individual's race, color, religion, sex, or national origin: (2) to limit, segregate, or classify his employees or applicants for employment in any way which would deprive or tend to deprive any individual of employment opportunity or otherwise adversely affect his status as an employee because of such individual's race, color, religion, sex, or national origin.

Title VII prohibited employers and unions from discriminating against their employees in the following areas:

1. Hiring Employees
2. Compensating Employees
3. Terms of Employment
4. Conditions of Employment
5. Privileges of Employment
6. Classifying Personnel
7. Assigning Personnel
8. Promoting Personnel
9. Disciplining Personnel
10. Demoting Employees
11. Providing Facilities
12. Assigning Facilities
13. Training Employees
14. Retraining Employees
15. Providing Apprenticeships

In an abrupt departure from past practice, Congress issued a clarion call for justice and equality in the workplace. The Civil Rights Act of 1964 was a major battle in the revolution of rising expectations (Hilgert and Haimann, 1991).

Under the authority of Title VII as amended in 1966, the Equal Employment Opportunity Commission (EEOC) was created as a regulatory agency. It was authorized to set standards and establish guidelines for compliance with the

requirements of the Civil Rights Act. The Commission issued a set of comprehensive Guidelines on Employee Selection Procedures in 1970.

In 1972, Congress extended the coverage of Title VII to include all state and local government operations with more than 15 employees. The amendment, known as the **Equal Employment Opportunity Act** of 1972, gave the Equal Employment Opportunity Commission more authority to formulate policies, procedures, rules and regulations designed to ensure compliance with the law. Many of the complaints filed with the Equal Employment Opportunity Commission and the cases that ended up in court arose from personnel practices involving the employment or supervision of police officers and fire fighters (Thibault, Lynch and McBride, 1990). These complaints and court cases ushered in a new era of affirmative action.

While the number of women and other minorities employed in state and local government increased, there was no really dramatic shift in the makeup of the public service. White males got most of the jobs and held on to them by virtue of their civil service status or seniority. In addition, nontraditional employees were not (for a variety of reasons) being promoted into the higher ranks as rapidly as had been originally anticipated. As a result, the EEOC adopted a proactive **affirmative action** strategy. Affirmative action required employers to take positive steps to overcome "present and past discrimination" in an effort to achieve equal employment opportunity. The affirmative action guidelines adopted by the Commission were designed to promote activism without creating the type of "reverse discrimination" prohibited by the Civil Rights Act. Section 703(j) provides that:

> Nothing contained in this title shall be interpreted to require any employer . . . subject to this title to grant preferential treatment to any individual or to any group because of the race, color, religion, sex, or national origin of such individuals or group on account of an imbalance which may exist, with respect to the total number or percentage of persons of any race, color, religion, sex or national origin employed by any employer . . . in comparison with the total number or percentage of persons of any race, color, religion, sex or national origin in any community, state, section, or other area, or in the available work force in any community, state, section or other area.

Affirmative action stressed the need for "goals," "timetables" and "actions" designed to deal with discrimination. The process involved four basic steps:

1. An analysis of all major job categories to ascertain if women and other minorities were being underutilized.

2. Development of goals, timetables and affirmative actions designed to correct identifiable deficiencies.

3. The maintenance of a comprehensive database for use in determining whether the goals were being accomplished.

4. Continuous assessment of utilization patterns to prevent the reintroduction of discriminatory practices.

Although goals, timetables and actions were (under appropriate circumstances) a proper means for implementing equal employment opportunity, the concept of "quotas" and "preferential treatment" based on race, color, national origin and sex were contrary to the law. In fact, the federal government issued the following policy statement:

> Under a system of goals, therefore, an employer is never required to hire a person who does not have the qualifications needed to perform the job successfully; and an employer is never required to hire such an unqualified person in preference to another applicant who is qualified; nor is an employer required to hire a less qualified person in preference to a better qualified person, provided that the qualifications used to make such relative judgment realistically measures the person's ability to do the job in question, or other jobs to which he is likely to progress. The terms "less qualified" and "better qualified" as used in this memorandum are not intended to distinguish among persons who are substantially equally qualified in terms of being able to perform the job successfully. Unlike quotas, therefore, which may call for a preference for the unqualified over the qualified, or for the less qualified over the better qualified to meet the numerical requirements, a goal recognizes that persons are to be judged on individual ability, and therefore is consistent with the principle of merit hiring (Equal Employment Opportunity Coordinating Council, 1973).

Some courts held that a statistical imbalance between minorities represented in the police department as compared to those residing in the community constituted prima facie evidence of discrimination. They imposed quotas (see Figure 13.1). In Alabama, for example, the court ordered the state Department of Public Safety to hire one black trooper for each white trooper hired until 25 percent of all troopers were black (*NAACP v. Allen*, 1972). The central thrust became to gauge equal employment opportunity not by the methods used but solely by the results achieved in the organization's work force (Stahl, 1983).

Most police departments used some type of written examination and a physical agility test to screen prospective personnel. The examinations often had a built-in cultural bias that discriminated against racial minorities. Physical agility tests, on the other hand, almost always discriminated against women. In order to ensure that **protected classes** (blacks, women and other nontraditional employees) were not tested out of equal employment opportunity, the Supreme Court ruled that screening devices like the ones discussed above had to be valid, reliable, job-related and based on **bona fide occupational qualifications** (BFOQ). These terms are best defined in the following manner:

1. **Validity.** Validity simply means that the test measures what it is supposed to measure.

2. **Reliability.** Reliability is the consistency with which any test yields accurate measurements.

3. **Job Relatedness.** Job relatedness means that the knowledge or skill being measured by the screening device is directly related to the actual job to be done.

4. **Bona Fide Occupational Qualification.** A bona fide occupational qualification is an attribute or skill that is actually required in order to do a particular job.

The *Griggs v. Duke Power Company* decision (1971) protected prospective police officers from arbitrary and discriminatory screening. It set a standard that is still in use today.

Police personnel administrators took the *Griggs* decision seriously and immediately began to modify their testing procedures. A great deal of time and energy was invested to make sure that examinations were job-related, valid, reliable and **nondiscriminatory**. A number of standardized entry-level and promotional tests were developed and are currently being marketed by groups like the International City Management Association (ICMA) and the International Association of Chiefs of Police (IACP).

Some police departments have moved away from using a comprehensive written test and now use the "assessment center" method to select personnel for entry-level positions or promotions. An assessment center is a multiple assessment strategy that involves using various techniques (job-related simulations, structured interviews, psychological evaluations, etc.) to screen candidates. "Behavioral samples" are obtained and submitted to a standardized evaluation based on multiple inputs by trained observers. Judgments are pooled by the observers at an evaluation meeting during which all relevant assessment data are reported and discussed. A final assessment is drafted and a recommendation is submitted to the hiring authority (Swanson, Territo and Taylor, 1993). Assessment centers have proven to be far less discriminatory than many other preemployment screening procedures.

While the assessment center approach is certainly superior to the standardized test, it is a fairly sophisticated process and requires a great deal of skill. It also costs more. Consequently, many medium-sized and small police departments are simply not able to make the switch.

Figure 13.1
Remediation through the Use of Quotas

U.S. Judge Gives Preliminary OK to Minority and Female Hiring Plan for the San Francisco Police Department

A federal judge gave preliminary approval January 26 to a landmark discrimination case settlement requiring that minorities receive 50% and women 20% of all the city police officer appointments for the next 10 years.

The out-of-court settlement was signed and submitted to chief U.S. Dist. Judge Robert F. Peckham, climaxing a six-year struggle over a controversial lawsuit charging the city police department with employment discrimination.

At present, the 1,670-member police force includes about 200 minority persons and 60 women. City officials expect to enroll more than 600 recruits in the next two years.

The agreement established hiring quotas described by attorneys as among the highest ever set in a police employment discrimination case. Among other things, it also requires that:

—The city expand its existing police force by 340 positions within two years, at a cost to the city estimated at $14 million.

—The city award about $400,000 in back pay to minorities and women who can prove they were victims of discrimination in the past. Also, the city must set aside $500,000 to recruit and train new officers.

—The city virtually abolish seniority credit for police promotions, in order to speed the advancement of minorities and women, and that ultimately police promotions reflect the racial and gender proportions of the officers seeking the promotions.

—The city pay up to $385,000 in attorneys' fees to Public Advocates, the San Francisco law firm that represented a coalition of minorities and women who brought the discrimination suit against the city six years ago.

The hiring quotas established in the settlement were officially called "goals," but attorneys expressed full confidence that should the city, as a party to the settlement, not reach those goals, the court action would quickly result.

"These goals are very court-enforceable," said Lois Salisbury, an attorney for Public Advocates. "And this city, which is about 50% minority now, should have no difficulty finding qualified applicants."

In the settlement, the city does not directly concede discrimination against minorities and women. But it does promise to refrain from discrimination in the future. The quota system the settlement imposes would exist at least until 45% of the force is made up of racial minorities. No such goal is set for women. Women minorities would count as credit towards both the 50% minority and 20% female quotas set for future hiring.

The settlement was signed in the form of a proposed consent decree by Attorneys for Officers for Justice, a group of black police officers, and the rest of the coalition of minority and women's groups that brought suit—along with lawyers for the city of San Francisco, the San Francisco Police Officers Assn. (a white officers' organization), and the U.S. Department of Justice.

The agreement had been approved earlier this week by a 7 to 3 vote of the San Francisco Boards of Supervisors.

The pact was approved with apparent reluctance by the supervisors, one of whom, Quentin Kopp, warned, "We're going to have a federal judge directing a substantial part of the operations of the police department."

Judge Peckham, receiving the proposed consent decree Thursday, noted that it formed a "substantial basis" for settlement of the long-standing suit. It was expected that the judge would give final approval soon.

The agreement was reached after six years of legal and political maneuvering, both in and out of court.

The organizations that brought the suit charged city officials manipulated police policies and physical and mental exams to effectively prevent racial minorities and women from being hired and promoted.

San Francisco homicide inspector Earl Sanders, a black officer, was the only witness ever called to testify in court proceedings.

He told the court that in 1964, when he took the police academy physical exam, city physicians found a "heart murmur" and "high blood pressure"—although his own doctor had said he was in excellent health.

Sanders said he heard a city physician say, "We already have 10 of them"—an apparent reference to 10 other black applicants.

Source: "Equal Opportunity Forum," *Affirmative Action Monthly,* February 1979, p. 22.

Case Study

Sergeant Jerry "Rex" Bell

Sergeant Rex Bell is the only command officer (besides the chief) in a small police department with an authorized strength of 15 full-time officers. He has 18 years of service and will, more than likely, become the next police chief executive. Sergeant Bell is respected by those in the political establishment, by his peers and by community leaders. He has earned a reputation for intelligence, decisiveness, integrity and professionalism. Sergeant Bell is a natural leader and a truly gifted spokesperson for his department.

The chief of police has entered into a consent decree with the local branch of the NAACP calling for an aggressive affirmative action campaign designed to establish an applicant pool that is representative of the minorities within the community. Blacks presently constitute 11 percent of the population. There are, however, no black police officers. The mayor has insisted that no black applicants applied in spite of the city's ongoing efforts to recruit and hire qualified minorities. Sergeant Bell is convinced that de facto discrimination has been a negative factor in recruitment and has communicated his feelings to the chief of police.

Sergeant Bell has been asked by the chief of police to assume responsibility for the recruitment, screening and selection of two new police officers. While there is no quota, there is an expectation that at least one of the positions will be filled by a qualified black. In order to ensure that qualified black applicants are not "tested out" unfairly during the screening process, Sergeant Bell is reviewing all requirements to make sure they are bona fide occupational qualifications (BFOQ). In addition, he is reviewing the written examination and the physical agility test to make certain they are fair to all candidates regardless of race, religion, sex or national origin.

If you were in Sergeant Bell's shoes, what specific criteria would you use to judge the fairness of the screening devices? If they are found to be discriminatory, what should be done with them? If none of the black applicants qualify for appointment to the police department, should the standards be lowered?

There is no doubt that Equal Employment Opportunity and Affirmative Action (EEO/AA) were designed to deal with and remediate a very serious social problem. The ideal (of social justice) was corrupted, however, when affirmative action goals became quotas and the noble end began to justify unscrupulous means in the hands of relatively unsophisticated police administrators. While EEO/AA opened the door for more blacks, women and other nontraditional employees, they also created deep wounds that have yet to heal. Many white police officers believe (rightly or wrongly) that they were victimized by reverse discrimination. They harbor a great deal of resentment and wear a

facade to mask their true feelings. White police officers cheered when the Supreme court ruled in the *Bakke* case (1978) that it was wrong for employers to use quotas designed to accommodate blacks and women in such a manner as to withhold gainful employment from eligible white males. The Reagan administration's de-emphasis of EEO/AA has reduced anxiety somewhat, and there is an uneasy truce between white male police officers and new nontraditional police officers.

The issue of reverse discrimination reemerged during the 1994 Republican landslide that captured both the U.S. House of Representatives and the U.S. Senate, with substantive changes in EEO/AA being considered by the 104th Congress.

Police sergeants find themselves in a very difficult spot. They, regardless of their ethnicity, race or sex, must work with and help to bridge the gap between the white male majority and various minority groups within the police department. It is a job that has been added to and yet transcends their other duties. If they perform this human relations function well, there will be a cooperative effort to accomplish the department's mission, goals and objectives. Failure, on the other hand, could serve to reignite the virulent racism and sexism of the past.

The Changing Face of America

It is estimated that there are 248.7 million people in the United States. Just over half of them are females. While the overwhelming majority of all Americans are Caucasian, 12.3 percent are African American and another 7 percent are Hispanic. Growing three times faster than the U.S. total, Hispanics may account for one-quarter of the nation's growth over the next 20 years. The Census Bureau's projections show that their 9 percent share of the population could grow to 19 percent by 2080. Even without immigration (legal or illegal) for the next 100 years, the Hispanic population will increase at twice the national rate. Asian and Native Americans round out the picture and contribute to the ethnic diversity of modern American society (*The World Almanac*, 1994).

It is clear that minorities and women remain underrepresented in virtually all specialties and at all ranks in law enforcement in spite of the aggressive EEO/AA programs of the past (see Figures 13.2, 13.3 and 13.4). In 1975, only 6.5 percent of all police officers were black, even though blacks represented 11 percent of the total population. While females constituted just over half of the population, somewhere between 2 and 4 percent of the sworn officers were women (Walker, 1992). The situation did not change much over the next decade. In a 1983 study of 1,173 cities with an average minority population of 7.6 percent, researchers found that a majority of the police departments had fewer than 3 percent minorities (Leonard and More, 1987). Statistics for 1992 show that, while the number of female police officers has more than tripled, only 9.1 percent of all sworn police officers are women (*Crime in the United States*, 1993). Black males now constitute approximately 13 percent of all sworn police personnel.

Figure 13.2

Full-Time Police Employees by Sex and Size of Place, On Oct. 31, 1992

(1992 estimated population)	Total police employees			Police officers (sworn)			Civilian employees		
Population group	Total	Percent male	Percent female	Total	Percent male	Percent female	Total	Percent male	Percent female
Total agencies: 13, 032 agencies:									
population 241,519,000	748,830	76.0%	24.0%	544,309	90.9%	9.1%	204,521	36.5%	63.5%
Total cities: 9,943 cities									
population 161,851,000	453,346	77.5	22.5	352,963	91.2	8.8	100,383	29.3	70.7
Group I									
63 cities, 250,000 and over:									
population 45,955,000	163,697	73.9	26.1	126,975	86.5	13.5	36,722	30.2	69.8
8 cities, 1,000,000 and over:									
population 20,365,000	86,620	73.1	26.9	67,351	85.3	14.7	19,269	30.3	69.7
17 cities, 500,000 to 999,999:									
population 11,694,000	38,185	75.7	24.3	29,890	87.9	12.1	8,295	31.7	68.3
38 cities, 250,000 to 499,999:									
population 13,897,000	38,892	74.0	26.0	29,734	87.5	12.0	9,158	28.8	71.2
Group II									
128 cities, 100,000 to 249,999:									
population 19,193,000	46,319	76.0	24.0	35,720	91.3	8.7	11,049	26.9	73.1
Group III									
335 cities, 50,000 to 99,999:									
population 23,180,000	51,586	77.7	22.3	39,680	93.5	6.5	11,906	25.2	74.8
Group IV									
680 cities, 25,000 to 49,999:									
population 23,596,000	52,093	79.6	20.4	40,937	94.4	5.6	11,156	25.2	74.8
Group V									
1,655 cities, 10,000 to 24,999:									
population 26,033,000	58,783	81.3	18.7	47,073	95.1	4.9	11,710	26.0	74.0
Group VI									
7,082 cities under 10,000:									
population 23,895,000	80,868	81.2	18.8	63,028	93.9	6.1	17,840	36.1	63.9
Suburban counties									
842 agencies:									
population 51,000,000	184,938	72.7	27.3	118,553	88.5	11.5	66,385	44.5	55.5
Rural counties									
2,247 agencies:									
population 28,667,000	110,546	75.5	24.5	72,793	93.2	6.8	37,753	41.5	58.5
Suburban areas[a]									
6,251 agencies:									
population 101,708,000	315,967	76.1	23.9	221,651	91.2	8.8	94,316	40.5	59.5

[a]Includes suburban city and county law enforcement agencies within metropolitan areas. Excludes central cities. Suburban cities and counties are also included in other groups.

Source: U.S. Department of Justice, Federal Bureau of Investigation, *Crime in the United States, 1992* (Washington, DC: USGPO, 1993), p. 294, Table 74.

Figure 13.3

Number of Police Officers and Number of Black Police Officers in the 50 Largest Cities, 1983 and 1992

City	Total number of officers		Black officers				Index of black representation		
			1983		1992				Percent
	1983	1992	Number	Percent	Number	Percent	1983	1992	Change
New York, NY	23,408	27,154	2,395	10.2%	3,121	11.4%	0.40	0.40	0.0%
Los Angeles, CA	6,928	8,020	657	9.4	1,127	14.1	0.55	1.00	81.8
Chicago, IL	12,472	12,291	2,508	20.1	3,063	24.9	0.51	0.64	25.4
Houston, TX	3,629	4,056	355	9.7	595	14.7	0.35	0.52	48.5
Philadelphia, PA	7,265	6,280	1,201	16.5	1,615	25.7	0.44	0.64	45.4
San Diego, CA	1,363	1,937	76	5.5	146	7.5	0.62	0.80	29.0
Detroit, MI	4,032	4,787	1,238	30.7	2,556	53.3	0.49	0.70	42.8
Dallas, TX	2,053	2,878	169	8.2	546	19.0	0.28	0.64	128.5
Phoenix, AZ	1,660	1,644	48	2.8	66	4.0	0.58	0.77	32.7
San Antonio, TX[a]	1,164	1,606	54	4.6	90	5.6	NA	0.80	NA
San Jose, CA	915	1,223	20	2.1	50	4.1	0.46	0.85	84.7
Baltimore, MD	3,056	2,822	537	17.5	851	30.2	0.32	0.51	59.3
Indianapolis, IN	936	979	123	13.1	174	17.8	0.60	0.78	30.0
San Francisco, CA	1,957	1,818	159	8.1	170	9.4	0.64	0.85	32.8
Jacksonville, FL[a]	1,263	1,205	78	6.1	232	19.2	0.24	0.76	216.6
Columbus, OH	1,197	1,444	133	11.1	256	17.7	0.50	0.78	56.0
Milwaukee, WI	1,438	1,971	168	11.6	283	14.4	0.50	0.47	-6.0
Memphis, TN	1,216	1,403	268	22.0	481	34.3	0.46	0.62	34.7
Washington, DC	3,851	4,396	1,931	50.1	2,980	67.8	0.71	1.03	45.0
Boston, MA	1,871	1,972	248	13.2	404	20.5	0.59	0.80	35.5
Seattle, WA	1,011	1,231	42	4.1	105	8.5	0.43	0.84	95.3
El Paso, TX	650	787	13	2.0	17	2.2	0.63	0.62	-1.5
Cleveland, OH	2,091	1,668	238	11.3	439	26.3	0.26	0.56	115.3
New Orleans, LA	1,317	1,551	276	20.9	608	39.2	0.38	0.63	65.7
Nashville, TN	969	1,058	114	11.7	139	13.1	0.50	0.54	8.0
Denver, CO	1,379	1,348	82	5.9	130	9.2	0.49	0.72	46.9
Austin, TX	607	830	43	7.0	81	9.8	0.57	0.78	36.8
Forth Worth, TX	766	967	43	5.6	112	11.6	0.25	0.52	108.0
Oklahoma City, OK	662	932	27	4.0	69	7.4	0.27	0.47	74.0
Portland, OR	688	877	19	2.7	32	3.6	0.36	0.46	27.7
Kansas City, MO	1,140	1,166	123	10.7	156	13.4	0.39	0.45	15.3
Long Beach, CA	637	696	20	3.1	39	5.6	0.27	0.41	51.8
Tucson, AZ	549	771	17	3.0	25	3.2	0.81	0.74	-8.6
St. Louis, MO	1,763	1,552	346	19.6	437	28.2	0.43	0.59	37.2
Charlotte, NC	644	872	144	22.3	167	19.2	0.72	0.60	-16.6
Atlanta, GA	1,313	1,223	602	45.8	668	54.6	0.69	0.81	17.3
Virginia Beach, VA	NA	599	NA	NA	50	8.3	NA	0.60	NA
Albuquerque, NM	561	765	14	2.4	16	2.0	0.96	0.67	-30.2
Oakland, CA	636	549	147	23.1	144	26.2	0.49	0.60	22.4
Pittsburgh, PA	1,222	1,128	175	14.3	289	25.6	0.60	0.99	65.0
Sacramento, CA	NA	607	NA	NA	38	6.3	NA	0.41	NA
Minneapolis, MN	672	840	20	2.9	46	5.5	0.38	0.42	10.5
Tulsa, OK	695	718	30	4.3	68	9.5	0.36	0.69	91.6
Honolulu, HI	1,557	1,870	11	0.7	28	1.4	0.58	1.07	84.4
Cincinnati, OH	971	927	89	9.1	176	19.0	0.27	0.50	85.1
Miami, FL	1,051	1,032	181	17.2	231	22.4	0.69	0.81	17.3
Fresno, CA	NA	412	NA	NA	33	8.0	NA	0.96	NA
Omaha, NE	551	610	46	8.3	70	11.5	0.69	0.87	26.0
Toledo, OH	757	639	139	18.3	119	18.8	1.05	0.94	-10.4
Buffalo, NY	1,018	963	86	8.4	195	20.2	0.37	0.66	78.3

Note: Data for 1983 were obtained through a questionnaire mailed to the office of the chief of police and the office of the municipal director of personnel (or equivalent position) in the 50 largest cities in the United States. Forty-seven cities returned completed questionnaires in 1983; all 50 cities returned completed questionnaires in 1992. Cities are listed in rank order of size based on the 1990 census of the population.

The index of black representation is calculated by dividing the percent of black police officers in a department by the percent of blacks in the local population. An index approaching 1.0 indicates that a city is closer to achieving a representation of black police officers equal to their proportion in the local population. The black population of a city is derived from the 1990 census of the population.

[a]Data for 1983 are based on 1980-81 information from the Police Executive Research Forum. *Survey of Police Operational and Administrative Practices 1981* (Washington, DC: Police Executive Research Forum, 1981).

Source: Samuel Walker, "Employment of Black and Hispanic Police Officers." *Review of Applied Urban Research* XI (October 1993), p. 3; and Samuel Walker and K.B. Turner, "A Decade of Modest Progress: Employment of Black and Hispanic Police Officers, 1983-1992." Department of Criminal Justice, University of Nebraska at Omaha, 1992. (Mimeographed.) Table adapted by SOURCEBOOK Staff.

Figure 13.4

Number of Police Officers and Number of Hispanic Police Officers in the 50 Largest Cities, 1983 and 1992

City	Total number of officers		Hispanic officers				Index of Hispanic representation		
			1983		1992				Percent
	1983	1992	Number	Percent	Number	Percent	1983	1992	Change
New York, NY	23,408	27,154	1,704	7.2%	3,688	13.6%	0.36	55.30	52.7%
Los Angeles, CA	6,928	8,020	943	13.6	1,787	22.3	0.49	0.56	14.2
Chicago, IL	12,472	12,291	432	3.4	925	7.5	0.24	0.38	58.3
Houston, TX	3,629	4,056	314	8.6	506	12.5	0.49	0.44	−10.2
Philadelphia, PA	7,265	6,280	46	0.6	202	3.2	0.16	0.57	256.2
San Diego, CA	1,363	1,937	107	7.8	226	11.6	0.52	0.56	7.6
Detroit, MI	4,032	4,787	32	0.7	62	1.2	0.29	0.43	48.2
Dallas, TX	2,053	2,878	96	4.6	234	8.1	0.37	0.39	5.4
Phoenix, AZ	1,660	1,644	156	9.3	211	12.8	0.63	0.64	1.5
San Antonio, TX[a]	1,164	1,606	384	32.9	583	36.3	NA	0.65	NA
San Jose, CA	915	1,223	159	17.3	240	19.6	0.78	0.74	−5.1
Baltimore, MD	3,056	2,822	10	0.3	14	0.5	0.30	0.40	33.3
Indianapolis, IN	936	979	1	0.1	0	X	0.11	0.00	−100.0
San Francisco, CA	1,957	1,818	159	8.1	189	10.4	0.66	0.74	12.1
Jacksonville, FL[a]	1,263	1,205	9	0.7	0	X	0.38	0.00	−100.0
Columbus, OH	1,197	1,444	0	X	1	0.1	0.00	0.05	0.0
Milwaukee, WI	1,438	1,971	66	4.5	109	5.5	1.09	0.87	−20.1
Memphis, TN	1,216	1,403	0	X	0	X	0.00	0.00	0.0
Washington, DC	3,851	4,396	40	1.0	132	3.0	0.36	0.56	55.5
Boston, MA	1,871	1,972	40	2.1	84	4.2	0.33	0.39	18.1
Seattle, WA	1,011	1,231	18	1.7	32	2.6	0.65	0.69	6.1
El Paso, TX	650	787	370	56.9	481	61.1	0.91	0.89	−2.1
Cleveland, OH	2,091	1,668	6	0.2	66	3.9	0.06	0.85	1,316.6
New Orleans, LA	1,317	1,551	26	1.9	25	1.6	0.56	0.46	−17.8
Nashville, TN	969	1,058	3	0.3	6	0.6	0.38	0.56	47.3
Denver, CO	1,379	1,348	180	13.0	122	9.1	0.69	0.40	−42.0
Austin, TX	607	830	73	12.0	123	14.8	0.64	0.64	0.0
Forth Worth, TX	766	967	51	6.6	85	8.8	0.52	0.45	−13.4
Oklahoma City, OK	662	932	5	0.7	16	1.7	0.25	0.34	38.0
Portland, OR	688	877	9	1.3	20	2.3	0.68	0.69	1.4
Kansas City, MO	1,140	1,166	18	1.5	32	2.7	0.45	0.69	53.3
Long Beach, CA	637	696	35	5.4	88	12.6	0.39	0.53	35.8
Tucson, AZ	549	771	95	17.3	151	19.6	0.69	0.67	−2.8
St. Louis, MO	1,763	1,552	0	X	7	0.5	0.00	0.31	100.0
Charlotte, NC	644	872	0	X	0	X	0.00	0.00	0.0
Atlanta, GA	1,313	1,223	9	0.6	0	X	0.43	0.00	−100.0
Virginia Beach, VA	NA	599	NA	NA	6	1.0	NA	0.32	NA
Albuquerque, NM	561	765	184	32.7	262	34.2	0.97	0.99	2.0
Oakland, CA	636	549	59	9.2	61	11.1	0.96	0.80	−16.6
Pittsburgh, PA	1,222	1,128	4	0.3	0	X	0.38	0.00	−100.0
Sacramento, CA	NA	607	NA	NA	70	11.5	NA	0.71	NA
Minneapolis, MN	672	840	8	1.1	24	2.9	0.85	1.38	62.3
Tulsa, OK	695	718	4	0.5	2	0.3	0.29	0.08	−72.4
Honolulu, HI	1,557	1,870	4	0.2	30	1.6	0.04	0.35	775.0
Cincinnati, OH	971	927	1	0.1	1	0.1	0.13	0.14	7.6
Miami, FL	1,051	1,032	413	39.2	487	47.2	0.70	0.75	7.1
Fresno, CA	NA	412	NA	NA	82	19.9	NA	0.67	NA
Omaha, NE	551	610	12	2.1	18	3.0	0.91	0.94	3.2
Toledo, OH	757	639	28	3.6	33	5.2	1.20	1.28	6.6
Buffalo, NY	1,018	963	21	2.0	64	6.6	0.74	1.35	82.4

Note: The index of Hispanic representation is calculated by dividing the percent of Hispanic police officers in a department by the percent of Hispanics in the local population. An index approaching 1.0 indicates that a city is closer to achieving a representation of Hispanic police officers equal to their proportion in the local population. The Hispanic population of a city is derived from the 1990 census of the population.

[a]Data for 1983 are based on 1980-81 information from the Police Executive Research Forum. *Survey of Police Operational and Administrative Practices 1981* (Washington, DC: Police Executive Research Forum, 1981).

Source: Samuel Walker, "Employment of Black and Hispanic Police Officers." *Review of Applied Urban Research* XI (October 1993), p. 3; and Samuel Walker and K.B. Turner, "A Decade of Modest Progress: Employment of Black and Hispanic Police Officers, 1983-1992." Department of Criminal Justice, University of Nebraska at Omaha, 1992. (Mimeographed.) Table adapted by SOURCEBOOK Staff.

Every precaution must be taken to protect the gains that blacks, women and other nontraditional employees have made in the past and to ensure equal employment opportunity for everyone in the future. Police managers, with the assistance of supervisory personnel, should work diligently to comply with the National Advisory Commission on Criminal Justice Standards and Goals' Standard 13.3. According to this particular standard:

> Every police agency immediately should insure that it presents no artificial or arbitrary barriers, cultural or institutional, to discourage qualified individuals from seeking employment or from being employed as police officers.

1. Every police agency should engage in positive efforts to employ ethnic minority group members. When a substantial ethnic minority population resides within the jurisdiction, the police agency should take affirmative action to achieve a ratio of minority group employees in approximate proportion to the makeup of the population.

2. Every police agency seeking to employ members of an ethnic minority group should direct recruitment efforts toward attracting large numbers of minority applicants. In establishing selection standards for recruitment, special abilities such as the ability to speak a foreign language, strength and agility, or any other compensating factor should be taken into consideration in addition to height and weight requirements.

3. Every police agency seeking to employ qualified ethnic minority members should research, develop and implement specialized minority recruitment methods. These methods should include:

    a. Assignment of minority police officers to the specialized recruitment effort.

    b. Liaison with local minority community leaders to emphasize police sincerity and encourage referral of minority applicants to the police agency.

    c. Recruitment advertising and other material that depict minority group police personnel performing the police function.

    d. Active cooperation of the minority media as well as the general media in minority recruitment efforts.

    e. Emphasis on the community service aspect of police work.

    f. Regular personal contact with the minority applicant from initial application to final determination of employability.

4. Every police chief executive should ensure that hiring, assignment and promotion policies and practices do not discriminate against minority group members.

5.   Every police agency should evaluate continually the effectiveness of specialized minority recruitment methods so that successful methods are emphasized and unsuccessful ones are discarded.

The employment of blacks, women and other nontraditional employees (like Hispanics, Native Americans, older workers, college graduates, etc.) should be a recruitment goal, not a quota governing the hiring of police personnel. The composition of the community should serve as a guide for recruitment policy, not discriminatory affirmative action. According to Leonard and More (1993), primary consideration should be given to employing the best qualified candidates available, regardless of ethnicity or sex (see Figure 13.5).

Figure 13.5
Employment of Women

Every police agency should immediately ensure that there exists no agency policy that discourages qualified women from seeking employment as sworn or civilian personnel or prevents them from realizing their full employment potential.

Every police agency should:

1.   Institute selection procedures to facilitate the employment of women; no agency, however, should alter selection standards solely to employ female personnel.

2.   Insure that recruitment, selection, training and salary policies neither favor nor discriminate against women.

3.   Provide career paths for women allowing each individual to attain a position classification commensurate with her particular degree of experience, skill and ability.

4.   Immediately abolish all separate organizational entities composed solely of police women except those which are identified by function or objective, such as female jail facility within a multi-unit police organization.

Source: National Advisory Commission on Criminal Justice Standards and Goals, 1973.

While members of minority groups and women have been and continue to be underrepresented in virtually all aspects of modern police work, we should not lose sight of the fact that a great deal of progress has already been made. More emphasis has been placed on creating an egalitarian process for choosing police personnel since Standard 13.3 was first issued by the National Advisory Commission on Criminal Justice Standards and Goals in 1973. Police personnel administrators have intensified their efforts to recruit, train and retrain qualified human resources from all segments of the community (Swank and Conser, 1983). As a result, the number of nontraditional employees in the work force has increased appreciably.

Figure 13.6

Accessing Police Work through Equal Opportunity

Despite cutbacks, a new police class

By Richard V. Sabatini
Inquirer Staff Writer

The first class to enter the Philadelphia Police Academy since the department's workforce was cut because of budget problems was sworn in yesterday.

Police Commissioner Willie L. Williams administered the oath of office to the 119 recruits at a 9 a.m. ceremony at the academy in Torresdale. The recruits immediately began their training classes.

After the ceremony, Williams said he hoped that this class would be "the first of two or three" classes in session by next spring.

He said a decision on the additional classes would be "made in the next few weeks after meetings with Mayor Goode and Managing Director James White to discuss funding and staffing levels."

The current force of 5,030 officers faces even further cuts through attrition, before graduation of this class, Williams said. But he said members of the new class "would help allay the losses we have already had."

Police officials would not release the number of applicants reviewed before the appointment of the current class, but one source said it was more than 500. Applicants for police officer are rejected for many reasons, among them physical problems and failure to pass background checks.

The new recruits, 81 men and 38 women, are to graduate April 3. Sixty-two are white, 48 are black and nine are Hispanic.

Police officials said that about 85 percent of the recruits were expected to graduate in April, based on the averages of past classes. The others are expected to either fail or drop out.

The class is also the first to be trained under the recently revised state Municipal Police Officer's Training Act, which sets a curriculum and requires that graduates meet certain physical standards, among them running $1\frac{1}{2}$ miles and demonstrating a certain level of agility. The most recent graduation was in June.

Funding for half of the recruit's $24,231 salary while in training and the total cost of training staff is paid by the state, according to Capt. Joseph Stine, head of recruit training.

Williams told recruits that they would be faced with challenges "that will test your personal integrity and personal values, for we live in a society in which everything is not perfect."

"And you have to recognize that," Williams said. "When those challenges come to you personally, you're going to be faced with a decision—a decision to walk tall with your head held high and upholding the principles of the Philadelphia Police Department or to turn your back on the oath you have just taken."

Williams warned that if they strayed "all of the weight and force of the Philadelphia Police Department will come down upon you."

He also told the recruits that they would be among the future supervisors of the department and that perhaps even one of them might someday be commissioner.

"Twenty-four years and nine months ago I sat where you are sitting today," he said. "Never in my wildest imagination did I think I would ever be standing here today as police commissioner. But anything is possible."

Source: *The Philadelphia Inquirer,* p. 4-B, Nov. 15, 1988.

Progressive police administrators are committed to ensuring equal employment opportunity. They favor an aggressive, proactive approach to recruitment. Their recruiters use a variety of innovative techniques to target specific ethnic and racial groups in a genuine effort to increase the number of nontraditional applicants and enrich the pool of qualified candidates.

Recruitment is a multidimensional process designed to encourage people to seek careers in police work and to select those individuals who are qualified to do the job. Researchers note that successful recruitment programs exhibit similar characteristics (Swanson, Territo and Taylor, 1988):

1. An internal commitment to equal employment opportunity.

2. A strong, well-managed minority recruitment component.

3. Utilization of minority police officers in recruitment.

4. Targeted recruitment of especially promising applicants.

5. Screening based on valid, reliable and fair procedures.

6. Appointment contingent on qualifications, not politics.

7. Promotion based on interest and on-the-job performance.

Police recruit classes (see Figure 13.6) are far different from those of the past. Based on pressure from minorities, changes in the law and our national commitment to social equality, the composition of the work force is slowly but surely being transformed into a mirror image of the community at large.

Supervising Minorities

With the increased emphasis on recruiting, hiring and nurturing nontraditional employees, first-line supervisors are more likely than ever to have supervisory responsibility for blacks, Hispanics and women. These employees, like all other employees, expect to be given a chance to succeed. They want to carry their own weight and to be appreciated for their potential contribution to the police department. Women and other minorities don't want to be patronized. They want and need to be respected as human beings. Due to the debilitating effects of past discrimination, they may need extra care, training and coaching to help them acclimate to their new environment. This is where the knowledge and human skills of the first-line supervisors come into play.

The supervisor is, according to Lawrence A. Johnson (1969), a "major key" to the minority worker's success or failure. A supervisor who wishes to change the status quo and improve human relations within the workplace must be prepared not only to avoid discrimination, but to actively help everyone overcome it. The bottom line is very clear. It is the supervisor's primary responsibility to

create and maintain an environment in which all employees are able to satisfy some of their needs while working cooperatively with others to accomplish the mission, goals and objectives of the department.

White male sergeants must begin to understand that many of their nontraditional employees have been conditioned to expect the worst. Blacks, Hispanics and women assume that they will face varying degrees of and be forced to deal with:

Prejudice	Hostility
Discrimination	Isolation
Resentment	Scapegoating
Rejection	

They may use selective perception to confirm these suspicions. Women and other minorities are often very sensitive to incidents, actions or events that nonminority workers brush aside. They are considered insults or personal attacks. In a longitudinal study of black police officers in the Metropolitan Police Department (Washington, D.C.), more than 65 percent reported that they trusted few or no white officers. This data was drawn from 947 (90 percent) of the black police officers in the District. Nearly 84 percent of the respondents were patrol officers and 80 percent believed that blacks were discriminated against in hiring, job assignments, enforcement of rules and regulations and job performance ratings (Thibault, Lynch and McBride, 1990). Until all subordinates feel that they are being treated as valued persons, there will always be a measure of discontent.

While it may be convenient to rationalize and reject these concerns as symptoms of unfounded paranoia, racial tension is a fact of life in the United States. John Leo, in a recent report on the neo-Nazi "skinhead" phenomenon, made the following sobering observation:

> The rampage of young toughs is the latest manifestation of racial violence that has resurfaced during the Reagan years. . . . The National Council of Churches warned that such violence has reached epidemic proportions in the U.S. . . . Bigoted violence has become the critical criminal-justice issue of the late 1980s (Leo, 1988).

Unfortunately there will always be a few police officers who will, regardless of their ethnic background or sex, try to take advantage of their supervisors. Some will be looking for special privileges. They may use their sex or minority status as a lever to gain favored treatment. This ploy, while it is understandable, must be prevented. The supervisor's success in working with other employees will be undercut if favoritism and privilege are allowed to flourish. Impartiality and fairness are absolutely essential in effective supervision.

Effective supervision always begins with an awareness of the individual and cultural differences among employees. These differences impact on performance and must be accepted as facts (Longenecker and Pringle, 1984). Knowing their subordinates and basing decisions on that knowledge helps supervisors avoid unreasonable expectations and provides a valid basis for under-

standing job-related behavior. Converting facts into performance-related information allows the supervisor to match the talents of the employee with the job to be done. If this approach is to be successful, supervisors must:

1. Be knowledgeable, approachable and empathetic when dealing with subordinates.

2. Learn to listen to and really understand the minority employee's point of view.

3. Communicate openly and honestly with their subordinates in all matters pertaining to the job.

4. Expect a considerable amount of testing and probing by minorities concerning the department's philosophy on human relations and the supervisor's attitude, sincerity and commitment related to equal employment opportunity.

5. Practice introspection and be aware of their own possible reactions to probable situations involving on-the-job relationships with minority employees (Plunkett, 1992).

The effectiveness of supervision can almost always be measured by the empathetic quality of the relationship between a good supervisor and receptive subordinates. Empathy (the capacity to participate in and appreciate another person's feelings or ideas) provides the foundation for positive human relations.

Sergeants may be required to make a special effort to motivate nontraditional employees. Consequently, they should analyze the situation and develop an action plan to:

1. **Make the Work Interesting.** Sergeants should examine each job in terms of how it could be "enriched" and made more challenging. There is a limit to the extent that employees will be satisfied performing repetitive or routine tasks.

2. **Relate Rewards to Performance.** While they may be limited by civil service regulations or collective bargaining agreements, sergeants should (whenever practical) try to relate rewards (special projects, recommendations for promotion, pay increases, etc.) to performance. The cost of failing to relate rewards to performance is high. Low performers will not be motivated to do a better job and top performers may be motivated to do less.

3. **Provide Valued Rewards.** Supervisors should do their best to determine the type of rewards that are valued most by employees. The most important thing is for supervisors to know what rewards they have at their disposal and exactly what the employees find most valuable.

4. **Treat Employees as Individuals.** As noted earlier in this chapter, different people have very different needs and want different things from their job. Individualized attention enhances self-esteem and makes the police officer feel like a valuable member of the organization. It also tends to produce more frequent and candid interaction between supervisors and minority employees.

5. **Encourage Participation and Cooperation.** It is natural for people to commit themselves to decisions that they help to make. Unfortunately, many supervisors do little to encourage active participation. They have not learned the value of sharing power with, rather than exercising power over, their employees.

6. **Explain Why the Action is Being Taken.** Police officers are usually more supportive and tend to perform better if they know why they have been asked to do something. Blind obedience to authority is passe in complex criminal justice organizations.

7. **Provide Accurate and Timely Feedback** A lack of feedback generally frustrates employees and has a negative impact on performance. Providing meaningful feedback is a normal part of supervision. People don't like to be left in the dark as far as their on-the-job performance is concerned. They want to know where they stand and resent being taken for granted. In fact, a negative performance evaluation may be better than no evaluation at all (Martin, 1987).

Nontraditional employees need **competent and supportive supervisors** who exercise good judgment and make reasonable decisions concerning them. In order to do the job right, police sergeants need a bag of tricks filled with technical, human, administrative and problem-solving skills.

Many of the municipal police departments that have actively recruited and hired nontraditional personnel did so because of federal EEO/AA initiatives, state Human Relations Commission regulations, court rulings, voluntary consent decrees (court supervised agreements hammered out and implemented in order to avoid future litigation) or a personal commitment to equal employment opportunity on the part of the chief police executive. Unfortunately, none of these decision-making processes do much to build mid-management or supervisory support for blacks, Hispanics, women or other minorities. According to Leonard Territo and Harold Vetter (1981), minority police officers are a very special breed. Not only are they subjected to the normal stressors of police work but to the additional stress of skepticism and rejection by their own kind. In addition, minority police officers are not likely to be fully accepted into the police culture (which is a source of support, camaraderie and occupational identity). A female officer is subject to additional and unique stressors. These include: (1) her own feeling of competence; (2) her perception of her peers' views of her competence,

Figure 13.7

How Good are Women Cops?

Kathy Burke has been a New York City cop for more than 15 years. For much of that time, the short, curly-haired detective worked undercover narcotics, buying drugs from pushers she would later arrest. She put more than 1000 dealers behind bars while risking exposure, rape and violent death. Now 41 and an investigator in the city's Major Case Squad, Burke obviously has paid her dues. Yet recently, while serving a subpoena, she encountered a clerk who could not believe she was a police officer.

"You mean that little girl's a detective?" said the clerk to Burke's partner.

"Yes, this little girl's a detective," Burke replied patiently. She is accustomed to such reaction. For female cops, it's part of the job.

It has been 12 years now since women began joining our police forces in significant numbers. The discriminatory hiring practices that deterred many women—and restricted those hired to largely clerical functions—were prohibited in 1972 by the Equal Opportunity Act. For the first time, women were allowed on patrol and to perform all the other duties previously reserved for men. As a result, the number of female officers is now 19,668, or almost 5 percent of total officers (up from 1.5 percent in 1972). New York, for example, has 2109 female officers; Chicago has 740; and Los Angeles has 506. Moreover, women continue to swell the ranks. By the end of the decade, they may constitute 20 percent of our police force.

Many of the initial objections to women cops—that they were too weak physically and couldn't handle the stress—have been widely dispelled. Countless studies have proved female officers equal in competence to their male colleagues. "Female police officers are essential," says Tom Sardino, the chief of police in Syracuse, N.Y., and president of the International Association of Chiefs of Police. "I have talked to hundreds of law enforcement executives throughout the world. I have not heard any of them register any kind of complaint regarding their ability." Clearly, women cops are up to the job.

But at what cost? Has it been hard for women, functioning in this hitherto all-male arena? What has been the impact on their personal lives, their families, their relationships in the community?

To find out how women officers are faring, I traveled around the country, talking to cops—both female and male—in big cities and small towns. I learned not only that the job has affected women but also that women, in turn, have had a decided impact on the job. Indeed, they are contributing to a whole new style of law enforcement emerging in America.

Why would a woman want to become a cop? Women become police officers for basically the same reasons as men: the excitement of the job, the opportunity for public service and the satisfaction of knowing that, out on the street, you're your own boss. Kathy Burke wanted to be a cop from the age of 13. "I had seen friends hurt from drugs," she recalls. "I wanted to rid the city of drugs."

Chris Lee and Marlene Willhoite, who are partners in San Francisco, left jobs in accounting and nursing to join the force. "I thought it would be a tremendous learning experience," says Chris, 32, "both the physical training and the use of firearms." Marlene, 32, explains that she was bored working in a hospital. "I thought police work would be more exciting, and I was right."

Another appeal, of course, is the money. Louise Vasquez, a 49-year-old Miami homicide detective, got married right out of high school and had four kids. When her youngest child was 5, she and her husband divorced, and she was left with no means of support. Attracted by the secure income police work offered, she took the test for officer—and was hired. Now a highly-decorated 18-year veteran, Vasquez has remarried, and her salary of more than $35,000 a year contributes to the raising of eight children.

Not that female cops don't earn their money. As demanding, dangerous and often thankless as police work is generally, for women the job has proven doubly taxing. First of all, they've had to deal with a public unaccustomed to the sight of a woman in uniform.

Mary Wamsley, 34, is a sergeant in Lakewood, Colo., a suburb of Denver. She started in 1974, the first year Lakewood allowed women on patrol. "The public was shocked," she recalls. "I remember getting a burglary-in-progress call one night and going up to the house, gun drawn. The man who called opened the door, saw me and slammed it. He called back to say, 'There's a girl outside with a gun who's part of the gang.' And this is even though I had my uniform on. They couldn't convince him I was a police officer. I had to wait in my car until a male officer showed up."

The surprise of the public was nothing compared with the initial reception female officers encountered from their male colleagues. "A lot of the men resented me," says Wamsley. "When I'd arrive as a backup, they'd act as if I wasn't there." Even worse than their cold shoulder was their protectiveness. "When I'd respond to something as minor as a barking dog or stolen bicycle, I'd get a backup," Wamsley recalls.

To prove her point, Vasquez confides that, during her entire career, she has rarely pulled her gun, and she has fired it only once. Her preferred method of dealing with murder suspects is talk.

continued

Figure 13.7, *continued*

"The toughest guy in the world can be talked to," she explains. "They're used to dealing with other tough guys, so if you come on nice, it works."

Whatever approach they use, female officers generally find that it's not hardened criminals who pose their biggest problem. Ironically, they have more difficulty with other women. "To this day, I find that women don't like to be arrested by other women," says Mary Wamsley. "They either call me a lesbian, a dyke or a whole string of profanities."

Understandably, the loudest critics of policewomen always have been policemen's wives. They fear that female officers will not adequately protect their husbands and, perhaps even worse, that the long hours together will lead to an affair. Bob Davis' wife hated it when he worked with women. She was particularly jealous of Adele, his partner. "It was my own fault," concedes Davis. "I talked about her all the time."

Lucille Burrascano thinks cops' wives have a perfect right to be jealous. "When you spend eight hours a day with a partner, delivering babies, protecting one another in shoot-outs, going from one high-tension job to another, you can't help but be close. Also, quite frankly, policing is a highly emotional job. You have moments of intense excitement. But to assume that two partners are going to have an affair is wrong. It depends on how good each of their marriages is. I'm single, and I rode for a while with a single man. He was great. But we never dated."

Kathy Burke had to sever a partnership because the man's wife felt threatened. But she herself has never experienced jealousy from her husband, maybe because she too is a cop. "He has always been supportive," she says.

Mary Wamsley has been married five years—her husband is a chief deputy district attorney—but when she was single, she found, as do many female cops, that her profession was a definite turnoff for most men. "I found in dating that a lot of men are intimidated by knowing that I carry a gun," says Wamsley. "Also, that if we were together and a fight broke out, I was more able to handle it than he was. My husband, however, doesn't give a rip."

But her husband *does* worry about her. "We have a code," says Wamsley. "I never go to work before he tells me to be careful. We've talked about the hazards of the job, and God knows he's seen me get injured (she has been stabbed and had her knee torn apart in the line of duty). But he knows I wouldn't be happy doing anything else."

Louise Vasquez says it's essential to separate family life from the job. Though encountering acts of violence almost daily, she does not allow herself to dwell on what she sees or relate any of it to her own family. Nevertheless, the mother of eight concedes that being a copy definitely influences the ways she acts at home. "I think I've become a much more demanding mother. As a cop, you come across so many parents who don't care about their kids. It's caused me to be more concerned and more aware of what my own kids were doing."

However, none of her children has ever accused her of *acting* like a cop. And she's obviously set a good example: Her daughter-in-law, Patricia, recently left her job in public relations to join the Miami Police Department, and her daughter Becky also is considering quitting the post office to join the force.

What will happen to Patricia and Becky as a result of putting on a uniform, strapping on a gun and joining all the other mothers and sisters on patrol? Without question, the job will change them as women. "I've become much more outspoken," says Marlene Willhoite. "Now, if I have something on my mind, I'll talk about it, whereas before I kept it to myself." And Mary Wamsley says: "I've become much more cynical than my friends who aren't cops. I've seen a side of human nature that I wish I didn't know. But it's done good things for me too. It's made me more self-confident. I was a starry-eyed debutante when I started. Now I'd like to think I'm a pretty good cop."

Mary Wamsley is not unique. Women like her all across the country are proving themselves as police officers. Of course, they still face hurdles. Kathy Burke still encounters "dinosaurs" who think she belongs at home and who condescendingly call her "honey," "sister" or "dear." Marlene Willhoite and Chris Lee have to endure wisecracks—"Hey, you're like Cagney and Lacey!"—at least once a night. Although Capt. Penny E. Harrington was just named police chief in Portland, Ore., so far only 6 percent of all women cops hold a rank higher than police officer. And Bob Davis predicts the real male resistance will develop when more women become supervisors, telling the men what to do. Lucille Burrascano goes so far as to say, "Women have two to three generations to go before they are truly accepted in a so-called 'man's job.'"

But women officers already have left their mark. They have shown that it is possible to be gentle and compassionate and still be a good cop. They have helped to humanize our police departments. They are a welcome addition to the ranks of America's finest.

Source: Tom Selligson, *Parade,* March 31, 1985, pp. 4-7.

particularly those of male officers; (3) reluctant acceptance into the male-dominated police culture; (4) unfavorable stereotypical reactions by some citizens; and (5) sexual harassment.

Sergeants must be trained not to place a value judgment on cultural differences. These differences must be understood and respected. Disregard for individual and cultural differences erodes productivity. Minority police officers may become disillusioned, resentful, bitter and resistant to supervision. Robert Fulmer and Stephen Franklin (1982) argue that supervisors who behave responsibly toward their subordinates know and consider them individually and personally. They cultivate sincere, honest, open, accepting and trusting relationships designed to instill self-confidence and a desire to achieve personal satisfaction through work. Competent sergeants are firm, fair and impartial. They possess a certain amount of charisma and the ability to focus their attention on the growth and development of their subordinates. This is particularly true in the case of minorities. The sergeant who takes this responsibility seriously may find the following guidelines helpful:

1. Consider minorities as individuals and important human beings at all times. Respect them and accept their individual and cultural differences. Know something about the "person" the police officer is when off duty.

2. Represent the interests and concerns of your employees to top management with understanding and candor. Listen very carefully to minorities as individuals and members of a group. Organize and communicate what you have heard so that police managers get the same message.

3. Make every effort to interpret and explain department policy accurately to nontraditional employees. Clarity is essential to compliance. Never withhold information that they need to know. Explain why policies have been adopted and the contribution the employee will make in achieving the department's mission, goals and objectives.

4. Be a role model for women, blacks, Hispanics and others. Forthrightness and fair play are critical variables in positive relationships. Keep a sense of humor and be prepared to laugh at yourself from time to time.

5. Reprimand minorities when necessary; remember to praise them for a job that is well done. Follow the golden rule: "praise in public and reprimand in private."

6. Let nontraditional workers know that they will be given every opportunity to develop and improve their skills and earnings. Always encourage questions and reply in a concise and straight-

forward manner. Share what you know with minority employees. Allow them to assist with work that may be routine but will teach them new and useful skills through active learning.

7. Evaluate performance and potential very carefully and objectively. Never permit individual personalities or prejudices to cloud objective opinions of any minority employee. Judgments must be based only on those aspects of personality which directly affect an employee's on-the-job performance.

8. Try to improve the minority worker's confidence by being considerate, firm, fair and impartial in dealing with ALL employees under your supervision. Never play favorites and never allow personality or cultural differences to cause you to abuse a subordinate.

9. Place minority workers in a job according to their skill, ability, attitude and (civil service or bargaining agreement) classification. Don't break probationary minority officers in by putting them on the toughest assignment. Whenever possible, do not assign nontraditional employees to jobs for which they are overqualified. They will feel bored and unchallenged.

10. Never "pass the buck" if something goes wrong. Always assume responsibility for the actions of minority employees when appropriate. This will encourage nontraditional employees to take responsibility for themselves. The final responsibility for the operation and on-site management of a work unit cannot be shifted to others by the first-line supervisor.

11. Learn as much as possible about how your minority workers relate to their occupational role. Develop an empathetic appreciation of their individual interests, likes and dislikes. Find out what nontraditional employees really enjoy about their job. Try to discover what frustrates them the most. Be on the lookout for small changes that might make a big difference in how minority workers view their job.

12. Always take time to give proper and adequate instructions to new nontraditional employees. Make them feel at home through a proper job orientation. Be patient. Use counseling, coaching and on-the-job training to help minorities overcome their anxieties.

13. Always stress the importance of safety. Be mindful of the fact that all people (including minorities) have a need for safety and security. A lack of attention to these needs will produce poor morale and a sense of alienation. Encourage employees to share their suggestions on how to make the job safer.

14. Assume responsibility for communicating, as accurately as possible, the feelings and attitudes of all line personnel to your superiors (middle-level managers). Police managers, on the other hand, expect (and sergeants should try to build) a team spirit, high morale, job satisfaction and harmony among all police employees regardless of race, color, creed, sex or national origin.

15. Set the moral and ethical tone for human relations within the police department with an absolute and unconditional commitment to equal employment opportunity. Anything less is an abdication of leadership and will serve to confirm the perception of a racist, sexist and ethnocentric criminal justice system.

These are awesome responsibilities that require a great deal of sensitivity, talent, knowledge, skill, training and courage. Sergeants are "change agents" and, as such, must take risks in order to do their job. Unfortunately, many sergeants are ill-equipped to carry out these duties. They do not have the experiential base or training needed to fulfill their role in personnel development. Far too many sergeants are, in fact, little more than promoted patrol officers.

Sergeants, of course, cannot (even if they are competent) do the job alone. Managers at all levels of complex criminal justice organizations must make a commitment to social justice through equal employment opportunity. It is up to the police chief executive to set the stage for change. The chief must formulate a no-nonsense policy in support of equal employment opportunity and be prepared to use all available resources to accomplish that policy. Continuous reinforcement is absolutely essential. The chief should be prepared to take immediate and appropriate action against any manager or supervisor who fails to support and carry out the department's policies in the area of human relations.

When all is said and done, however, it is the police sergeant who translates equal opportunity theory into practice within the police department. Without a genuine commitment on the sergeant's part, EEO/AA becomes ritualistic mumbo jumbo designed to placate supposedly naive minorities while perpetuating the status quo. Sergeants are in a position to activate and guide equal opportunity or turn it into a social placebo.

Dealing with Employees in a Protected Class

The phrase **protected class** has a special meaning when it comes to supervising employees who belong to certain minority groups. A protected class is composed of individuals who have been unfairly or illegally discriminated against in the past or who are believed to be entitled to preferential consideration due to past or present aspects of their life situation. The phrase protected class is currently used as a classification for individual employees based on their:

1. Racial or ethnic origin

2. Sex (gender or preference)

3. Age (over 40)

4. Physical status (disabilities)

5. Religion

Members of other groups, like veterans, have also been granted protected status based primarily on political grounds.

The identification of those individuals who are accorded special legal consideration when it comes to employment comes from federal civil rights legislation, equal employment opportunity regulations and court decisions. As a manager of human resources, it is in the sergeant's best interest to become familiar with the groups that have been granted "minority" status and to develop an understanding of why they are classified as such.

Irrespective of their social perspectives or personal biases, sergeants, as first-line supervisors who interact with a diverse work force on a daily basis, must be sensitive when it comes to potentially illegal (discriminatory) practices. They must also adjust their supervisory methods in a concerted effort to avoid these practices. The **OUCH test** is one effective strategy that is applicable to the supervision of employees who are members of a protected class (Hilgert and Haimann, 1991).

Being aware of and understanding the OUCH test helps to remind supervisors that ALL of their actions as first-line managers must be:

O — Objective
U — Uniform in application
C — Consistently applied
H — Have job-relatedness

While it is straightforward as well as simple, the OUCH acronym provides practical guidance for ethical, nondiscriminatory supervision in the context of modern police work.

From the OUCH perspective, a supervisor's action is objective when it addresses the employee's job-related behavior without being distorted by personal feelings. It is uniform in application when it is consistently applied to all employees. The action is consistent in effect when it has the same proportional impact on members of protected classes as it does on others in the work force. And finally, the action has job relatedness if it can be shown to deal with behavior that is necessary to perform the job.

The OUCH test should be viewed as much more than a statement of one's personal philosophy, however. It represents the criteria management and/or the courts use to determine whether or not real discrimination has occurred. By adopting the OUCH perspective as it relates to human resources management,

sergeants may well avoid allegations of discrimination and the lengthy administrative or legal entanglements that go along with them. Once again, the old adage may be correct: An ounce of prevention is often worth a pound of cure.

Handling Sexual Harassment in the Workplace

Recent studies indicate that there have been some positive changes in the status of women in police work. The percentage of women in the work force is up and continues to increase each year. Nearly 20 percent of the current applicant pool and recruits are female. This clearly indicates that there is no longer any systemic discrimination against women in the application process. On the downside, women police officers have much higher turnover rates than their male counterparts. Consequently, more women must be recruited and processed just to maintain the current sex ratio (Swanson, Territo and Taylor, 1993).

One cause of the high turnover rate for female police officers is **sexual harassment**. Sergeants are in a strategic position when it comes to dealing with this type of harassment in the workplace. As first-line supervisors and the representative of management, they are expected to be proactive rather than reactive in this regard.

Sexual harassment in the workplace is a major problem facing both public and private sector employers in this country. This is particularly true in male-dominated occupations. Twenty years of research has provided overwhelming evidence to indicate that unwelcome and offensive sexual conduct is both pandemic and problematic in many organizations. Conservative estimates suggest that about 40 percent of working women and 5 to 10 percent of their male counterparts have experienced some type of sexual harassment in the workplace (Thomann, Strickland and Gibbons, 1989).

In a recent study involving 81 of 122 female police officers in a metropolitan police department, 62 percent of the respondents reported that they had been subjected to sexual harassment by their male colleagues. Of these, one-third confronted the offender; 6 percent talked to their supervisors; a few contacted the Equal Employment Opportunity Commission; but 21 percent took no action at all. Very few took strong measures to deal with the problem (Daum and Johns, 1994). It appears that many female officers feel intimidated. Consequently, many of them make a conscious decision not to "rock the boat."

Sexual harassment is prohibited by the Civil Rights Act of 1964. The Act specifies that it is unlawful for an employer to discriminate against any individual with respect to his compensation, terms, conditions or privileges of employment because of such individual's race, color, religion, **sex** or national origin (42 U.S.C. 2000e-2(a)(1)). Sexual harassment can take one of two forms:

1. *Quid Pro Quo Sexual Harassment.* An individual is forced to grant sexual favors in order to obtain, maintain or improve employment status.

2. *Hostile Work Environment Sexual Harassment.* Individual employees are subjected to suggestive comments, photographs, jokes, obscene gestures or unwanted physical contacts. This type of harassment has the following four elements:

   a. The conduct is unwelcome.
   b. The conduct is sufficiently severe or pervasive to alter the conditions of the victim's employment and create an abusive work environment.
   c. The conduct is perceived by the victim as hostile or abusive.
   d. The conduct creates an environment that a reasonable person would find hostile or abusive.

Victims of sexual harassment report that they suffer from various physical and psychological maladies, diminished morale and a loss of productivity. Studies indicate that direct and indirect costs associated with sexual harassment are phenomenal. The federal government, for example, estimates that sexual harassment cost it $267 million dollars between 1985 and 1987—$204 million in lost productivity, $37 million to replace federal workers who left their jobs and $26 million in medical leaves due to stress induced by sexual harassment (U.S. Merit Systems Protection Board, 1987).

Litigation focusing on sexual harassment has also been very costly to an increasing number of public and private organizations. Some have been required to pay judgments and legal fees exceeding six figures (Thomann and Serritella, 1994). The array of compensatory and punitive damages awarded in sexual harassment cases has been truly mind boggling.

Under normal circumstances, sexual harassment between co-workers does not produce employer liability under Title VII of the Civil Rights Act because it is not considered an action of the employer. In addition, management will ordinarily not be held liable if it has taken "immediate" and "effective" steps to remedy sexual harassment occurring in the workplace. An exculpatory response includes a formal policy prohibiting sexual harassment, a user friendly and effective complaint procedure and appropriate disciplinary action in cases of sexual misconduct. As a general rule, when management acts "in good faith" to deal with known sexual harassment and management itself has clean hands, all liability is shifted to those engaged in the harassment.

Title VII provides a remedy for discrimination where there is an indication of employer responsibility in sexual harassment cases. Employers act through their supervisory agents. As a result, the police department (and the governmental entity of which it is a part) can be held liable if one of its supervisors actively participates in the harassment of one of its employees. It can also be held liable if its supervisors are responsible for, actively participate in or otherwise encourage the creation of a hostile work environment. Civil liability may also arise when first-line supervisors ignore open harassment, fail to assist subordinates who are seeking a remedy or otherwise attempt to subvert a remedy (IACP National Law Enforcement Policy Center, 1991).

Sergeants are key players in the ongoing battle against sexual harassment in police work. No police department can maintain a workplace free of harassment without the cooperation and support of its first-line supervisors. Apathetic, hostile or openly chauvinistic supervisors can quickly subvert an otherwise effective antiharassment policy due to their actions or inactions vis-à-vis that particular policy. On the other hand, supportive and proactive supervisors are in a strategic position to assist other police managers spot, stop and prevent sexual harassment.

According to the IACP Policy Center, supervisors play a unique role in preventing as well as dealing with sexual harassment:

1. Supervisors, based on their own actions and words, function as role models for their subordinates. They help to set the moral tone. Consequently, they must never initiate or participate in sexual harassment. On the contrary, supervisors must be prepared to stop the behavior of others that can be perceived as harassment and to take immediate steps to prevent further occurrences. Even the tacit acceptance of sexually inappropriate behavior on the part of employees sends the message that sexual harassment will be tolerated regardless of formal department policy.

2. Supervisors have an affirmative duty to deal effectively with and to report all known or reported cases of sexual harassment to the unit responsible for investigating employee misconduct. Failure to take appropriate action or the failure to report incidents of harassment as required by department policy is normally grounds for disciplinary action. This is essential if management wants to ensure the integrity of the anti-harassment effort at all levels of the process.

3. Each supervisor has a responsibility to reinforce the department's anti-harassment training and behavior modification efforts by actively counseling subordinates on the topic of sexual harassment in the workplace. Supervisors must make themselves accessible to victims and ensure them that their complaints will be handled in a proactive yet discreet and confidential manner. In situations where allegations of sexual harassment have been lodged, confirmed and resolved, the supervisor should continue to interact with the parties in order to ensure that the offensive behavior does not resume. The supervisor should also work with the victim to find ways of making the workplace more comfortable for all of the parties concerned.

Once again, these are awesome responsibilities that have been thrust upon first-line supervisors in the ever-changing social and cultural environment of modern police work. Being a successful police supervisor in the 1990s requires more commitment, knowledge and human skills than at any time in our history.

Supervising Gay and Lesbian Police Officers

A great deal has been written about the police subculture. It has been described as male-dominated, isolationist, elitist and authoritarian. Primarily a workplace phenomenon, the police subculture is the sum of the beliefs, values and norms shared by those within the law enforcement organization that both formally and informally communicates what is expected from members of the work group (Bennett and Hess, 1992).

While the police subculture has traditionally been homophobic, things are changing rather rapidly in some areas of the country and more slowly in others. Change, however, is the rule rather than the exception in regard to **sexual diversity** in the work force.

Many police departments have tacitly adopted a "don't ask, don't tell" philosophy regarding the sexual preferences of applicants and employees. Others actively recruit gay and lesbian police officers. These agencies do all that they can to create a positive workplace culture and hospitable environment for their homosexual employees. After a statewide study, the California Commission on Peace Officer Standards and Training singled out the gay community as a "key" pool for recruiting new police officers by police departments trying to bolster their sagging recruitment efforts. On the national level, the International Association of Chiefs of Police (IACP) rescinded its decades-old policy opposing the hiring of homosexual police officers (Law Enforcement News, 1990).

It is clear that the barriers blocking the employment as well as effective utilization of gay police officers are slowly but surely coming down. In all likelihood, most sergeants will, in their role as first-line supervisors, be responsible for supervising either discreet or openly gay police personnel at some point in their career. It is incumbent upon management to help them prepare for this task. It is up to individual first-line supervisors to prepare themselves as well.

Interviews with dozens of police officers and gay advocates indicate that the New York Police Department is successfully integrating gay and lesbian officers into virtually every policing function. According to one openly gay supervisor, "We are everywhere." In fact, the City's Gay Officers Action League (GOAL) claims to have a membership of nearly 800 police officers. GOAL recently opened chapters in Denver; Springfield, MA; San Francisco; Seattle; Chicago; and Marlboro, MD. It also has affiliates in London and Amsterdam (Blumenthal, 1993).

While no one should underestimate the homophobic hostility that remains in police work, change is on the horizon. First-line supervisors are in a position to help facilitate a meaningful change in human relations by embracing diversity rather than opposing it.

As supervisors, ranking officers must be open and accepting when it comes to gay personnel. While homosexual officers may have a radically different lifestyle, they are, nonetheless, human beings with distinctly human aspirations for a personally rewarding and successful career in their chosen field. Empathy is the key to understanding and utilizing the talents of these individuals. The supervisor's

strategy for dealing with homosexual employees must conform to the OUCH test in that his or her actions vis-à-vis gay subordinates must be objective, uniform in application, consistently applied and have specific job relatedness.

As leaders who set the ethical tone for their subordinates, supervisors have a professional obligation to act as role models for other police personnel. As part of the management team, they have an affirmative responsibility to assist top management facilitate meaningful change within the organization. These are critically important as well as awesome responsibilities that go with the turf.

A subcultural transformation like the employment of gay and lesbian police officers requires changes in the hearts and minds of heterosexual personnel. This means that those in management and first-line supervisory positions have to live the new culture and become the embodiment of it. They must also have their antenna up so that they can identify and reinforce other people whose behavior exemplifies the new values and norms they wish to inculcate in members of the work force.

In order to achieve these objectives, managers and supervisors need to adopt a viable personal strategy for facilitating changes in the workplace culture. The key elements in such a strategy are as follows:

1. Supervisors must really understand the old culture. They cannot chart a new course until they know exactly where they are at the present time.

2. Supervisors should familiarize themselves with the new culture and hold it up as an example from which others can learn. A genuine commitment is an essential element in the acceptance process.

3. Supervisors should encourage those police officers who are willing to discard the old culture and adopt the new one. Reinforcement is the key if new behaviors are to be adopted, internalized and retained by members of the work group.

4. Supervisors should not attack the tenets of the old culture head-on. As leaders, they should allow their subordinates to find new cultural perspectives for themselves and have faith that substantive change will follow.

5. Supervisors should not count on vision to work miracles. At best, vision acts only as a guiding principle for meaningful cultural change.

6. Supervisors should understand that they are in for the long haul. It takes anywhere from five to 10 years for substantive cultural change to become institutionalized.

7. Supervisors must learn to live the culture they advocate. As always, actions speak much louder than mere words (Dumaine, 1990).

Supervisors are change agents. They are, based on their rank and authority within the police department, also culture carriers. Without their commitment and support, both substantive and durable change will be very difficult to achieve. Since the employment and deployment of homosexuals in police work appears to be a fait accompli, first-line supervisors should climb aboard the bandwagon. By becoming proactive, they can help chart a new, more open and accepting course for the police subculture.

Managing a More Educated Work Force

Police supervisors are being called upon to **manage an increasingly more educated work force**. The educational level of American police officers has risen significantly over the past 20 years. While the vast majority of police agencies only require a high school diploma, about 60 percent of all sworn officers have more than two years of college education (Carter, Sapp and Stephens, 1989). This represents a dramatic departure from the past when a high school education was considered sufficient preparation for a career in law enforcement.

Based on a comprehensive study commissioned by the Police Executive Research Forum (PERF), the researchers were able to identify what they consider to be the advantages of a college education. College-educated men and women tend to have:

1. Greater knowledge of procedures, functions and principles related to their present and future assignments.

2. Better understanding of their professional role and its importance in the criminal justice system and in the society at large.

3. More desirable psychological makeup (including alertness, empathy, flexibility, initiative and intelligence).

4. Greater interpersonal skill focusing on the ability to communicate, to respond to the needs of others and to exercise compassionate leadership.

5. Greater ability to analyze situations, exercise discretion and resolve problems through appropriate decisionmaking.

6. Stronger moral character as reflected in a sense of conscience and qualities like honesty, reliability and tolerance.

7. More desirable system of personal values that is consistent with police work in a democratic society (Sapp and Carter, 1992).

On the downside, college-educated police officers seem to experience more stress than their less educated colleagues. This is due, in part, to the animosity

demonstrated by "street-wise" police officers, the unrealistic expectations of family and friends, misconceptions about advancement on the job, lack of input into policy formulation and decisionmaking, and boredom (Swanson, Territo and Taylor, 1993). According to data from the 1989 PERF survey, police administrators report that college-educated police officers are more likely to question orders, request more frequent reassignment, have lower morale and more absenteeism, and become more easily frustrated by bureaucratic procedures. Stress-induced productivity problems and high turnover rates are not uncommon.

First-line supervisors are granted the power to perform specific tasks in concert with and through the efforts of others. In order to work more collaboratively with their subordinates (especially college-educated men and women), sergeants must cast aside the traditional "overseer" mentality common in police work and accept the fact that their job is no longer one of supervision per se but one of sharing power and providing leadership.

The supervisor who chooses to share power with subordinates automatically expands his or her influence as a leader. By empowering others, the supervisor is in a much better position to accomplish assigned tasks. Delegation is the sharing of power. The sharing of power coupled with meaningful participation in the decision-making process leads to empowerment. Empowerment means that employees experience ownership in their job and accept 100 percent of the responsibility for doing it right. For all practical purposes, effective supervision is effective delegation (Whisenand and Rush, 1993).

Effective delegation does not just happen. It takes a great deal of thought and preparation. As Whisenand and Rush point out:

1. Recipients of the delegation must be well-trained to perform their job.

2. Training must be relevant, reliable and ongoing.

3. Supervisors should set high performance standards for themselves as well as their subordinates.

4. Supervisors should understand the needs and values of each of their employees.

5. There must be pertinent, open and frank communication between supervisors and their subordinates.

6. Those who fulfill their delegated responsibilities at an acceptable level should be rewarded.

7. Those who do not perform their delegated responsibilities at an acceptable level should be reprimanded.

8. There must be meaningful feedback systems in place to ensure the success of the delegation process.

The success or failure of this empowerment strategy will depend on the commitment and human skills possessed by the those seeking to implement it.

Four parties benefit from increased employee participation and the effective delegation power. They are the community, the police department, first-line supervisors and employees (Whisenand and Rush, 1993).

The local community benefits from the empowerment process. Empowered employees are ordinarily more skillful and dedicated to their job. Consequently, they tend to provide better and less costly police services. Better individual performance is likely to generate more respect and community support for the police department.

The police department benefits from the empowerment process. Employee participation, input into the decision-making process and acceptance of responsibility create an environment in which everyone is encouraged to pursue excellence. This strengthens the organization as it seeks to accomplish its mission, goals and objectives.

Supervisors benefit from the empowerment process. Supervisors benefit in that they are:

1. Instilling a commitment for getting the job done.

2. Strengthening mutual trust between themselves and their subordinates.

3. Enhancing their officers' knowledge and job skills.

4. Encouraging and reinforcing the feeling of job ownership.

5. Utilizing the power of leadership to provide quality police services through the efforts of their employees.

By empowering subordinates, supervisors empower themselves as effective leaders.

Rank-and-file police officers benefit from the empowerment process. Empowerment and its accompanying collegial status benefit employees in that they become much more:

1. Positive in terms of a commitment to their work.

2. Trusting, trustworthy and openly participatory.

3. Self-confident.

4. Competent.

5. Professional in their orientation.

6. Capable of working alone or with others to perform top-notch police work.

The empowerment of police personnel is essential if governments are to attract, field and retain college-educated officers.

Empowerment substitutes self-supervision for traditional organizational control mechanisms. An empowered organization is one in which individual police officers have the knowledge, skill, desire and opportunity to personally succeed in a way that leads to collective organizational success. Helpful systems and structures, win-win situations, self-supervision and personal accountability are at the heart of the empowerment process (Covey, 1992).

Once again, sergeants are the key players in the empowerment process. In order to succeed in this role, they must truly believe that people are their greatest asset. They must be trusting and be willing to take risks by delegating power to individual police officers while holding them and themselves accountable. Sergeants must be prepared to accept the mantle of leadership as they consciously reject the supervisor's traditional role as an overseer of "employees" in the workplace.

Training for the New Supervisor

As noted earlier, sergeants as first-line supervisors are in a strategic position to determine whether equal employment opportunity becomes a reality or remains a figment of our collective imagination. Even if they are committed to fairness and decency, sergeants cannot learn the information and human skills they need to play their staff-development role through osmosis. Whether they are traditional or nontraditional employees, **sergeants must be trained** for their new duties. They should also be given the opportunity to apply supervisory theory to real-life situations as part of an extended training process. Once they are on the job, new sergeants should be evaluated for competency and coached by a certified trainer (see Figure 13.8). Without extensive supervisory training and on-the-job coaching, there is little chance that new police sergeants will be able to cope with the human relations challenge of the 1990s.

Municipal governments are reluctant to spend money on supervisory training. Part of the problem is that training, itself, has taken a back seat to economic reality. Many police departments now receive minimum budgetary allocations. The abandonment of training for economic reasons borders on the absurd and will cost much more in the long run. Without adequate supervisory training, police departments run the risk of more vicarious liability suits and face potentially disruptive behavior by nontraditional employees in response to inadequate supervision. Proactive police managers know that the only way to guard against these potential problems is to strengthen the rank of sergeant through selective promotion, upgraded supervisory training and unequivocal support.

Figure 13.8
Supervisor's Training Guide

I. GENERAL SUPERVISION

	Trainer's Initials and Date	
	Instructed by trainer	Knowledge or ability has been demonstrated by supervisor
A. Role Identification: The supervisor will understand the role of first-line supervisor within the organization.		
1. Management's expectations of the supervisor		
2. Peer's expectations of the supervisor		
3. Subordinate's expectations of the supervisor		
B. Leadership: The supervisor will understand how to gain the cooperation of subordinates through the use of realistic and fair personnel management techniques.		
1. Personnel motivation		
2. Deployment of personnel/preparing work schedules		
3. Shows respect and a feeling of responsibility for subordinates		
4. Identifies poor performance		
5. Recognizes good performance		
6. Properly delegates work to subordinates		
7. Works at maintaining productive peer relations		
8. Resolves issues/problems through negotiation with subordinates, peers, and superiors		
9. Manages time effectively		
10. Understands the inspectional role of the supervisor		
a. Inspection of personnel		

I. GENERAL SUPERVISION *continued*

	Trainer's Initials and Date	
	Instructed by trainer	Knowledge or ability has been demonstrated by supervisor
b. Inspection of agency equipment		
c. Inspection of facility for safety of personnel and agency liability		
C. Employee Performance Appraisal: The supervisor will understand the complex issues relative to employee performance appraisal and how a fair system can improve productivity and accountability.		
1. Understands legal issues of performance appraisal		
a. Purpose of evaluations		
b. Agency policy in completing evaluations		
c. Agency policy in the use of evaluations		
2. Understands the performance/accountability cycle		
a. Use of contracts to improve performance		
b. Record of previous performance, good versus bad		
3. Understands the agency's acceptable standard		
a. Can write standards if necessary		
4. Understands common problems and errors supervisors should avoid		
5. Use of feedback		
a. Identifies poor performance		
b. Recognizes exceptional performance		

Figure 13.8, *continued*

I. GENERAL SUPERVISION *continued*	Instructed by trainer	Knowledge or ability has been demonstrated by supervisor
	Trainer's Initials and Date	
c. Lets the employees know where they stand		
D. Employee Counseling: The supervisor will understand the process of discussing work issues with subordinates. Includes discussing performance problems, resolving grievances and complaints, and resolving conflicts among employees.		
1. Understands how to prepare for an interview with an employee		
a. Identify problems		
b. Develop plan prior to interview		
c. Proper location, privacy		
d. Mutually agreed upon solution		
e. Set time to resolve and follow up		
2. Barriers to avoid		
3. Understands all elements necessary for a complete interview		
4. Contemporary counseling issues		
a. Issues unique to the agency, alcohol, marital problems, etc.		
E. Employee Discipline: The supervisor will understand the complex issues and the supervisor's role in the disciplinary process.		
1. Understands positive versus negative discipline and when to use it		
2. Understands agency policy on the use of discipline and the first-line supervisor's responsibilities/limits		

I. GENERAL SUPERVISION *continued*	Instructed by trainer	Knowledge or ability has been demonstrated by supervisor
	Trainer's Initials and Date	
3. Understands how to take a proactive approach to discipline		
a. Anticipate problems and be prepared to act		
4. Understands the agency's policy in the investigation of personnel complaints		
a. Who investigates		
b. Who initiates		
c. How to initiate if necessary		
5. Understands all elements of the Peace Officers Bill of Rights		
6. Understands the agency's grievance procedure		
7. Understands the agency's policy of the application of the Skelly Rule		
8. Understands the agency's policy in the maintenance of personnel files		
9. Understands the supervisor's role in the control of morale		
F. Employee Relations: The supervisor will understand the elements of an employee relations program and the supervisor's organizational responsibility to the program's maintenance.		
1. Understands employee unit bargaining agreements		
a. Both for sworn and non-sworn personnel		
2. Understands the agency's affirmative action program		

Figure 13.8, *continued*

I. GENERAL SUPERVISION *continued*

	Trainer's Initials and Date	
	Instructed by trainer	Knowledge or ability has been demonstrated by supervisor
3. Understands the agency's sexual harassment policy		
a. Must stress support of policy		
b. Must set a good example		
4. Understands EEOC/FEHC guidelines and how they apply to the agency		
a. Supervisor's role during investigation		
G. Administrative Support: The supervisor will understand the analytical process, the communication of policy, the process of problem-solving, decision-making, and the budget process.		
1. Understands how to analyze statistical data used by the agency		
2. Understands the need to communicate and support agency policy		
3. Understands the need for completed staff work		
a. How and why work is staffed within the agency		
b. Supervisor should be provided with the acceptable format used by the agency		
4. Understands the problem-solving system used by the agency		
5. Understands the decision-making process used by the agency		
a. How to provide input as a supervisor		
b. How to be an agency resource		

I. GENERAL SUPERVISION *continued*

	Trainer's Initials and Date	
	Instructed by trainer	Knowledge or ability has been demonstrated by supervisor
6. Understands the budget system used by the agency		
a. The budget cycle		
b. How to use agency purchase orders and the approval process		
c. The limits of the supervisor within the agency in making purchases		
7. Understands and supports organizational goals and objectives		
H. Communications: The supervisor will understand the importance of verbal/nonverbal communication skills, the art of listening, and the processing of information.		
1. Understands the need for proper verbal/nonverbal communication skills especially when dealing with subordinates		
2. Understands the art of listening and how it applies to supervision		
3. Understands the supervisor's role in citizen/officer conflict resolution		
a. Subordinate's expectations		
b. Citizen's expectations		
4. Understands the supervisor's responsibility for rumor control		
5. Understands the need to develop good public speaking skills		
6. Understand the agency's press release policy		

Source: California Commission on Peace Officer Standards and Training, 1983, *Supervisory Training Guide*.

Summary

Police work traditionally has been dominated by white males. It was, in many ways, an extension of the white power structure and represented a clannish "old boy" network. Nontraditional employees (women, blacks, Hispanics and other recognized minorities) were kept out of police work through blatant de jure and more subtle de facto discrimination. The prejudice, stereotyping and scapegoating so common in American society at large permeated nearly every aspect of law enforcement. Racism, sexism and other forms of bigotry were endemic to the infrastructure of the police culture. Overt prejudice and legalized discrimination became untenable in our multicultural pluralistic society, however. The situation began to change in the early 1960s.

The 1964 Civil Rights Act was landmark legislation. It outlawed discrimination based on race, religion, sex and national origin. Title VII prohibited discrimination in the workplace. The Equal Employment Opportunity Act of 1972 extended the coverage of the Civil Rights Act to municipal government and police departments. In an effort to curb prejudice and remedy past discrimination, the Equal Employment Opportunity Commission formulated affirmative action guidelines. These guidelines (which were often converted into quotas by bureaucrats and the courts) opened up police work for nontraditional employees Initial emphasis was placed on making police recruitment, screening and selection procedures nondiscriminatory. Additional federal and state EEO/AA guidelines have been designed to prevent discrimination in assigning, disciplining and promoting members of various protected classes.

As a result of these EEO/AA initiatives, blacks, Hispanics and women have been entering the work force in far larger numbers. Consequently, it is much more likely that police sergeants will come into contact with and be in a position to supervise nontraditional employees. Sergeants must adjust to a new role and different expectations. They must be objective and fair with those in protected classes, proactive in deterring the sexual harassment of female, gay and lesbian officers and nondefensive when it comes to empowering educated workers. As developers of the police department's human resources, they serve as mentors, coaches, trainers and positive role models. They act as coordinators rather than overseers. If they are to deal effectively with the emerging multicultural work force, sergeants must come to grips with their prejudices. They must be able to develop open, honest and empathetic relationships. Good sergeants strive to be helpful, firm, fair and impartial. They have a healthy respect for both individual and cultural differences. Sergeants, depending on their sensitivity, talent, knowledge, human skills and commitment to equal opportunity, will determine whether EEO/AA is fact or palatable fiction.

Case Study

Sergeant Kevin Kessler

Kevin Kessler is the senior sergeant in a fairly large metropolitan police department. He is considered to be an excellent first-line manager and is presented as a role model for all newly-promoted sergeants. The sergeant also serves as the chief instructor for an 80-hour supervisor training course offered by the regional criminal justice training and education center.

Sergeant Kessler just attended a seminar on instructional delivery systems offered by the California Police Officers Standards and Training Commission. The seminar focuses on newly promoted, nontraditional police personnel and their special training needs. As a result of the seminar, he became convinced that classroom training in supervision had to be supplemented by structured active learning in the field.

Upon his return, Sergeant Kessler contacted the captain in charge of the training center and volunteered to develop and implement a new training program for minority supervisors designed to integrate classroom learning with supervised field experience. The active learning would be coordinated by senior first-line supervisors.

A formal proposal was developed and forwarded to the chief of police for his review. The project was approved two weeks later, and Sergeant Kessler was authorized to proceed as soon as possible.

Using the Supervisory Training Guide prepared by the Training Program Service Bureau of California's Commission on Police Officer Standards and Training as a reference, what would you, if you were Sergeant Kessler, include in a general supervision course for newly promoted minority officers? How would you select the on-site trainers? What basic qualifications should they have?

Key Concepts

affirmative action

bona fide occupational qualifications

changing demographics

Civil Rights Act of 1964

competent and supportive supervisors

dealing with sexual harassment

discrimination

Equal Employment Opportunity Act

first-line supervisor's role

managing a more educated work force

nondiscriminatory selection process

nondiscriminatory supervisors

the OUCH test applied to supervision

prejudice

protected classes

sexual diversity in the work force

strategies for supervising minorities

supervising nontraditional employees

training supervisors to do their job

white male domination of police work

Discussion Topics and Questions

1. Policing has been dominated by white males from the working class. Why have the police been reluctant to accept blacks, Hispanics, women and other nontraditional employees? Should police managers try to build a more representative work force?

2. What is prejudice? How is it related to discrimination? Explain the difference between de jure and de facto discrimination. Give several examples.

3. EEO/AA initiatives are based on two separate federal laws. Identify them. Why did affirmative action (goals, timetables and action plans) degenerate into a not-so-subtle form of reverse discrimination? How has the Supreme Court reacted to this issue?

4. Federal law and court decisions require that the employee-selection process be nondiscriminatory. What criteria are used to determine whether the process is discriminatory? Are the criteria reasonable?

5. What is empathy? Why is empathy so important in forming positive supervisor-subordinate relationships?

6. What characteristics or traits do good supervisors have that help bridge the cultural gap between them and their nontraditional employees?

7. List at least seven things that a supervisor can do to enhance relationships with minority employees. Will these strategies work for white males? Is there any real difference?

8. What constitutes a protected class in terms of civil rights legislation? Discuss the OUCH test. What are the practical advantages of adopting this particular strategy?

9. Define the term sexual harassment. Differentiate between the two types of sexual harassment. What is the first-line supervisor's role in preventing as well as dealing with sexual harassment?

10. What is homophobia? Why is sexual preference becoming less of an issue in the hiring and retention of police personnel?

For Further Reading

Iannone, Nathan F. (1994). *Supervision of Police Personnel*, 5th ed. Englewood Cliffs, NJ: Prentice-Hall, Inc.

> Discusses the development of women as first-line supervisors. The author emphasizes that their effectiveness, like that of their male counterparts, will depend on whether they possess characteristics leaders must have and how well they apply the principles of leadership within the police department.

Martin, Susan E. (1989). "A Report on the Status of Women in Policing." *Police Foundation Reports*, May.

> Comprehensive examination of the status of women in American law enforcement. It explores the positive gains made by females and highlights some of the remaining problems.

Steinmetz, Lawrence L. and H. Ralph Todd (1986). *First-Line Management*. Plano, TX: Business Publications, Inc.

> Explores the legal, social and ethical responsibility of all first-line supervisors in relation to their subordinates. The authors stress the need for open and honest interaction.

Swanson, Charles R., Leonard Territo and Robert W. Taylor (1993). *Police Administration*, 3rd ed. New York: Macmillan Publishing Co.

> An excellent review of contemporary human relations within police organizations. The text elaborates on the needs of many nontraditional police personnel.

References

Bennett, Wayne W. and Karen M. Hess (1992). *Management and Supervision in Law Enforcement*. St. Paul, MN: West Publishing Company.

Blumenthal, Ralph (1993). "Gay, Lesbian Cops Gaining Acceptance in New York." *The Denver Post*, March 7: 33A.

Broderick, John J. (1987). *Police in a Time of Change*. Prospect Heights, IL: Waveland Press, Inc.

California Commission on Peace Officer Standards and Training (1983). *Supervisory Training Guide*. North Highlands, CA: Post.

Carter, David L., Allen D. Sapp and Darrel W. Stephens (1989). *The State of Police Education: Policy Direction for the Twenty-first Century*. Washington DC: Police Executive Research Forum.

Cole, George F. (1995). *The American System of Criminal Justice*, 7th ed. Boston: Wadsworth Publishing Co.

Covey, Stephen R. (1992). *Principle-Centered Leadership*. New York: Simon and Schuster, Inc.

Daum, James M. and Cindy M. Johns (1994). "Police Work From a Woman's Perspective." *The Police Chief*, Vol. LXI, No. 9.

Dumaine, Brian (1990). "Creating a New Company Culture." *Fortune*, Vol. 121, No. 1.

Equal Employment Opportunity Coordinating Council (1973). "Federal Policy on Remedies Concerning Equal Employment Opportunity in State and Local Government Personnel Systems." Washington, DC.

Fulmer, Robert M. and Stephen G. Franklin (1982). *Supervision*. New York: Macmillan Publishing Co.

Griggs v. Duke Power Co., 401 U.S. at 431 (1971).

Hilgert, Raymond L. and Theo Haimann (1991). *Supervision: Concepts and Practices of Management*, 5th ed. Cincinnati, OH: South-Western Publishing Company.

Holden, Richard N. (1986). *Modern Police Management*. Englewood Cliffs, NJ: Prentice-Hall, Inc.

IACP National Law Enforcement Policy Center (1991). "Harassment in the Workplace: A Proactive Approach." *The Police Chief*, Vol. LVIII, No. 12.

Johns, Gary (1988). *Organizational Behavior: Understanding Life at Work*, 2nd ed. Glenview, IL: Scott, Foresman and Company.

Johnson, Lawrence A. (1969). "Employing the Hard-Core Unemployed." New York: American Management Association.

Law Enforcement News (1990). "LAPD Gays' Hope: Mainstream Acceptance." Vol. XVII, No. 321.

Leo, John (1988). "A Chilling Wave of Racism." *Time,* Jan. 25.

Leonard, V.A. and Harry W. More (1993). *Police Organization and Management*, 7th ed. Westbury, NY: The Foundation Press.

Leonard, V.A. and Harry W. More (1993). *Police Organization and Management*, 8th ed. Westbury, NY: The Foundation Press.

Longenecker, Justin G. and Charles D. Pringle (1984). *Management*. Columbus, OH: Charles E. Merrill Publishing Co.

Martin, Randy (1987). *Personnel and Supervision in Criminal Justice*. Indiana, PA: Kinko Professor Publishing.

National Advisory Commission on Criminal Justice Standards and Goals (1973). *The Police*. Washington, DC: U.S. Government Printing Office.

NAACP v. Allen, 340 F. Supp. 703 (M.D., Ala., 1972).

Plunkett, W. Richard (1992). *Supervision: The Direction of People at Work*, 6th ed. Boston: Allyn and Bacon, Inc.

Sabatini, Richard V. (1988) "Despite Cutbacks, A New Police Class." *The Philadelphia Inquirer*, November 15:4-B.

Sapp, Allen D. and David L. Carter (1992). "Should All Policemen Be College Trained?" *The Police Chief*, Vol. 38, No. 12.

Stahl, O. Glenn (1983). *Public Personnel Administration*. New York: Harper and Row.

Swank, Calvin J. and James A. Conser (1983). *The Police Personnel System*. New York: John Wiley and Sons, Inc.

Swanson, Charles R., Leonard Territo and Robert W. Taylor (1993). *Police Administration: Structures, Processes and Behavior*, 3rd ed. New York: Macmillan Publishing Co.

Swanson, Charles R., Leonard Territo and Robert W. Taylor (1988). *Police Administration: Structures, Processes and Behavior*, 2nd ed. New York: Macmillan Publishing Co.

Territo, Leonard and Harold J. Vetter (1981). *Stress and Police Personnel*. Boston: Allyn and Bacon, Inc.

Thibault, Edward A., Lawrence M. Lynch and R. Bruce McBride (1990). *Proactive Police Management*, 2nd ed. Englewood Cliffs, NJ: Prentice-Hall, Inc.

Thomann, Daniel A. and Tina M. Serritella (1994). "Preventing Sexual Harassment in Law Enforcement Agencies." *The Police Chief*, Vol. LXI, No. 9.

Thomann, Daniel I., D.E. Strickland and J.L. Gibbons (1989). "An Organizational Development Approach to Preventing Sexual Harassment: Developing Shared Commitment Through Awareness Training." *College and University Personnel Association Journal* (Fall).

Turner, William W. (1968). *The Police Establishment*. New York: G.P. Putnam's Sons.

U.S. Department of Justice, Federal Bureau of Investigation (1993). *Crime in the United States*. Washington, DC: U.S. Government Printing Office.

U.S. Merit Systems Protection Board (1987). *Sexual Harassment of Federal Workers: An Update*. Washington DC: U.S. Government Printing Office.

U.S. Public Law 92-261, Section 703 (a) (1) (2).

Walker, Samuel (1992). *The Police in America*. New York: McGraw-Hill Book Company.

Whisenand, Paul M. and George E. Rush (1993). *Supervising Police Personnel*, 2nd ed. Englewood Cliffs, NJ: Prentice-Hall, Inc.

World Almanac (1994). Pittsburgh: The Pittsburgh Press, Inc.

Zastrow, Charles and Lee Bowker (1984). *Social Problems*. Chicago: Nelson-Hall, Inc.

Police Training—

An Investment in Human Resources

14

Introductory Case Study

Sergeant Julia Brightwell

Sergeant Julia Brightwell, a patrol supervisor, was recently transferred to the police academy. She has been assigned to develop and teach a new four-hour unit on the sexual abuse of children that will be incorporated into the basic training curriculum. When she tried to discuss the project with Lieutenant Bill Fisk, the police department's training coordinator, it became apparent that he was not particularly interested in working with a female trainer. After stuttering and stammering, he left Sergeant Brightwell on her own and advised her to do whatever she wanted to do in the course.

Sergeant Brightwell contacted Dr. James Brooks, a member of the American Society for Training and Development, and requested help. He asked her questions about the training. He also wanted more information about tasks, objectives, expected outcomes, style, methodology, the instructional process and various feedback mechanisms. Dr. Brooks went on to discuss job-relatedness, relevance, motivation, active learning and job performance assessment. It became obvious to Sergeant Brightwell that she had a lot of work to do to get ready for the task ahead. She realized, perhaps for the very first time, that effectiveness doesn't just happen. It takes time, energy and a great deal of expertise.

Put yourself in Sergeant Brightwell's place. If you had to go back to the drawing board, how would you, based on the input you received from Dr. Brooks, conceptualize, develop and implement an effective four-hour training module dealing with the sexual abuse of children? Use a management-by-objectives approach. Make yourself a flow chart that clearly indicates what needs to be done, the activities required to do it, the methods that will be used and the appropriate time frames. How would you try to evaluate the success of the training effort?

Sir Robert Peel has long been recognized as one of the greatest reformers in modern police history. He was the principal architect of the Metropolitan Police Act of 1829. This new law created Scotland Yard and emphasized the need for and importance of professionally oriented **police training**. The Peelian emphasis on formal training was echoed in this country by August Vollmer and other progressives in the International Association of Chiefs of Police (IACP). New York initiated formal police training in 1897. Chief Vollmer established a training school for Berkeley, California police officers in 1908. By 1930, nearly a dozen departments were operating large-scale police academies (Fogelson, 1977).

The motivating force behind the **training movement** was the perceived need to reform the police establishment. Reform-minded police administrators believed that training would help to:

1. Offset the adverse effects of partisan politics on police work.

2. Make police personnel much more efficient, effective and productive.

3. Bring recognition, higher wages and professional status to municipal police officers.

4. Prevent injustices caused by incompetent or negligent police officers.

5. Generate confidence in and financial support for police activities through improved police service.

The scope of the training was limited to the essentials, and quality control presented a nearly insurmountable managerial challenge.

While the merits of formal police training were self-evident, it was slow to develop in the United States. The Wickersham Commission (1931) found that only 20 percent of the 383 cities it surveyed provided any type of recruit training. In-service training was all but nonexistent. The Commission called for the establishment of mandatory minimum police training standards. The call for job-related recruit and in-service training was reiterated by the President's Commission on Law Enforcement and the Administration of Justice (1967), the National Advisory Commission on Civil Disorders (1968), the Commission on the Causes and Prevention of Violence (1969), the American Bar Association Project on Standards for Criminal Justice (1972), and the National Advisory Commission on Criminal Justice Standards and Goals (1973). California and New York became the first states to enact police officer standards and training (POST) legislation in 1959. By 1968, 31 states had enacted similar laws. According to Cal Swank and James Conser (1983), the quality of the legislation varied. Some statutes dealt with both in-service and recruit training. Others were far less comprehensive. Compliance was often voluntary rather than mandatory. Public interest was at times sacrificed for expediency.

Figure 14.1

Requirements for Police Entry-Level Training Programs

By type of competency area and state, as of December 1985

(In hours)

State	Total number of hours required	Competency area						
		Human relations	Force and weaponry	Communi-cations	Legal	Patrol and criminal investi-gations	Criminal justice systems	Adminis-tration
Hawaii	954	17	153	65	133	444	29	113
Rhode Island	661	42	65	0	48	480	0	26
Vermont	553	4	80	30	74	330	3	32
Maine	504	27	62	17	73	277	21	27
West Virginia	495	14	98	20	120	195	36	12
Pennsylvania	480	76	88	10	94	196	16	0
Maryland	471	0	0	0	73	366	0	32
Massachusetts	460	35	132	28	90	167	8	0
Utah	450	19	73	27	49	247	15	20
Connecticut	443	23	48	8	64	284	11	5
Indiana	440	21	73	4	83	192	32	35
Michigan	440	9	105	8	48	244	0	26
Washington	440	34	152	24	85	145	0	0
New Hampshire	426	20	75	8	60	205	8	50
New Mexico	421	30	69.5	18	56	238.5	9	0
Arizona	400	24	110	16	78	135	12	25
California	400	15	80	15	60	185	10	35
Iowa	400	33	75	12	44	175	13	48
Kentucky	400	6.5	84.5	3.5	75.5	182.5	6	41.5
South Carolina	382	18	77	12	72	178	2	23
Texas	381	14	48	18	68	233	0	0
North Carolina	369	28	64	20	72	170	0	15
Delaware	362	12	64	17	87	174	6	2
Montana	346	22	77.5	14	19.5	183.5	15	14.5
Nebraska	341	36	58	10	62	158	2	15
Colorado	334	19	55	22	79	141	18	0
Florida	320	24	39	18	54	158	9	18
Kansas	320	34	42	20	45	170	1	8
Mississippi	320	8	70	20	50	153	7	12
Wyoming	320	10	71	14	53	119	33	20
North Dakota	313	10	23	20	84	139	16	21
Idaho	310	0	47	9	51	169	16	18
New Jersey	310	26	40	13	49	116	17	49
Arkansas	304	14	60	6	19	190	0	15
New York	285	9	38	7	44	169	10	8
Alabama	280	14	49	8	48	138	3	20
Ohio	280	16	42	10	76	111	20	5
Oregon	280	14	64	12	62	104	8	16
Alaska	276	1	20	7	74	139	13	22
Georgia	240	18	45	5	47	110	2	13
Louisiana	240	16	57	8	36	78	5	40
Tennessee	240	2	50	7	31	136	8	6
Wisconsin	240	18	30	9	16	121	10	36
Nevada	200	8	28	11	46	96	2	9
South Dakota	200	17	32	8	22	109	6	6
Missouri	120	3	23	10	28	55	1	0

Note: These data were obtained through a mail survey of law enforcement training directors. Oklahoma, Illinois, Virginia, and Minnesota were omitted from the study due to incomplete data regarding their curriculum content. Each state mandates the minimum hourly requirements reported above, but police agencies within each state may establish entry-level training in addition to State requirements.

"Human relations" training stresses the development of the whole person in dealing with the problems of society. Training involves subjects such as human relations, crisis intervention, and stress awareness. "Force and weaponry" involves the development of skills in the use of firearms, chemical agents, hand to hand combat, and other measures of physical force. "Communications" is the development of interpersonal skills for conducting interviews and interrogations; included in this category are report writing, basic training in grammar, spelling, and body language. "Legal" training encompasses criminal law, rules of evidence, basic constitutional law, laws of arrest, search and seizure, civil rights, and liability. "Patrol and criminal investigation" training focuses on patrol techniques and procedures, defensive driving, basic criminal investigation, emergency medical aid, traffic control, physical fitness, accident investigation, jail/custody procedures, and other technical competencies. "Criminal justice systems" training stresses the knowledge needed for understanding the criminal justice system; included in this area are corrections and courts, and professional conduct and ethics. "Administration" covers training matters related to the use of equipment, basic orientation to the training program, and diagnostic testing and/or examination time. (Source, pp. 8-10.)

Source: Robert J. Meadows, "An Assessment of Police Entry Level Training in the United States: Conformity or Conflict with the Police Role?" Boone, NC: Appalachian State University, 1985. (Mimeographed.) Table 11. Table adapted by SOURCEBOOK staff.

As of 1988, all states had adopted either voluntary or mandatory minimum training standards for newly hired police personnel. The number of hours required for recruit training varies from state to state and ranges anywhere from 120 hours in Missouri to 954 hours in Hawaii (see Figure 14.1). Some states, for a variety of reasons, still do not require recruit training before deployment in the field. The Commonwealth of Pennsylvania, for example, currently mandates and pays for 520 hours of basic training for all municipal police personnel. Until recently, newly hired police officers were allowed to work for up to one year without the training (53 P.S. {740-749, 1974}). This legislation has been changed and now requires completion of a basic police training course before deployment.

While a few states have actually reduced the total number of hours required in the basic training curriculum, many have increased them, and in some cases, the increase has been rather substantial. The 1992 data gathered by the Pennsylvania Municipal Police Officers' Education and Training Commission tend to confirm this trend (see Figure 14.2). We can anticipate even more of an emphasis on recruit training in the near future.

State training commissions often tie curriculum revision in with a statutory change regulating the minimum number of mandatory training hours. In the Commonwealth of Pennsylvania, for example, the Municipal Police Officers' Education and Training Commission (based on a comprehensive task analysis) redesigned the training curriculum and increased the number of hours from 480 to 520. The new curriculum was developed by Temple University and is considered by many police trainers to be a model for the rest of the nation.

As of July 1, 1988, the State of Florida increased its mandatory minimum training requirement from 320 hours to 520 hours. The curriculum has been thoroughly updated and revised. It is keyed to the tasks performed by municipal police officers. The Criminal Justice Academy in South Florida offers an unusually comprehensive 800-hour basic law enforcement program. South Florida is also considered to be a trend setter when it comes to innovations in police education and training.

Police work has become one of the most complex and exacting occupations in contemporary American society. It is a labor-intensive governmental activity. A police department can best be described as a synergistic collection of human beings organized and equipped to protect and serve the community-at-large. People are its most valuable resource. The efficiency, effectiveness and productivity of the police department will depend on exactly how well these people have been trained. Training is the practical and applied side of education designed to transmit the knowledge, skills and attitudes needed to improve the employee's problem-solving ability or on-the-job performance in complex criminal justice organizations.

Selective recruitment, positive discipline, adequate supervision and effective training shape the department's style of policing and help to ensure the quality of its service. All newly hired police personnel need basic recruit training before they start to work. Veteran officers, on the other hand, need continuous "in-ser-

Figure 14.2
Supplemental Police Training Data

State	Previous Requirement	New Requirement	Change in Hours	Percent (%) Change
Alabama	280	480	+200	+71.4
Alaska	276	400	+124	+44.9
Arizona	400	440	+40	+10.0
Arkansas	304	280	−24	−7.9
California	400	560	+160	+40.0
Colorado	334	353	+19	+5.7
Connecticut	443	650	+207	+46.7
Delaware	362	502	+140	+38.7
Florida	320	520	+200	+62.5
Georgia	240	280	+40	+16.7
Hawaii	954	—	—	—
Idaho	310	390	+80	+25.8
Illinois	—	400	—	—
Indiana	440	480	+40	+9.1
Iowa	400	400	0	0
Kansas	320	320	0	0
Kentucky	400	400	0	0
Louisiana	240	240	0	0
Maine	504	320	−184	−36.5
Maryland	471	400	−71	−15.1
Massachusetts	460	480	+20	+4.4
Michigan	440	450	+10	+2.3
Minnesota	—	—	—	—
Mississippi	320	400	+80	+25.0
Missouri	120	120	0	0
Montana	346	540	+194	+56.1
Nebraska	341	500	+159	+46.6
Nevada	200	480	+280	+140.0
New Hampshire	426	510	+84	+19.7
New Jersey	310	—	—	—
New Mexico	421	504	+83	+19.7
New York	285	445	+160	+56.1
North Carolina	369	432	+63	+17.1
North Dakota	313	360	+47	+15.0
Ohio	280	444	+164	+58.6
Oklahoma	—	300	—	—
Oregon	280	370	+90	+32.1
Pennsylvania	480	520	+40	+8.3
Rhode Island	661	600	-61	-9.2
South Carolina	382	380	-2	-0.0[*]
South Dakota	200	240	+40	+20.0
Tennessee	240	320	+80	+33.3
Texas	381	400	+19	+4.9
Utah	450	440	-10	-2.2
Vermont	553	550	-3	-0.0[*]
Virginia	—	375	—	—
Washington	440	440	0	0
West Virginia	495	498	+3	+0.0[*]
Wisconsin	240	400	+160	+66.7
Wyoming	320	425	+105	+32.8

[*]less than ±0.001 change

Source: Pennsylvania Municipal Police Officer's Education and Training Commission, Hersery, Pennsylvania.

vice" training in order to keep up with the constantly changing demands of their jobs and to prepare for new assignments or promotions within the police department. Training must be relevant, job-related and focused on the realities of police work rather than the myths associated with it. Training is an ongoing process, not a one-shot activity. New knowledge, new procedures, new equipment and new jobs make training an absolute necessity in an ever-changing world. Effective training provides the police officer with an anchor for stability in a sea of change. It facilitates adaptability and helps to guard against human obsolescence in the workplace (Mathis and Jackson, 1991).

Relevant and effective training motivates mature police officers to work harder. Employees who really understand their jobs and have the skills needed to handle them are more likely to have high morale. They tend to see a much closer relationship between their own effort and successful performance on the job (Sayles and Strauss, 1981). As a result, they are usually willing to invest more of their time, effort, energy and talent in activities designed to accomplish the mission, goals and objectives of the police department. Well-trained police officers are competent and have confidence in themselves. They command respect. Qualified personnel plus a strong training program equals effective police work. Training is an investment in human resources and the passageway to police professionalism.

Training, in its many forms, is the one essential tool that is required to create, enhance and maintain effective police performance (Alpert and Dunham, 1992). The building blocks for a sound law enforcement training program are anchored by two common assumptions: (1) it should incorporate the appropriate mission statement and ethical considerations and (2) the training should be focused on what an officer actually does on a daily basis (Alpert and Smith, 1990).

While there may be some disagreement with the model, police work can be viewed as an emerging profession. It possesses, to one degree or another, all of the characteristics normally associated with a profession:

1. Social Grant of Authority. Members of the profession have the privilege, authority or license to practice a specialized occupation.

2. Autonomy of Practice. Members of the profession exercise a great deal of discretion in their work and are not subject to criticism by those outside their occupational group.

3. Systematic Body of Knowledge. Members of the profession are expected to have special competence because they have acquired a clearly defined body of knowledge and unique skills through specialized education and training.

4. Ongoing Education/Training. Members of the profession have an obligation to continue their education (theory) and to upgrade their skills (through training) in order to meet the needs of clients and the profession.

5. Self-Regulation. Members of the profession are expected to govern themselves by setting standards and controlling the entry of newcomers into the occupation.

6. Code of Ethics. Members of the profession formulate, internalize and live by an occupation-specific code of ethics designed to regularize relationships between members and/or clients (see Police Code of Conduct in Chapter 11).

7. Service Orientation. Members of the profession are expected to emphasize service to society and, when necessary, to willingly set aside their own personal interests to provide essential services.

There seems to be no clear-cut distinction between professional and nonprofessional occupations. The police appear to be somewhere in the middle of the continuum between fully professional and completely nonprofessional. There is no reason why dedicated police officers cannot, given adequate leadership, raise their occupation a few more notches up the scale of professionalism (Stone and DeLuca, 1985). They will need to emphasize selective recruitment, positive discipline, adequate supervision and effective life-long training. Formal courses and seminars dealing with topics like criminal law, violent death investigation, domestic intervention, interpersonal relations, principles of supervision, civil liability and so forth should be made available to all personnel on a regular basis.

In spite of the fact that training is considered to be the most important process for ensuring organizational efficiency, effectiveness and productivity, most police departments spend only about one percent of their budget on training programs. When municipal budgets are frozen or cut, even this meager amount is not safe. The training "line item" is often the first to go. Richard Holden (1994) has argued that the gross underfunding of the training function borders on criminal negligence. No community can expect adequate policing from untrained police officers regardless of their dedication. Police officers cannot legitimately claim full professional status until they resolve the training dilemma. In an era of deficit spending and cutback management, finding more money and administrative support for training may be an impossible dream.

The police department has a dual and interrelated responsibility to the community it was created to protect and serve and to the members of its workforce. The department has an obligation to develop its personnel to their full potential (Whisenand and Rush, 1993). Well-managed police departments achieve maximum productivity through people. They strive to create in all employees an awareness that their best efforts are essential and that they will (if they make a meaningful contribution) share in the rewards of success (Peters and Waterman, 1982).

The remainder of this chapter will discuss the mechanics of police training. The first section is for general information. It will explore the function and structure of formal preemployment, preservice and in-service training programs. Section two will analyze the sergeant's role as a counselor, coach and trainer. The third section will focus on the training needs of sergeants and other supervisory personnel.

Formal Police Training Programs

Until quite recently, professional police trainers could describe their world in fairly simple terms. There were two types of training: (1) recruit training and (2) in-service training. Recruit training was designed for newly sworn police personnel who, having met all the minimum qualifications for appointment, were commissioned as police officers contingent upon the successful completion of a rigorous (preservice) basic police training program. In-service training, on the other hand, focused almost exclusively on the occupational and professional development of certified police officers through various specialized job-related training programs. Things have been changing, however, and a new term must now be added to the lexicon of the police trainer, **preparatory preemployment police training**.

Preparatory preemployment police training is gaining popularity in many areas of the country. This term is used to describe an alternative approach to basic training. It is based on a proprietary vocational education model in which a civilian trainee pays tuition and fees to cover the cost of training in an attempt to access a career in law enforcement. These basic police training programs are offered by independent academies that are not affiliated with a police department. Some of these academies are operated by academic institutions; others are private, profit-driven businesses. The California Commission on Police Officer Standards and Training adopted an administrative policy allowing preparatory preemployment police training in 1962. Other states have experimented with the idea. Many conservative police administrators have opposed the concept of preparatory preemployment police training, and politicians have ignored it. The economic crunch of the 1980s muted much of the opposition and has given preparatory preemployment police training new impetus.

Reaganomics ushered in a new era of fiscal restraint and innovative programming. As the flow of federal dollars has been reduced, state and local governments have been faced with a hard choice: raise taxes or cut basic public services. Many local governments have chosen to cut back (or "retrench") rather than to risk further erosion in the tax base. In many economically depressed areas, postemployment (publicly financed) recruit training for police personnel has now become an endangered species. The Minnesota Peace Officer Standards and Training Board pointed out:

> Changing times and new economic realities have resulted in the phasing out of this kind of training. Local government bodies are increasingly reluctant to absorb the training costs of their peace officers, and the responsibility has now come to rest squarely on the shoulders of the potential officer. There is nothing unusual or unfair about this when you consider that aspirants to other professions have always had to personally finance their own lengthy training and education. The shift away from subsidized training for peace officers coincides with the overall change in emphasis from narrow training goals to the broader ideals of general education (Minnesota POST, 1987).

Preparatory preemployment police training represents a radical shift in public policy. It is a new paradigm in which those interested in police work are expected to utilize their own resources in order to prepare for a career in municipal law enforcement.

Very little has been written about preparatory preemployment police training. In most cases, national commissions have failed to mention the concept and state laws governing police officer standards and training remain silent on the subject. Roosevelt Shepherd and Thomas Austin (1986) believe that this is merely an oversight and not a rejection of the idea. They argue that state training commissions almost always have the administrative power and rule-making authority to allow preparatory preemployment police training. In fact, at least 17 states (34 percent) already permit it in one form or another. Several other states are in the process of exploring various policy options that would permit substitution of state-regulated college-based training for the traditional postemployment police academy.

Shepherd and Austin, after an exhaustive review of the literature and a careful analysis of the data derived from their applied research in the Commonwealth of Pennsylvania, have debunked many of the siege mentality myths used by opponents of preparatory preemployment police training. Based on their new theoretical model, police personnel (like all other aspiring professionals) should be expected to finance their own preemployment education and training as a condition of acceptance into the profession. Preparatory police training would no longer be controlled by line agencies. New police personnel should be recruited, screened and selected based on the quality, reputation and placement record of the "approved" basic police training academy they choose to attend. Shepherd and Austin view preparatory preemployment police training as a pathway to professionalism.

As police work moves closer to achieving **professional status**, there will be an increasing emphasis on preparatory preemployment police training. While the concept appears to be sound, it is not a panacea. Unbridled optimism and uncontrolled experimentation could lead to major quality control problems. Preparatory preemployment training programs should be monitored carefully in order to assess their overall impact on the delivery of police services.

Most of the police recruits in this country still attend traditional postemployment police academies. In addition to its training function, the academy also serves as a critical step in the employee selection process. Trainees who don't make it through the academy because of academic or adjustment problems (related to their suitability for police work) usually lose their jobs as well. Failure to successfully complete basic training is grounds for dismissal in almost all jurisdictions. In most civil service systems, the trainee can be separated from the police department with or without cause at any time during the probationary period.

All states encourage, and most actually require, basic training for all municipal police personnel. While it has not been fully implemented, Police Standard 16.3 (National Advisory Commission on Criminal Justice Standards and Goals, 1973) has been a catalyst for change. It recommended the following:

Every police agency should take immediate steps to provide training for every police employee prior to his first assignment within the agency, prior to his assignment to any specialized function requiring additional training, and prior to his promotion. In states where preparatory training is currently mandated by state law, every police agency should provide all such training by 1975; in other such states, every agency should provide all such training by 1978.

1. Every state should require that every sworn police employee satisfactorily complete a minimum of 400 hours of basic police training. In addition to traditional basic police subjects, the training should include:

    a. Instruction in law, psychology, and sociology specifically related to interpersonal communication, the police role and the community the police employee will serve.
    b. Assigned activities away from the training academy to enable the employee to gain specific insight into the community, criminal justice system and local government.
    c. Remedial training for individuals who are deficient in their training performance but who, in the opinion of the training staff and the employing agency, demonstrate potential for satisfactory performance.
    d. Additional training by the employing agency in its policies and procedures, if basic police training is not administered by that agency.

2. During the first year of employment with a police agency, and in addition to the minimum basic police training, every police agency should provide full-time sworn police employees with additional formal training, coached field training, and supervised field experience through methods that include at least:

    a. A minimum of four months of field training with a sworn police employee who has been certified as a training coach.
    b. Rotation in field assignments to expose the employee to varying operational and community experiences.
    c. Documentation of employee performance in specific field experiences to assist in evaluating the employee and to provide feedback on training program effectiveness.
    d. Self-paced training material, such as correspondence courses, to assist the employee in acquiring additional job knowledge and in preparing for subsequent formal training.

e. Periodic meetings between the coach, the employ-ee, and the training academy staff to identify additional training needs and to provide feedback on training program effectiveness.

f. A minimum of two weeks' additional training at the training academy six months after completion of basic training and again after one year's employment in field duties.

3. Every police agency should provide every unsworn police employee with sufficient training to enable him to perform satisfactorily his specific assignment and to provide him with a general knowledge of the police role and the organization of the police agency.

4. Every police agency should provide every police employee newly assigned to a specialized task the specific training he needs to enable him to perform the task acceptably.

5. Every police agency should provide sufficient training to enable every newly promoted employee to perform the intended assignment satisfactorily.

Most states have been content to specify the curriculum for recruit training and to leave implementation of the remaining recommendations in the hands of the individual police departments.

Once trainees have successfully completed their basic training, they are normally assigned to the uniformed patrol division. In small police departments this may signal the end of the formal training process. At this point, the sergeant assumes a traditional role as a counselor, coach and trainer. Many of the larger and more progressive police departments have adopted **Field Training Officer** (FTO) programs similar to the one developed by the San Jose, California, Police Department in 1972. The program was staffed by officers, sergeants and lieutenants who were selected based on their interest, desire, formal education, maturity, ability to teach, experience and skill in establishing positive interpersonal relationships. All the personnel assigned to the project were required to complete an intensive Field Training Officer course.

Field training officers are usually responsible for the post-academy training of all probationary police officers. They conduct performance audits in the field. The evaluation process includes an extensive review and reporting system. Probationary police officers are evaluated on their appearance, attitudes, job-related knowledge (laws, department policies, standard operating procedures, etc.), on-the-job performance and interpersonal relationships. Evaluations are anchored to actual performance rather than subjective judgments (Swank and Conser, 1983).

The FTO approach is a behaviorally based training process. It is designed to give recruits the specialized tools of their occupation in a structured environ-

ment. They are then evaluated on exactly how well they use those tools in real-life situations. It is a delicate and complex process. While the cost (in terms of budget, effort and displaced work) may be high, the benefits (in terms of efficiency, effectiveness and productivity) justify the expense. There is, according to Ronald Lynch (1995), an old saying: "If you think training is expensive, try ignorance!"

The FTO concept represents an alternative to traditional **pedagogy** that involves the one-way transfer of knowledge from the instructor to the student. It is rooted in **andragogy,** which promotes the mutual involvement of students and instructors in a learning process stressing analytical and conceptual skills in practical problem-solving situations (Roberg and Kuykendall, 1993).

While they may not be fully trained before they start to work, it is safe to say that almost all the police officers in this country receive some type of job-related basic training. This represents a shift in priorities and is a far cry from the benign neglect so common in the past.

Police training cannot cease once the basic program has been provided to recruits. Tenured police officers with civil service status must be given continuous **in-service training** in an effort to help them maintain adequate performance as well as to prepare them to cope with change and developments in their field (Bennett and Hess, 1992). The National Advisory Commission on Criminal Justice Standards and Goals (1973) was avant-garde in terms of in-service training; it recommended the following:

> Every police agency should, by 1975, provide for annual and routine training to maintain effective performance throughout every sworn employee's career.
>
> 1. Every police agency should provide 40 hours of formal in-service training annually to sworn police employees up to and including captain or its equivalent. This training should be designed to maintain, update, and improve necessary knowledge and skills. Where practical and beneficial, employees should receive training with persons employed in other parts of the criminal justice system, local government, and private business when there is a common interest and need.
>
> 2. Every police agency should recognize that formal training cannot satisfy all training needs and should provide for decentralized training. To meet these day-to-day training needs, every police agency should provide each police station with:
>
>   a. As soon as practicable, but not later than 1978, a minimum of one police employee who is a state certified instructor.
>   b. Audiovisual equipment compatible with training material available to the police agency.

    c.   Home study materials available to all police employees.

    d.   Periodic one-day on-duty training programs directed at the specific needs of the police employees.

3.   Every police agency should ensure that the information presented during annual and routine training is included, in part, in promotion examinations and that satisfactory completion of training programs is recorded in the police employee's personnel folder in order to encourage active participation in these training programs.

Due to the incremental nature and situational focus of in-service police training, it has been very difficult for most police departments to comply with Standard 16.5. While almost everyone gives it lip service, the track record has been mixed. Affluent communities tend to emphasize in-service training. In economically distressed communities it is often considered to be a luxury. In far too many cases, in-service training has taken a back seat to other more pressing needs.

Complexity, liability and professionalism have combined to create renewed emphasis on continuing education and formal in-service training for police personnel. In-service training programs normally range from one day to two weeks in length and may, depending on their rigor, carry college credit. The training is available from a variety of different sources:

1.   In-house police instructors

2.   Department police academies

3.   Regional police training centers

4.   State-level police organizations

5.   Federal law enforcement agencies

6.   Nonprofit service organizations

7.   Professional police associations

8.   Independent training consultants

9.   Private for-profit organizations

10.   Home study/correspondence courses

11.   College-related training centers

Effective in-service police training is tailored to meet the needs of the trainee and designed to maximize learning. Effective trainers are eclectic and use various teaching techniques (e.g., lecture, guided group discussion, computer-assisted instruction, computer modeling and interactive simulations). Police officers are able to choose from a wide variety of courses like those identified below:

1. Human Resource Management

2. Behavioral Aspects of Interviewing

3. Criminal Law Update

4. Stress Management for Police

5. Computer-Assisted Research Techniques

6. Street Drug Identification Seminar

7. Intelligence Gathering and Analysis

Florida currently requires all sworn police personnel to obtain a minimum of 40 hours of in-service training, at a state certified academy, every four years. There is an ongoing effort to require 40 hours per year. Pennsylvania is moving in a similar direction. A bill reauthorizing the Municipal Police Officers' Training and Education Commission also requires 40 hours of in-service training on an annual basis.

The Training Process

Training is something like an inchoate crime. It is never fully accomplished and is always in the process. Training is designed to focus knowledge so that it can be applied in specific situations. Department-sponsored police training has two very basic goals: (1) improve the officer's on-the-job performance and (2) develop the officer's capacity to handle even higher levels of responsibility. In other words, training should help the individual do a better job while preparing that same person for even more challenging duties. Training is unique in that it promotes both change and the unity of purpose within an organization. **Six philosophical planks** provide a foundation for modern police training (Whisenand and Rush, 1993).

1. Motivation plus acquired skills lead to positive action.

2. Learning is a complex phenomenon that is dependent upon the motivation and capacity of the individual, the norms of the training group, the instructional methods and behavior of the trainers, and the climate of the police department.

3. Improvement on the job is a complex function of factors like individual learning, the group shared expectations of the work force and the general climate of the department.

4. Training is the tripartite responsibility of the police department, the trainer and the trainee.

5. Training is a continuous process that serves as a vehicle for consistently updating the knowledge, attitudes and skills of the department's human resources.

6. Training is a continuous process and method for consistently improving the capacity of individual officers to act as a team.

Training, in its formal sense, is a consciously selected means to a particular end. Managers use various training techniques in order to achieve their specific objectives. These managerial objectives can be broken down into five general categories. The categories are as follows:

1. **Orientation.** An orientation introduces trainees to and provides them with a general overview of an issue, problem, procedure or process. The police academy's basic training curriculum is designed to give rookies an orientation to real police work as opposed to the Dirty Harry stereotype.

2. **Indoctrination.** Indoctrination is a deliberate attempt to inculcate acceptable perspectives, attitudes, norms and values in police trainees on the assumption that they will become internal control mechanisms capable of regulating the trainee's personal conduct and job-related behavior. Police instructors teach the right way to do things, reward conformity and emphasize the negative consequences of deviant behavior.

3. **Dissemination.** Dissemination involves the intentional and structured communication of specialized information needed by the trainee to function as an efficient, effective and productive member of the department or a specialized unit within the department. For example, a "Violent Death Investigation" seminar for patrol officers is designed to provide trainees with information relevant to their critical role in the preliminary investigation.

4. **Skill Aquisition.** Skill acquisition training gives the police trainee the opportunity to master a special skill through simulation or repetition. Combat shooting on the firing range allows the trainee to interact with an instructor and promotes proactive learning by doing.

5. **Problem Solving.** Problem-solving exercises require all police trainees to use comparative analysis in an effort to make decisions that fall within the range of solutions acceptable to management. The "in-basket" evaluation component of an assessment center is designed to judge each officer's promotability based on the overall quality of the decisions being made by that particular person.

Case Study

Sergeant Ray Whittle

Raymond Q. Whittle, a former detective, was promoted to sergeant and assigned to serve as a shift supervisor in a very progressive and well-financed police department. Sergeant Whittle is an intelligent and demanding person who becomes impatient with subordinates who are slow on the uptake. He is often insensitive to the needs of others. Consequently, he is having a very difficult time relating to his subordinates.

The department has adopted a sophisticated computerized Violent Criminal Apprehension Program (VICAP). The success of the program depends on the data base. Since much (if not most) of the data will come from the coded reports filed by patrol officers, Sergeant Whittle has volunteered to conduct a 3-hour training module on VICAP for all personnel assigned to the Patrol Division.

One day, without advance notice, all available patrol personnel were summoned to the assembly room at police headquarters. At this point, Sergeant Whittle began the lecture on VICAP. He went to great lengths to explain the technical aspects of the computer and how computers are used to process data, match MOs and identify suspects. He told them how to fill out the coded police report forms. Sergeant Whittle entertained only those questions that were directly related to the mechanics of VICAP and relied on technical jargon to outline the parameters of the project. He ended the training session by telling the officers that disciplinary action would be taken if they failed to fill out the coded report forms properly.

Three weeks later, the sergeant in charge of the data processing center contacted the chief of police and informed him that there were problems with VICAP. He complained that patrol personnel were skewing the data base. They were not filling out the coded report forms in the proper manner. He reminded the chief that computers are only as good as the quality of data base. The sergeant handed the chief a cartoon depicting a computer simulation of a horse that looked like a camel. The caption read: "Garbage in; Garbage out!"

The chief has asked you, as his administrative assistant, to find out what caused the problem and how to correct it. After discussing Sergeant Whittle's training session with some of the officers who attended it, you have come to the conclusion that he committed some basic errors. You must now write a report to the chief of police. Explain what went wrong (errors) and what should be done to correct the situation.

The success or failure of any training program will ultimately depend on the relevance of the training, the instructional methodology that is used, the capacity and receptivity of the trainee and the teaching ability of the trainer.

Adequate training ensures that police personnel have the necessary skills to perform well. This makes management's job much easier. It also lets the individual officer know that the police department and its managers are interested in developing people. According to Galvin and Sokolove (1989), it is absolutely imperative that police officers feel a sense of growth and development in their jobs because it contributes to a sense of well being. This often makes the difference between those who "graze from the public budget trough" and those who utilize their full potential at work to produce consistently high quality law enforcement services.

The training of police personnel is an expensive proposition, and yet many police departments throw their training dollars at what they perceive to be a problem without attempting to discover exactly what kind of training is actually needed. In order to ensure the relevance of training, there should be some type of task analysis. A task analysis is a detailed examination of a job and the role played by the employee in that job. This analysis aids in identifying all the tasks performed by the person holding that position. Once the role, tasks and job have been clearly defined, the training needs will be fairly easy to assess (Chruden and Sherman, 1984).

One of the first major task analyses involving police officers was **Project STAR** (System Training and Analysis of Requirements). Project STAR focused on the roles, tasks and training needs of police personnel in California, Michigan, New Jersey and Texas. The researchers found that police officers performed 13 roles fulfilled by 33 unique tasks (Smith et al., 1974). After the individual tasks were identified, specific performance objectives and a corresponding curriculum were developed. The curriculum was designed to provide police officers with the training necessary to ensure successful performance of the tasks. Through **task analysis**, police managers can now determine whether or not a training course provides the knowledge and skills required to do the job. If the training is inadequate to meet the needs of police officers, police managers have an obligation to reexamine the training methods that are being used or to update the training curriculum.

Project STAR spawned other task analysis protocols for use in law enforcement. An extensive task analysis project was undertaken in the Miami area in the early 1980s. The project produced a comprehensive database that led to a thorough curriculum revision. Based on the results of the analysis, Miami-Dade Community College revised its basic law enforcement and field training officer programs. It also factored job-relevant tasks (as standards against which to measure performance) into the entry-level assessment center process. The task analysis project has been credited with enhancing the efficiency, effectiveness and overall productivity of municipal police personnel throughout the area. The job task analysis prototype developed in South Florida has been adopted by and implemented in other areas of the country. Task analysis is action-oriented

applied research keyed to law enforcement's mission, goals and objectives. It also insures that the training experience is job-related and legally defensible.

The South Florida project discussed above was funded by the Law Enforcement Assistance Administration (LEAA) and was carried out under the direction of James D. Stinchcomb. The research data was derived by way of an assessment center process designed for entry-level police officers. The researchers identified and grouped 102 specific knowledge areas, skills and abilities required of entry-level police personnel. Based on analysis of the data, the researchers isolated eight traits or characteristics applicants need in order to become successful law enforcement officers.

1. **Directing Others.** Police officers must be able to initiate action and assume control of the situation. They assist, guide, direct and control others on a daily basis.

2. **Interpersonal Skills.** Police officers are expected to deal with the needs, feelings and problems of people in a courteous and considerate way that is consistent with the use of discretion in exercising police authority. Demeanor is a critical variable in successful police work.

3. **Perception.** Police work takes place in an environment of ambiguity. Police officers must be observant and must be able to identify and understand critical elements in a situation, recognize circumstances that require immediate action and comprehend the implications of that action.

4. **Decisionmaking.** Police officers must use logic and sound judgment in making a myriad of important decisions. Their decisions must reflect an understanding of the facts, definition of the problem, consideration of alternatives and formulation of solutions that are consistent with the department's policies, procedures, rules and regulations.

5. **Decisiveness.** Police officers are required to make on-the-spot decisions and take decisive action, based on the needs of the situation. They are expected to use judgment and must be able to defend their decisions or actions when confronted by others.

6. **Adaptability.** Police officers must be flexible in dealing with dynamic situations. They must be prepared to alter their course of action when there is a change in personal or environmental circumstances.

7. **Oral Communication.** Police officers must be able to communicate effectively with other people. Language skills, vocabulary, grammar, eye contact and a strong voice are invaluable assets.

8. **Written Communication.** The ability to write clearly and effectively is absolutely essential. Much of the police officer's work will be in vain unless it is backed up by clear, concise, accurate and well-written records that can withstand scrutiny in a confrontational system of law (Stinchcomb, 1984).

Performance objectives formulated as the result of a task analysis give direction to the training process and motivate trainees as long as they are relevant and achievable. Trainers must then specify the content of the curriculum and demonstrate exactly how the expected outcomes are related to the performance objectives. The next step is to select an appropriate **training strategy** or strategies (including a style and methodology) that will produce the desired outcome (see Figure 14.3). The success or failure of the training program will depend largely on the communication skills and teaching ability of the trainer. Once the training has been completed, various types of evaluative data should be analyzed to determine the overall effectiveness of the training in accomplishing its objectives. This data, known as feedback, is factored into the training process so that necessary and appropriate adjustments can be made (Fay, 1988).

Figure 14.3
Elements of the Training Process

1. Setting relevant, precise and achievable police training objectives.

2. Specifying the content of the training curriculum vis-a-vis police performance objectives.

3. Selecting the most appropriate police training strategy.

4. Adopting a suitable style and effective methodology for police training.

5. Measuring outcomes achieved by the participants in the police training program.

6. Evaluating the police training in terms of approach, content and effectiveness.

7. Factoring positive and negative feedback into the police training process.

Police trainers (and first-line supervisors or managers who counsel, coach and train subordinates) may perform their training function more effectively if they are aware of and understand the **principles of learning and teaching** that have emerged from studies by educators and psychologists. Findings from these studies clearly indicate that people learn according to some fairly well-established rules (Iannone, 1994). Some of these principles have special significance for police trainers and supervisors:

1. **Motivation.** The readiness to learn is one of the most important factors in successful training. A trainee is motivated to learn when (for whatever reason) conditions establish an attitude favorable to learning or the mastery of a special skill. Motivated trainees learn more than unmotivated trainees.

2. **Effect.** When a trainee is in a state of readiness in a more-or-less favorable environment, effective learning is possible. The effect of success in learning creates a pleasurable feeling of satisfaction. Consequently, the trainee strives to maintain this satisfaction. Thus, one continues to learn.

3. **Individualism.** Successful training is tailored to meet the needs of the officers as well as those of the police department. Every effort should be made to explain why the participants were selected for the program and what they can expect during the training process. Belief in and respect for the individual is the hallmark of good training.

4. **Relevancy.** All training should be directly related to the employee's current position or future job. Police officers should know the objectives of the training. They should also know what is expected of them, why they have been asked to learn the material and how their new learning will affect their work situation within the police department.

5. **Active Learning.** Proactive learning by doing is considered to be the best form of police training. New research shows that people learn more when they are directly involved in some type of "hands-on" training. Being able to apply what has been learned is, in and of itself, a positive reinforcement. As a general rule, positive results produce positive reinforcement and a heightened state of motivation (Preston and Zimmerer, 1983).

6. **Realism.** Police trainers should make the learning process as close to the real thing as possible (Plunkett, 1992). Realism piques interest and helps resolve the conflicts between theory and practice. When it is not feasible to conduct on-the-job training, simulation can be used effectively. The trainer should use examples and situations that accurately reflect actual problems the police officers are likely to encounter. The new knowledge or skill should be applied to actual situations in the workplace as soon as possible.

7. **Primacy.** Training should always come before, rather than after, the fact. Police trainers know that things learned first create a strong impression in the mind that is very difficult to change. Consequently, training police personnel how to perform properly the first time through is extremely important. Poor work

habits that are acquired first skew the learning process and make remediation very difficult.

8. **Recency.** Attitudes, skills or knowledge learned recently are, if reinforced, remembered best. Police trainers should use summarization, frequent review and repetition as tools to ensure that the learning is retained. Good communication and strong interpersonal skills are an asset to the trainer.

9. **Repetition.** Repetition builds habits which, if correct, lead to success, a sense of satisfaction and a desire to repeat those things that produce pleasure. Repeated use of what has been learned strengthens the trainee's subsequent performance. The failure to use what has been learned, on the other hand, weakens performance. This is referred to as "the law of use and disuse" (Hilgard and Bower, 1966). Nathan Iannone (1994) has noted that the better a trainee learns by using knowledge or a special skill, the longer that person will retain what has been learned. Since every learner forgets, to varying degrees over time, continuous retraining is required.

10. **Reinforcement.** Unless there is a reason to remember information or skills, trainees will forget them. Studies indicate that people forget 50 percent of what they hear and 25 percent of what they experience almost immediately. Practice, repetition and retraining are good reinforcers. They are usually built into an effective training program. More reinforcement is required, however. Management must emphasize the importance of training through the selective allocation of rewards. Training should be considered a pathway to tenure, promotion and pay raises.

11. **Feedback.** Feedback is a very important two-way street in law enforcement. Police officers need to know where they stand in the department and what they can do to improve their professional status. Since training is expensive and very time-consuming, management needs to know about the relevancy and quality of its training effort. By working together they can accomplish the goals of training, which are: (1) to provide better service to the community through improved on-the-job performance, and (2) to develop each officer's capacity to handle higher levels of responsibility within the police department.

Ongoing and effective police training, utilizing the principles discussed above, is the ticket to police professionalism. Police administrators are responsible for ensuring the quality of departmental training and have an obligation to protect training from the overzealous budget-cutter's axe.

Police officers graduating from training academies and going on the job often complain that the training given in the classroom was not realistic prepa-

ration for subsequent field assignments. This tends to undermine practitioner confidence in the training process and gives financially strapped police administrators an excuse to reduce funding for training. Great care must be taken to make sure that training is both relevant and effective. Lawrence Steinmetz and Ralph Todd (1986) believe that many of the problems associated with training could be resolved if trainers and supervisors followed a few fairly simple rules. Those rules are summarized below:

Errors to Avoid

1. **Trying to Teach Too Much.** Don't teach a complex task as one unit. Break it down into understandable parts. Praise those who perform the task correctly. Be prepared to work collaboratively with those in need of help.

2. **Trying to Teach Too Fast.** Don't push employees beyond their individual learning speed. Haste wastes human resources.

3. **Lack of Communication Concerning Training Plans.** Have formal plans established for training and let subordinates know what they are. The best surprise is no surprise.

4. **Failure to Recognize Individual Differences.** Do a careful analysis of trainee strengths and weaknesses as they relate to learning the task. Adjust the instructional methodology accordingly.

5. **Failure to Provide Practice Time.** Give employees time to practice a task in order to develop a proficiency before being required to do it on a regular basis. Practice enhances performance.

6. **Failure to Show Employees the Big Picture.** Trainees should see how their job fits in with the rest of the organization's work and exactly how important their efforts are to the success of the whole operation.

7. **Failure to Give Positive Reinforcement.** External and internal reinforcements work together much more effectively than either one does independently. Both serve as motivators, however.

8. **Intimidation of Employees.** Some people are ineffective as trainers because they tend to intimidate employees. The best way to ensure that there is no intimidation is to utilize instructors who understand the nature of training, who know what is going on with their personnel and who are in a position to give technical advice likely to be accepted by others.

9. **Lack of Common Vocabulary.** Use only language that is designed to help the trainee understand what is being taught. Avoid the use of language that will confuse the employee. Define esoteric as well as technical terms.

10. **The Pygmalion Effect.** Always make sure that your expectations for the employee are both realistic and appropriate. Do not prejudge a trainee's learning ability as being negative ("horns") or positive ("halo") before assessing actual performance. Skewed perceptions invariably lead to an erroneous evaluation.

While these are not earthshaking recommendations, they tend to humanize the training process. They focus on the interpersonal relations between the trainer and the trainee. Under these circumstances, the trainer becomes a developer of human resources rather than someone who merely exercises power over the police officer.

Training Cycle

There are four parts to a successful training effort. The **training cycle** consists of the following components:

1. **Identifying Training Needs.** Supervisors and managers scan the environment in such a way that they know when performances are not meeting expectations or standards. They compare performances to standards on a regular basis. Training becomes necessary when and where significant differences exist. These perceptions are translated into a list of tasks to be taught.

2. **Preparing Training Objectives.** Before training can take place or a person can learn, the trainer and the trainee must share common objectives. These objectives should be in writing and should state as clearly as possible what the trainee is expected to be able to do, the conditions under which the learner is expected to do it and how well that particular task is to be done. Criteria represent the standards the trainee must be able to meet in order to give a satisfactory performance.

3. **Preparing the Training Program.** Once the training needs have been identified and specific objectives have been articulated, those responsible for the training need to flesh out the instructional program by answering some questions concerning WHO (who is to do the training and who is to be trained); WHEN (when and how much time will be set aside for the training); WHERE (the specific physical area and equipment that will be needed for the training); HOW (in what chronological order will the tasks be taught and what specific methods of instruction are

to be used); and HOW MUCH (the amount of money and/or other resources that will be required to ensure a successful training effort).

4. **Conducting and Evaluating the Training.** Once all of the planning and preparation has been completed, execution begins. Effective training is designed to demonstrate the appropriate way of performing given tasks, permit trainees to apply what has been taught under real or simulated conditions, and elicit an evaluation as to whether or not the trainee is capable of performing all of the essential tasks taught and at the expected level of quality. Providing trainees with frequent and immediate feedback lets them know if their performance is acceptable or not. It also helps employees spot their own mistakes and gives them an opportunity to improve their own performance. Frequent and immediate feedback permits trainers to assess the effectiveness of the training effort and reteach the material if necessary (Plunkett, 1992).

Training Methodologies

There are a number of different approaches to training. Each has its advantages and disadvantages. The training methodology that is selected will depend on the human resources to be trained, the type of facilities that are available, costs (in relation to the funds allocated), the basic philosophy of the instructional personnel and the urgency of the situation. There is no ideal approach or single method that can be used effectively under all circumstances. Some of the more common **instructional methods** are listed below:

1. On-the-job training

2. Classroom instruction

3. Self-directed study

4. Role playing

5. Programmed learning

6. Job rotation

Training methods are the instructional tools used by police trainers to accomplish their objectives in relation to the development of the department's human resources.

On-the-job training is also known as job instruction training. It is one of the most commonly used methods for training employees. Police officers, after initial recruit training, are often placed under the supervision of an experienced

person and allowed to learn by doing. This provides trainees with first-hand experience under normal working conditions. The Field Training Officer program is a very good example of this approach. There are drawbacks to on-the-job training, however. In less sophisticated police departments, the trial-and-error method can create a number of problems. It has been noted that "doctors bury their mistakes, while lawyers send theirs to jail." Unfortunately, untrained police officers do a little of both.

Classroom instruction is a standard feature in almost every police training program, and the lecture method is the mainstay of classroom-based training. Lecture is an easy and cost-effective way to handle the maximum number of trainees with a minimum number of instructors. Lecture, unless it is supplemented with discussion, demonstration, simulation and role playing, is more useful for conveying general information than it is for training. Lecture is one of the least effective teaching methods because it is tailored primarily for speed of presentation rather than the trainees' capacity to learn. The effectiveness of the lecture method is also affected by the complexity of the subject, the size of the class and the instructor's knowledge, technical proficiency, personality, interpersonal skills and overall teaching ability.

Self-directed study, or self-instruction, is probably the most cost-effective means available for developing the department's human resources. A topic (such as department policies, procedures, rules or regulations) is assigned and trainees are expected to learn the material on their own. Self-directed study is totally dependent on the motivation of the trainee. Lacking motivation or incentives provided by a trainer, many police officers simply will not take the time to learn. Most people need direction and interaction with significant others in order to acquire the knowledge and skills needed to function effectively in complex criminal justice organizations like police departments. While self-study should be encouraged, it cannot take the place of ongoing, job-related police training.

Special attention should be given to the use of interactive simulation or *role playing*. Role playing is designed to simulate, as much as possible, those incidents the trainee is likely to face while on the job. It gives trainees hands-on experience in a practical setting and permits them to experience real-life effects. The scope of the training is limited only by the imagination and ingenuity of the instructional staff (Iannone, 1994). Confronting the armed intruder, body search and vehicle stop simulations, for example, convey certain attitudes as they help trainees develop skills. The key to effective simulation training is problem identification, scenario planning, on-site management and feedback. Many police trainers are convinced that simulation is the most meaningful way for new recruits to learn how to perform work-related tasks and enhance their self-confidence. As of September 1, 1988, mandatory role playing simulations were incorporated into Pennsylvania's new basic police training curriculum.

Programmed learning, which is also called programmed instruction or PI, is a self-study method that has proven to be quite useful in transmitting information or skills that need to be learned in logical order. The "instructor" is a specially structured workbook, a teaching machine or a computer (Halloran, 1981).

A program is designed to break down the subject matter into highly organized and logical sequences that require continuous responses from the trainee. Answers are provided for a series of questions. Trainees check the answers to determine whether they made the correct choices. This provides the trainee with immediate feedback, positive reinforcement and accurate information. Programmed learning, especially the computer-assisted type, works well with technical information. It is also being used in skill-development programs like interactive "shoot/don't shoot" computerized range training simulations.

Job rotation is an important element in a comprehensive police personnel development program. It is designed to help recruits and in-service personnel understand the work of the whole organization through job rotation. Every officer is assigned to and trained for a tour of duty in each unit of the department. This provides the trainee with both a "generalist" orientation and specialized training. It works particularly well with recruits who have not begun to identify themselves with a single police function. Richard Holden (1994) has pointed out that job rotation introduces new officers to a variety of different people within the department and helps to facilitate their entry and acceptance into the organization. Job rotation protocols have been perfected in many large police departments that emphasize the development of their human resources.

Police departments throughout the country now supplement their training efforts with professionally produced video presentations obtained from the Law Enforcement Television Network (LETN) of Dallas, Texas. LETN provides video training units covering just about every aspect of modern police work. Various training segments are offered on a repetitive schedule on a 24-hour a day basis. LETN makes valid, affordable and documentable training available to its subscribers. More than 2,000 police departments currently purchase educational products and services from the Law Enforcement Television Network (Haley, 1992).

Good police trainers take their role as a developer of human resources seriously. They respect individual differences, master the subject they teach, base their training effort on recognized rules of learning and do their best to choose an appropriate training method. Regardless of the method they select, good trainers usually adopt an instructional protocol that includes: preparing, motivating, presenting, reviewing, applying, testing and reinforcing learned behavior. The **instructional protocol** (see Figure 14.4) is the heart of the teaching process.

The Police Sergeant's Role as a Trainer

The sergeant's primary job is to obtain results through people. They are judged on their ability to get those who work for them to help accomplish the department's mission, goals and objectives in an efficient and effective manner. Training is the most important tool available to help sergeants achieve this end.

There is no doubt that training is a universal responsibility of all first-line supervisors. Sergeants won't get far unless they fulfill their training duties. Supervision and training are always interdependent. Everything a supervisor

Figure 14.4
The Instructional Protocol

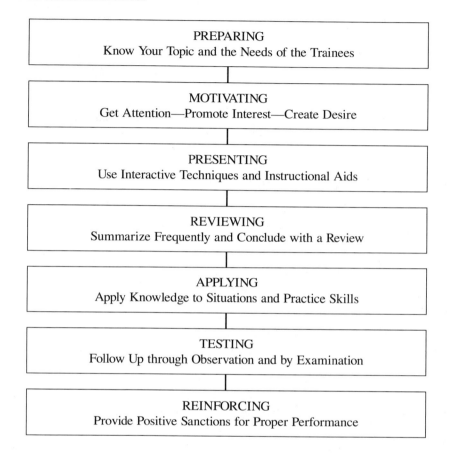

does in directing the work force has some element of training in it; conversely, every training activity involves an element of supervision. Supervision and training are inherent in the sergeant's role. Sergeants who take an active interest in their subordinates and perceive counseling, advising, coaching and teaching as part of their role make an incalculable contribution to the growth and development of the department's human resources.

Sergeants interact with their subordinates on a daily basis and, in most cases, are trusted by other police officers as street-level compatriots. Consequently, they are in an ideal position to influence the job-related behavior of the men and women who work for them. Mature sergeants who possess good interpersonal skills have the most influence. They are able to perform their training function in a low-key and nonthreatening manner. At the most elementary level, training takes place when the sergeant guides or assists subordinates in doing their work. In a more formal sense, training consists of guided interac-

tion, practice sessions, special seminars, planned courses or any other type of organized activity designed to produce a particular learning experience.

Good first-line supervisors tend to have what the late Douglas McGregor has referred to as a **Theory Y** orientation (Holden, 1994). They make certain assumptions about human beings and allow those assumptions to guide their behavior vis-à-vis their subordinates. Theory Y supervisors believe that:

1. Management is responsible for organizing the elements of productive enterprise, such as money, material, equipment and human resources, in order to achieve specified goals and objectives.

2. People are not, by their very nature, passive or resistant to the organization's needs. They become that way as the result of negative on-the-job experiences.

3. The motivation, potential for development, capacity for taking responsibility and readiness to direct behavior toward the organization's goals are all present in human beings. Supervisors don't put them there. In the final analysis, it is the sergeant's responsibility to make it possible for police officers to recognize and develop these characteristics for themselves.

4. The essential task of management and first-line police supervisors is to arrange the organization and methods of operation so that police officers can achieve their own goals by directing their efforts toward accomplishment of organizational objectives.

Modern police supervision is moving away from the view of individuals as static toward seeing them as being in process. The supervisor's job is to create opportunities, release potential, remove obstacles, encourage growth and provide guidance (Whisenand and Rush, 1993).

The Theory Y orientation, with its emphasis on developing employees beyond their present level, produces an empathetic supervisory style that treats police officers as professionals. Under these circumstances and based on a profession paradigm, they are often allowed to work out the details of their own job and to make many of the decisions concerning how it should be done. Since active learning is far more effective than passive learning, police officers benefit from resolving problems and making decisions for themselves. Training employees to govern themselves is an important concept in modern management.

In their capacity as developers of human resources, sergeants may be called upon to provide formal training to their subordinates. They normally conduct roll-call training and often are used to disseminate new department policies, procedures, rules and regulations. Sergeants use the principles of learning, instructional methods and teaching techniques that were discussed earlier to accomplish their objective. Much, if not most, of the training done by sergeants is informal, however. Sergeants train their subordinates by example. They serve as role models. In so doing, they set the ethical and professional tone for their

colleagues. Sergeants spend a great deal of their time counseling employees and coaching them on proper police procedures. They also give advice on how to handle delicate situations. In other words, sergeants are mentors.

Good sergeants monitor the professional growth and development of their personnel. When they detect a problem or a deficiency, they take immediate action to remedy the situation. If they do not have the counseling skills or training expertise to handle the problem, it will be referred up the ladder for an appropriate disposition.

Being a good supervisor/trainer is not an easy task. It requires ability, a positive attitude, human relations skills, **training** and a commitment to the concept of human resource development. While the job can be very frustrating, it has rewards. A few of the benefits are listed below:

1. You get to know your subordinates. The dual role helps you understand the needs, wants and potentials of those who work for you. This information can be factored into decisions concerning discipline, transfers, promotions and pay raises.

2. You promote good human relations. Through training, police officers gain self-confidence, pride and a sense of security. Your actions give them reasons to cooperate with their peers and the administration. Training helps establish unity of purpose, trust and mutual respect.

3. You feel good about your accomplishments. Training subordinates to do a good job produces a good feeling and motivates the supervisor to put forth even more effort. For all practical purposes, "success is its own reward."

4. You further your own career. As your subordinates grow in abilities, expertise and reputation, so will you. As your people look better, feel better and perform better, they enhance your reputation as a supervisor. Reputation is a product of positive training efforts.

5. You gain more time. Training helps to make people more confident and self-sufficient. As their performance improves, you will spend less time on corrections. This time can be invested in other supervisory functions like planning, organizing and coordinating. Coordinating is considered to be the essence of supervision if there is a well-trained work force.

There is no doubt that sergeants should be totally involved in and be held responsible for the professional development of all police personnel in the work unit. Whether or not sergeants assume this responsibility will depend on their status within the police department and the training they themselves have been given in order to fulfill this role.

Training First-Line Supervisors

Police sergeants have one of the most complex jobs in American law enforcement. They wear a multitude of different hats as they play a very complicated multifaceted role. Sergeants are the "spark plugs," so to speak, of the police establishment. Due to the strategic nature of their job, sergeants often determine the department's success or failure in achieving its mission, goals and objectives. There is no way for them to succeed in their role without adequate training. Unfortunately, comprehensive training for sergeants is the exception rather than the rule.

Police work is unique in many ways. Unlike most professions, there is no minimum educational standard. In addition, the only way to get ahead (in terms of pay and prestige) is to become a supervisor or a manager. Due to this vertical promotion system, many police officers are forced into roles for which they are not prepared and have no real interest. Consequently, it is not unusual for a newly promoted sergeant to revert to the role of a promoted patrol officer. While they may go through some of the rituals associated with the rank, they don't really do the job. Under these conditions, police work tends to become a rudderless enterprise consuming a huge amount of resources without meeting its basic obligation to protect and serve the local community. Ronald Lynch (1995) voiced his concern about this situation in his book, *The Police Manager*. He noted that police supervisors are often trained by the supervisor they served under, who, in many cases, may have been inadequate. Many police departments perpetuate inadequacy by not taking steps to improve the personnel development system. Formal training for first-line supervisors is all but nonexistent in most small police departments.

One way to deal with this problem is to create a realistic two-track career ladder system for sworn law enforcement personnel. The dual-ladder system refers to the side-by-side existence of the usual ladder of hierarchical rungs based on "rank" (and the exercise of authority), and another one consisting of "positions" like senior police officer or police agent (based on achievement) carrying successively higher salaries, more status, expanded responsibility and greater autonomy. This would help to reduce the drive of many officers to "get promoted." It would also motivate them to achieve higher levels of performance as police officers. The basic requirements for admission to the management track should be changed to reflect the qualifications needed by first-line supervisors (sergeants), middle-level managers (lieutenants) and police executives (captains and above). Those in the management track should be made to demonstrate that they have acquired the knowledge and skills needed to manage the department and its human resources. Extensive training will be required. The curriculum must emphasize human relations and the technical knowledge and management skills required to operate a complex criminal justice organization. A systemic change of this magnitude will take a commitment on the part of proactive police managers to plan for the future through the training process. Edward Thibault (1990) emphasized this point when he observed that police

supervisors can anticipate future events they have been trained to recognize as familiar situations. A proactive police department will try to synthesize planning and training so that its supervisors and managers will adopt a positive, plan-ahead philosophy.

Fortunately, more and more emphasis is now being placed on providing realistic and relevant first-line management training for supervisory personnel in police agencies at all levels of government. In one national study of 144 police agencies, including the two largest departments in each state, it was found that 97 percent provided in-house first-line supervisor training and that 78 percent made it mandatory. The training was provided before or at the time of promotion in 51 percent of the departments. The topics most frequently taught included the following (Armstrong and Longenecker, 1992):

1. Supervisory Techniques 95%
2. Use of the Disciplinary Process 92%
3. Counseling Techniques 80%
4. Performance Evaluation 79%
5. Motivational Strategies 73%
6. Management Theory 68%
7. Handling Empoyee Grievances 64%
8. Equal Employment Opportunity/Affirmative
   Action Compliance 62%
9. Personal Harassment Policies 52%

The State of California is very progressive and has been a leader in the field of police training. Its Peace Officer Standards and Training legislation (POST) can be traced back to 1959. There has been an emphasis on "supervisory training" since the inception of the program. All newly promoted supervisory personnel are now required to successfully complete an intensive 80-hour course in practical first-line supervision. The POST Supervisory Course Curriculum was revised and updated by subject matter experts in 1991.

After extensive applied research, California's Commission on Peace Officer Standards and Training came to the conclusion that one 80-hour course in police supervision was insufficient to prepare newly promoted supervisors for their very complicated role in contemporary law enforcement. The Commission reasoned that while many of the job tasks could be learned in the classroom, there were many, if not more, that needed to be taught in a one-on-one situation. The Commission's staff compiled a comprehensive Supervisory Training Guide. The new guide, similar to the Field Training Guide for new recruits, was developed as a tool for use by those responsible for training newly promoted first-line supervisors. It was designed to guide local police trainers through on-the-job training sequences in the proficiency required of supervisors performing specific assignments. The intent was to provide a desirable structure to reinforce the basic principles of supervision as well as the abilities needed to perform supervisory duties once the 80-hour supervisory course had been completed. Use of

the guide provides the police department with some consistency in on-the-job supervisor training and is an instrument to document abilities in the evaluation process. The required competencies were keyed to a thorough task analysis. The Supervisory Training Guide is broken down into the following categories:

1. General Supervision
2. Patrol Supervision
3. Jail Supervision
4. Traffic Supervision
5. Records Supervision
6. Investigative Supervision

Each category is subdivided into major instructional units related to specific field assignments. The units consist of very specific tasks. The trainer (an experienced supervisor or manager) is required to document and to sign off on each required task. Unit I of category 1 (General Supervision) outlines a sergeant's role in personnel development and training (see Figure 14.5).

The importance of training sergeants for their strategic role in police management should not be underestimated. An investment in training is an investment in the future.

The Payoff

Americans are beginning to think in terms of cost and benefit when it comes to their tax dollar. Police training is expensive, but the lack of it is ever more costly. One mistake by a police officer can take a human life, allow a predatory murderer to go free, generate massive civil disobedience or rob the community of confidence in the police establishment. Training is no panacea. Police work is so complex that there will always be mistakes; however, effective training will almost certainly reduce the frequency and severity of those mistakes. There is absolutely no doubt that effective police training benefits all concerned: the community, the police officer and the police department.

When the police are efficient, effective and productive (within constitutional constraints), the members of the community feel a collective sense of safety and security. They accept the police motto "to protect and serve" at face value and freely acquiesce to what is perceived as legitimate authority. While it is impossible to eliminate crime, delinquency and deviant behavior, the community expects the police to contain it at reasonable levels and to provide those essential services required to maintain the American way of life. Trained police officers function in harmony with and guarantee the survival of democratic institutions. The benefits of police training clearly outweigh the costs.

There is no doubt that effective training leads to competence and self-confidence. Police officers who have been nurtured, through training, to function as professionals and those who are permitted to have meaningful input into those decisions affecting them exhibit pride, positive discipline, high morale and an esprit de corps. Training is a catalyst for change and the harbinger of professional development. Well-trained police officers feel good about themselves and

Figure 14.5
General Supervision

General Supervision		
	Trainer's Initials and Date	
	Instructed by trainer	Knowledge or ability has been demonstrated by supervisor
Training: The supervisor will understand the responsibilities of being a trainer or subordinates.		
1. Understands the instructional role of the supervisor		
2. Understands the elements of the agency's field training program		
3. Understands the need to plan, schedule and conduct roll call training		
4. Understands the need to evaluate the training received by subordinates		
a. To ensure it is meeting training needs		
b. To ensure they are applying what they are learning		
5. Is aware of the training resources that are available within the agency		
6. Understands the career development process and provides guidance to subordinates		
7. Understands the concept of vicarious liability for failure to train		

see real value in their work. Consequently, they are more than willing to invest their time, energy, effort and expertise to make sure that the job they were hired to do gets done right. Here again, the benefits certainly outweigh the costs.

Civil Liability for the Failure to Train Police Personnel

Police departments (and individual police officers) are no longer immune to civil litigation. They can be sued for civil rights violations under federal law (42 U.S.C. Section 1983). Police departments are held to be liable if their policies or

procedures are responsible for any deprivation of rights enumerated in the U.S. Constitution. Police departments can also be sued for negligence in many states. The tort of negligence involves conduct (by an officer or a department) that presents an unreasonable risk of harm to others and which, in turn, is the proximate cause of the injury. State courts have extended liability to police departments when they have determined there was a duty to perform according to a reasonable standard of care and that the failure to perform appropriately caused a loss or injury. The major areas of concern are as follows:

1. Negligent Employment. It must be shown that the officer who caused the injury was unfit for appointment and the employer knew or should have known the person was unsuited for the job.

2. Negligent Supervision. It must be shown that a police manager had an affirmative duty to supervise an employee and that the failure to do so led to the injury or loss.

3. Negligent Training. It must be shown that the employer had improperly trained or failed to train police personnel in conceptual issues (like constitutional rights or minority relations) or skill areas such as pursuit driving, use of deadly force, firearms and first aid and that the injury or loss was the result.

Some of the compensatory and punitive damages awarded by the courts have been truly mind-boggling. Some communities have been forced into bankruptcy. Others have reached into the "deep pockets" of the local taxpayers. The courts have been sending a forceful message to police administrators: Hire the right people, train them and provide appropriate on-the-job supervision. Anything less is unacceptable. Under these circumstances, training is no longer a luxury. It is a legally mandated necessity.

The federal courts have ruled (in *Owens v. Haas*, 601 F.2d 1242 - 1979, and other cases) that local governments, agency administrators and supervisors have "an affirmative duty to train their employees." Failure to do so subjects them to **civil liability**. The following three cases help to illustrate this principle:

1. In *Harris v. The City of Canton,* 109 S. Ct. 1197 (1989), the plaintiff was arrested and transported to the police station in a police wagon. On arrival at the station, she was found sitting on the floor of the wagon. When asked if she needed medical assistance, she responded with an incoherent remark. During the booking process, Harris slumped to the floor. She was later released and taken by ambulance to a local hospital. The plaintiff was diagnosed as suffering from a variety of emotional ailments. Harris subsequently brought a Section 1983 action against the city and its officials claiming that they violated her constitutional right to due process of law. Evidence was presented which showed that shift commanders in the police department were authorized and

had the sole discretion to determine if a detainee required medical attention. Testimony was presented to establish the fact that shift commanders were not given any special training to make this determination. The District Court ruled in favor of the plaintiff on the medical claim, and the decision was affirmed by the Sixth Circuit Court of Appeals. The United States Supreme Court held that the failure to train can be the basis for liability under Section 1983 if that failure is based on "deliberate indifference" to the rights of citizens. The Court said "it may happen that in light of the duties assigned to specific officers or employees the need for more or different training is so obvious, and the inadequacy so likely to result in violation of constitutional rights, that the policy makers of the city can reasonably be said to have been deliberately indifferent to the need" (Kappeler, 1993).

2. In *Billings v. Vernal City*, U.S. District Court of Utah, C77-0295 (1982), a police officer on the job less than two weeks broke the arm of a plaintiff while trying to arrest him. The arrest was illegal. The officer had no probable cause to even attempt an arrest. The plaintiff filed suit, alleging that the chief of police was "grossly" negligent because he failed to train the officer correctly. The allegation was based on the fact that the officer was on duty before completing the basic training required by the state. The city argued that this was permissible because Utah law allowed a police officer to take formal training "within 18 months" of initial employment. The federal district judge ruled that anyone who would put a police officer on duty for "one minute" without proper training was grossly negligent. He awarded damages as follows: $12,500 against the chief and the city, $11,000 against the chief personally, $12,000 in costs and $25,000 in attorneys' fees. A broken arm cost more than $60,000.

3. In *Garcia v. City of Tucson,* Tucson Super. Ct. #177347; (Ariz. 1980)—LR# 10303 C/KD, Roy Garcia, a former Tucson police officer who was left paralyzed from the waist down after being shot by a South Tucson police officer, alleged the city was liable for its failure to train and supervise police personnel. Garcia, a dog handler, had been called by South Tucson police to assist in dislodging a suspect who was firing a gun from inside his home. The South Tucson officer in charge ordered Garcia onto the porch of the home and then ordered Tucson police officer David Novotny to kick down the door. In the ensuing gunfire, Novotny dived for cover and came up shooting at a silhouette in the doorway he thought was the suspect. Novotny was actually shooting at Garcia. In his suit, Roy Garcia alleged that the South Tucson officers acted "ad lib and without a plan" in trying to neutralize the suspect. The jury agreed and awarded Garcia $3.5 million. The verdict was $800,000 more than South Tucson's entire 1980 budget. Officer Novotny was cleared of any wrongdoing.

As noted above, the negligent failure to properly train police personnel is a legitimate cause for action under Title 42, United States Code, Section 1983. Meeting some minimum standard is simply not sufficient. It must be demonstrated that:

1. The training has been validated by a job task analysis.

2. Those who conduct training are qualified instructors.

3. Effective training takes place and can be documented.

4. The training is state-of-the-art and up-to-date.

5. Adequate performance measures are taken and documented.

6. Those being retrained learn the subject and/or master the skill.

7. Trainees are monitored, supervised and continuously evaluated.

The courts have made it clear that it is no longer good enough for the police department to say that it provides training. It must now prove that its job-related training is both sufficient and effective. Anything less than first-class training will leave the city, local police administrators and supervisors open to civil suits (Barrineau, 1994).

Police supervisors must realize and accept the fact that they can be sued, based on vicarious liability, for the wrongful acts of their subordinates. Two areas of negligence have been the prime source of litigation in recent years: "negligent supervision" and "negligent training." The courts have ruled that a deliberate indifference to supervision and/or training is proper grounds for civil liability. In some cases, meeting state-mandated minimum training standards may not be enough to avoid liability. In fact, the failure to provide training that is above and beyond the required minimum has been determined to be a "negligent failure to train" in some cases. Supervisors should become more familiar with case law concerning vicarious liability as it relates to their training function (Barrineau, 1987). Due to the complexity of this issue, it would behoove all first-line supervisors to review the "failure-to-train" cases listed below:

1. *Beverly v. Morris,* 470 F.2d 1356 (5th Cir., 1972)

2. *Dewell v. Lawson,* 489 F.2d 877 (10th Cir., 1974)

3. *Owens v. Haas,* 601 F.2d 1242 (1979)

4. *Sager v. City of Woodland Park,* 543 F.Supp. 282 (D.Colo., 1982)

5. *Languirano v. Hayden,* 717 F.2d 220 (1983)

6. *Tuttle v. Oklahoma City,* 728 F.2d 456 (10th Cir., 1984)

7. *Rock v. McCoy,* 763 F.2d 394 (10th Cir., 1985)

8. *Grandstaff v. City of Borger, Texas,* 767 F.2d 161 (5th Cir., 1985)

9. *Rymer v. Davis,* 754 F.2d 198 (6th Cir., 1985)

10. *Bordanaro v. McLoad,* 871 F.2nd 1151 (1st Cir. 1989)

The best defense against vicarious liability is a proactive strategy: police managers should hire the most qualified personnel, institute effective training programs and provide adequate supervision for all members of the department.

According to R.V. del Carmen and Victor E. Kappeler (1991), the courts have set forth what may be considered as prerequisites for civil liability based on the "deliberate indifference" standard. These include:

1. The focus is on the adequacy of the training program in relation to the tasks the particular officer must perform.

2. The fact that a given officer may not be satisfactorily trained will not alone result in vicarious liability because the officer's shortcomings may have resulted from factors other than a faulty training program.

3. It is not sufficient to impose liability just because it can be proven that an injury or accident could have been avoided if an officer had more and perhaps better training.

4. The identified deficiency in the police training program must be closely related to the ultimate cause of the injury.

While there are some safeguards against promiscuous, vicarious liability suits, the courts have been broadening the avenue for civil suit in failure-to-train cases. This liberalization in interpretation should raise red flags for police managers and first-line supervisors. They must heed the warnings and pay much more attention to their training responsibilities.

Documentation, Documentation and More Documentation

It is obvious that relevant and effective training is critically important from the professional standpoint as well as for defending against vicarious civil liability. Consequently, ALL informal (advising, coaching, counseling) and formal training activities should be thoroughly documented. Adequate record keeping is absolutely essential in the contemporary law enforcement milieu. These records should include but not be limited to the following:

1.   Individual training record forms

2.   Completed examinations and quizzes

3.   Hands-on performance demonstrations

4.   Lesson plans

Documentation should also include a compendium of what was actually said in class, which audio-visual and reference materials were used and which students attended. An evaluation of the training and these records will provide a basis for assessing future training needs, reducing civil liability and determining the competency of the instructional staff.

Documentation is particularly important in failure-to-train law suits. With the vicarious liability issue becoming more prominent all the time, police managers and first-line supervisors must understand that training records, course syllabi, attendance sheets, examinations, procedural manuals and policy statements are fair game and subject to subpoena by the plaintiff. (Chuda, 1995). In the worst case scenario, deficient or nonexistent documentation is tantamount to the "kiss of death."

Summary

Training is the practical and applied side of education designed to transmit the knowledge, skills and attitudes needed to improve an employee's problem-solving ability and on-the-job behavior. It focuses knowledge so that it can be applied in specific situations. Training is an ongoing process that promotes change, yet establishes a unity of purpose. Effective training is relevant and job-specific. It facilitates adaptability and guards against human obsolescence.

The emphasis on training in law enforcement can be traced from the Peelian reforms of 1829 through every national advisory commission to 1994. Every state has adopted police officer standards and training legislation. There are three basic approaches to formal police training: (1) preparatory preemployment training, (2) preservice recruit training and (3) in-service training. While training is emphasized as the pathway to professionalism for police personnel, departments spend less than one percent on police training. Many states still allow police officers to work in the field prior to completing recruit training. The status of in-service training in an era of cutback management remains unclear at this juncture.

Training is a means to an end. Whether it succeeds or fails will ultimately depend on its relevance, the instructional methodology that is used, the capacity and receptivity of the trainees and the teaching ability of the trainer. Good training is job-related training keyed to a task analysis and based on sound principles of learning. There has been too much emphasis on the lecture method in police training. Other interactive teaching methods have proven to be more reliable. Active learning by doing should be stressed whenever possible.

The sergeant's job is to obtain results through people. Training is a universal responsibility of all first-line supervisors. In fact, everything a supervisor does in directing the work force has some element of training in it. Conversely, every training activity involves an element of supervision. Sergeants instruct formal courses. They also instruct through example, advising, counseling and coaching. Police sergeants must have good human relations skills in order to carry out their role as supervisors/trainers.

Most supervisors learn their role from other supervisors. Many received no training before or after they were promoted. Due to the strategic role they play in the organization, training is critical. One of the best supervisory training programs has been developed in California. An 80-hour classroom experience is supplemented by extensive on-the-job training.

In today's qualification-oriented and litigious society, it would be a mistake to underestimate the importance of documenting informal and formal police training activities. Police managers and first-line supervisors who ignore this caveat are both penny wise and pound foolish. When it comes to training, the general rule is to document, document and document.

Everyone benefits from effective training. The community gets the protection and service that it deserves. Police officers do their jobs better and earn the professional status they crave. The department accomplishes some of its goals and objectives and mitigates some of its vicarious liability. Training is not a panacea, but it is a wise investment in the future.

Case Study

Sergeant Roland "Buddy" Bayer

Sergeant Buddy Bayer has been a shift supervisor for nearly 20 years. He is seriously thinking about retirement and has adopted a fairly ritualistic approach to his job. He is really not interested in making waves.

A recent U.S. Supreme Court decision invalidated the department's policy concerning shooting fleeing felons, and a new policy that is consistent with the decision has been formulated by the chief. All shift sergeants attended a training session conducted by the department's legal advisor and were ordered to disseminate the information during the next roll-call session. For some reason, Sergeant Bayer did not bring the new policy to the attention of his subordinates during roll call.

At approximately 10:30 p.m., the police received a call reporting a major disturbance. A patrol car was dispatched immediately. Upon arrival at the scene, the police officer was told that a man in a brown trench coat had just physically assaulted his brother-in-law. A witness reported that the suspect hit this guy in the nose with a bat. The officer put out an APB and requested a supervisor. Sergeant Bayer was off the air and unable to respond. No supervisor responded.

A few minutes later, the police officer observed the suspect on a deserted street a few blocks away from the scene of the assault. He ordered the man to halt. The suspect bolted from the officer. The officer drew his revolver, ordered the halt again and fired a shot. The suspect was killed immediately.

Based on the state law and department policy that had been invalidated by the Court, the officer's actions were "justifiable." Shooting a fleeing felon under these conditions, however, violated the new department policy. The family of the deceased brought an action under Section 1983 against the officer and a tort action for negligence against Sergeant Bayer and the police department.

If you were a member of the jury, based on current concepts of liability, would you find Sergeant Bayer negligent? How about the police department? How would you justify your decision?

Key Concepts

civil liability
documentation of training
field training officer (FTO)
human resources
in-service training
instructional methods
instructional protocol
minimum standards
pedagogy versus andragogy
preemployment training
preservice training
principles of learning and teaching

professional status
Project STAR
six philosophical planks
supervision as training
supervisory training
task analysis
Theory Y assumptions
training as supervision
training
the training cycle
training movement
training process

Discussion Topics and Questions

1. What is the training movement? Where did it originate? Who were the leading proponents? Why? What role did the national commissions play? What is the status today?

2. Define training. How does training differ from education? What are the goals of police training?

3. Police officers crave recognition as members of a profession. What are the characteristics of a profession? How does the concept of preemployment police training fit into the discussion? Do you feel that police work has achieved professional status? Why?

4. What is the basic difference between pedagogy and andragogy? Explain why the latter approach is being emphasized in modern American police work.

5. Explain the learning principles upon which a Field Training program is built. What role does the FTO play in personnel evaluation and the training process? Do you think that it is a realistic approach to on-the-job training? Why?

6. What are the "elements of the training process"? Why must the trainer be so specific in identifying training objectives and performance outcomes?

7. What are some of the errors instructors make that impact in a negative way on training? What can be done to correct the situation?

8. Do you accept the idea that there is a reciprocal and synergistic relationship between supervision and training? Explain your answer. What is the sergeant's role in formal training? How would you define informal training? What skills are necessary?

9. Define civil liability. Give some examples. What can you, as a sergeant, do to protect yourself from being held liable for your subordinate's negligence? Should you be concerned?

10. If you were assigned to teach a unit on ethics at the police academy, what would you do to get ready? How, based on the instructional protocol contained in this chapter, would you structure your presentation? Be creative.

11. Why is it so important to document ALL informal as well as formal training activities? Explain the various purposes for which this data can be used.

For Further Reading

Bittel, Lester R. and John W. Newstrom (1990). *What Every Supervisor Should Know,* 6th ed. New York: The McGraw-Hill Book Company.

> Comprehensive review of practical supervisory techniques with an emphasis on getting things done through others by ongoing informal, as well as formal, training.

DuBrin, Andrew J. (1985). *Contemporary Applied Management.* Plano, TX: Business Publications, Inc.

> Excellent analysis of management as a catalyst for change. It places an emphasis on the importance of training in all goal-directed and productive supervisory relationships.

Fay, John (1988). *Approaches to Criminal Justice Training.* Athens, GA: Carl Vinson Institute of Government, The University of Georgia.

> A comprehensive textbook dealing with all aspects of criminal justice training. It is an excellent practitioners guide emphasizing the practical application of the principles of learning accompanied by useable techniques designed to maximize the impact of the target-specific training.

References

Alpert, Geoffrey P. and Roger G. Dunham (1992). *Policing Urban America,* 2nd ed. Prospect Heights, IL: Waveland Press, Inc.

Alpert, Geoffrey P. and William Smith (1990). "Defensibility of Law Enforcement Training." *Criminal Law Bulletin,* No. 26.

Armstrong, L.D. and C.O. Longenecker (1992). "Police Management Training: A National Survey." *FBI Law Enforcement Bulletin,* Vol. 61, No.1.

Barrineau, H.E. III (1994). *Civil Liability in Criminal Justice,* 2nd ed. Cincinnati, OH: Pilgrimage Press, Anderson Publishing Co.

Bennett, Wayne W. and Karen M. Hess (1992). *Management and Supervision in Law Enforcement.* St. Paul, MN: West Publishing Co.

California Commission on Peace Officer Standards and Training (1983). *Supervisory Training Guide.* North Highlands, CA: Post.

Chruden, Herbert J. and Arthur W. Sherman (1984). *Managing Human Resources,* 7th ed. Cincinnati, OH: South-Western Publishing Company.

Chuda, Thomas T. (1995). "Taking Training Beyond the Basics." *Security Management,* Vol. 39, No. 2.

del Carmen, R.V. and V.E. Kappeler (1991). "Municipal and Police Agencies as Defendants: Liability for Official Policy and Custom." *American Journal of Police,* Vol. 10, No. 1.

Fay, John (1988). *Approaches to Criminal Justice Training,* 2nd ed. Athens, GA: Carl Vinson Institute of Government, University of Georgia.

Fogelson, R.M. (1977). *Big-City Police.* Cambridge, MA: Harvard University Press.

Galvin, Ralph H. and Bruce A. Sokolove (1989). "A Strategic Planning Approach to Law Enforcement Training." *The Police Chief,* Vol. LVI, No. 11.

Haley, K. (1992). "Training." In *What Works in Policing? Operations and Administration Examined,* G. Cordner and D. Hale (eds). Cincinnati, OH: Anderson Publishing Co.

Halloran, Jack (1981). *Supervision.* Englewood Cliffs, NJ: Prentice-Hall, Inc.

Hilgard, Ernest and Gordon H. Bower (1966). *Theories of Learning.* New York: Appleton-Century-Crofts.

Holden, Richard N. (1994). *Modern Police Management,* 2nd ed. Englewood Cliffs, NJ: Prentice-Hall, Inc.

Iannone, Nathan F. (1994). *Supervision of Police Personnel,* 5th ed. Englewood Cliffs, NJ: Prentice-Hall, Inc.

Kappeler, Victor E. (1993). *Critical Issues in Police Civil Liability.* Prospect Heights, IL: Waveland Press, Inc.

Lynch, Ronald G. (1995). *The Police Manager,* 4th ed. Cincinnati, OH: Anderson Publishing Co.

Mathis, R. L. and J. H. Jackson (1991). *Personnel: Human Resources Management.* St. Paul, MN: West Publishing Co.

Minnesota Police Officer Standards and Training Board (1987). "Index No. M-626.84," based on an interview with Mark Shields.

National Advisory Commission on Criminal Justice Standards and Goals (1973). *The Police.* Washington, DC: U.S. Government Printing Office.

Pennsylvania Consolidated Statutes (1974). "Title 53: 740-749," Harrisburg, PA.

Peters, Thomas J. and Robert H. Waterman, Jr. (1982). *In Search of Excellence.* New York: Warner Books.

Plunkett, W. Richard (1992). *Supervision: The Direction of People at Work.* Boston: Allyn and Bacon, Inc.

Preston, Paul and Thomas W. Zimmerer (1983). *Management for Supervisors.* Englewood Cliffs, NJ: Prentice-Hall, Inc.

Roberg, Roy R. and Jack Kuykendall (1993). *Police and Society.* Belmont, CA: Wadsworth Publishing Co.

Sayles, Leonard R. and George Strauss (1981). *Managing Human Resources,* 2nd ed. Englewood Cliffs, NJ: Prentice-Hall, Inc.

Shepherd, Roosevelt E. and Thomas L. Austin (1986). "Pre-Service Police Training: A Pennsylvania Perspective." Shippensburg, PA: Shippensburg University.

Smith, C.P. et al. (1974). *Project STAR.* Cincinnati, OH: Anderson-Davis, Inc.

Steinmetz, Lawrence L. and H. Ralph Todd (1986). *First-Line Management.* Plano, TX. Business Publications, Inc.

Stinchcomb, James D. (1984). *Opportunities in Law Enforcement and Criminal Justice.* Skokie, IL: VGM Career Horizons/National Textbook Co.

Stone, Alfred R. and Stuart M. DeLuca (1985). *Police Administration.* New York: John Wiley and Sons, Inc.

Swank, Calvin J. and James A. Conser (1983). *The Police Personnel System.* New York: John Wiley and Sons, Inc.

Thibault, Edward A. et al. (1990). *Proactive Police Management,* 2nd ed. Englewood Cliffs, NJ: Prentice-Hall, Inc.

Whisenand, Paul M. and George E. Rush (1993). *Supervising Police Personnel,* 2nd ed. Englewood Cliffs, NJ: Prentice-Hall, Inc.

Subject Index

Author Index